DOSE
OF MONEY."
—*Minneapolis Star Tribune*

"EXPLOSIVE…
BREATHTAKING!"
—Phil Donahue

"SUPER
INTENSE
TRUE CRIME"
—*Kirkus Reviews*

THE VERDICT IS IN FOR
FINAL JUSTICE

FINAL JUSTICE

The True Story of the Richest Man Ever Tried for Murder

▼

Steven Naifeh and Gregory White Smith

AN ONYX BOOK

ONYX
Published by the Penguin Group
Penguin Books USA Inc., 375 Hudson Street,
New York, New York 10014, U.S.A.
Penguin Books Ltd, 27 Wrights Lane,
London W8 5TZ, England
Penguin Books Australia Ltd, Ringwood,
Victoria, Australia
Penguin Books Canada Ltd, 10 Alcorn Avenue,
Toronto, Ontario, Canada M4V 3B2
Penguin Books (N.Z.) Ltd, 182–190 Wairau Road,
Auckland 10, New Zealand

Penguin Books Ltd, Registered Offices:
Harmondsworth, Middlesex, England

Published by Onyx,
an imprint of Dutton Signet,
a division of Penguin Books USA Inc.
Previously published in a Dutton edition.

First Onyx Printing, October, 1994
10 9 8 7 6 5 4 3 2

Author's Note:
In the interest of protecting the privacy of individuals whose identities are
not central to the true story told here, certain names and other descriptive
details have been altered in several instances.

In memory of Andrea Wilborn

ACKNOWLEDGMENTS

The story of Cullen Davis encompasses four criminal trials; interminable grand jury investigations; numerous bond hearings and bond appeals reaching up to the Supreme Court; five civil suits arising out of the shootings; several investigations by government regulatory agencies; Bill Davis's federal suit against his brothers and Kendavis Industries International; and a host of divorces. Between them, Cullen Davis, his family, friends, business associates, ex-wives, and enemies kept legions of lawyers busy for years, in the process filling literally hundreds of volumes of court transcripts.

In the media, too, Cullen Davis left a Shermanesque trail. For years, barely a day passed without an article on the Davis story, especially in the *Fort Worth Star-Telegram*, but in newspapers throughout Texas as well. Magazine articles followed, as did three books.

But our research only began with this mountain of paper. Far more important was the half year we spent in Texas, mostly in Fort Worth, interviewing and in some cases getting to know the principals in the drama.

We would like to take this opportunity to thank some of those people who contributed to our research: Wiley Alexander, Suzanne Arnold, Ronald Aultman, Clifton Bailey, Jim Bearden, Hugh Knox Bonifield, Marie Bonifield, Steve Brown, John Brutsche, Pat Burleson, Phil Burleson, Rachel Capote, Tom Cave, Marvin Collins, Claude Davis, Priscilla Davis, Sandra Davis, Dick de Guerin, George Dowlen, Grady Dukes, Lon Evans, Carl Freund, Brad Gandy, Gus Gavrel, Sr., Bob Gibbins, Gordon Gray, Sam Guiberson, Glenn Guzzo, Richard Haynes, Louise Helms, R. C. Hubbard, Marcelle Hull, Dorothy Humphrey, Wayne Ingram, Marie James, Jim

x   *Steven Naifeh and Gregory White Smith*

Jones, Walter Kaufman, Ron Knight, Albert Komatsu,
Bill Lane, Jerry Loftin, Lucy Lopez, Jim Mabe, Pat Mas-
sad, David McCrory, Judy McCrory, Hal Monk, Anne
Moore, Cecil Munn, Joe Meyers, Carolyn Naifeh, R. O.
Parkey, Hershel Payne, Sheila Phillips, Carolyn Poirot,
Ann Quinn, Mike Ramsay, Ben Reina, W. T. Rufner,
Leonard Sanders, Rich Sauer, Joe Shannon, Jr., Frank
Shiller, Don Shipe, Roger Shuy, Lucienne Potterfield Stec,
Cissy Stewart, Jack Strickland, Walter Strittmatter, Steve
Sumner, Larry Thomas, Andrea Tuinei, Russell Vorpagel,
Betty Wilborn, Jack Wilborn, Tolly Wilson, and many
others who requested anonymity.

When we began our research, almost fifteen years had
passed since the events in this book unfolded. Many people
were able to open up to us now in ways they could not
when emotions were still running hot and legal battles were
still in high gear. Most important was the vastly increased
access to information from within the defense camp: It is
the inside story of the Davis defense that remained virtually untold until now.

First, we were given notes from prosecution interviews
with a secretary at the firm of Burleson, Pate & Gibson
who was mortified by the actions of her employers—notes
so secret that they were unknown at the time even to some
key members of the prosecution. Second, an investigator
for Cullen Davis, infuriated because Davis failed to pay
his bills, confided some of the most damning details of the
work he was hired to do. And third, one of the defense
lawyers, Steve Sumner, provided us with detailed notes
from his interviews with witnesses and potential witnesses,
enabling us to portray the Cullen Davis "witness factory"
and permitting us a unique window into the world of high-
stakes criminal defense.

The names of several individuals mentioned in the book
have been changed for a variety of reasons: Craig Baker,
Marilyn Baker, Tracy Connors, Keith Harding, Randi
Matthiessen, Helen Murphy, Bart Newton, Bubba Palmer,
Nipper Perry, Sue Skinner, Martha Sloane, Bobby Smith,
Susan Spencer, and Cornelia Stratton.

Although almost everyone involved in the story was available to us and extremely helpful, there were a few individuals we could not interview, among whom Cullen Davis and the members of his immediate family were the most missed. Under the terms of their settlement agreement with Cullen Davis, Gus Gavrel, Jr., and his wife Beverly were precluded from speaking with us; and Judge Pete Moore, one of the heroes of our story, was too ill.

Speaking of heroes, we should mention our editor, Michaela Hamilton, our publisher, Elaine Koster, and our agent, Mel Berger, all of whom performed their many duties with the requisite grace under the inevitable pressure, which, come to think of it, is almost a definition of good publishing.

PART
ONE

1

"Help me, please. I've been shot." Priscilla Davis could hear a dog barking on the other side of the door. Through the window, she thought she saw shadows moving.

"Please!" she called out again, trying to make herself heard by the strangers inside but not by the man somewhere in the darkness behind her, the man with the gun.

"I'm very badly wounded! I need help."

She probed under her breasts for the hole. (The huge breasts were Cullen's idea. Her own breasts had been big enough for every other man, but not for Cullen.) It didn't feel like much—a three-inch slit with the edges sucked in, oozing warm wetness. It wasn't tender to the touch, but inside she could feel the throbbing all along the bullet's path and the hot trickle on her back where it had burst out of her. There wasn't much blood now, but any minute, with a sudden movement, a loud noise, or the sound of footsteps behind her, the throbbing would prove too much for her size-two body and all of her insides would explode out of that tiny, oozing hole.

"Please help me!" she called out again. *"Please!"*

Suddenly the porch lights flashed on, bright as headlights. Startled, she crouched behind a metal post to hide herself from the street. She felt the yellow light illuminating her teased mane of blonde hair—another of Cullen's ideas. She had bleached her long raven locks before, but he wasn't satisfied with just blonde. He wanted white blonde, ice blonde—platinum blonde. Perhaps he had known all along that this moment would come, that he would have to chase her down some night and kill her, using that torch of white hair as a homing beacon.

Her hands started to tremble, then her knees, then her whole body. The tide of adrenaline that had brought her alive through the long night despite a bullet hole in her chest was beginning to ebb.

"Who's out there?" came a woman's voice from the other side of the door. "What do you want?"

"I'm Priscilla Davis. I live in the big white house on the hill." She motioned west to a huge dark rise topped by the lights of a single house.

She knew the woman was looking at her through the glass in the door, sizing her up in the unflattering glare of the porch lights: the huge hive of surreally blonde hair, the extravagant breasts precariously bound up in the pink sling of a halter top, the plain features gilded into high drama by layers of makeup. This night, by chance, she had worn a long denim skirt, but it was gathered up in a bunch and she held it tight against the wound in her chest, exposing as much of her thighs as the briefest of her miniskirts. Since marrying Cullen, she had grown used to being sized up in this way by unwelcome eyes.

"My husband is calling the police," said the voice. But the door stayed shut.

A car rounded the curve on Hartwood Street. Its headlights raked the lunar landscape of lava rock that lined the little courtyard and washed the walls around Priscilla. The car seemed to slow.

It was him. He was looking for her.

Suddenly the throbbing in her chest exploded in her ears. She threw herself to the ground, hid her head, and waited for the sound of the car stopping, the door opening, his footsteps on the lava rock. In a few seconds she would look up to see one more time the black barrel of his gun, his hands bound in black plastic holding it, and, behind it, Cullen's smiling face.

But the car didn't stop.

As soon as it passed, she leapt to the door and jabbed frantically at the doorbell. *"You don't understand,"* she cried out, more desperate than ever. *"My husband has shot me. He's killing my children! He's killing everyone!"*

* * *

"Stop, stop, please stop!" Beverly Bass screamed as cars roared past on both sides. From the grassy median in the middle of Hulen Street, the dark rise with the single house on top still seemed terrifyingly close. She had been running from it for what seemed like hours and it was still right there, as in a dream, only footsteps away.

She darted into the southbound lanes, putting two lanes of hurtling traffic between her and the man with the gun. She waved her arms and ran directly into the oncoming headlights. A car screamed to a stop within arms' length. She ran to the passenger side and tried the door, but it was locked. The automatic window hummed open just a crack. She stuck her face in as far as it would go and pleaded frantically.

"My boyfriend's been shot! The man who owns that big house up there just shot my boyfriend, Bubba." She flung her arms in the direction of the dark rise. "I've known him for a long time, and I stood right there and looked at him when he did it. He shot Bubba, and then he came after me. You've got to help me! He could be dying!"

The driver unlocked the door and Bev flung herself into the front seat. "Hurry!" she ordered. "Take me to the police." Her breaths came short and fast. Less than a minute before she had been running for her life, racing barefoot across the moonlit fields trying to escape from a man she had known almost half her life.

Suddenly she remembered the others—Priscilla, Stan, Andrea—they were *all* up there, trapped in the same house with her dying Bubba and the man who had shot him.

"*Oh, my God!*" she cried out just as the car pulled into a parking lot next to a public phone. "*There are other people up there! Cullen will kill them all!*"

The Ray Crowder Funeral Home ambulance approached the house at 4208 Hartwood with its siren and flashers off. The dispatcher had reported a Signal 37—a shooting. The rulebook advised, "Approach with caution."

Before the driver had even stopped, he saw a woman

running limply toward him, doubled over in pain. She was blonde and bosomy and her skirt was gathered up against her chest. He jumped out and met her on the lawn.

"What happened?"

"I've been shot." Priscilla dropped the bundle of skirt and showed him the hole.

"Who shot you?"

"My husband."

"Who is your husband?"

"Cullen Davis."

"He's in a lady's black wig," she explained frantically as the driver and an attendant helped her into the back of the ambulance. "He's killing my kids and everyone in the house. He's gone crazy!" Just then another car rounded the curve on Hartwood, filling the back of the ambulance with the glare of its headlights. "Get me out of here!" she pleaded. "He's coming after me. He wants to kill me. *Get me away from here!*"

"Take me back!" Beverly Bass pleaded. The driver of the car that had picked her up had called the police and an ambulance was on its way, but the image of Bubba lying on the ground dying would not go away. "Take me back to the house," she demanded again.

The driver refused. He told her to wait for the police.

"What if he's bleeding to death?" she wailed. "What if he's already . . ."

A car turned off Hulen onto Bellaire. Bev recognized the Homeguard Security Jeep and ran to meet it, waving her arms wildly.

"You've got to help me. There's been a shooting. My boyfriend has been shot and he's dying."

The uniformed driver reflexively touched his Colt .357 magnum. "Where's your boyfriend now, Miss?"

"At Priscilla's."

"You mean Priscilla Davis?" The guard knew the house on the hill. Friends of his had worked security at the wild parties there. They told stories that he had never believed.

"You've got to take me up there," Bev insisted, choking back sobs of exasperation. "I've got to go back. He shot my boyfriend! I saw him do it. He was trying to kill me! I just ran. He chased me across the whole place."

"You saw *who* do it?" the guard asked.

"It was *Cullen!*" she screamed—suddenly, murderously focused. "Cullen did it. I saw his ugly fucking face!"

2

Patrol Sergeant Gordon Box was ready to write off the night of August 2, 1976, as one of the deadest in his twelve years with the Fort Worth police. At half past midnight, he was sitting in his marked car in a parking lot near Texas Christian University on the city's west side listening to Officer Jimmy Soders complain about the boredom.

"Dammit, Sergeant," Soders was whining, "I'm about to go to sleep. It's dull as dirt out here." Box nodded in solemn agreement. For the past three nights they had been working relief in east Fort Worth: mostly poor, mostly black, and the busiest part of town for a cop. A typical night east would be a dozen calls, more on weekends. The adrenaline never stopped pumping. Tonight they were on the west side, with its tony suburbs, country clubs, and the TCU campus. Their shift was already half over and Box hadn't responded to a single call.

Soders was still grumbling when he rolled up his window and pulled away. Tonight he's complaining about no action, Box thought, tomorrow, on the east side, he'll be complaining about no rest. "Cops have to learn to take it as it comes," he always said. "The trick is to be ready."

Only seconds after Soders's departure, a call came through: a Signal 37 at the corner of Hulen and Bellaire. Box let Soders and another officer in the area, Jimmy Perez, handle it. They would call if they needed help.

Boredom didn't bother Gordon Box, a tall, brickhouse-solid, straightbacked and deep-voiced man, who saw himself more as a lifestyle cop than a blue knight. At thirty-four, after two calamitous marriages, he had lost his taste for adrenaline. Besides, he knew what adrenaline could do. In east Fort Worth he had seen a man kill another man over a twenty-five-cent pool game. As the father of a beautiful thirteen-year-old girl, Box could no longer afford to be addicted to highs like that.

A few minutes after the first call, another came in. This time it was a Signal 63—officers requesting assistance. The address was 4200 Mockingbird Lane.

Soders and Perez needed help.

"He's gone!" Beverly Bass screamed. "Bubba's gone! He was right here!" She started to run toward the spot on the sidewalk where she had last seen her boyfriend's body, but Officer Perez caught her arm and pulled her back.

"You stay behind us!" he barked.

Soders and Perez made their way along the rough stucco walls of the garage toward the back door of the Davis mansion. Ahead of them, the walkway was strewn with shards of glass glinting in the porch light. A plate-glass window to the left of the back door had been shattered. Beyond its jagged remnants they could see a body. Bev was the first to recognize it.

"Bubba! Bubba!" she shouted and ran toward him.

Officer Perez caught her again, just at the threshold of the door. "You stay outside here," he ordered, pulling her backward. "We'll check the house."

It was then that they both saw the blood. The floor was awash with it, as if someone had mopped the elegant wood parquet with it. Slivers of glass floated in it, whorls of it led off into another room. A phone lying next to the body was smeared with it. "Bubba!" Bev screamed, certain he would never answer.

But he did answer. "I need a drink of water," he groaned softly as his eyes flickered open.

Bev lunged fearlessly through the broken window, announcing, "I'm going to get him a drink of water."

Then, suddenly, Bubba's face screwed up in pain and terror as he recognized where he was. "Get me out of here," he pleaded. "He's gonna come back and get me!"

Perez yanked Bev back from the threshold and drew his gun. Soders simultaneously drew his gun, motioned Perez to stay with the two civilians, then moved slowly toward the kitchen where the trail of blood led. He crouched behind a peninsula of cabinets that jutted into the room, pressed flat against them so hard he could feel a little pocket of suction form in the small of his back each time he paused. At the end of the peninsula, where the trail of blood disappeared around the corner, he stopped. He flashed back to the conversation with Sergeant Box earlier that night—was it just fifteen minutes ago?—about what a boring night it had been.

He gripped his gun with both hands and rounded the corner. Two feet in front of him, the trail of blood ended in another body—a huge white male, lying on his stomach like a whale beached in a tidal pool of its own blood. He must have been six feet, no, *seven* feet, and three hundred pounds, Soders guessed. By the quantity of blood, it was clear he had been shot or stabbed repeatedly.

Soders let out a long breath. "I think we've got another 12," he called to Perez, using the police code for a dead body. "Better call for backup."

Minutes later, Sergeant Box arrived. He found Soders and Perez questioning Beverly Bass. "I thought he was breaking into the house," she explained, still frantic, pausing only for great gulps of air, "but then I recognized him—it was Cullen."

"Cullen who?" Box asked.

"Cullen *Davis*, the man who owns the house! Cullen and Priscilla—that's his wife—have been getting a divorce. Cullen shot Bubba, and then he came after me."

"Are you sure it was Cullen Davis?" Box pressed.

"Absolutely. I've known him since I was a little girl. I begged him not to hurt me. When he started running after me I ran down to Hulen. He chased me almost the whole way."

She gave them a description of Cullen and his white-over-blue late-model Cadillac. Box ran to his car to call in a "pickup" on Davis, but another report was already coming through. The ambulance carrying Priscilla Davis had stopped at the Hulen Street entrance to the mansion. The driver had told the officer at the gate that Priscilla thought Cullen could still be in the house.

They would have to search the mansion.

With the mike still in hand, Box backed out of the car and took a good look at the house. He hadn't really noticed it when he first pulled up, except that it was big and modern and sat alone on a huge expanse of horizon. Now he saw for the first time just how big it was. Beyond the three-car garage in front of him, he could see a dozen tall stone walls, pale white in the moonlight, jutting everywhere into the darkness like the sails of some ghost armada. Between them, huge panes of dark glass reflected the silver night clouds. The stark black and whiteness of it seemed to go on forever. No doubt about it: This was the biggest damn house he had ever seen.

"I'll think we'll need more backup," he informed the dispatcher.

As reinforcements arrived, Box posted men at the doors and formed separate upstairs and downstairs search parties. He sent men to seal off the guest quarters at the north end of the grounds, as well as the staff quarters and stables. Soon after the search began, a detective from homicide appeared. Then a canine officer with a German shepherd. Then the inevitable press. A helicopter unit was called in to comb the grounds from the air.

The search of the house proceeded at a crawl: room by room, with guns drawn. Beyond the kitchen where the enormous corpse lay, they searched the dining room with its huge glass table and sparkling chandelier; the living room with its conversation pit of built-in sofas surrounding a floating fireplace; the game room with several billiard tables; and, on a balcony overlooking it, an elaborate track for toy racing cars. They searched the paneled library with its wall of jade, malachite, and alabaster statues and its leopardskin chairs. In one room an enormous portrait of a dark-haired man and a pretty blonde woman hung on the wall.

They searched the main hall, from the massive bronze doors at one end to the vast palm-lined indoor swimming pool at the other. Up the winding stairs, they searched the master bedroom with its double-sided fireplace and banks of televisions. They searched a bathroom lined in suede, and another lined in pink patent leather. They opened every door and shined their flashlights into every closet— and there were dozens.

The search was almost finished when another message came through on the radio. In the emergency room at John Peter Smith Hospital, Priscilla Davis was frantic to know if her twelve-year-old daughter, Andrea Wilborn, was all right. "I'll repeat that," the dispatcher said, in a rare display of concern. "There is a twelve-year-old girl reportedly still in the house."

"There must be some mistake," Box responded. "We've been through almost the whole daggum place and there's no sign of anyone. Tell Mrs. Davis . . ."

"Come here, Sergeant." It was Perez's voice coming from the kitchen. Box found him standing at the head of the basement stairs pointing to a dark smudge on the wall. It was a partial handprint, in blood. Box whistled for the dog and his handler. They would lead the way down. Box and Perez would follow.

The stairs gave out into a vast storage room scattered with boxes and mattresses, a couch, a nest of tables, a rug, an old television. On the left wall were two doors. Perez opened the first door slowly, flashlight in one hand, gun in the other, taking care to stand out of the way when the door swung open. He swept the blackness inside with his flashlight. Nothing but lawn furniture stacked away haphazardly. He moved to the second door. All other movement in the room stopped. Perez unlatched the second door and slowly pushed it open, three inches, four inches . . .

The shaft of light fell across a pair of small feet pointing toward the door.

Perez yanked the door shut and motioned Box to the other side of the doorway. Then he swung the door open again, quickly this time, thrusting his flashlight into the dark space. Box leapt into the doorway, gun drawn.

On the floor lay the body of a young girl. The light from Perez's flashlight played across her brown-and-white-striped tube top, her brown corduroy skirt, and her long, silky dark hair. It caught her eyes, still open, and glinted off the pool of blood beneath her. Perez's hand began to tremble so badly that he couldn't keep the flashlight steady on the body. He turned and lurched out of the room.

Someone found a light switch, but the sight was worse in the light. The girl was lying on her back, sprawled across the floor, her arms thrown up over her head, which was turned to the left. Her eyes looked startled. One leg was crossed over the other, hiking her skirt high on her legs. It was a strangely lifelike pose, except for the hole in her chest.

If she had looked more like a dead body, if he had seen her in a morgue drawer or in the bloodless black-and-white limbo of a crime scene photograph (in which even the cops standing around look dead), Gordon Box might have found her easier to look at. But this little girl looked too real, too much like a little girl, too much like his own daughter, Connie.

"This is gonna be tough," he muttered behind his clenched teeth as he walked away from the door, fighting to keep his thoughts focused on the job ahead. But the image had already burned itself into his memory. "Tough, tough, tough." He had certainly seen his share of dead adults—suicides, murders, accidents, so many that they no longer bothered him much. Like a lot of cops, he took some spartan pride in his casual relationship with death. But a child . . .

He thought about the juvenile killings he had seen, all

of them on the east side. He remembered a father standing
over a child whom he had beaten to death, saying, "Maybe
I went a little too far with the discipline"; another telling
the police, "She fell and hit her head." Almost always it
was the mother's boyfriend or a stepfather. He's babysit-
ting while she's working. It's not his child. And after the
child's dead, no one wants to testify. Mom and Dad are
back together again before the trial begins.

But that was the east side.

What went through her mind in the last minute, Box
wondered. It wasn't hard to speculate. He knew what his
own daughter would have thought: "He's just going to
lock me in here." A thirteen-year-old child has faith in
adults. People don't do things like this to each other, and
certainly not to beautiful little girls. "The worst he's gonna
do is lock me in this closet."

From a safe distance, despite himself, he looked back
at the little body sprawled in the doorway on the other
side of the room. If he was a policeman for a hundred
years, he thought, he would never get used to this. More
cops were coming down now as word spread through the
search parties upstairs, but no one spoke. They came down
the stairs laughing and joking, but as soon as they saw,
they shut up.

Beverly Bass was still waiting outside when Sergeant
Box emerged from the back door. An ambulance had already taken Bubba to the hospital, but the police wouldn't
let her ride with him. When she saw Box, she ran toward
him. "Where's Andrea?" she called out. "Have you found
Andrea yet?" She had heard the radio report that Priscilla's daughter was still in the house.

Box did his duty. "She's dead, too," he said.

After hours of anguish and dread, hours in which she
had barely stopped talking, Bev suddenly fell silent. She
had been with Andrea earlier that day. They had gone
shopping together. She had helped Andrea pick out a
brown-and-white-striped tube top to wear shopping, that

Andrea thought her new boyfriend would like. He was her first boyfriend and she wanted to please him.

Bev didn't know what to say. She turned to the officer assigned to watch her and take her home whenever she was ready. "Let's go," she said with a sigh.

As she was getting into the car, Box called out, "Do you know where Cullen Davis lives?"

"He's living with his girlfriend, Karen Master, in Edgecliff," Bev said. "But you better hurry. Cullen has two jets at Meacham Field."

3

The sound of the phone ringing jolted Karen Master out of a dead sleep. The pills she had taken at ten had done their job with heavy-handed efficiency. She couldn't find the phone. She gazed at the clock for a long time before it came into focus: a few minutes past four. Only then did she discover Cullen lying next to her. He hadn't been there when she fell asleep.

Cullen was the reason Karen needed pills. Recently she had been so worried about the stress he was under that *she* needed help sleeping. If he wasn't battling his brothers for control of their father's $700 million empire, he was brawling with Priscilla's lawyers over the divorce. Just the day before, the divorce judge had raised Priscilla's allowance from $3,500 to $5,000 a month and delayed the start of the trial yet again. Karen knew what a blow that had been to Cullen and suspected it was the reason he had come home so late. But she didn't dare ask.

After the first few rings, Cullen began to stir. "Dammit," Karen muttered, mostly for his benefit, "who would be calling at this hour?" Although certain it was for him, she picked it up.

It was Cullen's brother Ken. A friendly call, at least. Ken was an ally of Cullen's in the family warfare.

She handed the phone to Cullen, who shook off sleep with surprising ease.

"What are you doing?" Ken asked.

"Well, actually, I was in bed," said Cullen, closing his eyes.

"Have you been there all night?"

"Well, most of it."

"Have you heard what happened?"

"No."

"There's been a shooting at your house."

Cullen's eyes remained closed. "Who was shot?"

"Stan Farr and a little girl were killed, and Priscilla has been shot and she is in the hospital." Ken expected his brother would want to know more about the identity of the little girl, even though he had nothing more to tell him.

Instead, Cullen asked evenly, "How did you find out?"

Ken explained how the news had come to him, through a contact at the *Fort Worth Star-Telegram*. Again he expected a question about the dead girl.

"Who did it?" Cullen asked.

"Well, I don't know," Ken replied, then paused. "But the police are looking for you."

No response.

Ken tolerated the silence as long as he could. "Well, what are you going to do about it?" he finally pressed.

Another long pause before Cullen yawned, "Well, I guess I'm going back to bed."

When Gordon Box and his commander, Lieutenant B. J. Erby, arrived at Karen Master's house on Arthur Drive in Edgecliff at 4:30 A.M., Davis's white-over-blue Cadillac was parked in the garage. Two patrol cars were already positioned in front with their lights out. "Don't go in by yourselves," the dispatcher had warned them. "This man has shot four people."

Box and Erby were followed by several more patrol units, the canine unit, and four Tarrant County sheriff's deputies. Box looked around at the restless crowd of uniforms. Most of them already knew that a little girl had been shot and killed. They were ready, even eager, to do what had to be done.

Lieutenant Erby radioed the police dispatch supervisor, Henry Ford, and instructed him to "call the Arthur Drive address and ask the subject to come out and surrender to the officers."

Cullen Davis calmly relayed his brother's news about the shootings to Karen, then nestled back into bed.

Karen didn't take it nearly as well. Frantic, she called her mother, Dorothy York, who lived only ten blocks away. "Mother, I need you right now. The most awful . . ." Suddenly the line made a clicking sound and a third voice broke in. "This is the police department. Please release the line."

"Yes, of course," Karen said. She started to explain to her mother what was happening, but her mother was gone.

"Is this Karen Master?" the voice asked.

"Yes."

"Ms. Master, this is Officer Ford with the Fort Worth Police Department. I would like to speak with Cullen Davis if he is there."

"Just a moment, please," said Karen. She put her hand over the receiver, turned to Cullen, and mouthed the word: "Police."

After a long pause, Cullen took the receiver.

"Mr. Davis, this is Officer Henry Ford. We have officers completely around the house and out in front and they would like for you to come out peacefully with your hands up where they can be seen, and talk to them in reference to a shooting that occurred at 4200 Mockingbird Lane."

Silence.

"Please, Mr. Davis. There has been enough trouble tonight." An innocent man, Ford thought, would have asked, "What kind of trouble?"

Looking at his pants neatly laid flat on the floor so the

crease would stay in them and nothing would fall out of the pockets, Davis asked for time to dress.

Ford gave him two minutes. "But that's all, Mr. Davis."

"Thank you," said Davis curtly. His voice was eerily calm, thought Ford, icily calm.

Ford called Lieutenant Erby and told him Davis would be out in two minutes, then called Davis back to keep the line open.

Karen was on the phone with her mother again. "Please, Ms. Master," Ford broke in. "Stay on the line until Mr. Davis goes outside." Then, after a pause, as if idly making conversation to fill the silence: "What time did Mr. Davis arrive at your house tonight, Ms. Master?"

Karen answered, "I don't remember."

Two minutes came and went. Within five minutes, a dozen more policemen had arrived. The lights from their cars turned the yard into a brilliantly lit stage. Box and the others crouched on the dark side of the cars with their guns drawn, waiting for some hint of movement inside the house. Finally, Erby reached for the microphone of his car's public address system. "Mr. Davis?" he called out in his distinctive Arkansas drawl. His granite voice cracked through the neighborhood. "Mr. Davis, your time is up. Will you please come outside?"

Silence. More minutes passed. Someone thought he saw a rustling at the curtains in one window, but it was followed only by more dead stillness. "Mr. Davis," Erby tried again, "I said your time is up. Would you please walk out into the front yard?"

After another long wait, the front door opened and a man emerged. He was short and slender, dressed in a beige business suit, his wavy dark hair cut short and slicked back. He walked straight out toward the street and the waiting cars in even, tailored steps.

Sergeant Box and Lieutenant Erby came forward from behind the line of cars to meet him. Normally they would have ordered the suspect to raise his arms. But not this suspect. There was something disarming about Davis's manner, his walk. By the time Box and Erby met him in the middle of the yard, in the glare of the headlights, they had holstered their guns.

"Are you Cullen Davis?" Erby's tone was strangely courteous, Box thought. More the voice a cop would use with a victim.

"Yes," said Davis, very calm, very businesslike.

"You're under arrest." By now Erby's tone was almost apologetic. Where were the handcuffs, Box wondered. This man was suspected of shooting four people, killing two, including a little girl.

Erby read Davis his rights, then asked: "Do you understand everything, sir?"

"Yes, I do."

A group of reporters who had gathered behind the police line were listening to the conversation on the lawn. One of them, Bob Rayel, a reporter for a local radio station, had seen hundreds of arrests in his career, but never one like this, never one so . . . polite.

Box showed Davis to the backseat of a police car. Rayel noticed that the prisoner, still without handcuffs, was allowed to sit directly behind the driver—another violation of police procedure.

"What the hell is going on here?" Rayel asked the reporter next to him.

"I'll tell you what's going on," the reporter shouted back as he ran to keep up with the parade of press cars following Davis to jail. "One of the richest men in town, from one of the most powerful families in town, just got arrested for murder. That doesn't happen every day of the year."

Box and Erby took Davis to "the chute," a holding area in the basement of the Fort Worth City Jail. Davis sat stiff-backed against the cinderblock wall, but not leaning on it, his eyes straight ahead, avoiding the crowd of reporters not far away, as well as the other prisoners strewn on the benches and concrete floor. Within minutes, a man approached him.

"Mr. Davis? I'm Claude Davis, the homicide detective on this case. If you don't mind, I would like for you to come upstairs and talk with me for a minute."

"I'm Cullen Davis," Cullen responded, as if introduced at a country club buffet. "Glad to meet you, Mr. Davis. No relation, I assume. No, I don't mind going upstairs. It's been a long night." So polite, thought Bob Rayel, standing in the pack of reporters nearby, so damn polite.

Detective Davis led his prisoner past the semiconscious drunks and frightened youngsters, some of whom had been waiting for hours.

Upstairs, the first thing Detective Davis noticed was the suspect's perfectly pressed suit, a subtle plaid with razor-sharp creases. Rumors were already ricocheting around homicide—figures like one hundred million, two hundred million, even a billion. That's what the rumors were saying this man was worth. Detective Davis tried to divide his annual salary into the lowest of those figures but lost track of the zeroes.

He pulled out his little blue Miranda card and read Cullen his rights again. "Do you want a lawyer?" he asked when he was done.

"I don't need a lawyer," Cullen replied in a thin, expressionless voice.

"All right. What do you know about the shooting out at your place?"

Cullen didn't blink, or look to either side, but there was a pause, a dropped beat. "Perhaps I had better talk to my lawyer first," he finally allowed.

Detective Davis leaned back in his squeaky chair and waved his hand. "I don't want you to sign anything," he said in an extravagantly reassuring voice, summoned up from the front porch of his childhood home in Bishop, Texas. "I just want you to tell me what took place out there, and why two people had to get killed. What would be a good enough reason for two people ending up getting killed like this?"

For the first time Cullen looked directly at him. It was like having ice water thrown in his face. "Sometimes," said Cullen, "a man doesn't need a reason."

Detective Davis knew it would never hold up in court, but as far as he was concerned, it was a confession.

PART
TWO

4

Less than twenty-four hours after his arrest, Cullen Davis was released from the Tarrant County Jail, where he'd been moved, on bond. Instead of returning to Karen Master's house, he was taken in secret to the Schick Hospital, a small, private drug and alcohol rehabilitation facility in Dallas. There, on the advice of his attorneys, he was given a battery of psychological tests, one of which instructed him to "finish the incomplete sentences by writing the thought that comes to your mind." Cullen scribbled his terse answers in the awkward script of a schoolboy.

When I was a child . . . *I was happy*.

The Packards and Lincolns were backed up all the way out the long driveway and down Westridge as the elite of Fort Worth dropped their children off in front of the big white clapboard house on a September 22 sometime in the 1930s. The rest of Fort Worth, the rest of Texas, the rest of the United States might have been mired in the worst economic depression in history, but on the vast lawns that spread here in every direction there were no signs of it.

A clown in a rust-red wig, billowing suit, and size-26 shoes trundled back and forth, buoyed by a huge bouquet of balloons. Honey-colored ponies with red ribbons in their manes and sparkling saddles pawed patiently in a row. Long tables covered in red-and-white bunting were laden with ginger and lemon cookies and huge pitchers of lemonade. On one table sat an enormous round red devil's-food cake with marshmallow icing. On the top, in sweet red script: "HAPPY BIRTHDAY CULLEN."

But there was something odd about this party. When the children climbed down from their parents' shiny cars, there were no squeals of pleasure, no darting off to try the pony ride or grab a handful of cookies. Despite the guileless smile and friendly greeting of Alice Davis, the small guests moved tentatively away from the security of their parents' cars, as if afraid of the house, or the people who lived there.

In fact, they were afraid. Not of Mrs. Davis. Everyone loved Alice Davis, the gentle, gracious daughter of West Texas aristocrats, whose prestige came from the oldest and most respectable source of all—cotton. Not of little Cullen, whom many in fact hardly knew. Even in a small class, Cullen was, in one classmate's word, "a nonentity." Strange, perhaps, but hardly frightening. Excruciatingly shy and awkward in groups, he barely made an impression even at his own extravagant birthday parties. When it came time to blow out the candles or open the presents, he would disappear completely, leaving his mother to smile forlornly and explain, "Cullen is such a shy boy."

What frightened the children at the house on Westridge was Cullen's father, Mr. Davis—Kenneth W. Davis— called "K. W." by those who served him, "Stinky" by everyone else.

Children feared him because their parents hated him. When oil was discovered in nearby Ranger, Texas, just after World War I, Fort Worth became a one-business town, and that business was oil. Most of Cullen's classmates were the children of oil families. They had heard their fathers tell how Stinky Davis stole the Mid-Continent Supply Company from "the widow Holmes," a pretty blonde lady whose gentility was much admired around town. How Stinky began as a clerk, but within a few years had moved into the widow Holmes's bed, and then into her office. How she jumped to her death one night from the tenth floor of the Forest Park Apartments. Some people even thought that Stinky pushed her—if not with his hands, with his hard heart. After bedding her and beating her out of the company, he had abandoned her.

Charges were never brought, but then Stinky had a way of dodging the law. He was sued for stealing Mid-

Continent Supply, but nothing came of it. Everyone knew that he cheated on deals. In the oil fraternity, where most deals were sealed with a handshake, cheating was easy. He stole business by secretly underbidding competitors— "cutting prices to cut throats," one oilman called it. He showed up at major fires and paid distraught property owners pennies on the dollar for property that was still ablaze. With a reassuring smile, he would lend a company money one day, then foreclose the next, collecting enormous assets for paltry investments. People compared him to H. L. Hunt, with his three wives and three sets of children, who cheated ranchers out of their drilling rights by assuring them there was no oil to be found on their land. "Butter wouldn't melt in their mouths," people used to say about men like Hunt and Stinky Davis.

My father . . . *was a forceful person.*

Parties were a rarity at the house on the corner of Westridge and Vickery. Stinky Davis expected his sons to spend their time either working or studying—and Stinky took a personal hand in both. He would sit for hours with a terrified Cullen, going over his lessons, screaming abuse, exploding at every mistake. "You're stupid, stupid, stupid," he would yell, his round, hard face flushed with anger. "You have to be the stupidest son a man ever had!" If Cullen tried to defend himself, Stinky would rear up on his short legs and roar, "If you're talking, you're not listening!"

Once, in a fit of exasperation, Stinky lifted Cullen out of his chair and threw him bodily into a closet. "If you don't know the lesson when you come out," he bellowed, "you're gonna be in there for the rest of your life!" Another time, after one mistake too many, Stinky showed Cullen the hard back of his hand, catapulting his son over backward in his chair. On many nights, Stinky would end "study period" by stalking into his room and returning with a wooden paddle that he kept for one purpose only. The crack of wood against flesh would echo through the house as Stinky went at it with a small man's abandon.

Almost from the time he could speak, Cullen was unable to finish a sentence in his father's presence. Around everyone else, he was shy but articulate. Around Stinky, he was paralyzed. Whenever Stinky asked him a question, he would stutter uncontrollably, which only made Stinky angrier and the beatings fiercer.

If my father had . . . *not made me work so hard I would probably have regretted it today*.

Like most of the oil pioneers who despised him, Stinky Davis was a self-made man. He had sold newspapers on street corners, hawked scorecards at baseball games and postcards at Coney Island, forged steel, and, during World War I, shot down German planes over France. In the oil business, he tried just about everything—roustabout, tool dresser, driller—before settling down as a clerk in a supply store. Through it all, from the day he quit school in sixth grade to the day he took over Mid-Continent Supply in 1929, he never asked for a favor from any man, and never gave one.

Cullen, on the other hand, never understood why he had to work at all. As a child, he balked at mowing the lawn for a measly 25¢ an hour. Someday he planned to run his father's huge company, Cullen told friends, and that was the only work that interested him. When Stinky ordered him to find a part-time job *or else*, Alice Davis secretly arranged a paper route for him. To sweeten the offer, she even promised to pay for the papers, which meant Cullen could pocket all the money he took in. But getting up early and carting papers around proved too much trouble for Cullen. After only two months, he quit.

People whom I consider my superiors . . . *don't exist*.
The men over me . . . *none*.
I know it is silly but I am afraid of . . . *nothing*.
When I was young, I felt guilty about . . . *nothing*.

* * *

Finally, at age fourteen, Cullen got a chance at the job he'd been born to.

At the six-story red-brick Mid-Continent Supply building in downtown Fort Worth, Cullen strode through the lobby, took the elevator to the fifth floor, passed the john with the sign on the door, "NO READING OF ANY KIND PERMITTED IN THIS LAVORATORY," and reverently entered his father's office. Stinky was standing next to the desk, screaming into a phone. He was known to rage like this for hours—cussing, threatening, bullying, ridiculing. The target of abuse could be a banker—banking was a profession he hated with something approaching biblical passion. It could be one of his own employees, caught wearing cowboy boots, or a green tie, or a mustache, all of which were strictly forbidden under Stinky's draconian dress code. Back and forth he stomped on the eighteen-inch platform that he had ordered built under his desk to give his 5'4" frame a boost, hurling abuse, spitting profanities, baring his bantam-rooster chest to a world he knew hated him.

This was the man Cullen Davis worshipped.

It didn't matter what his friends' parents said, it didn't matter how often Stinky beat him, it didn't matter that his older brother, Ken, was always his father's favorite. It didn't even matter when Stinky turned to him and, with an unceremonious wave of the hand, condemned him to a job in the mailroom stamping dates on incoming letters.

Once inside Mid-Continent, Cullen saw a different side of Stinky Davis. At first he wondered why almost every woman working in the executive offices on the fifth floor, Stinky's floor, was blonde and attractive—the sole exception being Stinky's private secretary, Cornelia Stratton, a dragonish, hatchet-faced old maid who served her boss with maniacal devotion. (People used to say that if he ordered her to fight a circular saw, "she'd head straight into it.")

But the mystery was cleared up the next time he saw his father "touring" the building. On summer afternoons he would strut around the place looking the girls up and down, leering at them over the water fountain, pinching them in the elevator. If he saw one he liked, she would receive a notice the next day from Cornelia Stratton reassigning her to the fifth floor. After that, she belonged to Stinky. Supervisors eager to keep good workers would warn young blonde newcomers: "Don't go up to the fifth floor alone. If Stinky sees you, you'll never come back." If the new recruit's husband also worked for the company, Stinky would quietly have him transferred out of town temporarily, or send him on a long "goodwill trip," visiting the distant corners of the far-flung Davis empire. If the husband worked elsewhere, Stinky might hire him, *then* ship him out of town. If anyone objected to the scheme —employee, husband, or supervisor—they were fired the same day.

This was the man Cullen Davis worshipped.

My mother . . . *was like every mother should be.*
My feeling about married life . . . *is I like living with a woman but I don't like being married to her.*

To ensure that his marital vows never interfered with his sex life, Stinky Davis spent a half-million dollars building a "retreat" on land he owned on the shore of Eagle Mountain Lake, not far from Fort Worth. He even imported a set designer from MGM to give the interiors the look of a 1930s Hollywood romance.

Such care was not wasted. Stinky spent many nights on the lake, both weekdays and weekends, while Alice Davis hosted her bridge games, church teas, and P. E. O. club meetings, first on Westridge, and then later, at the big house he bought for her in Rivercrest. If she knew, which she must have, she never complained.

One Davis Alice truly cared for was Bill, her third son. If Ken was Stinky's child, Bill was Alice's. Throughout her life, she quietly but fiercely protected him from Stinky's abusive rages at home and remorseless demands at work, turning her other sons against him in the process. She never neglected her duties to Ken and Cullen, encouraging them (mostly in vain) to attend church, behave civilly, act modestly, and treat each other more generously. But on her deathbed, it was Bill, not Ken or Cullen or even Stinky, that she cried out for.

"Bill's not here," her nurse responded, "but Cullen's home."

"I don't *want* Cullen," Alice snapped back. "I want *Bill*!"

When both Bill and Cullen appeared at her bedside, Alice took off her rings and handed them to Bill. "Keep them for me," she said, clasping his hands in hers.

After his mother's death, Cullen refused to mourn. Recollecting her exhortations to patience and prayer, he often complained, "She bitched a lot."

**My greatest weakness is . . . *a good-looking woman*.
I think most women . . . *are greedy*.**

If Cullen Davis had a weakness for attractive women, it was a secret to his classmates at Arlington Heights High School. A big school that drew from a cross-section of Fort Worth society, Arlington Heights was a place where football talked louder than oil. Student life and social status centered around the Friday game and the big fight afterward between players from the rival teams.

Cullen did his best to fit in: He went out for football and joined ROTC, a jock-heavy marching unit, but his short, slender frame was no match for a team full of country bruisers and he quit after his sophomore year. He then proceeded to turn the one social asset his father's wealth conferred on him—a shiny new Chevy Power glide—into a liability by charging classmates for the privilege of riding in it: five cents for a trip to Weber's Drive-in or the Triple-X. In Stinky's eyes, that may have looked like a sharp bit of business, but in the eyes of Cullen's classmates, it looked like the clueless act of a grade-A geek.

Cullen did little to counter the impression. By high school, his childhood shyness had evolved into a bizarre adolescent blankness—part brooding, part evasiveness, part insecurity, part catatonia. His face had only two expressions, barely distinguishable: distraction and incomprehension, the former for conversation, the latter for questions—which he would answer, if at all, only after a long, awkward pause. When told a joke, he would stare blankly straight ahead and laugh—if he laughed—only later, after the conversation had moved on. He developed an irritating habit of responding to questions indirectly, with acknowledgments rather than answers: "all right" instead of yes or no.

Not surprisingly, dates during these years were few and far between. He did go out with one girl, on and off, for most of his junior and senior years, although more out of desperation than devotion. Both continued to insist to friends that they were "not going steady."

At Stinky's insistence, he enrolled at Texas A&M, a men-only, military-style engineering school dropped in the empty hill country of east Texas—"West Point on the Brazos," it was called. Stinky chose it for its isolation, its discipline, and because it wasn't *too* good a school. "I sent 'em all to A&M," he would chuckle, "because I didn't want 'em to be smarter than me."

After graduation, Cullen spent three dimly lit years in the Navy (stationed, strangely, in Indiana). In letters home, he complained bitterly about the indignity of taking orders from anybody other than his father. But Stinky considered military experience good discipline and advised his son to use the time "learning managerial skills," which Cullen took to mean "how to order people around."

Not until he returned to the strange sexual incubator of Mid-Continent Supply—now under a spreading corporate umbrella called Kendavis Industries International —did Cullen's "weakness" begin to emerge. It was hard to see at first. Like Stinky's own sexual exploits, Cullen's early indiscretions were sucked back into the black hole of Davis family privacy and payoffs. But slowly, one by one, like bodies bobbing to the surface after a shipwreck, stories began to circulate: How Cullen had a taste for "bad girls" from the other side of town, carhops and barmaids

and worse. How he liked to dress them up, show them a
little of the good life, then dump them. How he wallpa-
pered his bathroom with *Playboy* foldouts, but kept the
really raunchy stuff in his car.

In a bar, he would pull out an especially lurid scrap of
pornography—picture playing cards were a particular
favorite—and slip it under the eyes of a prostitute, or a
pimp, or just an unsuspecting patron. His eyes would dart
back and forth and he would whisper in a breathy voice,
"Looks interesting, huh?" If someone jumped away in
disgust, he would stuff the photo back into his pocket and
laugh his squeaky laugh, as if to say, "Can't take a joke,
huh?"

A woman who saw him prowling from bar to bar
thought "he just *looked* like a trick, a John Doe. You
could tell right away he was looking for sexual favors. He
would say suggestive things, goofy things, then laugh at
his own jokes and leer at you, like, 'Get it?' " Down at
company headquarters, they told the story about how Cullen approached a company executive at the Ridglea Country Club and whispered in his ear, "Your daughter is the
best piece of ass of all the employees in this company."

There were stories about "Jekyll and Hyde" parties at
Stinky's lakeside retreat, where friends from the bars,
brothels, and pool halls of Fort Worth would congregate
and Cullen could satisfy his increasingly bizarre sexual
appetites.

Outsiders got their first glimpse of Cullen's dark private
world at a bachelor party thrown for a friend at the Western Hills Inn in 1960. More than a hundred guests frolicked
around the striped poolside cabanas, among them Tim
Curry, future Fort Worth district attorney. The bars were
open, the liquor free, and the anticipation level high as
the drummer struck up a grinding "Bump-a-dump, bump-
a-dump, bump-a-dump." To a chorus of cowboy whoops
and whistles, three glitter-clad women popped out of the
crowd, breasts jiggling, tassels whirling, hips undulating,
huge smiles pasted on their faces like price tags. A little
vortex of energy and forbiddenness formed around them,

and the whooping men gave it space, scrambling to avoid being touched by these jiggling objects of their desire. Only after the two groups had separated themselves, spectators on one side, dancers on the other, did the crowd finally erupt with erotic fervor.

Just at that moment, Cullen Davis broke through the front line of spectators. He stared full bore at one of the three nude women in front of him. She stared back. Before anyone could move, he grabbed her by the arm and jerked her violently out of sight of the crowd. Someone heard her say as she disappeared, "I'm sorry, Cullen." A few minutes later, someone else saw him dragging her, now with a robe thrown around her, to his car. He opened the door, pushed her in, then sped away.

Two years later, on August 18, 1962, Cullen married Sandra Masters, a pretty honey blonde from a middle-class family in Fort Worth. After three months of dating, he told her one night, "I'm going to marry you." And that was that.

Stinky was harder to convince. Although Sandra qualified for a night at the lake, she did not have the social pedigree that Stinky considered the only rationale for marriage. At a command dinner appearance, Sandra found her future father-in-law a "frightening, hellacious" man. That was before Stinky paid a visit to her parents. "I want to make it perfectly clear," he told them. "Cullen's foremost concern is his work. His work comes before anything." Finally, relieved that at least she wasn't a stripper or a whore, Stinky gave his consent.

Sandra knew that Cullen was rich, but not until after the wedding did she discover how rich. For six weeks, they traveled Europe and North Africa in the grandest manner. In Paris, he took her to a private showing at Christian Dior. He bought her a $10,000 mink coat as a honeymoon present. Back in Fort Worth, she had to learn how to call a caterer and how to use the personal shopper service at Neiman-Marcus. They settled into a charming yellow brick house with blue trim in an upscale subdivision, Embassy West. It had a patio.

In return for this shower of luxuries, Cullen demanded surprisingly little from Sandra: a child—she was pregnant within three months of the marriage—and a chance to play Pygmalion. Instead of honey blonde, he wanted her hair yellow blonde; he picked the shade himself. He also wanted her breasts bigger, and she dutifully underwent breast enlargement surgery. When it was done, Cullen had what he could have found in another woman but preferred to create in this one—a busty blonde.

No amount of silicone or peroxide, however, could keep Cullen's eyes from wandering for long. Even before their first child, Thomas Cullen Davis II, was born on August 3, 1963, he began to spend more time away from home. One of his favorite stops on frequent out-of-town trips was the Playboy mansion in Chicago, where he could combine two of his favorite activities: women and pool. Closer to home, he made no effort to hide his wandering attentions. One morning, when Sandra woke up and discovered that Cullen hadn't come home, she drove down the street and saw his car in a neighbor's driveway. Through the front window she could see Cullen and the neighbor embracing. He hadn't even bothered to close the curtains.

Next came the beatings. They began with a slap during a tennis match at the Ridglea Country Club. She beat him—at tennis—so he hit her. Some time later, a visiting neighbor found Sandra sitting in the dining room, curtains closed, her face covered with bruises. She had already called Stinky. He was on his way.

Stinky took one look at his daughter-in-law and ordered Cullen to come home. When the two were face to face, he stabbed his stubby finger at Cullen's chest. "I want to tell you this," he said, his face flashing red. "If I *ever* hear of you touching her again you will be out of the company!"

For Sandra, it was a hollow victory. True, with Stinky on her side, she would never have to worry about Cullen hitting her again. "The only restraining influence Cullen ever had on him was his daddy," said one family friend. "Ol' Stinky was smarter than Cullen and meaner than Cullen. And he had control of the money—the *real* restraining influence."

But what would happen when the old man died?

Fortunately, Sandra would never have to face that question. On the same tennis court where Cullen had struck her, he met someone else. The rumors were already flying back to her: There was another woman. She, too, was pretty, blonde, and buxom.

And her name was Priscilla.

5

He was everything Priscilla Lee Childers had dreamed about in a man. Big and tall, a full foot taller and twice her weight, affectionate and "artistic," Jasper Baker was just out of the Marines, lean and tawny and hungry for fun. No wonder all the girls in the swirl of nightlife that Priscilla called home were after him, fondling the bristly back of his head, tracing his tattoos with their long red nails. At twenty-one, he seemed almost as old and worldly as her father, the handsome rodeo cowboy whom she knew only from her mother's pictures. "If you ever met him, you'd like him," was all her mother would say when Priscilla came to her cradling the little mother-of-pearl frame and asked about the exotic, dark-eyed man in the photograph.

Audie Childers had warned her daughter about marrying too young. She herself had spent ten hard, childless years with the wrong man in California before returning to Houston and marrying Richard Childers, the man in the mother-of-pearl frame. Childers stuck around just long enough to sire three children, then he too "wandered off."

But Jasper wasn't like that, Priscilla protested. He wasn't just another soldier on leave looking for a good time.

Priscilla had learned the hard way about the boys in uniform who hunted the sleazy Naugahyde bars and strip joints hard by the port of Houston. When she was fifteen, one of them had told her how beautiful she was and how much he loved her and how he would never hurt her. And then he raped her. Or at least that's what it seemed like: She kept saying no and he kept saying yes yes yes as he pressed his weight down on her. At the time, there was no one else in her life, so she forgave him. She even saw him off at the train station when his leave was up. It was a scene right out of a movie, she thought: his face pressed against the window, his lips forming the words, "I'm sorry." But then, when he didn't write or call, she began to wonder how honest he had been after all, if the lips had really said "I'm sorry," and she hardened against him.

But that was ages ago. She was sixteen now, and far more worldly. Besides, Jasper loved her.

They married in the fall of 1957, and in July of the next year, Priscilla had a daughter, Angela Dee. They called her simply "Dee."

But father or not, Jasper Baker wasn't about to miss his fix of cheap women and cheaper booze. He would stagger in unapologetically at five in the morning reeking of perfume and whiskey. One night, Priscilla followed him to a local hamburger drive-in where he met up with one of the carhops as she got off work. Priscilla couldn't decide what was more appalling, that her husband was cheating on her or that the carhop was twenty-four years old. "I couldn't believe it," she said later. "With an old woman!"

Less than a year after the marriage, Priscilla packed her bags and moved back to her mother's house. When Jasper called to apologize and plead for her return, she told him, "I've been hurt one time too many." She was seventeen years old.

After a brief trip to California and an even briefer affair with a drag racer at the Bakersfield Speedway, she returned to the nightlife of Houston, the only place, it seemed, where she felt sure of attracting attention. She tried a daytime job, gift wrapping at a local department store, but the quota system strangled her creativity. One day she walked off to lunch and kept on walking.

Besides, she preferred the night. In the daylight she was just a short girl with strangely oversized breasts, a pallid complexion, plain features, and limp brown hair. At night, in the gilded glow of a club like the Tidelands, surrounded by rich velour, brass rails, and veils of cigarette smoke, she could be a voluptuous raven-haired beauty.

Among the many men whose nocturnal attentions she attracted at the Tidelands was a tall, tan, sandy-haired Oklahoman named Jack Wilborn. He had a soft, manly voice and the handsome lived-in face of a Hollywood cowboy just past his prime—but only just past. And, best of all, like the cowboys in the movies, he had come to rescue her.

Unfazed by the twenty-year age difference—he was arrestingly handsome even for a forty-year-old—Priscilla leapt onto his horse and they rode off together into what looked like a sunset of marital bliss. Jack built a small used-car dealership into a huge and prosperous enterprise using the unlikeliest formula—honesty. Like his father, a dairyman who refused to cut off milk supplies to any of his customers during the Depression no matter how much they owed him, Jack earned a statewide reputation for square dealing, and the money poured in: three million in a good year. He became a pillar of the Fort Worth business community, joined the prestigious Petroleum Club, where he could rub shoulders with oil tycoons, and the exclusive Ridglea Country Club, where their wives played tennis.

In the meantime, Priscilla's tiny body bore two more children: Jack, Jr. (called Jackie) in 1961, and Andrea in 1964. With six-year-old Dee, that brought her brood to three. When the time came, she joined the PTA and headed a Brownie troop. Thanks to the success of Jack's business, she always had a new car to drive and a maid to clean the succession of new houses she needed as her family expanded.

Jack was not only a good provider and an ardent lover, he was a loving father. The oil tycoons down at the Petroleum Club, the Basses and the Davises, meant nothing to him. He would rather stay home and watch Andrea make miniature roses out of clay. On those occasions when he had to travel, he would call home two or three times a day, often stopping at a phone booth on the road just to hear his children's voices. And they would line up to hear his.

He loved all three of his children, but there was no hiding the special bond he felt with Andrea. When Priscilla went into the hospital to give birth to their first child, Jack prayed for a girl. He even bought Priscilla a car—a dusty-rose Cadillac—"to bring my daughter home in," he predicted confidently. But the first child turned out to be a boy.

Three years later, Andrea answered those prayers. "When Andrea was born," Priscilla told friends, "there was no one in the world more excited than Jack." She grew up tall and beautiful, with her mother's raven hair and her father's umber skin. From an early age, she spoke the careful, perfect English that her grandmother taught her—when she spoke at all. Friends called her "deep-thinking," not because she was morose or studious, but because she lacked the giggly frivolity so common to girls her age.

Her teachers said she had a "gift" in art. They meant drawing and sculpting, but Jack knew her gift went much deeper than that. Her touch was magic. She could take the most common object, a box, a comb, a tissue, and transform it into something beautiful, often with no more than a twist or a fold or a piece of colored paper. And when she touched him, when she hugged him every morning without fail, and said in her sweet, soft voice, "I love you, Daddy," *he* was transformed.

Priscilla had everything she ever wanted: a good family, a good home, a good husband, a good life. During the lonely nights along the waterfront in the port of Houston, she had fantasized this kind of life—"a little cottage with a white picket fence" is the way she described it to skeptical friends. But on a slow night, in the velour darkness of the Tidelands, even she had begun to doubt if it could ever be. No doubt about it: Seventeen-year-old Priscilla would have thought twenty-five-year-old Priscilla was living in heaven.

There was just one problem. If this was heaven, why was she so bored?

Soon the old fantasies were replaced by new, more glamorous ones. On the eve of a trip to Mexico with Jack, a friend told her that Mexican men went wild for blondes. Priscilla had her long beautiful hair bleached a honey blonde. Her wardrobe changed: from high necks, full sleeves, and knee-length skirts to décolletage, sleeveless blouses, tight jeans, and halter tops. For more than a year, she had scoffed at the most recent fashion fad sweeping the country, especially Texas—miniskirts. Now she embraced it. Inch by inch, her hemlines crept closer and closer to her pencil-thin waist. "They make me look younger," she explained with a coy smile.

She began seeing a psychiatrist. She spent hours, then afternoons, then days away from the house. Her new friends were other women with troubled marriages. They would talk endlessly about "self-discovery" and the "wrong turns" they had taken. She had a hysterectomy. She complained about too much time on her hands even as she became a virtual stranger to her children. To "keep herself from going crazy," she took up tennis, joining the other wives in the daily rituals of ennui at the Ridglea Country Club.

The next step was inevitable.

"Are you okay?" asked Susan Spencer, a friend and frequent tennis partner of Priscilla's at the Ridglea Country Club. Priscilla hadn't been her usual fiercely competitive self on the court this day. She had, in fact, been acting more like the club matrons she so detested, the ladies in the latest whites from Neiman's who would wait for an hour in the blazing sun, sipping iced tea on the little deck behind the tennis house, only to lose interest once they glided onto the court.

"Jack's here," Priscilla said absently, as if the comment were not responsive, although clearly it was. She had been coming to the club almost once a day recently, and usually alone, but on weekends there was no way to keep him from coming along. They saw each other so little already. For months now, Jack had been getting home late in the evenings, even on weekday nights, after playing gin and gambling. Priscilla knew he was waiting for her to complain—but she never did.

Susan changed the subject. "I like your hair." After returning from Mexico, Priscilla had decided to keep her hair blonde, even lighten it a little.

"It's Jack's idea," she lied. "First it was a wig. Now it's peroxide. Next thing you know, he'll want me to get these enlarged." She grabbed one of her breasts and hoisted it in the air. They both laughed.

Like most of Priscilla's friends, Susan didn't believe for a minute that the blonde hair was Jack's idea. She had watched Priscilla's transformation from den mother to country club vamp too closely. More recently, she had seen Priscilla around the club between matches, flicking her new blonde hair and nuzzling up to the waiters and lifeguards. To Susan, the evidence pointed in the oddest possible direction: At age twenty-six, Priscilla Wilborn was terrified of getting old. Perhaps it was her recent hysterectomy, Susan thought. Or perhaps the reality of being married to a fifty-year-old man had finally caught up to her.

The two women had just begun another volley when Priscilla noticed a man and a woman holding rackets standing at the edge of the court. She recognized the woman, a slender blonde with a pretty face and a hard look.

"Priscilla," the woman called out. "How about doubles?"

Not in the mood for more company, Priscilla was about to offer the court to the woman when she saw the man standing next to her. He was almost as slender and taller only by an inch or two—the size of a boy. His dark, wavy hair was combed straight back and glistened in the sunlight like a 1930s movie star's. That's the way she thought he looked: sophisticated, continental, exotic, even a little dangerous—"like a ballroom dancer."

"Priscilla," said the woman with a gesture toward the dark-haired man. "I don't believe you've met my husband, Cullen."

6

Less than a month later, Jack Wilborn found himself in the office of his used car dealership with tears in his eyes talking to a complete stranger. He had been through the worst week in his life. He hadn't changed clothes or slept in days, hadn't spent two consecutive nights under the same roof in a week. Not since the night in Okmulgee, Oklahoma, when he was eight years old had he felt so lonely, angry, frustrated, and hurt all at once. That was the night his retarded brother set fire to the family house and it burned to the ground along with everything he owned except the pair of shorts he was wearing.

He had thought walking out on Priscilla would help. But it didn't. He had thought filing the divorce papers would help. But it didn't. There was a fire inside him and nothing he did could put it out. So he hid his handsome, tanned face in his hands and cried like an eight-year-old boy who's lost everything.

"I love my children very much," he finally said, "and I want to get them from my wife. What kind of chance do you think I have?"

The stranger with him was Cliff Bailey, head of one of Fort Worth's largest private investigation firms. "Who has the kids now?" he asked.

"The judge gave me temporary custody," Wilborn replied, collecting himself.

"I assume she disputes that," said Bailey. He had heard scores of these stories. He kept a staff of almost one hundred busy, mostly with cases just like Wilborn's.

"Yeah. She says she wants the girls, Dee and Andrea, but she really doesn't." Of all the possible outcomes, losing Andrea was to Wilborn the most unthinkable.

"You know it's typical in these cases for the mother to get custody."

Wilborn grew suddenly indignant. "Priscilla doesn't want to raise these kids!"

Bailey wasn't surprised by the outburst. He had seen far worse. In fact, Wilborn seemed to him surprisingly free of the usual bitterness. No wild denunciations, no threats, no blood vows to "keep the bitch from getting a single penny." Not one use of the word "whore." All Wilborn seemed to feel was regret and sadness.

"What do you think my chances are?" he asked again.

"Well, I have succeeded in sixty-eight out of seventy cases in getting custody of the children for my client." Wilborn felt a wave of warmth, the first in a long time. "But you must have proof that the mother is unfit for some reason."

Wilborn was ready. He told Bailey how Priscilla used foul language in front of the children; how she spent all day, every day, at the club playing tennis, leaving their children in the care of a babysitter; how, when she was home, she never cooked them a hot meal, but instead served crackers and peanut butter on the living room floor; and, last but not least, how she ran around the house in her underwear in front of the kids.

"It's not enough," said Bailey, shaking his head. "There's only one way to persuade a Texas judge that a mother's unfit and that's to show that she's running around on you."

Wilborn paused. He didn't want to destroy Priscilla, he just wanted his kids. There had to be another way.

Bailey read his thoughts. "That's the only way."

"I'm sure she is," Wilborn conceded softly. He didn't have any details, but he didn't have any doubts either.

"Do you have any proof?" Bailey pressed.

"No," said Wilborn.

"Then we'll just have to get some."

A few weeks later, Jack Wilborn closed the door of his office and switched on the big reel-to-reel tape recorder that Bailey had supplied. On the tape were the last two days of calls on Priscilla's phone. He had thought his biggest problem would be getting into the house to hook up the tap in the first place. But thanks to the maid, May, that part had been easy. The real problem was finding time for the dozens of hours of tape the tap produced.

Listening was sheer agony. Not for what was on the tapes—in the first few weeks the tap had produced nothing incriminating—but for what might be on them. All the time he was listening, Wilborn kept thinking: The next call could be the one. He would hear Priscilla's sultry voice, and then a man's voice—undoubtedly a young man's voice—and then what? Did he really want to hear a conversation between his wife and her lover?

This night, he found out.

"I'm sorry we couldn't be together tonight." It was Priscilla's voice: soft and petulant and ten years younger, the voice of a schoolgirl seductress.

"Will I see you tomorrow?" It was a man's voice—a young man's voice.

"I don't know." Priscilla was being coy. Wilborn recognized the tone.

"I can't hardly wait till then," he said.

"Maybe we shouldn't." Priscilla, still coy.

"Priscilla!" Mock exasperation.

"You're crowding me." Mock warning.

"Don't be mean," he cooed.

"I could never be mean to you," she cooed back. "It's just that distance is sometimes good for two people."

"But we're not just any two people."

"You wouldn't want me to be easy, like that woman I saw you with on the court today."

"She's not my type."

"What is your type? What kind of girl do you like."

"A girl just like you, Priscilla. Beautiful blonde hair, pretty eyes, good legs, forty-two cups . . ."

Wilborn snapped off the machine.

He didn't sleep that night. The next morning, he seized the first pretext to call Priscilla. In no time, the conversation grew heated and bitter. Insults ricocheted back and forth. Finally, it burst out of him. "And just when are you gonna grow into forty-two cups?"

Priscilla exploded. "You son of a bitch, you're tapping my phone. You son of a . . ." Wilborn slammed the phone down and immediately called Bailey. "Get that tap off now or we're in big trouble," Bailey ordered.

The tap disappeared in time, but with it went Bailey's best chance of making the case. Hours of purring and cooing, however hard it was for Jack Wilborn to listen to, did not constitute proof of an extramarital affair. And without that, Bailey told Wilborn, keeping his kids was a long shot.

Not long afterward, Wilborn received a phone call from a total stranger. "My name is Sandra Davis," she said. "Did you know that your wife and my husband are seeing each other?"

The romance was slow getting started. A few days after the tennis court meeting, Priscilla and Cullen ran into each other in the Terrace Room of the Colonial Country Club. It was the week of the Colonial PGA golf tournament, a sports extravaganza that threw the spotlight of national attention briefly on the social elite of Fort Worth. Cullen, who was without Sandra, invited Priscilla, who was without Jack, to join the group at his table. There he proceeded to flirt like an awkward schoolboy the rest of the afternoon, winking and blinking and twitching his nose and smiling for no discernible reason.

It was an odd smile. It didn't turn up at the ends and

it didn't show any teeth. Because his mouth was so wide and his lips so thin, it really wasn't much more than a long horizontal scar—an old incision that had healed badly. He would stare at her for five or ten minutes straight with that unchanging smile and eyes that never seemed to focus.

Still, thought Priscilla, he was sophisticated, even courtly. His clothes were well made, his hair well cut. The others at the table treated him with deference. They didn't seem to mind the awkward smile or the occasional crude remark. They laughed lustily at his barnyard jokes. Once, when she got up to leave, he scuttled around the table and cut off her exit, stepping in close, his face six inches from hers. "I hope I didn't say anything to offend you?" he said in a soft, shy voice—like a boy's, Priscilla thought. Later that night, he wedged his slender body between Priscilla and another guest. He put his face six inches from hers and said, almost in a whisper, "Excuse me." The smell of his cologne was overpowering.

The next day, like some fairy-tale prince, he disappeared. Priscilla didn't know it at the time, but he had gone to Paris for the annual international air show. (While he was there, also unknown to Priscilla, Sandra Davis filed for divorce.) All Priscilla knew was that he didn't call.

Finally, in August 1967, she called him.

"Do you remember me?" she asked in her coyest voice. Cullen said he surely did.

There was a long pause. She had to restart the conversation. "I called to see if you can get me some tickets for the game"—the upcoming exhibition football game between the Dallas Cowboys and the Green Bay Packers.

Cullen chuckled deep in his throat. "Your chances of getting tickets to that game are slim to none."

Another long pause as Priscilla waited for a "but." It didn't come. "Well, thanks," she finally said, and then hung up.

After that Priscilla never expected to hear from the ballroom dancer again. But it was only a few days before he called back. "I still haven't got those tickets you're looking for," said Cullen. "But I have got a night free for dinner."

For their first rendezvous, Cullen picked an obscure barbecue joint. It was probably better, he explained, not to be seen in public together given the "nasty situations they currently found themselves in."

For several months, they saw each other now and then: only at night, only in out-of-the-way places, preferably in Dallas, thirty-five miles away. He smuggled her tickets to the Cowboys games but always at the other end of the stadium, far from his company box. Whenever Priscilla complained, Cullen just reiterated the need for "absolute discretion."

Then one day he disappeared. Again. Priscilla waited, but the phone never rang. A few days later she heard that Cullen had left for New York City to host Kendavis Industries' annual Christmas extravaganza for VIP customers at the Waldorf-Astoria. On the night of the party, after most of the guests had staggered up to their rooms or to waiting limousines, Cullen finally called.

"I know this isn't the best timing," he said, his voice a little too earnest, "both of us getting divorced and everything. But I want to marry you."

Priscilla was struck speechless. This was the first mention of marriage—by either of them.

Before she could answer, he asked her to spend the New Year's holiday with him in Acapulco—"to hell with the lawyers." Priscilla was thrilled. She saw herself sipping margaritas in a seaside cabana and welcoming in the new year, 1968, with a kiss under a tropical moon.

Then came news that Cullen had taken Sandra and their children to Stinky Davis's big house in Rivercrest for a family holiday celebration. Priscilla spent a wretched Christmas Day, sullen and distraught. She confided her fears to a friend: "What if Sandra is trying to use Cullen's father and his money to make him come back to her?" She knew Cullen well enough to know that Stinky was the only power in the world he feared.

But on December 26, Cullen called again. "I'm leaving

Sandra," he reassured her. "She's trying to blackmail me
with some Polaroid pictures of furniture she says I broke.
She says she'll prove in court that I have a violent temper.
I've had it. I need to get out of here. Are we still on for
Acapulco?"

Priscilla's heart leapt at the word *Acapulco*. The rest
was lost. "You bet!" she squealed.

7

"Did you know Cullen and Priscilla have gone to Acapulco
for the holiday?" Jack Wilborn recognized Sandra Davis's
reedy, indignant voice.

She had been calling regularly for several months, ostensibly to share intelligence—she had a remarkable network of informants—but mostly to commiserate, and
occasionally rail against the injustice of adultery.

Somehow Sandra had learned the flight number and
arrival time of Cullen's return from Acapulco. Wilborn
immediately called Cliff Bailey. For months they had been
searching for proof that Priscilla and Cullen were sleeping
together. Now it was about to fall into their hands. "We've
got the bastard!" Wilborn exulted. Bailey had expected
him to say "bitch."

On the evening of January 2, 1968, the flight from
Mexico touched down on a foggy, cold runway at Love
Field in Dallas. Cullen Davis and Priscilla Wilborn walked
off the plane hand in hand, she in a huge sombrero and
white miniskirt—the better to show off her tan thighs—
and carrying a teddy bear almost half her size, he in a
sports coat and no tie. They walked casually to the arrival
area and waited for their bags. Neither noticed the five
figures standing at a mezzanine rail overlooking the baggage claim area.

Wilborn was the first to spot them. He turned to Sandra, Bailey, and two of Bailey's investigators and pointed. "There are our lovebirds now."

Cullen and Priscilla left the airport in Priscilla's white Cadillac. Wilborn and Sandra followed with Bailey's two men. Bailey left on other business but gave instructions to call him if anything developed.

After a stop at Cullen's office in the Mid-Continent Building, the Cadillac proceeded to the Green Oaks Inn, Fort Worth's fanciest hostelry and, since leaving the mansion, Cullen Davis's home between homes.

Separated only by a few dozen feet of darkness, the two cars pulled into the huge parking lot. From one of its green, parklike meridians, Wilborn watched as Cullen picked up the key from the lobby desk. When he came out, he offered Priscilla his arm and the two walked arm-in-arm up the stairs and out of sight. Wilborn felt his face go red under his perpetual tan.

Wilborn started to follow, but Bailey's men held him back. They might be spotted if they followed closely enough to see which room Cullen had been given. The motel was a labyrinth of courtyards and exposed hallways. They could make a wrong turn and meet Cullen and Priscilla coming back at them. Instead, an investigator named Swain "liberated" the registration card from the front desk. It confirmed that Cullen and Priscilla had checked into the same room. It was time to call in Bailey.

While they waited, they searched the Cadillac, using Wilborn's extra set of keys. In the trunk they found a camera and several rolls of film, presumably from the Acapulco trip, which they also liberated. Meanwhile, Wilborn opened the hood, pulled out the coil wire, and threw it as far as he could into the darkness at the edge of the parking lot. Whatever happened that night, Cullen wouldn't be able to follow them.

When Bailey arrived, he found Wilborn, Sandra, and his two men, cameras ready, waiting near the door to Cullen's room. "Jack," he whispered, "you and Mrs. Davis wait downstairs."

Reluctantly, Sandra left; Wilborn didn't budge.

"There's no way in hell I'm gonna miss this," he shot back in a fierce whisper.

Bailey nodded. He took one last look down both ends of the hall and out into the darkened courtyard. He looked at Swain. "Now!"

Swain's huge foot was the first to hit the door. Before the echo came back from the other side of the courtyard, three more blows landed and the dark wood door, which had looked so solid, splintered into kindling. The two investigators jumped through first. One held out a can of Mace and sprayed into the darkness ahead of him. The other one pointed his camera in the direction of the bed and started snapping.

The first brilliant flash of the bulbs caught Cullen in midair, leaping out of bed in bikini underwear. "You can't do this!" he screamed. "You can't do this and get away . . ." He inhaled a cloud of Mace and exploded in a fit of coughing.

In the second flash, Wilborn saw Priscilla, a tiny statue of flesh, her huge blonde hair in disarray. She kept her head down to avoid the camera, but the light of the third flash caught her naked body in midflight as she scrambled toward the bathroom screaming, "Wilborn, you son of a bitch! If you don't get out of here, I'll call the police." Another flash. Cullen had reached the balcony door, trying to curse but only gasping for air. Priscilla had reached the bathroom, but before she could slam the door, another flash. There she was, standing straight up in the bathroom doorway, buck naked, her untanned breasts staring out of the darkness, her face screwed up in an expression of utter fury. Darkness again. The sound of the door slamming and Priscilla continuing her screams from the other side. "I'm gonna call the police."

"Open the door," Wilborn called to her, "and I'll hand you the phone."

Another flash. Sandra Davis appeared in the hall doorway. On the other side of the room, her husband had made it out onto the balcony. "Cullen," she screamed at him in a voice that carried to the far end of the courtyard, "you dirty sonofabitch! You'll never see the kids again!"

Bailey's men made a quick check of the room for incriminating evidence, then ran out, dragging Wilborn and Sandra with them. On the way back to the parking lot, Swain pulled Bailey aside. "It's a good thing we used that Mace," he said. "Cullen had a gun under his pillow."

At eight o'clock the next morning, Wilborn's phone rang. It was Cullen Davis. "Jack, this is Cullen." The voice betrayed nothing—a stony monotone. He could have wanted to buy a car. "I want you to know I intend to marry Priscilla," he said. "Would you come down to my office so we can talk?"

If Cullen's purpose was to throw Wilborn off base, he succeeded. "Let me think about it and call you back," was all he could think to say. As soon as he hung up, he called Bailey.

The private investigator and his men had already been on the carpet that morning in front of an irate captain at the Fort Worth Police Department who also happened to be, in his off-duty hours, head of security for the Green Oaks Inn. Unless they wanted to face criminal charges, he informed them, they would have to pay for the broken door, return the purloined registration card, and hand over all the photos. It might have been worse except that the police captain was the brother-in-law of one of Jack Wilborn's closest friends. Cullen may have had connections, but Wilborn had friends.

Bailey didn't like the sound of the meeting at all. "I don't think you should do it," he told Wilborn, "but if you do, I want to be there." He also insisted the meeting take place at the Continental Inn on East Lancaster, where he rented an office and "had contacts." Remembering the pistol under Cullen's pillow, Bailey wanted a place where he could provide protection—"just in case."

Cullen was already sitting at a booth in the motel restaurant when Wilborn and Bailey arrived. As they approached, he refused to look at them—a bad sign, thought

Bailey. Even from a distance, Cullen looked edgy and on guard. Wilborn couldn't blame him for that. He couldn't have slept very well the night before. Wilborn sat down across from him. Bailey rode the outside edge of the seat. He motioned to a waiter to get them something to drink. The waiter, in fact, was one of his men. With a man like Cullen, it wasn't possible to be too safe.

As soon as Wilborn was seated, Cullen thrust his head across the table and said fiercely, "You're not going to get any of my money!"

Wilborn was visibly relieved. "I'm not interested in your money," he said, waving away the suggestion. Cullen had apparently convinced himself that Wilborn—like everybody else—was trying to hold him up. A suit for alienation of affection could cost him dearly. "The only thing I want," Wilborn said slowly, "is custody of my children."

In an instant, all the tension went out of Cullen's face. He leaned back in the booth and put one arm up on the seatback. There was a long, satisfied pause. "I don't suppose you'd consider splitting the children up? Say, you keep Jackie and let Priscilla have the girls."

After a lifetime of selling cars, Wilborn knew when a deal was a deal. Cullen was still bargaining, but his heart wasn't in it. "No, sir!" said Wilborn.

"What about Dee? How about letting Priscilla have Dee? After all, Dee's hers, not yours."

"No, sir!" Wilborn repeated. "And you can tell Priscilla she isn't going to get the Cadillac or the thousand dollars a month she's asked for either. Tell her that for me."

Cullen bristled at being bullied, but he didn't retract anything. The best he could do was save face. "Of course, I haven't decided yet whether I am ready to take on the responsibility of Priscilla," he said, his eyes darting back and forth. Then he stood up and walked out.

"You know," Wilborn mused to Bailey, "Cullen sure seemed relieved when he found out I wasn't after his money!"

* * *

Less than a week later, a man walked into the small, ramshackle office of Jerry Hittson, a Fort Worth private investigator with a past variously described as both "colorful" and "shadowy." According to Hittson, the man who came to his office that day was short and slender, with wavy black hair and a strange smile. He wanted Hittson to tap the phone of a woman he was seeing. Her name was Priscilla. He said he suspected her of seeing other men.

And there was something else the man wanted done, Hittson said. He called it "special work." He had heard of Hittson's underworld contacts. He offered Hittson several thousand dollars to find some "heavy shooters" in Detroit who would perform these special services. First, he wanted his wife killed. Her name was Sandra. "This is the only way I can get custody of my boys," he told Hittson. He also wanted four men killed. They were Jack Wilborn, Cliff Bailey, and two investigators who worked for Bailey whose names he didn't know. He was willing to pay tens of thousands of dollars for each "service."

Hittson took the money but did nothing.

8

"Do you, Cullen, take this woman to be your lawfully wedded wife? . . ."

Cullen could finally relax; everything had been taken care of. After the meeting at the Continental Inn, he had told Priscilla, "Let Jack have custody for now and don't worry about getting anything out of the divorce. I won't just duplicate what you had with Jack, I'll give you ten thousand times more than he ever thought about giving you." Priscilla sulked about the kids for weeks, but the two leopardskin coats Cullen bought in Europe cheered her back up. As for Wilborn, for reasons unfathomable to Cullen, he had stuck to his pledge not to sue for alienation of affection.

Sandra, too, after all her troublemaking, had turned out to be a cheap payoff. She got the house on Ridgehaven Road (which Cullen never liked anyway), a new car, her personal belongings (mostly things Cullen had given her over the years), and a paltry $20,000 in cash—paid out over a year and a half. That was *it*. Her share of the half-billion-dollar Davis family fortune: nothing.

The last piece of the plan had fallen into place at the Green Oaks Inn two days before the ceremony, where, in the presence of a notary, Priscilla had signed an agreement giving up all rights to any of Cullen's money or property. "It is [our] mutual desire that the separate property and estate now owned or hereafter acquired by Cullen as well as the income accruing on the separate property of Cullen, shall become and be the separate property of Cullen . . ." He had the words memorized. When he recited them to himself, a great feeling of peace descended on him and he could say, without reservation:

"I do."

"Do you, Priscilla, take this man to be your lawfully wedded husband? . . ."

Priscilla wished her kids were with her. No matter what Cullen said, she should never have given them up. "Just don't fight Jack," he kept saying. "Let him have the kids." She couldn't understand why he was so adamant, but she couldn't say no to him. Now it was coming back to haunt her—as everything did, it seemed.

Cullen had also been adamant about the prenuptial agreement. "You have to sign this before we can get married," he had said in his coldest tone. When he put it that way, what else could she do? Besides, she wasn't interested in his money; she didn't even know how much he had. If the rumors she was hearing were true, then it was a lot, but the Davis family was notoriously private and rumors were notoriously exaggerated. A friend had asked her what she would do if someday they divorced. "That won't happen," she replied confidently. "We're in love." With that thought, she answered without hesitation:

"I do."

The minister pronounced them man and wife and the small group assembled in the First Methodist Church on a hot day in August, 1968, adjourned to a reception on the porch of the big house in Rivercrest. Priscilla, in her Geoffrey Beene wedding gown cut ten inches above her knees, kissed the beaming groom. There was food and cake and extravagant flowers, and the Rivercrest house with its stately brick-and-timber facade and huge old trees made a splendid backdrop for a wedding party.

But the mood was strangely somber that night. So somber that a casual observer might have taken the subdued gathering on the porch for a group of mourners at a funeral.

Which, in fact, is exactly what it was.

Only a few hours before the ceremony, Stinky Davis had died.

Later, Cullen insisted that the timing of the wedding was purely coincidental. The florist, the gown, the food, and the minister had all been arranged for days. But then, Stinky had been near death for days. Priscilla herself wanted to know why, given the parade of visitors filing past Stinky's deathbed, Cullen never allowed her near him. Wouldn't he want to meet his new daughter-in-law, she wondered? When news came of his death, Priscilla offered to delay the ceremony, but Cullen insisted on going through with it.

Over the next few days, when people approached Cullen to offer their condolences, he would nod in appreciation, "Thank you," and then gesture toward Priscilla. "And I'd like for you to meet my new wife." He loved to watch their jaws drop.

The first year of marriage was like "finding a genie in a bottle and having all your wishes come true," Priscilla told a friend. They traveled to Europe—Paris, Rome, Amsterdam, Berlin—then to South America—Caracas and

Rio—then back to Europe for a car trip along the Riviera—Nice, Cannes, Monte Carlo. At first they flew first class. Then, when an airline lost Cullen's luggage, he bought a Learjet and they went in a class by themselves. ("If you want anything done right," he screamed at the Braniff supervisor, "you've got to do it yourself.") New York City became a favorite weekend getaway spot. They would stay at the company suite in the Waldorf, see a show, and shop, shop, shop. One time, they "popped over to Paris" on a few hours' notice for a single business meeting. To immortalize her journeys, Priscilla bought a gold charm in the shape of a globe and studded it with diamond chips to mark the places they had been.

At home in Fort Worth, she became the lady of the house in the baronial Rivercrest mansion. If she needed anything, a servant would fetch it. If she wanted to shop, which she always did, she had only to pick up the phone. Cullen had arranged "unlimited accounts" at all the right stores. For jewelry and furs, she needed his permission, but that was always easy to get. Before long she had added two sable coats, a white mink jacket, and five mink coats—two in white, one each in beige, brown, and pink —to the two leopards Cullen had wooed her with. If she wanted anything else, she would simply drive her latest-model Lincoln Continental down to Neiman's. In leaner times, she had applied for a job in the store's portrait studio and been rejected. Now she swept through the place, chatting with every salesgirl, stopping at every counter, buying with a wave of her hand. In the "precious jewelry" department, her favorite, she would trade the latest social gossip with the manager while trying on a diamond-and-emerald necklace and ordering yet another chip for her globetrotter bracelet. "I'm always falling behind," she complained.

For $120,000 a season, he bought her a box at Cowboy Stadium in Dallas: even more than jewelry or private jets, the ultimate status symbol in football-crazy Texas. Then he gave her money to decorate it.

In return for so much, Cullen asked only two things of

Priscilla. First, to transform her. Just as he had done with Sandra years before, he persuaded Priscilla to bleach her hair even lighter, as light as it would go, to a blonde as dry and white as the sand in Acapulco. Then, to her utter bewilderment, he coaxed her into having her already enormous breasts enlarged. She agreed partly because she was never able to grant his second request—that she quit smoking, her one habit that infuriated him. The best she could do was hide it from him.

Eventually, Cullen even bought Priscilla a daughter. Whenever ten-year-old Dee came to visit her mother, he lavished gifts on her and filled her pockets with spending money. Before long, the investment paid off. One day Priscilla called Wilborn. "Why don't you let Dee come live with us?"

Wilborn talked to Dee. "Is that what you want to do, sweetheart?" It was.

Soon Priscilla suggested that she and Cullen adopt Dee. Wilborn agreed. Dee, after all, was more Priscilla's than his. Later, over Dee's objections, Cullen legally changed her name to Dee Davis.

But the greatest gift was yet to come.

One day in the summer of 1969, Cullen drove Priscilla to a huge tract of empty land off Hulen Street. He called it "the farm." Together they hiked to the top of the rise that dominated the site. From its crest, they could see all of downtown Fort Worth to the east. "My father always wanted to build here," Cullen said, surveying the 180 acres Stinky had bought from a hard-pressed, heartbroken widow during World War II. "He had his chance. Now it's my turn."

The next day, Cullen walked into the offices of Albert Komatsu, a local architect who had done some work on Stinky's lakeside house. He dropped on Komatsu's desk a heavy file filled with pictures he had clipped from newspapers, rough sketches of floorplans, and scribbled notes on everything from plumbing fixtures to building materials. It took two years and cost almost as many headaches as dollars, but Cullen got the house he wanted. Like the Basses and the Tandys, who were commissioning modern architects to design huge new houses as monuments to their modern fortunes, Cullen wanted a contemporary look. Rivercrest's fake Tudor was fine for Stinky, but Cullen was "a man of the seventies," and he wanted a house that was, like him, unbeholden to the past.

It sat on the crest of the hill like a fortress, its blank painted-stone facades and courtyard walls ready to repel any assault. Indeed, with its own power plant, water source, and a system of concrete tunnels and electronic gates connecting the various outbuildings, the house seemed almost designed with that purpose in mind. A security system more suited to Fort Knox than Fort Worth monitored movement in every room, every window and door, as well as every light fixture throughout the seventeen-thousand-square-foot main house. All thirty-one major doors were fitted with electronic bolts that clamped into place at the push of a button. The ominous clunk of their simultaneous closing, like the sound of a prison lockdown, could be heard throughout the house. Any door or window could be locked or unlocked, any light turned on or off, from the two central security panels: one downstairs near the back door, one upstairs in the master bedroom.

Within the walls and the locks, Cullen created an eccentric, opulent private world: a specially made dining room table for twenty; library chairs upholstered in leopardskin; a huge indoor swimming pool festooned with potted palms, a bar, and a popcorn wagon from Hammacher-Schlemmer; a "presidential" bank of three televisions arrayed over the fireplace in the master suite; a silver-fox spread across the twin double beds; his and hers bathrooms, his in brown suede with a tigereye pattern, hers in mirrors and pink patent leather, a sunken marble tub surrounded by plants, and an antique crystal chandelier.

Cullen bought the chandelier on a shopping trip to New Orleans, one of many foraging expeditions through the antique shops and galleries of the world in search of "trinkets" to fill his Xanadu. Determined that the huge rooms not look empty, he bought paintings, bronzes, and marbles by the truckload. On a trip to New York, he saw a painting of a ship in a shop window and ordered his limousine driver to stop. Within five minutes, he had bought the painting in the window and 115 other works of art and was back on the road. If it was cheap, he wasn't interested. He wanted the $85,000 chess set of marble and gold, or the $350,000 jade pagoda, or the $400,000 Renoir painting for the powder room. He would walk down the aisle of a shop, pointing from left to right, saying, "I'll take this, I'll take this, I'll take this": a jade collection in a silver case; "I'll take this": a miniature chariot of beaten gold decorated with precious stones; "I'll take this": a copy of the Taj Mahal fashioned of gold and studded with diamonds, rubies, emeralds, and sapphires.

Priscilla tried to persuade him to hire an art consultant, but he waved the suggestion away like a bad odor. "No fags! I don't want any goddamn fags!"

As the centerpiece of his collection and his house, Cullen commissioned a gigantic portrait of himself from Wayne Ingram, Fort Worth's premier society portrait painter. The big six-by-eight-foot canvas showed Cullen enthroned wearing a business suit and smiling his strange smile. Priscilla was in the picture, too, although smaller, floating in space above him, her blonde hair cascading over her shoulders, dressed as Cullen liked her best: a low neckline and a high hemline. Circling around the two central figures, like putti in a Renaissance altarpiece, smaller images depicted Cullen at play: shooting pool, skiing, playing tennis; and Priscilla wearing different outfits, a ball gown, a leather microminiskirt and boots, but not *doing* much at all.

Said one friend when the painting was unveiled, "Priscilla just looks like something else Cullen does."

Almost overnight, it seemed, the fatherless waif from the Houston wharfs had been transformed into the belle of Fort Worth. Lured like pilgrims to the castle on the hill, all of the city's most prestigious organizations and fund-raisers found their way to Priscilla's big bronze doors: charity balls, opera association teas, and outdoor galas. More and more often, the "new Davises" showed up on the society pages of the *Star-Telegram*.

There they were, standing next to President Nixon and his daughters, watching Apollo 11 lift off. There they were, arm in arm, at the Jewel Charity Ball, the Opera Ball, the Steeplechase, the Colonial Golf Tournament. There was Priscilla, hosting a tea for the women's board of the Fort Worth Children's Hospital. At the Rivercrest Club, the Colonial Country Club, the Petroleum Club, the Ridglea Country Club, among the thousand-dollar tables filled with powerful men and beautiful women, there were Cullen and Priscilla.

But the transplant never really took. Surrounded by money and attention, Priscilla was still Priscilla—perhaps even more so. Uncowed by the faux-English finery of the Rivercrest house, she filled the old rooms with her randy humor and raucous laughter. To Cullen's mortification, she befriended the staff with the same bubbly breathless-ness that made her the favorite hostess of Cullen's friends (if not their wives). Dressed in a lime-green miniskirt the size of a face towel, she jetted around the house, bringing more raw, tart life to the gloomy old manse in one after-noon than Stinky and Alice had in decades.

On their glamorous trips abroad, while Cullen met with clients, Priscilla spent most days in her hotel room smoking and talking on the phone to friends back in Fort Worth. In Paris, she left the phone off the hook while she ran down to the hotel gift shop to buy more cigarettes. At fine restaurants, she would pick her courses according to price, constructing the most expensive meal possible, then leave most of it uneaten and retreat to the restroom to have what she really wanted: a cigarette.

At the charity balls and society galas, her costumes drew gasps from the crowd: gowns with backs or fronts or sides missing, or transparent, or cut to the navel; shim-mering black sheaths with diamond-shaped cutouts along the sides, rimmed with rhinestones; skirts so brief they revealed more flesh than a bathing suit. At the Rivercrest or Colonial Country clubs, the other wives made their entrances in linen dresses and smart hats. Priscilla came in cutoff jeans and headbands. She was dressed that way the day she walked into the board room of the First National Bank to rendezvous with Cullen just as a directors' meeting was breaking up. The bank's chairman saw her and his mouth fell open. "Who the hell is *that*?" he exclaimed, forgetting that his microphone was still on.

At Cowboy Stadium, she decorated their private box in hot pink—hot pink fabric on the walls, hot pink carpeting—with white leather armchairs. Mirrors in every size hung from the black ceiling over a bar made of marble studded with gold fixtures. One guest described it as "whorehouse moderne." Wives invited to a game with their husbands would walk twenty feet behind Priscilla on the way to the box so no one would know they were with "that woman."

Unlike many of the club ladies, Priscilla made no effort to hide her past. When a rumor spread that she had been a "working girl" at the Caravan, a seedy local motel, she laughed, "The Caravan! Surely I could do better than that!" Posing beside the giant Ingram portrait, she was asked: "Cullen seems to have so many activities. What is it that you do?"

"I do Cullen," she replied with a little-girl smile.

When asked if she ever worried about Cullen straying, she snapped back, "Hell, no! He can't even take care of what he's got at home." A rumor went around that during dinner in a fine Dallas restaurant, Priscilla disappeared under the table to satisfy another of Cullen's appetites. No one thought it sounded farfetched.

When friends gave her a costume jewelry necklace that spelled out "RICH BITCH" in rhinestones, she laughed and loved it. "It's me!" she exulted. When it was lost, she had a new one made—with diamonds this time.

* * *

Just as Cullen would cup his hands under his chest and brag about how he had "transformed" Priscilla, Priscilla would brag about the changes she had wrought in Cullen. Before their marriage, he would never have worn a pastel coat and two-toned shoes to the Rivercrest Club, or a dark blue tux with velvet lapels and cascades of ruffles to the Opera Ball. She even convinced him to wear a leather sports jacket once or twice instead of the ubiquitous suit, but he drew the line at leather pants and she never managed to coax him into a pair of jeans.

She did introduce him to a whole new world: nightclubs.

Cullen had seen the noisy, bawdy, boozy world of Fort Worth and Dallas after dark in his younger days, but only from a distance, as one of the lonely men in suits who sat at the far end of every bar, near the restrooms and the telephones, holding the same drink for hours, staring at the dance floor, beating bad time to the music. They might occasionally share some passing insight or, in Cullen's case, some scrap of pornography, with the bartender or a neighbor, but mostly they just watched. People who passed one of them on the way to the restroom might assume he was an out-of-town salesman or just another john looking for a lay.

Now, when Cullen entered a club with Priscilla on his arm, everyone noticed. At the Round Up Inn, or the Old San Francisco Saloon, or the Rangoon Racquet Club, he no longer had to slink to the shadows. He was greeted boisterously by name and led to the best table in the very heart of the din. People dropped by, not on their way to the restroom, but to share a gaudy laugh with Priscilla or yell intimacies over the music. Handsome strangers in cowboy hats would amble back and forth in front of the table, competing with each other to catch Priscilla's eye. Sooner or later, the club's manager would appear and snap his fingers for a free round of drinks.

Cullen may not have been the center of attention, but he was nearer to it than he had ever been before. Sometimes, when they entered a club, he would walk a few paces behind Priscilla just so he could watch other men's eyes follow her across the room. "He treated her like a 1908 Ford," said a club friend admiringly. "It was like everyone would like to have her, but he knew nobody else could afford her."

In other ways, Cullen hadn't changed at all. On trips to Europe and Latin America, the only sights that interested him were those in nude stage shows and live sex shows. In Mexico, he sought out the nearest "donkey show," featuring bestiality as well as audience-participation group sex. At every stop he spent hours shopping for pornography to take home. Once, returning from Caracas, Venezuela, Priscilla caught him looking at some of the child pornography he had stocked up on. "That is *sick*," she said firmly, "and you're going to have no part of it!" But the next time he found himself alone in a bar, he would pull it from his wallet and flash it furtively to anyone who would look.

At the annual Colonial Golf Tournament, he had a Winnebago RV hoisted over the club wall to provide "recreation" for him and his friends. Inside, the movie *Deep Throat* ran continuously. Between showings, Cullen would hold court, explaining how it was possible to tell an honest Jew from a dishonest one by the shape of his head, and sharing some "hilarious" new erotica from his latest trip to Europe. (For his older guests, he had a picture of a very young girl with a very old man. "I'll never speak to you again if you don't throw that away," Priscilla said when he showed it to her.)

If Cullen had changed, it was not at play but at work. After years of frugal management and conservative investment, Cullen had thrown open the coffers of Kendavis Industries. Cash sluiced out of company accounts: a million for a plane; then another million for a second plane; hundreds of thousands for travel; hundreds of thousands for clothes and cars and servants; six million for the fortress on the hill, not including the value of the foregone profit from the sale of 180 acres of prime land on which it stood—the largest undeveloped tract left so close to downtown Fort Worth. When Cullen couldn't charge something to a company account, he would use the company's credit to back up a personal loan.

At the same time, those parts of the Davis empire under Cullen's control also went on a buying spree, acquiring new companies at breakneck speed and extravagant prices. For the first time, Cullen was making investment decisions on his own, without consulting his brothers. Company money bypassed the usual controls and poured directly into pet projects.

While skiing in Aspen, Cullen met a shadowy Fort Worth "dealmaker" named Roy Rimmer, and soon afterward the cash began to flow in new and even stranger directions.

Rimmer and Cullen looked strangely alike: both short and slight, with predatory features, black wavy hair slicked back, and pencil-thin smiles. Rimmer dressed differently, preferring silk shirts open to the navel, gold chains, silk slacks, alligator shoes, and a Vegas showgirl on each arm. Cullen apparently admired the style, however; not long after meeting Rimmer, he bought his first gold chain.

Cullen bought everything Roy Rimmer had to sell: $1,500,000 in investments the first year, $1,000,000 the second year, $2,000,000 the third year. Rimmer made every deal sound like a winner, but out of dozens, only one showed a profit in the first three years. When Cullen's lawyer, Hershel Payne, tried to warn him away—"There's no way these can work," he said again and again—Rimmer would cut him off with a sharp "That's not your job. You're just supposed to draw up the papers." Unchecked, the deals got stranger and stranger: a California winery, a Las Vegas casino, uranium mines. Meanwhile, company debts as well as personal debts climbed toward eight figures.

No one understood Rimmer's hold on Cullen. The two men never made appointments, they just showed up at each other's offices. On their frequent trips in the company Learjet, they often made unscheduled stops. "I don't know what it is," complained one of Cullen's lawyers, "but Roy must have caught Cullen doing something worse than having oral sex with a Chinaman."

Those who knew Cullen best had a better explanation. Cullen Davis *had* changed since marrying Priscilla, but it wasn't Priscilla's arrival that had changed him. It was the departure, on the very same day, of Stinky Davis. This wasn't a new Cullen they were seeing, this was the real Cullen. "K. W. was the only one who could control Cullen," one worried family member told another. "Now that K. W.'s gone, there's no controlling him."

9

They had come to Palm Springs for a convention. The sky was a cloudless blue, and the palms around the hotel pool quivered in the desert breeze. The room was white and filled with sunlight, and Priscilla was ready to spend the lazy afternoon sunning on a chaise longue and sipping margaritas.

Then Cullen arrived.

He stormed through the door, screaming obscenities. She tried to talk to him, but everything she said only infuriated him more and darkened the already dark look in his eyes. Suddenly he lashed out, slapping her hard. The blow caught her off balance and she fell against a chair. He picked her up and hit her again, this time with his fist. She went down again. He kicked her as hard as he could. Reflexively, she curled up in a ball to protect herself. He kicked her again, square in the small of her back.

She scrambled to her feet and tried to run, but he caught her bathing suit and pulled her back toward him. He tried to hit her face with his clenched fist, but she put her arms up and bent down to ward off the blows. She fell to the floor again—to protect herself this time. She was safer on the floor. All he could do was kick her back and buttocks and legs. It seemed like an hour before he finally stopped.

She never got to the pool that day, or any day the rest of the trip. She couldn't wear a bathing suit in public: her back and legs were too black and blue. Even after she returned to Fort Worth, the blood clots, dozens of them, lingered for weeks.

It wasn't the first time.

Priscilla hated to admit it, but the first time was before they married. They were at the Eagle Mountain Lake house visiting Cullen's brother Bill and his wife, Mitzi. Cullen announced he was ready to leave and stood up. Priscilla said, "Well, I'm not," and laughed. As quick as a snake, Cullen reached down, grabbed her arm, and jerked her off the couch. Before she could find her feet, they were out the door. On the way to the car, he batted her head back and forth with the heel of his hand. "When I say we go, we go!" he barked as she bent down to ward off the blows. "Don't contradict me!" Another cuff. "Do you understand? Don't contradict me!"

She should have known right then, she told herself whenever she recalled the incident—which was more and more often as she approached her third anniversary with Cullen.

Members of the All Saints Episcopal Church attending a "spring coffee" at the home of Mr. and Mrs. Cullen Davis were shocked to be greeted at the door by the hostess wearing a microminiskirt, a mini-fur, and a black eye the size of a coaster.

When he lost a pool game—which was often—he might beat her on the way home. She pleaded with Judy McCrory, whose husband often won his pool matches with Cullen, "*Please* tell David not to win so often and not to gloat so much, 'cause when we leave here, I get the shit beat out of me." When she won an argument in a restaurant, he jerked the chair out from under her. Whereas before he was flattered when men flirted with her, now he was incensed. He would never challenge the men, but instead threaten her darkly under his breath: "You'll pay for this later."

Friends pleaded with her. "If you're gonna stay with him, have enough sense not to provoke him," advised Pat Burleson, a handsome, muscular ex-Navy boxer who ran a karate studio and knew Priscilla from the club circuit. "Don't just hang around and irritate him." But no matter what she did, no matter how hard she tried to avoid it, Cullen always found a way to be provoked.

Neighbors in Rivercrest often heard the squeal of tires as Priscilla's big Continental rounded the corner on Western Avenue, heading home to Stinky Davis's old house at breakneck speed. Cullen had laid down the law: Priscilla was supposed to be there when he arrived home from work in the evening. If she wasn't, she would be in "a heap of shit."

Most nights she made it, even if Western Avenue was cross-hatched with the tire marks she left getting there. One night, however, when she squealed around the last corner, she saw Cullen standing on the front porch waiting for her. "What do you think this *is*," he screamed, purple veins bulging from his neck, "your goddamn motherfucking private street!" On and on he went for ten minutes while Priscilla stood in the doorway, hands clutching her head, partly to dampen his screams, partly to shield herself from what she knew would follow. Finally, he grabbed her by the arm and dragged her into the house.

And still Priscilla made excuses. "There are good times with Cullen as well as bad," she told Judy McCrory, who was quickly becoming her closest friend. "I just live to have that one more good time with him."

"My God," said Judy, pointing to a black eye or one of the huge bruises that were appearing with increasing frequency, "when do you say enough is enough?"

Priscilla thought for a minute. The firmness of the answer made it clear she had given the question careful thought: "If it spills over to the kids."

* * *

For the first time in years, the big house in Rivercrest echoed with the sound of children's voices. The occasion: a celebration of Dee's official name change from Wilborn to Davis. Clutches of twelve-year-old girls raced in and out of every downstairs room in the old house, talking in excited whispers, screeching with laughter, dissolving and reforming, while stoic boys in long hair and bell-bottom jeans stood their ground. Much of the whispering concerned Dee's new stepfather: how rich he was, how lucky she was.

Suddenly, in the pool room at the back of the house, an adult appeared. A whisper went around, "That's him. That's Dee's new stepfather."

"Dee!" Cullen called out. The noise level dropped a notch. "Dee!" he called again. No one answered. Cullen saw a familiar face in the crowd, a friend of Dee's who had spent the night several times.

"Bev!" he called to her.

Beverly Bass approached Cullen warily. She had seen him before but never actually spoken to him. He scared her a little. "Bev, do you know where Dee is?"

She didn't. Cullen, stiff with anger, wheeled around and headed outside, his eyes scanning back and forth over the suddenly subdued crowd of young faces.

Outside, he found Dee necking with a boy. He grabbed her away and flung her toward the door. "Get upstairs," he ordered. Dee hesitated and started to say something. Before she could, Cullen kicked her hard in the buttocks. Anger flared on her face. She hesitated again. Cullen kicked her again, harder this time. Now she began to move slowly toward the staircase. He kicked her again, and again and again at each slow step toward the stairs. Even after she started up, he continued kicking her. Dee's friends stared in disbelief as the strange procession lurched up the stairs.

Half an hour later, Bev Bass felt a tug at her sleeve. It was Dee, motioning her into the bathroom. There, Dee pulled up her dress and showed Bev her buttocks. They were angry red, raw and crisscrossed with long white welts.

Bev was horrified. "What did he use?"

"His belt," said Dee, her jaw locked in anger.

For the first year, the belt was good enough. It came out every time Cullen caught Dee not studying—she was supposed to study from the moment she arrived home from school to the moment she went to bed, with time out only for dinner. If she received anything less than an A on her report card, the belt came out. He would take her to some deserted spot, force her to lower her dress and her panties, and whip her.

Then one day, while searching the attic of the Rivercrest house, Cullen found the board that Stinky had used to beat him. The next time he caught Dee sneaking out of the house, he marched her to the basement; ordered her to bare herself, hit her sixty-three times with the board (she counted), then warned her, "Don't tell your mother."

After the move to the big house on Mockingbird, he would always march her to the basement before administering punishment.

He beat her so often and so ferociously that blood began to appear in her urine. A doctor diagnosed it as kidney damage caused by the board and insisted that the beatings stop.

So Cullen went back to the belt.

Cullen put a tap on Dee's phone. Then, when he overheard her calling him a "butt," he whipped her savagely.

Late one night, a week before her fourteenth birthday in July 1972, Dee was awakened by her stepfather's fierce voice. "What did we forget to do tonight?" he yelled, yanking her out of bed and pushing her down the back stairs so hard she almost fell. In the kitchen, he pointed at the door and again demanded: "What did we forget to do tonight?"

"I forgot to lock it," Dee admitted sheepishly.

"You're damn right you did," he raged, swinging his arm around and hitting the girl a heavy blow square in the face. Dee knew instantly that her nose was broken. More from the shock than the pain, she exploded into tears.

Cullen stood over her, his face still red with rage. "What did I tell you about locking the doors?"

The only emotion Dee felt was defiance. "Let me guess," she spat back at him, holding her bloody nose.

Cullen hit her again—in the face, on the nose.

Priscilla appeared in the stairway wearing a robe and carrying a kitten—an early birthday present for Dee—in her arms. She arrived just in time to see the last blow fall. "What the hell are you doing?" she screamed.

Cullen came at her. He snatched the kitten from her arms, held it in the air with one hand for a second, then flung it down as hard as he could. The little body twitched on the floor. He picked it up again and threw it down again. The twitching stopped.

He grabbed a table with both hands and hurled it across the room, where it crashed against the wall and exploded into pieces. He lunged at Priscilla. She turned to run, but he caught the back of her robe and pulled her to the floor. He hit her again and again. She held her arms up against the blows, squirming frantically to escape his grip, screaming for him to stop. Finally she broke free, groped toward the security panel, and pushed the alarm button.

The police arrived within minutes. Priscilla and Dee spent the next three nights at the lake house under the protection of Cullen's sister-in-law Mitzi; then Priscilla sent Dee to stay with friends in San Antonio. Cora, the maid, dutifully cleaned up the mess in the kitchen.

Cullen never said a word about the episode until years later when his lawyers asked him if what they had heard about the kitten was true. "Yeah," he said. "I killed the little motherfucker."

10

"Stupid, stupid, stupid!"

Priscilla could hear Cullen's voice, coarse and threatening, coming from the room where Andrea was staying. After much pleading, Jack Wilborn had allowed her to visit her mother for a few days. Now, Priscilla was sure, they both would regret it.

"It's *not* hard!" Cullen was yelling again. "The reason you can't get it is because you're stupid and lazy!"

Priscilla had tried more than once to explain to him that Andrea wasn't stupid or lazy, she was just a slow learner. "She's a dreamer," Priscilla would say. "She's an artist." She was more interested in the pattern of sunlight on a leaf than in something so evanescent as homework.

In fact, as she grew up, Andrea was becoming more and more like her mother, except taller and thinner and more genuinely beautiful. She had her mother's weakness for stray animals. Every visit she brought along a new pet: a parakeet, a baby alligator, a bat, a wild duck, in addition to the usual entourage of Pussycat, the dog, and Cinnamon, the cat. The mess they made only wore Cullen's patience thinner.

"Goddammit!" Cullen shouted. "You're so fucking stupid!" Priscilla couldn't hear Andrea, but she knew she was crying. Unlike her mother, Andrea had a tiny, choked cry that barely made a sound. She wanted so badly for everyone to be happy that she would do anything, even accept punishment for things she didn't do.

"I can't believe how fucking stupid you are!" Cullen roared. "What a fucking dimwit! You're going to stay here at this desk until you get it right, I don't care if it takes all night!"

Priscilla wanted to rush into the next room and protect

her "Pussycat," as she called Andrea, but she knew better than to cross Cullen in the heat of a rage. There were far worse abuses than words.

The next morning, Andrea called Jack Wilborn from school. "Please come get me, Daddy!" she pleaded. "Please. I don't want to go back there again."

When Cullen came home and found Andrea missing, he exploded. "This is the thanks I get for caring about her school?" he ranted. "This is what I get for being a good parent? She runs away!" He dragged Priscilla to the phone and ordered her to call Wilborn's house and get Andrea on the line. He wanted to talk to her. As soon as Andrea picked up, Cullen grabbed the phone.

"Why didn't you come back here after school?"

Andrea tried desperately to avoid a confrontation while choking back tears. " 'Cause I had things to do with my father."

"Then I want you to come over this weekend," Cullen demanded.

"I have plans," Andrea whimpered.

Cullen couldn't hold it in any longer. "Goddammit, if you don't get back here this minute," he screamed into the phone, "you'll never be welcome in this house again!"

Andrea began to cry. "I *can't!*"

Cullen sputtered. "Then I want you to gather up everything your mother has ever given you, and bring it back to this goddamn house!"

Andrea burst into wails of weeping, dropped the phone, and ran to her room. Jack Wilborn, who had been listening on an extension, rushed to console her. She was lying on her bed, trembling with fear and weeping hysterically, something he had never seen her do. He sat down beside her and put his arm around her. Twice before, she had returned from trips to her mother's saying she was afraid of Cullen. Wilborn had assumed it was just the usual friction between stepdaughter and stepfather. He knew better now. "You don't have to be afraid of him ever again," he told her softly. "You will never, ever have to go back to that house again."

* * *

In January 1973, six months after the incident in the kitchen, on a family vacation to Aspen, Colorado, Cullen hit Dee with his fist and knocked her across the room, splitting her lip open. She was fourteen years old.

When they returned from vacation, Dee's grades arrived. Priscilla held her breath as Cullen opened the envelope; a single B would mean a brutal whipping. But this time, for the first time ever, Dee had received all A's. For once, it looked like there would be peace in the house.

Then Cullen discovered that Dee had altered the report card.

He dragged her to the basement, ordered her to pull down her jeans and her panties, and went to work with his belt. Calmly, methodically, for the next thirty minutes, he whipped her. Dee tried to count the number of lashes but lost count around one hundred. When he finally stopped, she was black and blue from the middle of her back to the back of her knees, the welts running together in one huge swollen mass.

That night, hiding from her stepfather at a friend's house, Dee called the Department of Public Welfare. The night intake worker, David Sheets, came to talk with her and examine her wounds. Even in east Fort Worth, Sheets had rarely seen a case where a spanking had gotten more out of hand.

The next day, a Public Welfare caseworker, Alyson Roberts, called Cullen. "I would like to hear your side of the story, Mr. Davis."

"I had to punish her," Cullen bristled, angry at the very idea of an inquiry. "What Dee really needs is more discipline," he insisted. "That's the only way to make her shape up."

Roberts carefully broached another idea. "Would you consider family counseling?"

"Absolutely not," Cullen snapped. If there was one thing he could not abide, it was shrinks. "Dee and her mother can go if they like, but *I* don't need any counseling."

The next day, Priscilla called Roberts and asked to meet with her alone—without Cullen.

"Do you think your husband presents a real danger?" Roberts asked.

Priscilla looked down into her lap, at the thighs that had so often been too badly bruised to wear a short skirt, at the arms that had warded off innumerable blows. The long silence was all the answer that Roberts needed, but Priscilla added one of her own. "Not right now," she said. "Ever since you got involved, Cullen's been worried that he might get into some kind of legal trouble for what he did to Dee. I don't think he'll do it again," she added confidently.

Privately, though, Priscilla was terrified. With Andrea removed and Dee off-limits, that left only one target for Cullen's rage.

11

In November 1972, only days before they were scheduled to move into the big new house on Mockingbird Lane, Cullen cornered Priscilla in her bathroom. She would always remember it as "the last fight in the old house." A month later, she wouldn't remember how it started—perhaps he had discovered her sneaking a cigarette—but years later she would be able to point to the scar on her forehead as a reminder of its ferocity.

He hit her ten or fifteen times, back and forth across the slick bathroom floor. Bottles and jars and makeup paraphernalia flew through the air. She used everything she could put her hands on—towels, robes, dirty clothes —to fend him off. But he kept coming. He caught her one good blow on the side of the face, and her head jerked around and hit the edge of the door. The impact dazed her. She reached up to feel her forehead. It was strangely numb. Then the whole room turned red as the blood streamed down over her eyes. But that didn't stop Cullen.

Eventually he wound down, more from exhaustion than compassion, and collapsed against the doorway of the bathroom, panting and wiping the sweat from his forehead.

"You know," he said between gulps of air, "the new house can't take this."

"You're right," Priscilla replied. "Neither can I."

For a while, at least, after they moved into the new house, Cullen kept his word—he saved the most savage beatings for out of town.

On the skiing vacation to Aspen in January 1973, the rage came on in the hotel room where they were staying. He beat Priscilla to the floor, then began kicking her, slamming his boot again and again into her side, her stomach, her back, her legs, her arms, her head. At one point, he stomped down hard with his heel on her breast. The soft mass shifted so violently she feared her silicone implant would burst.

Priscilla returned from that trip with a broken ankle. She told friends that it was the result of a skiing accident, but not all of them believed her. Two months later she was still hobbling around on a crutch, taking Percodan to kill the pain, when the rage came over Cullen again. He jerked the crutch out from under her, pushed her to the ground, and began hitting her with the broad end of the crutch. She was badly hurt but refused to go to the hospital. Instead, she took more Percodan.

By the following spring, she was nursing an ulcer, and her breasts, probably due to the repeated beatings, were developing fibroid cysts. To make matters worse, she had proved highly resistant to painkillers. Normal doses of Percodan did almost nothing to relieve the pain, so she started taking them more often—eight, ten, a dozen a day—in a vain search for some relief. Friends joked grimly that the real pain wasn't in her stomach or her breasts or even her ankle; it was in her marriage.

* * *

What most of Priscilla's friends didn't know was that there was no longer a marriage. Sex—the engine that had driven them to the altar in the first place—had begun cooling down soon after the move into the big house on Mockingbird. Priscilla could identify the exact moment when the change began: when Cullen met Roy Rimmer. She often wondered what bizarre secret sexual outlet Cullen had been introduced to by his strange new friend and business partner.

The word "affair" flashed into Priscilla's mind. She tried to dismiss it—lately Cullen hadn't been potent enough to satisfy *her* sexual demands, let alone someone else's—but it wouldn't go away. More and more, when she nuzzled his neck or slid her arms around his waist, he would push her away impatiently and complain about "not feeling well" or "being tired." One day he snapped: "I can't even take my clothes off without you grabbing at me. Can't you keep your damn hands off of me?"

For Priscilla, that was the final proof: He was seeing someone else.

Determined to catch him in the act, she waited until he was in the shower to search his wallet for unfamiliar phone numbers. She checked the clothes in his closet for unusual stains and sniffed for strange perfumes; she called the places he said he would be.

With the help of Judy McCrory, she began following him when he left work in the afternoon or left the house without her at night. Judy started calling her "Dick Tracy." His first stop was usually the Albatross, a hole-in-the-wall bar owned by two lawyers, Bill Magnusson and Tim Curry. It was an odd mixed salad of a bar, especially during happy hour, when Mexican factory workers crowded the standing counter while attorneys and their secretaries pawed each other at the tables. Cullen came for the pool, often playing for money with Curry.

To do her spying inside a bar, whether in Fort Worth or out of town, Priscilla maintained a network of informants, mostly bartenders and waitresses. If someone needed extra money for an emergency, they knew where to find it. Priscilla once gave a waitress the money for an abortion.

Eventually the effort paid off. One night she and Judy followed Cullen to the Captain's Den, a cheap ship-ahoy dive on East Seminary in south Fort Worth. They waited until he began chatting up a petite, attractive redhead in a tiny denim skirt and tall black boots. Judy recognized her: a notorious "happiness girl" named Lola—"a working girl," as they said in Fort Worth, "and it ain't the five and dime." Just as Cullen shimmied his chair closer to Lola, Priscilla burst through the door with Judy trailing three feet behind. She strode straight up to the table, inches from Lola's chair, and spat at her, "You fucking whore!"

Lola leapt up and grabbed a fistful of Priscilla's hair. Priscilla returned the favor. The two women were suddenly wheeling around the room, tugging at each other's hair and exchanging kicks. Before either one could land a blow, the manager, a burly man with big hairy arms, lumbered out from behind the bar and pried them apart. "I am not going to have any of this shit," he said as he dragged Priscilla to the office, threw her in, and slammed the door behind her.

Lola brushed herself off, combed her big red hair with her fingers, and walked over to Cullen, who had retreated to the bar. They whispered a few words and Lola left. Judy McCrory slipped into the office, where she found Priscilla "trying to straighten her face" even as her anger ricocheted back and forth between "that fucking Cullen" and "that fucking whore." Suddenly the little office was filled with a tremendous cracking sound, then another. Someone was kicking the door down. Then they heard Cullen's voice, loud and ferocious. *"Priscilla!* You get the fuck out here right now! Come out here, you *bitch!* Come out here right now or I will fucking break this door down and *drag* you out!"

Priscilla made a move toward the door. Judy jumped in front of her. "You aren't *seriously* thinking of going out there, are you? You gotta be crazy!"

"Priscilla!" Another deafening crack. The door bowed visibly with each blow.

Priscilla came to her senses. "I guess not," she said. "I don't think I need that tonight."

The kicking at the door stopped and a minute later the manager came in. "I made him go home," he reassured them. As they left, he added, "I know it's not my business, but I think your husband's a little crazy." He tapped the side of his head with his big finger, "Up here."

After that night, Priscilla decided it would be safer if someone else followed Cullen. She hired a Dallas private detective to shadow his every movement outside work and, she hoped, record the sordid details with a telescopic lens. But for reasons that were never clear, the investigator failed to produce a single photograph or scrap of usable information. His explanation was that Cullen drove too fast. "We just can't keep up with him," said the report that accompanied the bill.

Priscilla knew that Cullen was a wild driver. "No one can keep up with him," she would say, "and the cops won't touch him." In fact, the Fort Worth police had awarded him an "Honorary Sheriff's Posse Badge," which he would flash whenever he was pulled over. But Judy McCrory suspected that Cullen had spotted the tail and paid him off. "There are only two rooms at the Ramada Inn that have hot tubs," she reminded Priscilla. "All they have to do is stay put around those rooms and Cullen will come to them. That's where he ends up taking all his broads."

Terrified of what Cullen might do if he discovered she was spying on him, Priscilla waited three months to confront him with his cheating ways.

It was the spring of 1974, at a hotel in Marina del Rey, California. The fight began like every other fight. Then, in the heat of anger, without really planning to, she let it out: "I know you've been running around with other women."

"How the fuck do you know that?" he demanded. "Have you been spying on me?"

It wasn't really a question. She could tell by the acid

in his voice that he already knew the answer. It wouldn't
have done any good to deny it. He pounded her with his
feet and his fists, chasing her back and forth across the
hotel room, blocking every escape. She clambered onto
the bed, hoping that it would soften the blows, but he
yanked her off and threw her hard against the floor. As
she hit it, she heard a crunching sound in her shoulder.
She struggled to get to her feet but a sudden explosion of
pain and weakness pushed her back down. Her collarbone
was broken.

But Cullen kept coming. In fact, this time he showed
no signs of letting up. "He's gonna kill me," Priscilla
thought as she writhed on the floor in pain and fear. "This
time he's not gonna stop."

12

Priscilla sat by the window at Marilyn Baker's house gingerly testing her shoulder. She had only recently stopped
wearing the brace that Dr. Lipscomb had given her to help
the collarbone heal properly. He wanted her to wear it a
few more weeks yet, but what did he know? Had he ever
tried to wear a shoulder brace with a halter top or a white
mink mini-fur?

Besides, if the shoulder gave her trouble she could
always just take a few more Percodans. She sometimes
wondered, as she emptied her second bottle in a week, if
she was becoming addicted to the painkillers. But she
never worried for long. It wasn't as if Percodan were heroin, for Chrissakes.

Priscilla enjoyed her visits to the Bakers' little gray-
shingle bungalow on Pershing Avenue. Marilyn, a pear-
shaped lady with huge thighs and a perpetual tan ("it's the
only way to make my cellulite look good," she explained),
was an ex-hippie with a cleaning compulsion. Her living

room, where she did business, was filled with roach clips, pipes, and cigarette cases filled with joints, but she was always renting carpet-shampooing machines to clean up after the guests. She would smoke a joint while cleaning the baseboards. Her husband, Craig, another ex-hippie, kept their little yard immaculately manicured.

Priscilla stopped at the Bakers' two or three times a week to have a wig "freshened up." She was wearing wigs or falls more and more these days as the weekly bleaching to keep her roots from showing began to take its toll on her real hair. Marilyn warned her that it was getting thin —eventually she might even go bald in spots. But what choice did she have? Cullen wanted a blonde—*platinum* blonde, roots and all. She and Marilyn laughed about it sometimes. "Sooner or later Cullen's gonna have to decide if he wants you brunette or bald," Marilyn would joke.

"If that's his choice, I think he'd rather not have me at all," Priscilla would reply with a black laugh.

Marilyn's was also the place where Priscilla could talk about her love life—or, increasingly, her lack of one. She complained about Cullen's coldness and chronicled for Marilyn her attempts, so far unsuccessful, to find out exactly who he was sleeping with. There had been some amusing diversions along the way, of course. Like the handsome cop Priscilla had "pulled off the street." After a few steamy weeks, he found out who her husband was, zipped up his pants, and bailed out, saying, "This is too much for me, I can't handle the heat."

This day, however, Priscilla had no interest in reliving old chapters from her love life. She was thinking of starting a new one. Across the room, a tall, sandy-haired man sat sprawled and cross-legged in the low-slung chair beneath a bullet-shaped amber light that Marilyn had acquired in exchange for a blow job. The man was saying, "I'm a union electrician and damn proud of it."

Priscilla wrinkled her nose. All she knew about unions was what she had heard from Cullen, and it was all bad. "You know, most Communist governments in the world started with unions," she offered, paraphrasing Cullen.

The man pulled at his wiry goatee and showed a slow, lopsided grin. They had only been talking for a few minutes—while Marilyn worked on a wig—but Priscilla already liked him. There was something both sexy and boyish in the way his sad gray-blue eyes peered out from underneath that unruly mat of thin hair. With his long arms and long legs and the sharp angles at his elbows and knees, he seemed to occupy more space than he rightly should. He didn't move much, except to scratch, or underscore a point with a long, lazily hooked finger.

Priscilla repeated something else she had heard Cullen say about unions and the man rolled his eyes. "That's enough," he announced, his gaze zeroing in on Priscilla. He leaned forward in the chair and, with his big hand, reached down and grabbed his crotch. "Listen, lady," he said slowly, shaking his genitals, "you ain't got a set of these, so you can't fucking talk to me." Then he got up, shook his legs one at a time, and walked out.

"Who the hell was that?" Priscilla demanded of Marilyn, watching out the window as the man climbed into an old turquoise Fairlane.

Marilyn smiled. "That was 'T.' "

Not long afterward, Priscilla saw "T" again, at a party given by David and Judy McCrory. Not long after that, she drove to a house at 5613 King's Court in Arlington, where "T" lived with a huge Doberman named Heidi.

The first time she came, he put his arm around her and said in his sweet-butter Texas drawl, "Even though I have long hair and am an arrogant sonofabitch, and an alcoholic, and a drug addict, you may find I know something." Priscilla laughed. She didn't believe it. As she visited more often, she realized it was all true. "T" was nothing if not honest. And after years of Cullen's cold stares and cryptic sighs, she needed honesty almost as much as she needed sex.

Between rounds of lovemaking and tequila with orange juice, "T" told Priscilla his story.

* * *

His name was William Tasker Rufner. He answered to "W. T." or "T-man," but his friends called him just plain "T." And his friends were everywhere. He was the kind of man who, for better or worse, drew crowds, both men and women. According to W. T., that was because his mother "didn't like for me to go to other people's houses, so they all came to mine."

W. T. talked a lot about his "old lady," Sadie Marie, a hard-working lady from Emporia, Kansas, and about his other love, motorcycle racing. "I thought the only thing in the world was a motorcycle and a pretty girl." By the time he was twenty, he had an expert plate; by twenty-one, a national number. Out of thousands of motorcycle racers around the country, only ninety-nine had national numbers. "It was born and bred into me to go fast," he confessed, "and that's just the way I am. Fuck, I've said it before, if I thought I was ever gonna live this long, I might have taken better care of my body."

W. T. drained two cans of beer and smoked a joint for each sip Priscilla took of her tequila and orange juice. Every now and then he offered her a toke, but she turned it down. "It doesn't do anything for me," she said. She was happy enough just to drink and smoke the cigarettes Cullen wouldn't let her smoke at home. Eventually, W. T. offered her just about everything—coke, speed, Quaaludes—but she turned them all down.

In March 1974, Priscilla flew to Boston to visit Judy McCrory—and to escape Cullen, whose moods were growing increasingly dark and dangerous.

Judy had followed her ne'er-do-well husband David, Cullen's ex–pool partner, to Framingham, Massachusetts, in pursuit of yet another get-rich-quick scheme. The departure of her best friend had devastated Priscilla, who could never understand what a bright, beautiful girl like Judy saw in an overweight, baby-faced would-be high roller like David McCrory. "He's just a scuffer," Judy would say defensively when Priscilla and others complained about David's endless con games, but even Judy couldn't deny that his grip on reality was, at times, "slippery."

Strangely, it was Judy who suggested calling W. T. As far as Priscilla knew, Judy and W. T. had never been close. He was just one of the local dealers from whom she had occasionally bought $30 bags of "little crosses"—speed—back in her speed-freak days. "He has a magnetic personality," was about the best thing she had ever heard Judy say about W. T.; "a little bit goes a long ways," about the worst.

Judy made the call and W. T. seemed pleased enough to hear from her. But when she told him Priscilla was there with her in Boston, his tone changed. "Oh shit," he said, "I'm not doin' nothing. Why don't I just come up there?"

The next day they picked him up at the airport and drove straight to Cape Cod. Normal visitors might have found the Cape a little bleak in March—too early and too cold for the usual tourist activities. But the carful of Texans that local fishermen glimpsed speeding by on Route 3 was anything but normal: in the front seat, the long-legged, long-haired Judy and her gawky, pubescent husband; in the back, a rangy, shady man in cowboy boots and a short, huge-breasted, platinum-headed woman in a white rabbit mini-fur.

And they weren't interested in the normal tourist activities, either. When they pulled off the road, it wasn't to watch the waves roll in or take pictures of the quaint villages; it was to smoke some pot, snort some cocaine, or buy some liquor. It wasn't long before everyone was high on something and everything that happened seemed uproariously funny.

W. T. contributed the drugs. He kept each substance in a different pocket of his coat: speed in one, 'ludes in another, pot in yet another. He described himself as "a walking fucking drugstore." A true gentleman, he always offered whatever he pulled out to Priscilla first, even though he knew she would refuse. "It's okay if you want to," she would say, "but it's not for me." Alcohol was all she needed.

The party lasted through dinner, then they turned around and headed home, the car rocking with laughter. W. T. dubbed the trip "a honeymoon," and Priscilla howled. She hadn't enjoyed herself as much since the early days with Cullen—and maybe not even then.

The day ended on a sour note when David McCrory and W. T. almost came to blows in the parking lot outside the McCrorys' apartment. Ostensibly, the fight was over who was to blame that they had almost run out of gas on the way home. But the real fight was over Judy. David had heard rumors about W. T. and his wife back in Fort Worth. Now W. T. had materialized on his doorstep to pass out free dope and good times and maybe something else.

As they pulled into the parking lot, W. T. jumped out before the car had come to a stop. "Hey, motherfucker, bail your ass out!" he snarled, ripping his shirt off, forgetting that he was in Boston, not Texas, and the temperature was in the twenties. "Get outta your fuckin' car."

McCrory emerged warily and tried to smile. "Hey, them girls think we're gonna fight," he said, trying to laugh behind clenched teeth.

"We ain't gonna *fight*," W. T. growled. "I'm gonna whup your ass!"

Eventually W. T. decided McCrory was too pathetic to fight. "Oh, fuck it," he said, throwing his hands in the air. "You're just a fucking blowhard who wants to talk his way out of everything. Fuck you, I'm leaving!" Then he turned to Priscilla and his voice softened. "You're invited to come with me, if you want."

The next day, Priscilla and W. T. flew to Baltimore to visit an old friend of "T"'s from the racing circuit, Gary Nixon, a short, coarse, red-headed man with an insatiable appetite for stimulation, and his wife, Mary, a pretty, petite Englishwoman. W. T. introduced Nixon to Priscilla as "Number Fucking One." And, in fact, he had been the number-one motorcycle driver in the country for three straight years, 1968–1970, a phenomenal record. But

W. T. meant it another way. "I can call him up anytime and say, 'Hey, I'm bringing a friend of mine—we need a place to crash,'" he explained to Priscilla. "We're that close."

W. T. introduced Priscilla to Nixon as "Bunch-of-bucks."

They left Baltimore on Sunday, W. T. moaning and cursing under the weight of Priscilla's half dozen bags, including one just for jewelry. When they arrived at the Fort Worth airport that night, Priscilla spotted a familiar silhouette from a distance. "Oh, my God," she cried. "It's Cullen!"

13

W. T. dismissed it as a bad joke. "Bullshit!"

"No, it's Cullen!" Priscilla choked. She was frantic. "What the hell is *he* doing here?" But there was no way out; he had seen them. "Pretend like you're somebody I met on the plane," Priscilla whispered urgently out of the side of her mouth. "You're just picking up my bags for me."

W. T. was drunk, had been drunk for three days. This was the wrong time for reality. "Aw, fuck it!" he said, still not bothering to look. "You're full of shit! Nobody knows where we went."

"I'm telling you, it's *him*! He's meeting the plane."

"Why would he be meeting a fucking plane that's coming from Baltimore instead of Boston?"

But Priscilla didn't have time for questions now. She slipped the baggage tickets into W. T.'s hand and pushed him away just in time to run toward Cullen. Out of the corner of his eye, W. T. saw them embrace and kiss.

At the baggage carousel, W. T. piled Priscilla's bags,

all six of them, on a porter's cart and slung his lone briefcase on top. The gravity of the situation was finally beginning to burn its way through the fog in his head. "If
somebody is gonna be in for a surprise," he said to himself,
"it isn't gonna be me." He opened the briefcase a crack,
pulled out a .380 Browning, and slipped it into his coat
pocket.

When he raised his head and looked around, he saw
that the porter was staring directly at him. W. T. smiled
reassuringly. "The lady is carrying a shitload of jewelry
and money," he said, motioning toward the tall stack of
pink bags. "I'm protecting her." The porter pushed ahead
without a word.

W. T. waited at the curb for five minutes before Priscilla's long white Continental pulled out of the basement
parking area. Right behind her was another car. W. T.
felt for the bulge in his pocket. He had fooled around with
the wives of other men, but never a man as rich or—if
Priscilla's bruises and broken bones were any indication
—as violent.

Priscilla jumped out of the Continental in a froth of
forced levity. Cullen stepped out of the car behind her.
W. T. tried to read his face, without success. "Cullen,"
Priscilla bubbled, "this is . . . what's your name? T?
Ruf . . . ?"

"W. T. Rufner," W. T. supplied. Cullen stuck out his
hand, very stiff and very steady. W. T. shook it. "Cullen
Davis," he said calmly. "I appreciate you entertaining my
wife on the plane and getting her luggage for her."

"No problem."

"I was just dropping someone off," Cullen added.

W. T. didn't believe it.

"I didn't even see you," he said to Priscilla.

Priscilla didn't believe it.

Cullen turned back to W. T. "Let me take you home."

All W. T. said was, "No, no," but his mind, suddenly
revved, couldn't stop thinking: If some strange man had
fetched *his* wife's luggage, he would at least have asked
him, "Did you two have a drink on the plane?" or "Where

did you come in from?" But no, Cullen wasn't asking anything. Somehow Cullen knew what flight they were going to be on. That meant he knew the whole fucking deal.

Meanwhile, Cullen was strangely insisting on taking W. T. home. "We're gonna go have a drink," Cullen said. "Why don't you join us?"

"No, no," W. T. fumbled. "Someone will be here in a little bit to pick me up. He's probably just drunk. He's just late. No problem." There was no way he was going to get into Cullen's car.

"I insist that I take you home."

Another refusal would be as good as a confession. "But I'm not going to get in that fucking car," W. T. kept telling himself.

"Oh, you got to let us take you home," Priscilla chirped in a desperate bid to throw Cullen off the scent. "Cullen will drive you home, and I'll just follow you all."

Finally, W. T. gave in. "Fuck it, I'm in this game," he thought. "I'll play it out." He got in the car with Cullen.

Priscilla pulled out in front of them. At the parking lot tollbooth, she leaned out the window and called back to Cullen, "Pay this, will you, hon?" Cullen nodded. When he got to the window, he discovered Priscilla's bill was $200—she had parked in the short-term parking garage. To W. T.'s astonishment, Cullen didn't flinch. He pulled out his wallet, riffled through a dozen hundred-dollar bills, and calmly pulled out two.

"I can't believe it," W. T. thought to himself again and again as the car slipped onto the freeway. "I'm fucking sleeping with his *wife* and he acts like he doesn't know it —or like he doesn't give a fuck if I am. He's just cool and calm and collected, the two of us sitting right here next to each other very nice. It just doesn't make any fucking sense."

Cullen was the first to break the silence. "What do you do for a living?" he asked politely.

"I'm an electrician. Have been for years."

"Where have you worked?"

W. T. gave him a capsule personal history. But his mind was elsewhere: "Why doesn't he ask the obvious questions, like 'Where have you been? What flight were you on?' Why? Because he *knows*, he fuckin' KNOWS. Why? 'Cause there was some motherfucker on the airplane *telling* him where we came from. Cullen must have had Priscilla followed all the way to Boston, and from Boston to Baltimore." He crossed his arms, slipping his right hand into his coat and resting it on the butt of the gun. He kept the muzzle pointed at Cullen the whole trip.

"And what do *you* do for a living?" W. T. asked.

"I'm in the oil business," Cullen said, and then let the subject drop. W. T. spent the rest of the trip talking on and off about racing.

By the time they reached W. T.'s house on a dead-end street in east Fort Worth, Cullen had managed to lose Priscilla. It was pitch black on a moonless night and the streets were deserted. W. T. noticed that his car wasn't parked in the usual spot. In its place were two unfamiliar cars, a rare and generally suspicious sight in this part of town. There was no sign of Pee Wee, a racing buddy who shared the house with him. But most alarming was the silence. Where was his big Doberman, Heidi? Usually, if anyone came within a hundred yards of the place, Heidi would wake the neighborhood. But on this night, as he stood alone on a dark, deserted street with his lover's husband, clutching a gun with the safety off under his coat, there was no sign of her. Surveying the empty street and his dark house, he wondered if Cullen had prepared a surprise for him inside. Was that why he was so cool at the airport?

When the car stopped, both men jumped out. They looked at each other over the roof of the car. "I'll get my things out," W. T. said. Cullen walked to the trunk. W. T. followed, his hand still under his coat. W. T. pitched his briefcase on the ground, then turned back to Cullen. He didn't want to take his eyes off him. "Thanks a lot," he said.

Just then Priscilla drove up and got out of her car.

W. T. caught the anxious look on her face and wondered if Cullen had. "Thank you very much for getting my luggage," Priscilla said, waving at him from a safe distance. "I really appreciate it."

"Yes, thank you," Cullen added flatly.

Both cars drove off, leaving W. T. alone in the darkness. All he had to do now was walk through the front door. He'd never been so scared—even on a motorcycle. He pulled the gun out of his coat and ran around to the back of the house, climbed the fence, and peered in the living room window.

There was no hit man. All he saw was Pee Wee and Pee Wee's wife watching television with the lights off and Heidi fast asleep on a beanbag chair. "Fuck, man," he muttered to himself as he slinked inside, "get rid of her. No woman is worth this kind of hassle."

The next morning, Priscilla called.

"What happened after you two left?" W. T. asked.

"Would you believe, nothing? We just went on down to the Hungry Eye Club and had a few drinks."

"Did you go home and fuck?"

"No," Priscilla cooed.

It was the wrong answer. "Shit!" thought W. T. "Cullen's really gonna be out for my ass now."

Two days later, W. T. returned from a long lunch with too many beers and found the police in his house. That very morning, he had been on the phone with a friend, Sandy Myers, telling her how he was ready to retire. "I'm gonna go to California and fuck around on the beach," he told her. "I just got things handled to where I don't have to work anymore."

"Aren't we gonna see you again?" Sandy asked in a worried voice.

"Well, we better have us a drink soon, because in about five hours this house will be clean as a hound's tooth, and I'm gonna be gone to California in the morning, honey." Minutes after that conversation, unknown to W. T., the police arrested Sandy for selling cocaine to an undercover narcotics agent. An hour later, Sandy's husband, Larry, showed up at W. T.'s door to take him to a bar for some "farewell" beers. He didn't bother to mention Sandy's arrest. Two hours later, the police arrived at W. T.'s little gray and white house on King's Court.

When W. T. returned home after lunch and found the police tearing the house apart, he realized what had happened: "They sent Larry to take me to lunch for a reason, to get me loaded and to keep me out of the house, 'cause they knew I was crazy and had a lot of guns." Later, he figured that Sandy must have tried to buy herself some slack by tipping the cops that he was leaving town. That was why they had to come down on him the same day. Fortunately for W. T., it was also why they found so little: 705 grams of marijuana, a few amphetamines, and a potpourri of pills. They found the coat he had worn in Boston, but the pockets had been pretty much emptied out during the trip. There were a few vials and a baggie with a couple of crosses left in it. But no heroin and no cocaine—what they were really looking for.

They charged him with possession with intent to sell and recommended a $100,000 bond. He couldn't make that, so they locked him up.

Jail gave him a chance to do some clearheaded thinking for a change. Sandy Myers may have tipped the police that he was planning to leave town, but according to the search warrant, his house had been under DEA surveillance for five days. That meant the original tip had been phoned in the previous Friday, the day W. T. and Priscilla left Boston for Baltimore—the day after the fight with David McCrory. Suddenly everything began to make sense. McCrory had called Cullen on Friday and told him Priscilla was headed to Baltimore with W. T. That was how Cullen knew where they had been and what plane they were coming in on. Either McCrory or Cullen had called the cops and told them to stake out the house. W. T. put his money on Cullen. McCrory didn't have the nuts.

On Friday, the D.A.'s office dropped the bail to $25,000 and W. T. walked out of jail after three days—

"a long time when they're fuckin' scarin' you," he said. It was almost dark when they released him. He considered returning to the house on King's Court for the night, but the prospect terrified him. What if Cullen had planned another welcome for him, something worse than a drug bust this time?

Then he thought about all the whiskey that was still at the house and decided there was no point in letting a lot of good booze go to waste.

14

Priscilla and W. T. couldn't stay away from each other for long. Within a week of W. T.'s release on bail, they were sneaking off to Dallas clubs in Priscilla's white Continental. "We used to drink two fucking quarts of tequila a day," W. T. bragged. "She would buy that shit by the case— Cheval 1800 Gold, $20 bucks a bottle—and we would drink two quarts a day driving in that white fuckin' Continental. And that doesn't count the shooters we drank in the bar when we got there. I'd get to drinking scotch and oh, hey, I could put it away. Boy, did I get *intelligent*."

One night in a Dallas bar, she told him, "Cullen and I were very much in love when we first met. We used to go across the lake from his father's house and I'd suck his dick right there in the boat." The memory made her smile briefly between gulps of tequila and orange juice. "After we got married, though, the whole deal ended. That's the reason we have two beds—yeah, can you believe it, two queen-size beds, side by side. He sleeps in his bed and I sleep in mine." Another long swig. "When he fucks me, I don't get in his bed, you know, he gets in mine."

"You know what your fuckin' problem is," W. T. began, feeling particularly intelligent this night. "Cullen has never given you a chance to be a person. You never had a fuckin' chance. Any dog that's never been off the leash is gonna wonder what it feels like. You didn't do anything that wasn't natural. It's his fuckin' fault that you're here tonight."

After that, Priscilla was silent for a long time—"takin' it all in," W. T. hoped.

Priscilla had planned a trip to California to shop for a dress—something special for the ceremonies dedicating the new Dallas–Fort Worth International Airport. She and Cullen would be seated at the main table with Vice President Gerald Ford, so, of course, just any dress wouldn't do, she told Cullen. "It *has* to be from out of town."

W. T. was waiting on the plane when she boarded.

Priscilla found the dress she was looking for in a shop off Rodeo Drive. W. T. described it as "one of these places where you go in, and they bring you champagne, cigarettes, cigars, and there's always someone right there with a fucking ashtray." When Priscilla emerged from the dressing room, W. T. let out a whistle that turned every well-coiffed head in the store. "You can damn near see through it!" he exclaimed. "Tits and all!" Then she told him the price; $17,000. W. T. thought it "looked like it had thirty cents worth of material in it," but still, he liked it. "It impresses the shit out of me," he reassured Priscilla. "I only wish *I* could buy it for you."

On the morning of July 4, 1974, Priscilla Davis's long white Continental pulled into the driveway of a small suburban tract house in west Fort Worth. Parked in the same driveway was the light brown Winnebago camper she had rented the day before. Priscilla, looking pale and vexed by the early hour, got out of her car and joined the group that had already gathered in the camper. W. T. welcomed her on board with a hug. He wanted to ask, "What the fuck did you tell Cullen?" but decided it didn't matter. They would be together for the next three days—three days and nights of "down home music, dancin', draft beer, dickin', and drugs" at the annual July 4 Willie Nelson concert, known to everyone in Texas simply as "the Picnic."

Together, but hardly alone. By the time the camper left later that morning, there were nine on board, including Dee, who would soon celebrate her sixteenth birthday. It was for Dee that Priscilla had originally dreamed up the idea of a trip to the Picnic. She wanted to have some time together with her daughter away from school, away from the house, and especially away from Cullen. To sweeten the offer, she also invited Dee's new boyfriend, Tommy Brown, as well as two of her girlfriends, Randi Matthiessen and Valerie Marazzi. Also along was W. T.'s sometime friend Larry Myers—W. T. hadn't forgiven him for helping the cops with the bust, but he hadn't figured out how to get back at him either. As soon as the last person boarded and the last bag of provisions was loaded, W. T. grabbed the wheel and let out a whoop. The big camper bounced out of the driveway headed for Interstate 35 and, 225 miles away, College Station, Texas.

By the time they arrived, a crowd was already forming in the vast infield of the two-mile firecracker racetrack just northeast of Austin. By the time the musicians started warming up, the crowd had swollen to more than 100,000—a prairie of cowboy hats, bandanas, bare shoulders, and ice chests full of beer. Speakers the size of boxcars roared music so loud that Priscilla and W. T. could barely hear each other talk as they sat on the roof of the Winnebago, at the far edge of the racetrack grounds.

Once the tidal wave of music began to roll out over the Central Texas plains, everything was chaos. No one could hear anyone else, so there was no point in trying to work together. Like survivors of a shipwreck on the high seas, everybody was on his or her own. Priscilla spent much of the first day searching vainly for Dee. People ran in and out of the Winnebago, blurs of bathing suits and shorts, grabbing sandwiches, beers, or one of the bags of drugs lying everywhere. "If there's a drug made," W. T. had promised, "we'll have it." W. T. mostly smoked pot, but occasionally shared a Percodan haze with Priscilla. Others did "mild acid and shit like that."

By the second day, everyone was on a drug and decibel high. No one noticed when musicians changed: Kris Kristofferson sounded just like Waylon Jennings and they both could have been Willie. People in the same camper lost each other for hours. Outside, in the huge, sweltering throng of gyrating humanity, celebrants fainted by the score. And still the music throbbed on.

Priscilla was among the second day's casualties. In searching for Dee, she had managed to lose herself. That evening, Dee showed up at the Winnebago and W. T. spent hours looking for Priscilla. He talked his way into the special backstage party, vacuumed up whatever scotch he could find, and waited until midnight, but there was still no sign of Priscilla. He had planned to take the Winnebago to a nearby campground for the night. It would give him a chance to spend a few quiet hours with Priscilla. Now it looked like they would have to leave without her.

Just about the time he started to crank the Winnebago up, W. T. looked down the little dusty lane that led away from the concert site and "here comes this big titty, good-looking sonofabitch." They drove to the spot on the lake that W. T. had found. "We partied that night and then Priscilla and I made up. We got on top of the Winnebago and made love when the sun was coming up, the waves was lappin' on the lake, and all that romantic shit."

The night Fort Worth celebrated the opening of its new international airport, W. T. watched the festivities on the local news. He saw Vice President Gerald Ford sitting at the center of the head table, and there next to him was Priscilla Davis. "There's fucking Priscilla!" he shouted to a friend who was watching with him. "Doesn't she look terrific!" She was wearing the $17,000 sequined gown she had bought with him in Los Angeles. "She's sitting right next to the fucking Vice President of the United States. To me, that would be, God, the biggest thrill," W. T.

thought. "I'd love to shoot the shit and get my picture taken with him."

A few minutes later, there was a knock at the door. It was Priscilla, standing in the doorway of W. T.'s little gray and white house in her $17,000 dress "looking like ten million bucks."

"Fuck," W. T. thought, genuinely moved, "she is sitting next to Gerald Ford, the Vice President of the fucking United States. And as soon as she can, as soon as the dinner is over—she doesn't stay to have her picture taken, she doesn't stay for the speech—she leaves to come to *my house*."

The next morning, Priscilla awoke early, anxious about returning to the big house on Mockingbird. To smooth the way, she called first. When Cullen answered, she launched immediately into an elaborate excuse: "I had to leave the party early, honey, because . . ." But she only got a few words out before Cullen erupted. W. T., who had been half asleep in the bed next to her, sprung bolt upright at the sound of Cullen's voice screaming on the other end of the line.

By the time she hung up, Priscilla was almost in tears. "I'm afraid of going home," she whimpered, leaning against W. T.'s shoulder.

"Then don't," he whispered. "Stay with me. I'll take care of you."

But Priscilla wasn't listening. "I'm afraid," she repeated several times, then got up and dressed.

15

A few days later, Cullen got his revenge.

After her disappearance from the airport gala, Priscilla had decided to lie low for a few days: no nocturnal bar-hopping, no late nights out, no mysterious phone calls behind closed doors, and most of all, no W. T. It was just for a few days, she told herself, until Cullen cooled down. Besides, it gave her a chance to catch up on old friends and pursue her second-favorite activity: solving other people's problems.

On this particular night, she was counseling Tracy Connors, a friend from Dallas who had fought with her boyfriend and summoned Priscilla to rescue her. Priscilla had driven all the way to Dallas and brought her back to the mansion for a long soul-to-soul. With Cullen safely preoccupied in the billiard room, they curled up on the big master bed and talked until past midnight.

Finally, around one, Priscilla concluded, "Well, I think everything will be okay if we just get something to eat!" But no sooner had they picked up hamburgers at a nearby fast-food restaurant than she insisted on showing Tracy a new club that had just opened. "It's called the Sea-Hag and it's kinda cute," she bubbled, suddenly reinvigorated by the night air. When they arrived, however, and Tracy saw the roomful of couples dancing and laughing, she had only one thought: "I gotta go back to Dallas and see my boyfriend."

Priscilla didn't think that was such a good idea. Dallas was an hour away even at the hellish speed Priscilla drove. That put the round trip at two hours or more. It could be dawn by the time she got back to the mansion.

"But I've got to see him," Tracy pleaded. *"Tonight."*

Reluctantly, Priscilla agreed and headed the white Continental east on Interstate 30.

Just past the last Arlington exit, about halfway to Dallas, she had second thoughts and turned the car around, promising Tracy she would make the trip first thing the next morning.

When they arrived back at the house, Priscilla ran to the billiard room to check on Cullen.

He was waiting for her.

"Where the hell have you been?" he screamed. This time there was no lead-up, no warning. All that had happened while she was gone. His face and hands were swollen

with rage, his cheeks flushed crimson, the knuckles where he grasped the side of the pool table white as bone. His voice was stretched as high and tight as she had ever heard it: *"Where the hell have you been? Out with another one of your lovers?"*

He didn't wait for an answer. His arm flew out and caught Priscilla on the side of the head. The force of the blow lifted her off the floor and threw her up onto the pool table. Tracy backed out of the room in horror. Priscilla screamed and reached for the far side of the table in an effort to pull herself free, but before she could get a hand-hold, Cullen grabbed her by the ankles and yanked as hard as he could. She flew backward, landing hard against the side of the table. He moved in close and punched her square in the face. Her skull reverberated with a loud crack, the sound of her nose breaking.

"Please, Cullen," Tracy pleaded from the safety of the doorway. "Please, it wasn't like that. We just went out for something to eat, and then I asked her to take me home . . ."

But Cullen wasn't listening. He grabbed Priscilla's ankles again and yanked her away from the table, flat on the floor.

"Let her explain," Tracy pleaded.

Priscilla tried to speak, but when she went to take a lungful of air, nothing came in. She couldn't breathe. Her nose felt like a solid block of flesh and blood and bone.

"There's nothing to explain," Cullen shouted between deep, angry breaths. "She fucks other men. No big deal. I fuck other women. Didn't you know?"

He lifted her up by the ankles, then threw her down again, hard, against the walnut parquet floor.

"I want a divorce!" he screamed.

Then again, holding onto her the whole time, up and back down again, hard, as if he were beating the dust out of a rug.

"I want a divorce!"

Priscilla felt the back of her head crack against the hard

floor, then she was up in the air again. He was trying to beat the life out of her.

"I want a divorce!"

In the predawn hours, Tracy drove Priscilla to the hospital. Examining her broken nose, deep facial lacerations, and extensive bruises, the doctor asked, "What the hell happened to you?"

Priscilla smiled at him wanly. "My horse fell on me."

The next day, Priscilla called Cullen at his office.

"My jewelry's missing," she shouted. The long silence on the other end of the line confirmed her suspicions.

"It's here in my office safe," said Cullen, "and it's going to stay here awhile."

"Oh, no it's not!" Priscilla lashed back. "You goddamn cocksucking sonofabitch, I'm coming down there right now and if you don't have my jewelry ready for me, I will tear that place apart! I will make a scene so ugly that no one in goddamn Kendavis Industries will ever forget it—and you know I can do it. I'll be there in fifteen minutes."

Priscilla ran to her white Continental and raced downtown. Stopping in front of the Mid-Continent Building, she left the car in the middle of the street.

Cullen was waiting at the door with the jewelry in a big manila envelope. It passed between them without a word. But as she walked out, without looking back, she shouted over her shoulder, "You want a divorce? Well, you're gonna *get* one."

"That's all right," Cullen called after her coolly, "I've been there before."

Priscilla wheeled around in the doorway and faced him. Her eyes were on fire. "Oh, no, you *haven't*!" she spat. "Not like this you haven't!"

16

To attorney Ronald Aultman, the well-dressed platinum blonde woman sitting down in front of his desk was just another of the legions of middle-aged ladies who wanted to divorce their husbands. She had called him at home the night before to make the appointment, and he had hastily scribbled down her name: Priscilla Davis.

"I've heard that if you're going to get a divorce, you should get a criminal lawyer to handle it," Priscilla began.

Actually, Aultman split his time between crimes and divorces, partly because they were so much alike, and partly because they were both in such abundant supply. Lawyers around the courthouse often joked that after oil, divorce was Texas's biggest industry.

With a line of people in his waiting room, Aultman wanted to skip the small talk. Before agreeing to take the case, he needed to know how much it was worth.

"Where do you and Mr. Davis live?" he asked. The neighborhood would tell him a lot.

"On Hulen," Priscilla answered, "south of the railroad."

"Do you own your own home?"

"Yes, we do."

"Is it paid for?"

"Oh, yes."

Aultman made a note on his pad. "About what is your home worth?"

Priscilla did a quick calculation. "I believe it's six million dollars."

Aultman started to write, then looked up. "Now, Mrs. Davis," he began impatiently, "as you see, I have quite a few clients waiting, so, if you would, let's stay within reason."

"I know it cost a minimum of six million," Priscilla repeated firmly. "But I'm sure it's worth more."

Aultman was still skeptical. "Well, Mrs. Davis, what on earth does your husband do for a living?"

Priscilla thought for a moment. "You name it," she said brightly.

"No, no," Aultman corrected, "*you* name it."

Priscilla looked at the ceiling and concentrated. "Well, he's president of about a hundred corporations all over the world . . ."

Finally Aultman's eyes opened. Later, he described the moment: "Lights began turning on and bells began ringing and buzzers buzzing. Suddenly this wasn't just another divorce."

He did manage to subdue the bells and buzzers long enough to ask one more question: "What would you estimate your estate to be worth?"

"Oh . . ." said Priscilla, thinking hard, "I would say in the area of one hundred million."

In a flash Aultman produced a contract for Priscilla to sign.

There was just one problem: Priscilla didn't have any money. Cullen had opened accounts for her at every store in town but scrupulously kept cash out of her hands. To pay Aultman's retainer, she had to go to a bank and write a $1,500 check against her MasterCharge card. As she left the bank to deliver the money to Aultman, she looked at a calendar and saw that it was July 31. She held up the envelope that contained the cash and muttered under her breath: "Happy Birthday, Priscilla!"

She spent a sleepless night with friends. The next morning, she waited until she was sure Cullen had been served with the papers ordering him out of the mansion. Then she waited some more, just to be safe. Then, finally, she returned home.

Cullen was waiting for her in the billiard room.

"How about a game of pool?" he said, bouncing a cue ball off the bumper and smiling his reptilian smile. He rolled the cue ball across the table, then moved toward her. He wanted a kiss.

Priscilla recoiled. "Don't you touch me."

"But, Priscilla . . ." he began, almost in a whisper.

"Leave me alone," she cut him off, then hurried from the room.

A few hours later, after talking to his lawyers on the phone, Cullen packed a bag and left for the Ramada Inn Central, boasting confidently that he wouldn't be gone for long.

He was wrong.

Aultman moved with astonishing speed to make good on Priscilla's threat. In a matter of days, he had won for his client temporary possession of her Lincoln Continental Mark IV, her clothes, and her jewelry, even the Mockingbird Lane house and everything in it. The divorce judge, Joe Eidson, also ordered Cullen to pay $2,500 a month for Priscilla's living expenses, plus support payments for Dee, plus medical expenses, plus her legal bills, plus maintenance expenses on the house that he couldn't enter.

But even all that didn't buy Cullen peace of mind. Those were only temporary awards until the case could go to trial—in a year, maybe two. Rumors floated back to Cullen that, at trial, Priscilla would demand not only the cars, the house, the jewelry, and the art, but also fifty million dollars—maybe more.

When he first heard the rumors, Cullen laughed. He had protected himself against just such threats by having Priscilla sign a prenuptial agreement, he told himself. "She can't touch me," he told his attorneys.

But Priscilla remembered it differently. "Do you recall signing such an instrument?" one of Cullen's lawyers asked her during a deposition.

"Well, looking back on it, I recall signing *something*," she said, "but as for this"—she held up a copy of the prenuptial agreement the attorney had given her—"I've never seen it before. I've never read it."

"But you don't deny that you signed it at that time?"

"I remember Cullen asking me to sign something because he said that we would be traveling out of the country, and I think he said his brothers wanted me to sign something to do with the company, stocks and bonds. I just said, 'Okay.' "

"When Cullen told you to sign it, that it just pertained to some stocks and taxes, did you believe it?" Ronald Aultman asked.

"Yes, sir," said Priscilla.

"Now, throughout your marriage, did he show any kind of irritableness or irritation when you would want to read things he asked you to sign?"

"Oh, yes, sir. On occasion, I would start to read something and he would just say, you know, 'Sign it, damn it. You don't need to read it, just sign it.' "

When his attorneys delivered the bad news that the prenuptial agreement might not stand up in court, Cullen exploded. How could she lay claim to any of the assets of Kendavis Industries? he demanded to know.

Had he ever promised her anything, they asked: a share of the business, perhaps, or a sum of money.

No, he insisted.

But Priscilla remembered it differently.

"Before the time you were married," Aultman asked her at the same deposition, "did you have any agreement with Mr. Davis as to any specific property that you would get at any particular time?"

"At the time I got my divorce from Jack Wilborn, Cullen told me he would darn sure give me a heck of a lot more than Jack ever gave me."

Could she be more specific? Aultman prodded.

"Jack had been offering me a $5,000 settlement," Priscilla explained, "and Cullen told me he could give me ten thousand times as much."

Five thousand times ten thousand was exactly fifty million dollars.

Then there were Priscilla's charges of brutality. Every time Cullen's attorneys asked if they were true, Cullen waved them off with a terse, "She exaggerates." Not until

Aultman cornered Cullen at a deposition did they hear the truth about their client.

"Now, you heard the testimony of Mrs. Davis about some physical abuse," Aultman asked. "Do you recall striking her on numerous occasions?"

"I can recall striking her on four, maybe five, different occasions," Cullen responded nonchalantly.

"Can you recall breaking her nose?"

"Well," Cullen hesitated, "she went to the doctor one time and came home and *said* that her nose was broken. Other than the fact that she had a black eye, I couldn't tell you, to look at it, that it was broken."

Aultman pressed. "Do you remember that occurring as much as twice? I'm talking about the nose."

"Yes."

"And do you recall breaking her collarbone?"

"Yes."

"And did you do that by striking her?"

"Well, no . . ." Another hesitation. "Well, yes. I threw her down on the floor."

"And do you recall striking the daughter, Dee?"

Giving up. "Yes."

"Do you recall killing the cat?"

"Yes."

"And the incident in the billiard room?"

"Yes."

"And you admit doing those things, do you?"

"Yes."

Cullen's attorneys tried to caution him that Priscilla had a credible case—not strong, necessarily, but strong enough to wage a long and costly battle. But Cullen refused to listen. "She can't touch me," he repeated over and over. "She can't fucking touch me."

He was wrong about that, too.

One day Priscilla dropped by his room at the Ramada Inn Central during a Dallas Cowboys football game. She just had one little favor to ask, she said, sitting down on the edge of the bed and shimmying over to him. The new 1975-model Lincoln Continental Mark IVs would arrive in the showrooms soon, and she really needed to replace her last year's model. Cullen's eyes didn't leave the football game. There was a long silence while they sat on the bed and watched together.

After a few minutes, she began to reminisce about the good times they had shared in the box at Cowboy Stadium. She recalled fondly the splendor of the hot pink Pucci walls, the white chairs, the marble bar, the mirrored ceiling. How much more fun it was to watch that way, she lamented, as the little figures flickered back and forth on the television screen. There were drawbacks, of course, she added enigmatically. In the box they could never do this . . . she ran her hand down between his legs. Or this . . . she rubbed his crotch with a soft, circular motion.

They had sex with the Dallas Cowboys flickering to a lopsided win in the background, like candlelight. Afterward, as Priscilla nestled on the bed next to him, Cullen heard himself say yes to the new Continental. "The woman can't live without me," he told a friend afterward.

A week later, he heard that W. T. Rufner had moved into his mansion.

In fact, W. T. had begun slipping into the mansion for a few hours at a time almost from the day Cullen left it. In October, he moved into the huge master bedroom, bringing with him only "some cutoffs, a couple of T-shirts, and some jeans" to put in Cullen's mammoth, suede-lined closet.

They spent the mornings watching television and having sex, the afternoons driving around town. After six years of playing the rich society wife, Priscilla was ready to cut loose. Racing down the highway to nowhere in particular, she would throw off her blouse and let her huge breasts revel in the rushing air. If a car pulled up on W. T.'s side, she might make a dramatic open-mouthed lunge for his crotch, or, if she caught the attention of a woman driver, reach quickly into W. T.'s pants, hoist out his penis, and smile triumphantly. "She's just bein' affectionate," W. T. would explain to the startled onlooker.

"The most important thing you gave me," she told W. T. one night, "of all the other things that you gave me, was the strength to get away from Cullen."

"Hey, fuck," W. T. cooed back. "You've got a marker on me, lady. If you ever call it in, I'll deliver. No matter what it is."

W. T. never traveled alone. He was used to having people around, playing rough host to friends, or friends of friends, or just some stranded, down-on-his-luck son-ofabitch he met in a bar. Over the years of racing, bumming around the country, and provisioning friends with drugs, he had "shaken hands, gotten high, or gone to bed with just about every form of life known to man." And sooner or later, if he stayed in one place long enough, almost all of it showed up at his door.

The first to arrive was Sandy Guthrie Myers, the "friend" who had snitched on W. T. the day of his arrest. (W. T. was never one to hold a grudge.) Priscilla was impressed by Sandy's dramatic looks—not really attractive, but arresting. With her slender body, long, wild hair, dark almond eyes, and thick, masklike makeup, she reminded Priscilla of a vampiress in a B horror movie. Sandy, in fact, had told people she was studying to be a witch, and when she moved into the mansion, brought with her boxes of books on witchcraft, occult paraphernalia, and dozens of candles that she proceeded to arrange around her room.

Priscilla had suspected that Sandy was yet another of W. T.'s former girlfriends—"chicks," he called them—from the moment W. T. introduced them during a riotously debauched weekend at his boathouse on Possum Kingdom Lake earlier that summer. In fact, W. T. and Sandy had met on a pool table and gotten to know each other better as they stripped away each other's clothes, at which point Sandy threw a pie at W. T.'s groin and proceeded to lick it off.

It wasn't long before Sandy brought her girlfriend, Sue Skinner, to Priscilla's doorstep. Sue, a young, petite brunette, looked straight enough: How much trouble could she be? If she did a little too much dope or slept around, that wasn't Priscilla's business. Which of W. T.'s friends didn't? No formal invitation was issued. None was needed. She just showed up, stayed overnight, left some things. When the next morning came and Priscilla didn't object, she returned the next night and left more things. Before long, she had moved in.

It wasn't long before the boyfriends started coming around. Sue attracted Nipper Perry, a weary-eyed doper who slapped hamburgers and hauled boats in and out of the water at the Benbrook Marina, which was where W. T. met him. Sandy brought her common-law husband, Larry Myers, also known as "Squinch." Myers had done a little drug business with W. T. since the two first met in 1970, but otherwise no one, including his wife, knew what the hell he did. He never seemed to work but always had money in his pocket and a woman at his side (usually not Sandy), a combination that suggested something less than Rotary Club respectability.

Why W. T. remained friendly with Myers, and vice versa, was another mystery to Priscilla—and not just because Squinch had snitched on him to the police. Earlier that year, during a party at Myers's house, Priscilla and W. T. had retreated to a bedroom to have sex when Myers burst through the door, buck naked, dragging Valerie Marazzi, the seventeen-year-old from the Winnebago trip, also naked. But no sooner had the two jumped into bed alongside Priscilla and W. T. than Myers's attention began to wander. As W. T. reached for a drink, Myers scrambled over Valerie and squirmed on top of Priscilla. Rufner looked back around just as Priscilla began to buck and scream, "Get the fuck off me, you bastard. Forget it!"

W. T.'s hazy mind came instantly into focus. "Why, you cocksucker," he shouted as he shoved Myers hard, spilling his scotch in Myers's face just as he was reeling backwards across Valerie. W. T. and Priscilla stormed out of the party after that—and hadn't been back to Myers's house since.

But now, with Sandy settled down in her candlelit coven upstairs, there wasn't much Priscilla could do to keep Squinch away.

After a birthday party that Priscilla threw for W. T. at the Benbrook Marina, Bart Newton started showing up at the mansion. Like Nipper Perry, Newton worked at the marina hauling boats and grilling burgers, although, at age thirty-six, he had less of an excuse. Newton loved only two things in life: dope and "young dollies"—the younger the better. He also liked to abuse them. Still, despite everything, he always seemed to have a seventeen- or eighteen-year-old hanging around his neck, stroking his long, stringy, receding hair and kissing the mouth with the big black gap where a tooth had been knocked out. It was the dope that attracted them—and the abuse. The current one was Randi Matthiessen, a pretty high school dropout. She was sixteen.

When Delbert McClinton, a rhythm-and-blues singer struggling to make a living with a wife and new baby, called, W. T.'s heart went out to him. "You got a place?" he asked. "No," said McClinton. "Well, I got a BIG fuckin' place," W. T. laughed. Soon afterward, McClinton and his family arrived, pulling their house trailer behind a pickup.

McClinton had a musician friend named Sonny Fortner whose promising talent had gone up years ago in a cloud of marijuana smoke. One day he was jamming in blues clubs; the next, dealing pot out of his garage. His young wife, Debbie, was the next "guest" to make a place for herself at the mansion. W. T. described her as "not very pretty but a hell of a mount." By the time Sonny, a Charles Manson lookalike in ponytail and bandana, showed up weeks later, there wasn't much Priscilla could do about it.

For the most part, it was a sorry group. "Between them," said W. T., "they couldn't pour piss out of a boot if the directions were on the heel." But at least they came and went quickly. Some stayed only once; some, like Debbie Fortner, stayed for several months at a stretch; some, like Sandy Myers, were in and out: in when Larry was

busted for dealing, out when he made bond. Most of the
men—Newton, Perry, Sonny, Larry—came and went like
they were visiting girlfriends who shared an apartment.
The house never seemed full—there were only two guest
rooms, plus a maid's room where Dee stayed, all of these
in distant wings of the house, far from the master bedroom.

Which suited Priscilla just fine. She liked having people
around, but she didn't care much who they were. Faces
were interchangeable. Besides, she spent most days with
her real friends like Judy McCrory (who had returned from
Massachusetts after yet another of David's get-rich-quick
schemes fell through)—or with W. T.

When Priscilla did appear, usually in the evenings for
the almost nightly impromptu parties, her houseguests
flocked around her. "Your place is just so fucking beautiful," they would say. "It's like fucking Buckingham Pal-
ace." After years of tiptoeing around Cullen, Priscilla
welcomed the flattery, sincere or not. She came to think
of her houseguests the way Andrea thought of the stray
animals she took under her wing. Sure they were a mangy,
wayward, abused, and often abusive group; sure it wasn't
the vine-covered cottage with window boxes and white
picket fence that she sometimes dreamed would *really*
make her happy, but it was a family, of sorts.

When Dee's friend Bev Bass learned she was pregnant,
she came first to "Mother Davis"—a title Priscilla relished.
Mother Davis drove her to the clinic, sat up with her at
night, and paid for the abortion. Similar "motherhood
attacks" would send Priscilla scurrying to the kitchen at
odd hours to cook for whatever guests happened to be in
the house.

As the rumors poured in about Priscilla and Rufner
and their houseful of guests, Cullen sat alone in the Ramada Inn's Butch Cassidy Suite—two standard, sunless
motel rooms with a hot tub that reeked of commercial
disinfectant—spending most nights and weekends watching television and circling classified advertisements for
"swinger partners."

While Priscilla partied every night in the splendor of his six-million-dollar house, Cullen hit the club circuit: the Jet Set and the Swingers Club, places known for "partner swapping"; the Albatross, Tim Curry's place, for a game of pool; or the hotel bar just downstairs, the Two Minnies. Friends saw him there, standing at the bar, one elbow on the counter, one foot propped up, coolly surveying the crowd, waiting for some girl, any girl with blonde hair and a halter top, to notice him. When approached, he would make a crude remark and smile his awkward, thin-lipped facsimile of a smile. By all accounts, there were few takers. "He worked real hard at the title of 'swinger,' " recalled a business associate who saw him at the Albatross one night, "but he always seemed to be alone."

Eventually—on a blind date—he found Karen Master, a part-time Kelly girl and divorced mother of two. Or, perhaps more accurately, she found him.

With no solid job and two handicapped sons, Karen Master was in desperate straits when she accepted the blind date arranged by a nurse friend. It had been three years since the head-on collision in which her sons, ages four and six months, had sustained brain injuries that left one epileptic and deaf and the other partially blind. Soon afterward, her husband divorced her, leaving her with a stack of overdue medical bills and no way to pay for the expensive rehabilitation her sons needed. With little work experience—selling shoes at Thom McAn—and no high school diploma, Karen was reduced to taking part-time jobs, borrowing from her father, and praying that the right man would find her—quick.

When she heard from a friend and former Kendavis employee who her mystery date was, Karen was sure her prayers had been answered.

Cullen took a little longer to come around. Karen was very attractive, in fact, with honey-blonde hair, soft feminine features, ample breasts, poise, and a pleasing, if slightly apologetic, girlish manner. In 1965, at age seventeen, she had even been chosen "Miss Flame" by the Fort Worth Volunteer Fire Fighters Association. But that wasn't good enough for Cullen. He wanted someone more brilliantly blonde, more heartstoppingly buxom—in short, more like Priscilla. Within months of their first date, Karen's hair began to lighten, her busts began to show more bulge and her clothes more flesh. He gave her flashy jewelry and mini-furs and paraded her at all the nightspots.

From a distance, people often mistook her for Priscilla and wondered why they hadn't heard about the reconciliation. "Congratulations," someone shouted to Cullen at a club one night as he and Karen passed through a crowd. "I'll bet it feels good to be back in your own house."

17

"You're just like Cullen," Priscilla screamed. *"It's just like having Cullen back in the house!"*

"I just want to know where the fuck you were until eight o'clock this morning?" W. T. was drunk, but not so drunk he didn't know he was mad. He had been up all night too, not exactly waiting for her—some motorcycle friends had dropped in to play pool and smoke some pot —but worried about her.

"If it's any of your fucking business, I was playing backgammon," she snapped.

"That piss-ass game." W. T. actually liked backgammon, which Priscilla had taught him to play, but not the way she played it until seven or eight in the morning.

"That's it!" W. T. declared the argument closed. "Fuck it!" He went to Cullen's big closet and got out his small suitcase.

It wasn't the first time W. T. had thrown his cutoffs, T-shirts, and jeans into a suitcase and headed out the door. And it wasn't just about backgammon. Their fights— "yow-yows," W. T. called them—had begun almost the minute Cullen walked out and Rufner moved in. Mostly they fought about "the zoo"—W. T.'s term for Priscilla's houseguests, many of them his own friends. "It's a helluva responsibility to take care of this place," he complained. "All these people coming and going and I'm saying to myself, 'Hey, what happens if this fucking stuff disappears? Who the hell is gonna get nailed for it? Gonna be me for sure.' "

When his racing buddy from Baltimore, Gary Nixon, showed up with a rowdy crew of bikers, W. T. didn't know whether to smile or scream. "It was kinda like Hell's Angels visits the Kimball Art Museum," said Judy McCrory, who was there. W. T. trusted Nixon, but it was easy to see that some in his entourage "had larceny in their hearts." When W. T. herded them toward the swimming pool, away from the main part of the house, they began stripping and jumping into the pool, boozily whooping and hollering as they leapt through the air buck naked, followed by wives and girlfriends.

The next morning, while Priscilla made the survivors breakfast, Rufner discovered that two ivory objects were missing from the display case in the living room, which sparked another yow-yow.

The problems went from bad to worse when Priscilla started spending more evenings away from home without W. T. Around midnight, he would hear her big Continental pull into the courtyard, followed a few seconds later by another car, then another, then another—sometimes as many as a dozen cars escorting her home from whatever bar she'd been to last. "These are fucking strangers," W. T. would complain as she paraded in with her awestruck, spaced-out entourage. "Don't you think we have enough shit to deal with from the people we *know*?" But Priscilla didn't want to hear it. She liked playing the hostess; she liked the attention she got in bars and clubs, and she especially liked bringing that attention home with her.

Finally, one night in mid-1976, W. T. had enough. "That's it," he hollered. "I'm fuckin' finished! I don't wanna be tied up in none of this bullshit." If Priscilla didn't care what went on in her house, then he sure as hell didn't either. He was through playing policeman.

"That's it," he said, hanging his head. "I'm gone." As he drove away, he turned his car onto the vast lawn, tearing deep muddy ruts in the perfect grass.

Later that night, Judy spent an hour on the phone with W. T., trying to ease his pain. "We all know you've been good for Priscilla," she offered. "You're the one who gave her the self-confidence and the courage to break out of that shitty marriage with Cullen."

"Yeah, but look what it's done to *me*," W. T. moaned.

It was the first time Judy had heard him cry.

Unchecked by W. T.'s hard eye, the parties downstairs spun out of control. Larry and Sandy Myers moved in and began to work the nightly crowds, selling 'ludes, coke, junk, acid—Quaaludes, cocaine, heroin, LSD—and anything else that came through the pipeline. If Myers was feeling particularly flush, he might distribute free samples as a "promotional gimmick." It was easy to hide from Priscilla; by midnight she was usually flying above the crowd on a potent mix of Percodan and margaritas.

The next thing W. T. heard, Priscilla was being seen around town with "some big cowboy."

18

"Big" was an understatement. Stan Farr was huge: 6'9", almost three hundred pounds. When he stood next to Priscilla, they looked like a trick photograph on the front page of a tabloid. When someone asked Priscilla how she made love to a man almost two feet taller and three times her weight, she smiled and said, "Some dicks are for fucking and some are for sucking."

From the moment Stan Farr first saw Priscilla Davis

standing in the Round Up Inn during Fort Worth's big
annual stock show, he knew the lady had class. He didn't
need to be introduced; he knew her story already: her
husband, her separation, her big house, her multimillion-
dollar divorce battle. "I met *the* Priscilla Davis," he
boasted to his sister after that first encounter. With his
college friend, Rich Sauer, he couldn't stop bubbling about
her expensive clothes, her white Continental, her "substantial balcony." "She's the big time!" Farr exulted.

It wasn't the first time Farr's friends had heard that
story. "Stan always had an eye for the rich ladies," one
of them recalled. "He invariably had one full-time mama,
and invariably she was loaded. He wanted so desperately
to be big time."

For Farr, Priscilla represented the top rung on a ladder
he had been climbing his whole life. Since first striking out
on his own, he had always been ambitious for something
better. First it was the House Of Pizza, near TCU, which
he bought while still in college. It was a modest start, but
successful enough for him to sell it and move up to a *real*
restaurant, and then to a "supper club"—a nice place with
tablecloths and imported beer. He let customers open
charge accounts so they could say "put it on my tab,"
because that's the way they did it at fancy clubs like the
Petroleum and the Cattleman's. From the supper club, he
hoped someday to make the final step up—to nightclubs.

Unfortunately, Farr's luck wasn't up to his ambitions.
As a teenager he enrolled at TCU, with a head full of
plans. Then, just before school began, his girlfriend
showed up pregnant. After a hasty ceremony arranged by
her family, he arrived at school with a wife and child in
tow. He had great hopes for a high-paying career in pro
basketball, until a knee injury laid him low. After divorcing
his first wife, he started seeing a girl who seemed just right
for him. Then, one night, in a motel room, while he went
to the bathroom, she stole his car.

The supper club went bust because half the customers
thought it too fancy for Fort Worth and the other half
opened charge accounts but never paid them. After that,

Stan tried his luck at construction, his father's business, but spent so long trying to put together financing for an apartment complex that he missed the building boom by ten months. Then his partners backed out, leaving him with nothing to show for his efforts but debts and lawsuits.

When he met Priscilla in the lobby of the Round Up Inn, surrounded by throngs of rodeo fans and the sweet smell of cow chips, he was recovering from a failed second marriage and a long, lean year working for his father in Meridian, Texas.

W. T. was still in the mansion, but that didn't faze Priscilla. They would rendezvous at the Sea Hag, the Old San Francisco Saloon, the Rangoon Racquet Club, the Merrimac, the Colonial, the Western Hills, the Green Oaks, or the Carriage House, anywhere he could order his usual dozen beers and she her vodka with three limes. Stan was such a welcome change from W. T., whose threats and tantrums had become almost as suffocating as Cullen's. Where Rufner was explosive, Stan was affable and gentle. What else could one expect from a man who had, for years, made a career out of drinking beer (working for Miller Brewing Co.) and whose friends called him "The Bear" for the way he grabbed them with his huge arms and suffocated them in a hug? He liked to go out almost as much as Priscilla did, and best of all, unlike W. T., he made no demands.

By midsummer, W. T. had moved out.

By fall, Stan had moved in.

They grew on each other gradually. "We were slow to realize we loved each other," Priscilla admitted later, which was her way of saying that sex was not the glue of their relationship.

The glue was good times. Almost every night, they would show up together at the latest hot spot: the "jolly giant" in his "cosmic cowboy" outfit of beaver-hide hunter hat, lizardskin boots, bear-claw belt buckle, and polyester leisure suit; and the petite blonde bombshell in her cutoff jeans and "Daisy Mae" halter top with an eye-popping flesh-to-cloth ratio (the furs and sequins went out with

Cullen). Both were so used to heads turning when they walked into a bar that being together seemed strangely inevitable. Women would flutter around Stan, men around Priscilla. "Stan was propositioned probably more than once a day," a friend said later. "He had to lock himself in the back room sometimes to keep some of the ladies that were chasin' him away." Priscilla's tolerance for such behavior was limited. One night she caught a girl hanging on Stan's bear-claw belt, slowly removing her blouse. "Get the hell out!" Priscilla screamed.

Soon after Farr moved into the mansion, he bought the lease on the Sea Hag, an ailing bar next to a pancake house in a small shopping center on Camp Bowie Boulevard. With borrowed money, he transformed the place into the Rhinestone Cowboy. With dark zigzag-pattern wallpaper, wooden seats upholstered in blue vinyl, and formica tables in yellow and red, it was the fulfillment of Farr's dream of a big-time club: half western, half disco—the perfect mix for Fort Worth. Now he and Priscilla had their own place to hang out.

Despite so much togetherness, it was a long time before they started talking about the future. Even then, the talk was usually offhand and halfhearted. They were having too much fun every night. Occasionally Stan would complain that he never felt comfortable in Cullen's big house and Priscilla would suggest playfully that they build a dream house of their own someday. They even talked about what it would look like. Stan wanted something classy: "a big central room with a real merry-go-round in the middle which would be the bar."

But mostly they avoided the subject. To his friends, Farr called Priscilla "my investment." She might not pay off for a while—until the divorce was settled—but if what her lawyers were telling her was true, she could be his long-awaited ticket to the big time. Fifty million could buy a lot of class. To her friends, Priscilla described Farr as "a trinket"—an affectionate trinket, to be sure—and a no-hassles companion. "Going out with Stan was like a three-ring circus," she said. His presence allowed her to breathe easier at night when the big house was otherwise empty, kept W. T. and his roughneck friends away, and, last but not least, made Cullen mad as hell.

They were visiting the Old San Francisco Saloon one night, keeping an eye on the competition, when Priscilla felt a tap on her shoulder.

"What's a nice girl like you doing in a place like this?" said a familiar voice. She turned around and found herself staring into Cullen's face. His eyes were red-rimmed and his smile unconvincing even by Davis standards. He looked older than she remembered him: sunken cheeks, creases in his forehead, dark bags and crow's-feet around his eyes.

Next to him and a few steps behind stood a woman with platinum blonde hair and big breasts popping out of a low-cut dress. Priscilla recognized Karen Master. She was prettier—and younger—than Priscilla had expected. Before Priscilla could respond, Cullen moved past and headed for Stan. Karen followed him, giving Priscilla only a quick sidelong glance as she passed.

Standing next to Stan, immense in his cowboy boots and beaver-skin hat, Cullen looked like a child. "Bob Lilly is looking for you," he said, referring to the equally gigantic tackle for the Dallas Cowboys. It was a feeble attempt at humor. Priscilla figured he had been rehearsing it for weeks.

Again, Cullen didn't wait for a reply. He introduced Karen and then quickly disappeared into the crowd, leaving Stan with a half-formed "howdy" on his lips.

The moment passed so quickly that Priscilla wondered later if it had really happened at all. Had Cullen's eyes really been red? Was she just flattering herself, or did he really look like a man on the verge of a breakdown?

19

On one side of the boardroom table of Kendavis Industries, within shouting distance of Stinky Davis's old office,
Cullen Davis sat head in hand, looking unusually pale.
The tan from his January skiing trip to Aspen had worn
off, leaving his skin the color of someone abandoned in a
hospital hallway. In fact, he hadn't been feeling well lately.
Karen worried about his losing weight, although it was
only a few pounds, and urged him to see a doctor. "Just
as soon as this meeting with Ken is over with," he told
her. Someone on his staff suggested that it was the meeting
itself that was making him sick.

On the other side of the table sat Ken Davis, Jr., a
short, slick sliver of a man, squinting through thick black-
rimmed glasses at a stack of papers that obviously dis-
pleased him. There was no mistaking him for anything
other than a Davis: high forehead, thin lips, protruding
ears. Everyone agreed he was the least attractive of the
three brothers—as well as the shortest—and the most like
his father: cunning, cold, and ruthless. To illustrate just
how bad Ken Jr. could be, family friends would joke knowingly that after Stinky's death, he was the only man whom
Cullen Davis feared.

On this day, Cullen had every reason to be afraid. Ken
Jr., had been reviewing the books of Stratoflex, Inc., and
Cummins Sales and Service, the two branches of the Kendavis empire over which Cullen had virtually complete
control. He was also looking over Cullen's personal finances. It was clear from the pained expression on his face
that big brother didn't like what he saw.

Ken put the papers down and threw his glasses on top
of them. "When is this going to end?" he asked.

Cullen explained, for the hundredth time, that the di-

vorce case was bleeding him dry. The judge, Joe Eidson
—Cullen invariably referred to him as "fucking Eidson"
—had given Priscilla virtually everything she asked for:
the mansion, the art, the car, as well as $2,500 a month
in support payments. A few months later, he raised the
payment to $3,500. Along the way he ordered tens of
thousands of additional dollars for everything from school
fees to bathroom bowl cleaner. Add to that the cost of the
Butch Cassidy Suite at the Ramada Inn and the divorce
was costing him more than $100,000 a year. Then there
was the nearly $120,000 he was spending on Karen Master,
including jewelry, furs, cars, and mortgage payments. The
room at the motel was, in fact, just a cover to fool Eidson;
he had been living at Karen's house for some months.

Ken pointed out the obvious: With an annual salary of
less than $200,000, Cullen was spending more than he was
making.

"What about the freeze?" he wanted to know. Judge
Eidson had put a freeze on all of Cullen's assets. Nothing
could move out of any of the companies in which Cullen
had a stake without Eidson's permission. Securing that
permission was a time-consuming, not to say humiliating,
process—and not always a successful one. In November
1974, Cullen had asked permission to sell 44,930 shares of
Western Drilling Company stock for $1,403,163 in order
to meet payments on $14,000,000 in short-term loans. Eid-
son had refused the request.

Ken had railed about that for days. What would Stinky
say? For fifty years he had obsessed over family privacy
and corporate independence. *No one* told Stinky he
couldn't do something with his own company, not even a
judge. It was a damn good thing that Daddy wasn't alive
to see it, Ken remarked ominously. *He* would have hit
somebody.

Which brought him back to his first question: "When
is it going to end?"

"Just as soon as I can get rid of this thing with Priscilla,"
Cullen insisted.

But Ken knew well that the problem wasn't just the

divorce. Ever since Stinky's death, Cullen had been spending money like a drunken sailor. The house that Priscilla now lived in, the art that decorated her debaucheries, had cost almost $6 million. That might not seem like so much to a man of Cullen's net worth *on paper*, but the company wasn't set up to generate that kind of cash. Never in his wildest dreams did their father contemplate extravagance on such a scale. To him, profits were for reinvesting, for building the empire ever bigger, not for squandering on gold and silver chess sets and jade temples. That was why he paid himself, and his sons, such modest salaries, why their companies rarely declared dividends and virtually never sold shares to outsiders.

But being worth $200 million wasn't good enough for Cullen. Cullen wasn't happy just being rich, he had to *act* rich. So what did he do? He went out and borrowed from *banks*—the very word used to make Stinky spit. He borrowed to build the house, borrowed to buy the art, borrowed for vacations, for furs, for jewelry, for parties, even for charities. He called them "personal loans," but in fact, as Ken knew well, they were nothing of the kind. The only way the banks would take Cullen's shares as collateral was if the company agreed to purchase them on demand at a set price. That turned Cullen's debts into company debts.

It wasn't his fault, Cullen protested. It was Priscilla's. *She* was the one with the extravagant life-style. *She* demanded the clothes and the furs and the jewelry. He didn't mind driving the company truck, it was Priscilla who had to have a new Continental every year. It was Priscilla who decorated the house so extravagantly, not him. It was all Priscilla's doing.

And what about the deals with Roy Rimmer? Was Priscilla to blame for those, too? In just a few years, Cullen had poured millions of dollars, some of it borrowed from banks using company shares as collateral, down the drain of Rimmer's get-rich-quick schemes. Why did Cullen invest in deals "on the side" at all? Did he feel a need to have his own money? Was that why he now found himself $14 million in debt?

Their brother Bill was so appalled by Cullen's extravagant life-style that he had filed a lawsuit accusing Cullen of "gross mismanagement" and making business decisions "based on emotional needs rather than any exercise of business judgment." Cullen was "out of control," Bill contended, and Rimmer was "a bad egg." If the two of them kept trying to make a killing, sooner or later Cullen's entire one-third share in Kendavis Industries would be hostage to the banks. Even worse, his suit demanded that the court appoint a receiver—an outsider—to take the empire out of the brothers' hands and either manage it properly or liquidate it entirely. If Stinky Davis hadn't died already, Ken fumed, this would surely have killed him.

All of it was Priscilla's fault, Cullen insisted. She was the reason he needed extra money, the reason he had to go to the banks for loans. He didn't want to have to come to his brothers and ask for more than his share. So he started doing deals with Rimmer, searching for the big score that would allow him to pay off his loans and continue to maintain Priscilla in the style to which she had become accustomed.

Ken thought it over for a few minutes, then came back to where he began. "I'm only interested in one thing," he said. "When is it all going to end?"

To that, Cullen had no answer.

20

On March 15, 1976, the divorce trial was postponed again.

Karen Master was worried about Cullen. The repeated delays in the divorce, the lawsuit with his brother, the sour deals with Rimmer, all had begun to take their toll.

She worried about his health. She feared those "minor problems" he had been ignoring for months would turn out to require major surgery. In April, he checked into

Harris Hospital for a catalogue of operations: hernia removal, hemorrhoidectomy, laminectomy (spinal fusion), appendectomy, tonsillectomy.

She worried about his mind. Cullen Davis, of course, wasn't the kind of man to show it, but Karen could tell the stress was getting to him. His triphammer temper went off even more easily now, and more often. When it did, he struck out more violently. That summer, he hit her six-year-old son Brian in the face with a clenched fist, knocking him to the ground and bloodying his lip. "I'll do it again if you tell your mama," Cullen snarled.

Every day brought some new provocation, like the reports from his various spies at the mansion detailing Priscilla's latest outrages. The maid submitted almost weekly accounts of wild parties, shady houseguests, and broken furniture. The gardener dutifully reported W. T.'s angry exit from the mansion the night he left his tire tracks on the lawn. Soon afterward, Cullen began to hear stories about Priscilla's new beau, "the ten-gallon cowboy with the two-ounce brain," Stan Farr. Cullen didn't like W. T. because he was tall. Even before their first meeting in the Old San Francisco Saloon, he loathed Stan Farr.

Their second meeting, at Dee's high school graduation, wasn't nearly as cordial. Farr lumbered over to Cullen and reached out to shake hands. Cullen took one look at Farr's huge hand, spun around on his heel, and stalked off.

Incidents like that, increasingly common, worried Karen. Was the stress of so many problems finally getting to Cullen? Was he losing control?

Cullen made lavish, obsessive preparations for his twenty-fifth high school reunion in June 1976. At the "get-reacquainted" party the first night, he cock-walked around the room with Karen, in a white halter-neck dress slit to the navel, clutched possessively at his side. When his classmates voted him "Biggest Playboy," he gave a brief speech, thanking them "on behalf of my ex-wife, my present wife, and my girlfriend." Only once did his temper flash through the cheerful fakery when he heard someone refer to Karen as "a carbon copy of Priscilla." By the end of the party, people were comparing notes on Cullen's "wild mood swings."

Later, at a dinner for a few "old friends"—most of whom barely remembered him—Cullen told dirty jokes in Spanish and bragged about "how easy it is to be rich if you're smart." By way of demonstration, he predicted that "by the year 1990, the entire world's oil supply will be used up. That's right, gone! That's why I'm buying up companies outside the oil business. I just bought number eighty." Everyone nodded politely except at the next table, where Cullen's comment met with derisive whispering followed by laughter. Cullen's face turned flame red. "I heard that," he exploded, leaping to his feet and zeroing in on the offender. "How would you like to step outside?" The man at the next table, a big fellow, just smiled and turned back to his companions, leaving Cullen to sputter.

The reunion speaker was Cullen's classmate Tommy Thompson, author of a recent bestselling book, *Blood and Money*, the bizarre story of a prominent Houston doctor who was tried for murdering his wife—and acquitted. Cullen found the story "mesmerizing" and at another dinner party the next night couldn't stop talking about it. When someone tried to change the subject by pointing out that there was not a single doctor in the class, Cullen interrupted. "Did you know we have one alleged murderer?"

No one knew.

With great gusto, Cullen proceeded to tell the story of Ronald Blankenship, a marginal troublemaker in school whose fiancée's charred body was found amid the ashes of a house that had burned to the ground. Originally, Fort Worth police thought she had died in the flames, but an autopsy revealed she was dead before the fire started. Classmate Ronnie was accused of killing her and then burning the house down to cover up the murder.

"But this is the best part," Cullen added, grinning. "He was *acquitted!*"

* * *

Later that summer, Cullen and Karen attended a large cocktail party at the mansion of a wealthy oilman. Soon after they arrived, Cullen disappeared. A half hour later, a rumor began to buzz through the crowd that Cullen Davis was planning some sort of surprise. Karen held her breath. A minute later, she heard a commotion around the foot of the grand main staircase. She looked up to the top of the stairs and saw a strange blonde woman dressed in a gaudy costume slowly descending. The commotion spread across the room, louder and louder. Someone said, "It's Priscilla." She looked back at the woman. It could have been Priscilla—cascades of platinum-blonde hair, impossibly huge breasts. But then she saw the face.

It was Cullen in drag.

21

"Where's Cullen?"

Ken Davis, Jr., looked around the fifth-floor conference room of the Mid-Continent Building, tapping his pencil impatiently. It was bad enough that Cullen would keep him waiting—he hated these trips to Fort Worth from his office in Tulsa, especially for meetings to plot strategy for the legal battles with his brother. But seated across the table from him were Cecil Munn and S. G. "John" Johndroe, two of the biggest names in the biggest law firm in town, Cantey, Hanger, Gooch, Cravens & Munn. Their time was costing the company hundreds of dollars an hour.

Ken Jr. double-checked the date and time in his notes: Monday, August 2, 1976, 8:00 A.M. It was right. Where the hell was Cullen?

Recently Cullen had been making a habit of arriving late. And his mind tended to wander more often when he did arrive. What could he possibly be thinking about, Ken wondered, that was more important than the fate of their father's empire?

He summoned a secretary. "Find my brother," he ordered through clenched teeth, "and tell him to get his ass in here."

An hour and a half later, Cullen arrived. Ken greeted him with a blood-chilling scowl. Cecil Munn thought Cullen looked strange: not like a man who had overslept—more like a man who hadn't slept at all.

Andrea Wilborn slept long and late that August morning. She had returned the day before from vacation Bible school in Houston and at the last minute decided to spend some time with her mother. With Cullen gone, she had finally begun to enjoy her stays in the big house and took advantage of every opportunity to visit. Dee was there, too, or at least she spent her days there. Most nights she preferred the company of her boyfriend Brent Cruz.

That was the other reason Andrea had come to the mansion: she wanted to share with her sister the excitement of her latest discovery—boys. Just before leaving for Bible school, she had approached her stepmother, Betty Wilborn, with an awkward question—"But you have to promise not to laugh," she insisted.

Betty promised.

"How do you know when you're in love?"

Boys had been pursuing Andrea for some time. Although only twelve, she was already a leggy 5'7", with thick auburn hair and breasts that demanded a C cup. When she dressed up—which was rarely—she could pass for fifteen or sixteen, so it wasn't any surprise that the boys showed interest in her.

What was new and startling was that she showed interest back. Earlier that summer, during a daylong hot-air balloon event on the mansion grounds, Priscilla discovered Andrea missing. After a frantic search she found her in the remote reaches of the basement, supposedly showing a young boy, John Buckley, the house's network of tunnels. Not until later that night did the light go on in Priscilla's head. "What do you mean to that boy?" she asked. But Andrea only shrugged her shoulders. Later, Priscilla lamented to Judy McCrory, "First it was Dee, now it's Andrea. I'm gonna have to watch *her* now."

Andrea and Dee were sitting on the bed in Dee's room listening to records and talking about boys when Bev Bass arrived.

"Aren't you ready yet?" she said to Andrea, looking at her watch. "It's almost noon."

"Oh my God!" Dee yelped, jumping off the bed and running for the door. "I've got lunch with Cullen!" Before Bev could ask for an explanation, she was gone. Andrea lingered on the bed listening to the music in a world all her own.

"Andrea!" Bev shouted over the music. She hated to break into that world, but they had arranged to spend the afternoon shopping for a gift for Bev's father. It wasn't Andrea's fault, Bev told herself. She was just a dreamy kid. You could send her upstairs to brush her hair and she'd be gone for an hour. How could you be angry at a girl who took in stray animals and wrote poems on kitten stationery? "When I die," she had written to Bev from Bible school, "I'll be with the animals."

Six years separated the two girls—a huge gap to a child of twelve—but Bev rarely thought about it. She had been Dee's friend originally, but now she felt closer to Andrea. They were like sisters. "She's the sweetest, most innocent, beautiful child you've ever seen," she would tell her friends. Andrea, in turn, adored Bev. She said she wanted to be just like her when *she* grew up—tall and leggy with long, sexy hair—and she seemed well on her way. Andrea gave Bev a charm bracelet she had made herself; the charms spelled out "I LOVE YOU 2." Bev wore it everywhere.

"You can't go like that," Bev said, looking at Andrea's T-shirt and blue jeans. "Let me pick out something for you." For such a pretty girl, Andrea paid shockingly little attention to the way she looked, Bev thought, but that would change now that she had discovered boys. She picked out a corduroy skirt like the one she was wearing and a brown striped tube top, then helped Andrea comb her hair. About half past noon, they set out in Bev's 1972 Buick Skylark.

In the second-floor dining room of the Fort Worth Sheraton, Cullen stared into his drink, then across the room, then out the window at the Water Gardens, anywhere but at Dee. He could cover the hatred in his voice, but not in his eyes. Minutes before, he had told his brother Ken that he couldn't have lunch at the Century II Club with attorneys Munn and Johndroe because he had an appointment with Dee. Ken didn't say anything, but Cullen knew how his brother felt about Priscilla and the leeches she called children. He had warned Cullen dozens of times about the folly of adopting Dee: Once she had her legal claws in him, she would never let go. "You can't divorce a child," he would say. What would Cullen do if she claimed part of the Davis empire? "She'll be nothing but trouble 'til the day you die," he predicted ominously.

At times like this, it seemed like he was right.

"What am I going to do about school?" Dee finally asked, with a whine of helplessness. "Money-wise, I mean." She hated it when he made her ask.

Dee always needed money, or so it seemed to Cullen. He reached for his wallet and pulled out a $50 bill.

Dee rolled her eyes—a lousy fifty bucks! She almost said it out loud, but decided not to risk a fight. She had been trying for months to persuade Priscilla or Cullen or Jack Wilborn or *somebody* to buy her a Maserati to take to college. This might be her last chance before school started.

"About the money . . ." she tried again.

"Here's what I want you to do about that," Cullen said with great seriousness. "I want you to go home, *tonight*, and sit down with your mother and make out a detailed budget."

"But . . ."

"No buts. Do it. *Tonight*."

The Maserati would have to wait.

By the time Cullen arrived back at his office, he had a splitting headache. He called his chiropractor, Dr. Tom Chames, and made an appointment for that afternoon "before six."

Andrea wanted to know all about Bev's new boyfriend, Gus Gavrel.

They called him "Bubba," Bev explained as they drove to Cox's, a department store on Camp Bowie Boulevard. He was twenty-one—three years her senior—and he had quit high school his senior year. Not because he wasn't smart, she was quick to add; he was just unhappy there. Well, he wasn't that smart, Bev conceded, but he was affectionate, faithful, and good-hearted—about as much as you could expect from a man. The two girls giggled in the front seat of the Skylark.

On the way back home from Cox's, where Bev bought a golf shirt for her father, Andrea spotted a pet store and pleaded with Bev to stop. Andrea may have developed a new fascination with boys, but she hadn't yet lost her old—and not unrelated—fascination with small, helpless, cuddly creatures of all kinds. This time her eye was caught by a pygmy goat, shaking and stumbling in a small pen. "Do you think Mom would mind if I brought it home?" she asked.

As they walked to the door, Andrea turned and took a long, last wistful look at the rows of cages, pens, and glass bowls lining the walls. "Look at all of them," she whispered to Bev. "I wish I could set them all free."

They returned to the mansion between four and five, and Bev stayed another hour, talking mostly about boys. Andrea didn't want her to leave. Priscilla and Stan were going out to a party, Dee would spend most of the night with Brent, and, of course, Bev would be with Bubba. That left Andrea the only one without a date. "I have to stay home alone tonight," she said as Bev prepared to leave. "Sometimes I get scared."

* * *

"Goddamn, fucking Cullen!" Dee slammed the break- fast room door so hard the glass trembled and the dishes in the kitchen rattled. "What the fuck am I supposed to do for money! Fifty lousy dollars! Oh, thank you, Daddy, thank you very fucking much!"

She flung her bag across the room and reached for the telephone. When the number she dialed produced only a busy signal, she raised the phone over her head and hurled it against the floor. "Fucking Cullen!"

A secretary poked her head in the door just as the meeting with Ken and the lawyers was resuming. "Mr. Davis, Mr. Wessler is here to see you." The name brought a sudden silence to the conference room. Everyone knew that Jack Wessler was representing Cullen in his divorce. They also knew that there had been a hearing before Judge Eidson the previous Friday to argue Priscilla's latest re- quest for a delay in the trial. A delay meant more months of paralysis at Kendavis Industries, more months of Judge Eidson's prying eyes watching over every move they made in response to Bill Davis's suit. Another delay could cost the company millions, even tens of millions.

Eidson's decision was due today. Wessler was deliv- ering it.

"How did it go?" Cullen asked when they were alone in his office. His voice betrayed nothing. He could have been asking a secretary what she had for lunch.

Wessler hesitated. "Not well, I'm afraid." Then he braced for an explosion. He knew how much this delay meant to Cullen and the business, and Cullen, as everyone knew, had his father's temper.

Instead, all he heard was a thin, emotionless "Okay."

He looked up at Cullen through his gold-rimmed spec- tacles. Had Cullen heard right? Did he understand? Wes- sler, a distinguished, silver-maned lawyer who spent most of his time dealing with far more decorous banking busi- ness, tried again. "Eidson granted the delay," he repeated.

Again. "Okay." Cullen's eyes looked past Wessler as he spoke, and his thin lips barely moved.

Wessler plunged ahead, unnerved by Cullen's exaggerated calm. "Eidson also increased Priscilla's monthly support from $3,500 a month to $5,000 a month." Surely that would elicit a reaction, Wessler thought. The delay had been expected, if dreaded; the boost in payments was an ugly surprise.

But Cullen didn't blink or raise his voice. Just "Okay."

"At least that's only for another two or three months —only until the trial begins." Wessler was having a conversation with himself. He tried again: "Eidson also ordered you to pay her attorneys $25,000 and to pay about $27,000 for some bills she has accumulated . . ."

"Okay."

There was a long silence while Wessler waited for questions. None came. Finally Cullen ushered him out the door, still without a word. After he had gone, Cullen turned to his secretary, Joyce Knowles. "Call Karen," he instructed, his face flushing red and his knuckles on her desk white as paper, but his voice still expressionless. "Tell her I won't be home for supper."

"Wouldn't you just love to see Cullen's face when he hears about this," Priscilla bubbled to secretary Beann Sizemore as she skipped out of her lawyer, Ronald Aultman's, office.

She had stopped by to find out how Judge Eidson had ruled on her request for a postponement of the trial, and was elated with the news. Now she could pay some bills and even buy Dee a car—although certainly not the Maserati she was always angling for.

Finally, she had beaten Cullen at his own game of mendacity and manipulation. He would hate her for this. He hated her already, but this would hurt him where she had never been able to hurt him before—in his pride. *She* was in control, not him, and she knew that nothing in the world made him madder than not being in control.

Unfortunately, she also knew that he wouldn't just give up. That thought made her suddenly, deeply gloomy. "Maybe I won this battle," she mused to Sizemore, who was startled by the quick change in mood. "But it's not over yet. Cullen doesn't like to lose. It's not the money—it's the battle. He always has to be the winner."

Cullen wasn't the only one upset by the news that the trial had been delayed. Stan Farr had been waiting almost a year for Priseilla to make good on her promises. "Just wait till the divorce comes through," she would say, "and we'll be set for life. Count on it." And that's exactly what Farr had done. Convinced that "big money" was just around the corner, he had found an old honky-tonk bar, Panther Hall, and drawn up plans to convert it into a country-western "disco-saloon."

After the last delay in the trial, he had been forced to seek investors to put up the necessary $350,000. That job was made even harder when he was fired as manager of the Rhinestone Cowboy in July because the cash tallies at the end of each night were routinely coming up several hundred dollars short. One of his partners suspected Farr of having his big hand in the till; others thought he was so busy gladhanding customers and coming on to girls that *anybody* could have walked off with the money.

Even with that cloud over him, Farr had been able to interest several investors in his Panther Hall project—on the condition that he put up $50,000 of his own funds. But Farr didn't have that kind of money, even after he sold off his interest in the Rhinestone Cowboy; and until the divorce came through, neither did Priscilla.

Priscilla returned from her lawyers' office feeling better than she had in months. Her ulcer had finally settled down, and, for the first time since a $2,500 nip-and-tuck in the spring, her face felt "right" again. Friends like Judy McCrory were still warning her about taking too much Percodan, now as many as 200 pills a week, but they didn't understand how much she *needed* it. Her back still hurt from a skiing accident in 1971, and regular doses just didn't do any good. She had a right to live her life free from pain. This two-month delay in the trial would give her a chance to really get her strength back.

Farr received her "good news" about the divorce with a long, stony silence. Then, glumly, "I've got a meeting tonight with Dejarno and Cashion"—two of the potential investors in Panther Hall.

Priscilla tried to be upbeat. "Oh, why don't you forget about that old place? Aren't you tired of clubs? You can find something better to do."

In fact, after a year of almost nightly clubhopping and backgammon at the Rhinestone Cowboy, Priscilla was tired of the club life. "I want a break," she had told a stunned Judy McCrory. "I need to get back to some normalcy. My health can't take this going out every night."

What Priscilla really wanted a break from was Stan Farr. On a recent night at the Rhinestone Cowboy, before Farr was fired, they had fought so furiously, and so publicly, that it was almost like being married to Cullen again. "You dumb son of a bitch," she screamed at him. "You big dumb fucking cowboy!" Then she grabbed his beloved beaver-hide hat, threw it to the ground, and stomped all over it. As slow as he was, Farr got the message.

For Priscilla, the idea of marrying Farr, once a real possibility, had become almost laughable. "She knows she can't settle for what Stan has to offer," Judy McCrory told a friend. "To go from Mrs. Cullen Davis to Mrs. Stan Farr is too big a leap off the totem pole as far as life-style is concerned." Priscilla hadn't worried about such things when she thought she could win twenty or thirty million dollars from Cullen in the divorce. With that kind of money, she could be "Mrs. Cullen Davis" for the rest of her life. But recently, unknown to Farr, her attorneys had retreated from their astronomical early estimates of what they could pry from Cullen. More and more, it looked like she would not be able to divorce Cullen while staying married to his money. More and more, it appeared, the two were a package deal.

As that realization dawned, Priscilla began to give Cullen another look. "Maybe he isn't so terrible after all," she mused to a horrified Judy McCrory one day.

"My God, Priscilla," Judy exclaimed. "After all you've

been through—the broken bones, the black eyes, the mind games, the emotional torture. What does it take? A fucking brick?"

Then Priscilla decided to go *see* him.

It was while he was in the hospital for the operations on his back and appendix. "I'm seriously considering asking him to come back," she told Judy.

"Priscilla," Judy pleaded, "have you *really* thought about this?" It was beyond her comprehension.

"I *have* thought about it," Priscilla insisted. "I'm going to the hospital. I am seriously going to make amends, and ask him to come back."

"My God," Judy muttered to herself after Priscilla left. "She's still in love."

Priscilla did go, armed only with a funny get-well card she had spent hours choosing. When she walked into the hospital room, she saw Cullen lying on his back after the surgery and Karen Master sitting in a chair next to him, with her feet propped up on the bed and nestled under his covers. Priscilla didn't know whether to scream or cry.

Karen didn't get up. She didn't even take her feet down, Priscilla noted as the anger rose to her throat. She just sat there and said, "Hello," inflecting it with a coy smile.

With as few words as possible, Priscilla left the card and fled the room. For days afterward, she cursed Karen Master and cried over Cullen.

Cullen left the Mid-Continent garage in his old Chevrolet pickup around 5:30, the day's meetings swimming together in his head. After the news from Wessler about the postponement, he and Ken had called in Walter Strittmatter, the company's chief financial officer, and an accountant from Price Waterhouse. A day that had begun with a strategy session ended in panicked damage control. "That's a hell of a note!" Ken railed when he heard of the delay. "As far as I'm concerned, this damn thing has already gone on too long. It's already been two fucking

years! If there's gonna be a divorce, then get it over with.
I don't care what you have to do to solve this problem,
just get it done."

Around 7:00, Bubba picked Bev up in his 1975 Chevy
Blazer. They drove to Mansfield, about twenty miles
southeast of Fort Worth, and had a barbecued chicken
dinner with Bubba's friends Scott and Jan Herr. Bev, who
loved kids and wanted to teach school someday, spent most
of her time on the floor with the Herrs' two small children.
Around 8:15, she and Bubba met Dee at Brent Cruz's
house. While Bubba and Brent stayed behind, Bev and
Dee delivered the golf shirt birthday present to Bev's father. There they discovered that Bev's water bed had
sprung a leak. To patch it, her father would have to drain
it, leaving Bev with no place to sleep except the couch.
Dee jumped in and invited Bev to spend the night at the
mansion—she kept some extra clothes there for just such
occasions. Bev accepted the invitation eagerly.

When the girls returned to Brent's house, Bubba suggested that the four of them go out to a club, but Dee
begged off. She wanted to spend a quiet evening with
Brent. Later, when Cruz asked her if she planned to return
that night to prepare a budget for college, as Cullen had
instructed, she looked at his baby face in indignant astonishment. "You gotta be fucking joking!"

Priscilla heard the heavy "clunk," like distant thunder,
as the hydraulic locks throughout the house clamped into
place. On the way out to Farr's black Thunderbird, she
watched Andrea lock the back door behind them and then
checked the door from the house to the garage herself to
make sure it was locked.

She and Stan were the last to arrive at the Old Swiss
House, an aging fantasyland brick cottage with a steeply
pitched roof, half-timbered gable, and a little columned
portico. "I know why they're late," Judy McCrory whispered as they appeared at the door. Priscilla's latest facelift

had just healed and she had decided to stop wearing a wig. "She wants to make a grand entrance to show off her new face and real hair."

The occasion was a combination birthday party for Larry Thomas, husband of Priscilla's good friend Carmen, and an anniversary party for Judy and David McCrory, although no one made too much of the latter, since it was widely known that the McCrorys' marriage was in trouble. The party took a large circular table directly in front of the bar, ordered a round of drinks, then another, then dinner—mostly steaks—and a bottle of wine. Because of her ulcer, Priscilla drank only half a glass of white wine, but still had to take two antacid tablets to quell her indigestion.

After a brief visit to his chiropractor to treat a pinched nerve that had been giving him headaches for years, Cullen returned to the Mid-Continent Building. He stayed until just before 8:00, when he walked out to the truck for a second time, bid the security guard good night, and disappeared.

By 11:00, the party at the Old Swiss House was in full, noisy swing. Priscilla seemed unusually buoyant, Judy thought, and assumed it was because of her success in the courtroom that day. All her friends knew how badly she wanted to put the trial off. She needed to be at her best to face Cullen in court. But when someone asked Priscilla about it, instead of lighting up, she became suddenly very somber. "It scares me," she said. "*I* know how mad Cullen can get about these things."

The topic seemed to throw a permanent pall over the evening for Priscilla, until someone brought her back to life by asking about Andrea. Now that Andrea was beginning to show some interest in boys and clothes, she and Priscilla finally had something to talk about. The thought of shepherding a second daughter—and a beautiful one at that—through the years of dating, with all its thrills and heartbreaks, both excited Priscilla and scared her. She summed it all up with a brave laugh: "Here we go again!"

Andrea rattled around in the mansion's big kitchen until 9:00, baking a cake, then summoned up the courage to make a phone call.

"Hi," she said. "Is Kip there?"

Barbara Fischer knew who it was, and she didn't like it one bit. It wasn't "healthy" for their fifteen-year-old son, Kip, to be seeing a twelve-year-old girl, no matter how "developed" she was. Mrs. Fischer didn't care much for Andrea's so-called mother, either. "She's not a responsible person," was the way she put it to Kip after he met Andrea at the Windy Ryon Memorial Roping two months before.

When Kip heard that he had a phone call, he, too, knew who it was. Andrea wasn't just the only girl who called this late; she was the only girl who ever called. "Tell her I'm asleep," he whispered to his father.

Fred Fischer relayed the message.

"Oh, he's asleep?" Andrea sounded heartbroken. "This is Andrea. Will you ask him to call me in the morning? I'm at my mother's." Her little voice sounded far away and lonely.

The party at the Old Swiss House broke up suddenly around 11:10 when Larry and Carmen had to relieve their babysitter.

Next on the night's itinerary was the Rangoon Racquet Club, a popular night spot in a converted house just off Camp Bowie not far from the Old Swiss House. Stan howdyed the bartender and walked to the outdoor "beer garden" in the back. As soon as he and Priscilla entered, a girl sitting at one of the booths jumped up and ran toward them. It was Bev Bass. She hugged and kissed them both. "What a great surprise," she giggled. "Did y'all's party break up early?"

Priscilla nuzzled up to her ear and whispered, "Who're you with?"

"Bubba," Bev whispered back, and giggled some more.

"Why don't you join us?" Priscilla offered as they headed for a table near the gate that led to the parking lot. Bev went back to her booth and fetched Bubba, along with two high school friends, Linda Albee and Debbie Bumgardner. Everybody ordered hard drinks except Priscilla, who stuck with white wine.

At one point, Priscilla leaned over and whispered to Bev: "I was in court today, and I got what I wanted. I'll tell you about it later."

"You can tell me tonight," Bev grinned. "I'm spending the night at your house."

Around 11:30, Stan and Priscilla left for home. Bev and Bubba decided to stay a few more minutes with their friends.

Around 10:40, the phone rang at the mansion. The sound of fifteen phones ringing at once echoed through the empty house. Andrea, who was sitting alone in her room, answered it eagerly.

The caller was Lynda Arnold, Stan Farr's sister. She was looking for Priscilla.

"She's not here," said Andrea, disappointed that it wasn't Kip. "She and Stan went to a birthday party for Larry Thomas." At least it was *someone* to talk to.

Just then Lynda's daughter, Dana, walked into her mother's bedroom. Dana and Andrea were close friends. They would often get together to play with Andrea's animals, or wander to the Trinity River, or cook—although Priscilla considered it closer to "creative mess-making," since they rarely finished what they started. Sometimes Dana just liked to come over and sit in one of the mansion's living rooms. "It makes you feel so *rich*," she said.

When Dana discovered Andrea was on the line, she grabbed the phone from her mother and insisted on talking to her. The two girls chattered for the next twenty minutes. Finally, at her mother's urging, Dana said, "I've got to go now, it's getting late." Andrea didn't want to hang up, but finally resigned herself to it.

"Okay," she said mournfully. "Good night."

22

"Andrea?" Priscilla knew before she entered that something was wrong. She could see through the kitchen window that the security system had been turned off. The row of four red lights was dark.

This wasn't like Andrea.

It was like Dee, however, and for a second Priscilla thought maybe Dee and Brent had already returned. She scanned the parking area for a car, thinking maybe she had looked right past it on the way in.

But the only cars there were Stan's black Thunderbird and her own snowy white Lincoln gleaming in the moonlight.

Priscilla checked the back door. It was locked—just as she had left it. As she opened it, she noticed that the kitchen lights were all on. That was strange, too. Usually by this time—past midnight—Andrea had retreated upstairs, either to her room or to her mother's fox-covered bed.

"Andrea?" she called again, still more puzzled than urgent.

She turned left, past the back stairs and toward the kitchen. It seemed like every light in the house was on, even the light leading to the basement, which she could just see at the far end of the kitchen. She looked around the counters for some sign of activity. She could tell that Andrea had done some baking, but that had obviously been hours ago.

"Andrea?"

Still no answer. That too was strange. Andrea was usually so happy to see someone after being alone in the house all evening. She would bound down the stairs and position herself at the door before they were even out of the car. She had a sixth sense that told her when someone was approaching.

"Andrea?" Priscilla called again, loud enough to be heard through most of the downstairs. Again, no response. "Stan," she instructed, in a flat, tense voice, "go see if she's upstairs." Farr lumbered up the back stairs.

Priscilla had a sixth sense, too, and she didn't like the warning signals it was giving off. Her mind ran through all the possibilities: Dee or a friend had visited, then left, and Andrea had forgotten to turn the system back on; Andrea was in the bathroom; the system had shut down by mistake. She wanted to believe any one of them, but couldn't stop doubting all of them.

"Andrea?"

Automatically she began turning off lights. Her mind was still racing but her body moved slowly, deliberately, from one light switch to the next, working her way around the kitchen cabinets and toward the basement door. Something inside told her to stop shouting Andrea's name. Instead she began to repeat it softly, in long, muttered chains: "Andrea, Andrea, Andrea, Andrea, Andrea," as if puzzling out a riddle.

She turned the corner to the basement door and reached absently for the light switch. Suddenly she broke out of her trance and saw something on the wall near the switch, only a few inches from where she was standing. It was a bloody handprint.

In an instant the puzzle was solved.

"ANDREA!" she screamed. "ANDREA! MY BABY!" Her eyes still fixed on the bloody smear, she screamed for Farr. "STAN, COME HERE. STAN! I NEED HELP!"

When Farr didn't appear, she turned to run after him. At the bottom of the stairs, she stopped to call him again. Just as the muscles of her throat tightened, she saw movement out of the corner of her eye. She looked and saw a

man step out from the darkened hall on the other side of
the breakfast room. He was dressed in black and wore a
shoulder-length black wig. His hands were holding something wrapped in a black plastic bag. He stepped forward
out of the darkness so calmly that for a second or two she
wasn't in the least alarmed. He was even smiling at her—
a bizarre, thin-lipped, smile. Familiar.

"Hi," the man said, then fired.

Priscilla clutched her chest as soon as she heard the
gunshot, but the hole was already there. An instant later,
the blood came. She stumbled backward and fell. Then
the pain came, long knives of it, stabbing straight through
her.

She heard Farr's heavy footsteps on the stairs. "Stan,"
she screamed. "I've been shot!" With every word, the pain
stabbed her again. "Stan, go back!"

But Farr was already at the bottom of the stairs. As
the man in black rushed toward him, Farr slammed the
door leading to the stairway. The two men struggled over
the door, pushing against each other, feet slipping, grunt-
ing frantically. Farr finally managed to shut the door from
the inside, leaving the man in black slamming his shoulder
against it from the outside. Panting and angry, he stepped
back and fired through the door.

From the other side Priscilla heard a grotesque cry of
pain, so loud it didn't sound human at all. The pressure
on the door went slack and the man in black pushed it
open. Farr fell on top of him, half wrestling, half clinging,
his massive arms locked around the other man, who staggered backward, struggling to free himself from the huge
body and its deadweight grip. From somewhere between
them, muffled by the struggle, Priscilla heard another shot.
Farr's body jerked back and then toppled over like an
ancient tree, falling hard on its side not far from her. His
face was toward her, looking up. She could see there was
still life in it. He lifted his chin, as if to roll over or stand
up. He tried to speak, but the only sound he made was
the gurgling of blood deep in his throat.

The man in black walked over and stood at Farr's feet.

He raised his gun and fired into Farr's body. There was no sign of impact, no flinch of pain. Priscilla saw Stan's chin begin to sink. He was no longer trying to get up. The man in black fired again. Farr's chin sank farther toward the floor. He laid his head all the way down and his eyes rolled slowly backward. From the floor across the room, Priscilla watched him die.

The man in black grabbed Farr's ankles and began dragging him toward the kitchen, away from the breakfast room door where he could be seen through the plate-glass window.

As soon as he disappeared around the corner, Priscilla scrambled to her feet and lunged for a nearby sliding glass door. The lock wouldn't open. The noise of her fumbling alerted the man in black. He dropped Farr's legs and leapt over them toward her. Just then the lock gave way. She flung the door open and ran into the courtyard, her hand pressed against the hole in her chest. When she turned around to see how close he was, her shoe caught the edge of a paving stone and she fell at the foot of a statue. It was a statue of Aphrodite, goddess of love. A second later, when she looked up, he was standing over her, pointing his gun down at her.

"I love you," she pleaded. "I didn't—I have never loved anybody else. Please, let's talk. *Please* sit down and talk with me. . . . *Please!*"

He reached down, grabbed her arm, and yanked her to her feet. "Come on," he said in a soft, calm, terrifying voice as he dragged her back toward the house.

"Please, don't, you're hurting me," she protested, struggling to keep one hand over her wound, convinced that if she let go her insides would burst out of her.

"Come on," was all he said.

As they neared the kitchen door—he would take her inside and kill her, she knew it, just as he had killed Stan—she began to scream. "Why are you doing this? I love you. *I love you!*"

Suddenly he stopped and stood bolt upright, as if listening. Priscilla felt his grip loosen as he strained to hear something. Then he let go and headed back into the house.

Priscilla ran. In the corner of the courtyard, she hid behind a bank of shrubs, jerked off her shoes, and gathered up her long denim skirt in a bundle which she pressed against the hole in her chest. She lay very still for a few seconds listening to the drumming of her heart, then looked back toward the house.

He was coming toward her again.

Her heart was pounding so loudly that she almost didn't hear the voices floating over the courtyard wall from the parking area. The man in black heard them, though, and stopped to listen. Then he walked right past her on his way to the driveway gate.

For a moment Priscilla felt a rush of relief. Then she heard the voices again. One of them was a girl's voice. "My God, it's Dee!" Priscilla thought. "He'll kill her too!" She wanted to scream, but it was too late. All she could do now was run for help. "Just run, you stupid broad," she screamed in her head, "just run!" Holding her dress against her breast, she headed out the gate, past the ring of oaks that circled the house, and out into the darkness.

Standing on his toes, Bubba could just see over the courtyard wall. The light was dim, only moonlight really, but he could make out a man dragging a woman with blonde hair by the arm toward the house. The woman was saying, "I love you, I love you," and the man was saying, "Come on, come on." The man appeared to be carrying a bag in his other hand.

"Who is it?" Bev demanded in a whisper. She could only hear the voices, not the words. "Is somebody trying to rob the house?"

They walked a little farther and the figures in the courtyard disappeared from Bubba's view. The night air, which had seemed so reassuringly warm when they stepped out of the air-conditioned Blazer, suddenly felt hot and oppressive.

When they arrived at the gate to the courtyard, Bubba decided to announce their presence. "Hey, what's going on here?" he called out in a loud, aggressive voice. "Where is everybody?"

From out of nowhere, a man appeared behind them. He was dressed all in black—black turtleneck, black pants, black shoes—and he kept his head bowed to hide his face. He held a crumpled black plastic bag in his hands.

"Right this way," he said, leading them around the garage toward the back door. "Let's go inside."

Bubba was suspicious. "What are you doing?" he demanded.

The man didn't respond. "Just come on," was all he said.

Bev turned to Bubba. "I think he's taken something from the house," she whispered. "I think he's broken in." Bubba nodded and motioned her to stay behind him.

The lights over the three garage doors had been flickering for several days. Tonight they had all blinked out at once. The route to the back door was dark, except for the light from a sliver of moon. As they turned the corner of the garage and headed up the walkway with the house on one side and a low wall on the other, the man in black began to walk faster. He was almost ten feet ahead of them now.

He's trying to make a run for it, Bubba thought, convinced that Bev was right, that they had interrupted a burglary. He quickened his pace to keep up. "I can take him," Bubba decided. The man was only 5'4", maybe 5'6", slightly built, not carrying a gun. He didn't appear to pose any real threat.

They turned another corner into a small paved courtyard, and Bubba saw the back door ahead of them. A spotlight flooded the area in front of the door, and the man's pace slowed as he entered the pool of light. The sudden change in speed brought Bubba and then Bev up close on the man's heels—no more than three feet behind—but his back was still all they could see. "If I'm gonna jump him," Bubba thought, "now's my . . ."

Before he could finish the thought, the man turned

around and confronted them. The light streaked across his face.

"Bubba," Bev shouted. "That's Cullen!"

Instantly the man raised his black bag, pointed it at Bubba, and fired. Bubba just had time to look down and see a dark spot below his shirt pocket before his legs gave way and he crumpled backward to the ground next to a row of garbage cans. His roar of pain was almost drowned out in the reverberations of the gunshot in the walled courtyard.

The man in black walked calmly to where Bubba lay, eyes open, in a widening pool of blood. He leaned over and pointed the gun at Bubba's head.

"No!" Bev screamed from where she stood, frozen in place, only a few feet away.

"Run!" Bubba yelled to her. "Run!"

The man looked at her. They were eye to eye, only feet apart. "Cullen," she heard herself say, "it's me, Bev."

"Run!" Bubba shouted.

This time, she heard him. But even as she flew terrified back down the walkway toward the driveway, she continued to shout: "It's me, Cullen. It's Bev! Please don't shoot me! Cullen!" She couldn't tell if he heard her. All she could hear was the reverberations of the gunshot, still screaming in her ears. Then she looked back. He was chasing her.

At the end of the walkway, she jumped over the wall instead of using the gate. That gave her a few more seconds' lead. Once she reached the dirt driveway and headed toward Hulen, years of running track in high school came back to her and she hit her stride. But every time she glanced back, she could still see him, 150 feet behind, 100. Was he shooting at her? Her ears still heard only the first gunshot, but once or twice, when she looked over her shoulder, she caught a glimpse of him raising the black bag and pointing it at her. She began to weave back and forth, on and off the driveway, praying he would miss. At some point she felt the cool grass on her feet and realized her sandals had come off.

It wasn't until she reached the Hulen Street gate and saw the traffic darting back and forth that she felt safe enough to take a long look behind her.

He was gone.

Lying on his back, staring at the night sky, his feeling and hearing numbed by the gunshot, Bubba felt disconnected from the world. He wondered if this was what it felt like to die.

He tried to raise himself up but couldn't. It felt as if his body were attached at the waist to a thousand-pound weight. He couldn't move his legs. They didn't hurt—the pain was all in his chest—but they wouldn't budge. He rolled over on his stomach and dragged himself toward the back door. It was only twenty feet away, but it seemed like two hundred, moving a few inches at a time. As horrendous as the pain was, it didn't frighten him as much as the thought that at any moment the man might return. There would be nothing he could do then, so he had to do what he could now.

The door was locked. He reached up and rang the doorbell. No answer. He pulled himself over to the glass panel to the left of the door and peered through. The first thing he saw was a phone, only ten feet inside the door. Then he saw the blood—swirls of it, clots of it, covering the floor inside. If someone was at home, someone still alive, he thought, they weren't about to let him in.

But he had to get to the phone.

He tried breaking the glass with his fist, then butting it with his head. He knew he could cut himself, but what choice did he have? It seemed like an hour since the man in black had taken off after Bev. When he came back, cuts wouldn't matter.

But the glass refused to break. He looked around for something to hit it with. His boot. He reached down to take it off, but no matter how hard he tugged, the lifeless leg inside wouldn't give it up. More minutes lost. Maybe he could throw something through the window. He crawled down the two steps into the courtyard and tried to pry up a paving stone. It wouldn't budge. More minutes lost. He tried another stone.

Then he heard footsteps on the walkway. Someone was running toward the house. There was no time to crawl back to the spot by the garbage cans or drag himself to cover. Right where he was, a few feet from the back door, he put his head down and played dead. He closed his eyes to a narrow slit, and, as soon as he saw a figure emerge from around the corner, held his breath.

It was the man in black.

The man ran past him—no more than five feet from Bubba's paralyzed legs. At the back door, he reloaded his gun, fired three quick shots into the glass panel, knocked some shards away with his hand, and jumped through.

Five minutes later, the man reappeared and jumped back through the broken glass. This time he stopped when he reached the motionless body lying at the edge of the courtyard. Bubba held his breath and waited in agonized silence.

"Oh, my God!" he heard the man say, and then the footsteps started up again.

As soon as the sound disappeared, Bubba dragged himself back to the window. Ignoring the jagged shards of glass and the deep cuts they made in his head and arms, he crawled through the opening onto the slippery breakfast room floor. Blood was all around him—his own mixing with what was already there—as he scrambled toward the phone.

When he reached the table, he yanked the cord and the phone fell on the floor next to him. He grabbed the receiver and started to dial. Then he realized there was no dial tone. He pushed another button for another line. No tone. The phone was broken.

With that, all the fear and panic suddenly left him. He rested his shoulders and head against the bloody wall and closed his eyes, trying to forget the pain and a sudden, overwhelming thirst.

The next thing he heard was Bev's voice, distant, as in a dream. "Bubba? Are you all right?"

PART
THREE

23

Joe Shannon reached for the copy of the *Fort Worth Star-Telegram* on his front porch and saw the huge headline even before he picked it up:

TWO SLAIN: CULLEN DAVIS SOUGHT
EX-TCU CAGER FARR, GIRL DEAD

Shannon knew of Cullen Davis and his infamous wife Priscilla, and he pieced together the triangle behind the headline even before reading the story. He looked at the file picture of Stan Farr, beardless and youthful, taken when he was playing basketball for Texas Christian University, and muttered to his wife, Carol, as she passed on the way to the kitchen, "What's a kid like that doing with an older woman?"

He wondered if the police had apprehended Cullen Davis yet. He considered calling his boss, District Attorney Tim Curry, to find out, but decided to save the time, dress quickly, and get to the office early. After a murder like this, the first twenty-four hours were always the craziest.

Like most lawyers, and all prosecutors, Shannon calculated other people's misfortunes in hours. A minor theft was a few hours; a robbery a week; a murder, several weeks. If the defendant was poor, he could divide those figures in half; if rich, double them. Hours, in turn, translated almost directly into late nights at the office. Somehow work never seemed to get done between nine and five. So a misdemeanor might equal one evening and a murder one or two dozen, depending on how rich the defendant was and how many prosecutors were working the case.

Given Cullen Davis's wealth and status, Shannon realized, it was useless to calculate hours or evenings. Suffice it to say that he wouldn't be eating dinner at home for a long time.

The prospect wasn't entirely dispiriting, however. After all, there was nothing like a dramatic courtroom shoot-out with a high-paid hired-gun defense lawyer (Davis wouldn't hire anything less) to make a prosecutor feel like a champion of justice again, like Gary Cooper in *High Noon*. It sure beat running the usual waste disposal system, prosecuting the spaced-out, doped-up, child-abused, no-other-way-out, and just plain vicious dregs that the system chewed up and spat out daily.

He wondered what his father would say if he saw the long line of blacks and Hispanics and blue-collar hoodlums that led from his office to the county jail—and often back again. These were exactly the kinds of people Joe Shannon, Sr., had taken such plain, populist pride in defending. Of course, Joe Sr. started his little practice during the Depression, when nobody had money, not even Stinky Davis. He got by on DWI cases mostly, once winning thirteen of them in a row—a record of some obscure sort.

Shannon had first learned about the law watching his father in the old Fort Worth courthouse. They had night sessions then, and the families of lawyers were allowed to sit inside the rail. In the days before television, it was often the best show in town, and people packed the gallery to watch his father. "He's a craftsman," men would say as they passed and patted Joe Jr. on the head after his father had won a case. "Your father's an artist."

Since then, all Joe Shannon had ever wanted to be was a lawyer. Let the other boys daydream about being firemen or policemen or cowboys when they grew up. That was all kids' stuff as far as Joe was concerned. Lawyers were the real heroes. They were the ones who helped the underdogs win against the bullies of adult life—policemen and prosecutors. "If someone is little and getting kicked around in the world," his father would say, "I want to help him."

Like his father, Joe Jr. served his time in the Texas State Legislature ("Dad felt that the law was to be used for the benefit of society," Joe Jr. would tell people, "and not just to make money") before settling down where he most wanted to be: at his father's side, practicing law in his father's firm. Little had changed since his boyhood: The clients were still mostly "average blue-collar-type folk," Hispanics and blacks and "anyone who walked through the door." The work was almost 100 percent criminal, with civil cases as rare as rich clients.

Then, in 1972, Shannon's old friend Tim Curry was elected district attorney for Tarrant County. The first person Curry asked to join his staff was Joe Shannon, Jr. To everyone's surprise, not least his own, Shannon accepted, explaining his sudden jump to the other side of the criminal bar in his usual aw-shucks way: "It sounded sorta interestin'."

He didn't intend to do it for long. A few years walking around in a prosecutor's shoes, he figured, might make him a better defense lawyer—get to know your enemy and all that. But soon something strange began to happen. The word "victim" began to take on new meaning. It no longer referred to the underdog caught in an oppressive system. Now it was the woman who had been raped, the man mugged, or the child abused. It was the families that crowded the hall outside his office: families who had lost a loved one, or been scammed out of their life savings, or had their business robbed. Suddenly he found himself "defending" their rights by prosecuting the worthless, lying, drug-dealing, recidivist human refuse that poured into the bedpan of the Tarrant County Jail every night.

One day Joe Shannon woke up and realized, after a lifetime of opposing it, that he believed in the death penalty. "In a lot of cases," he would concede, "there is not a satisfactory solution other than capital punishment." What would his father say?

Fortunately, he never found out. In January 1975, Joe Sr. died. Almost two years later, Shannon was no longer exactly in mourning for his father, but he still felt strangely "on his own."

"Cullen must be off his rocker!"

It was an odd way for Tim Curry to begin the meeting, Shannon thought. A district attorney is supposed to prosecute murderers, not explain them.

"There's just no other explanation," Curry went on. Shannon knew that Curry and Cullen were friends— maybe not close friends, but under the circumstances, any kind of friendship was, to say the least, awkward.

"It's possible he did it in cold blood," Shannon gently reminded his boss. After all, there was a good chance that he, Shannon, would have to spend the next year proving that, in fact, Cullen Davis was *not* "off his rocker" at the time of the murders; that there were, in fact, "other explanations."

Curry finally got the point. "Oh, right. True."

Shannon could see already this was going to be a problem. Not because Curry was corrupt—far from it. He ran a tight, professional D.A.'s office and would never try to block a full and rigorous prosecution of Cullen Davis just because they had played pool together now and then, or just because Cullen had contributed $250 to Curry's last reelection campaign. That was more a PR problem, Shannon concluded, than a prosecutorial one. Shannon had known Tim Curry since junior high school. Both their fathers had been lawyers, with offices across the hall from one another. Tim was a stand-up, by-the-book government bureaucrat.

That was the problem. He was an administrator, not a lawyer. In four years as district attorney, he had tried only one murder case and a handful of felonies and misdemeanors. He rarely even appeared alone in front of a judge anymore. Standing in his trophy-lined office in cowboy boots and jeans (the suits stayed in the closet until the last possible second), he might just as well have been the manager of a king-size cattle ranch or a country-western saloon. His real enthusiasms, attested to by the mounted fish and huge stuffed deer's head on the wall, lay far from the courtroom, in the fields and streams of Texas and New Mexico, where he spent every minute he could squeeze from his schedule.

A lifetime of living in the shadow of a more colorful lawyer-father and a more talented lawyer-brother had left Curry without either the ambition or the self-confidence to make his mark in the courtroom. He liked the shadows too much, and was inevitably attracted to their vocational equivalent: government bureaucracy. Only by chance had he ended up in a high-profile elective office like district attorney: A group of local lawyers, in search of someone qualified, but not *too* qualified, had recruited him to run for the job.

Once safely ensconced, however, Curry showed the tenacious instinct for self-preservation common to all true bureaucrats. His formula: pick easy targets, like pornography; stay out of the limelight; and, above all, avoid controversy. For four years the formula had worked well. If the local criminal bar made fun of him—"If you're gonna commit a serious crime, this is the county to do it in!" they would joke—he didn't seem to mind. The voters of Tarrant County had already reelected him once and, by all indications, would do so again, gumption or no.

But all that was about to change.

"We've got to treat Cullen Davis like any other murder defendant," said Joe Shannon, trying not to look directly at Curry. The very fact that he felt the need to say it scared him. Were they already treating Cullen differently, he wondered, even in the way they insisted that this was just another case?

Curry filled in the details of the murders—or at least what they knew so far. The police had three eyewitnesses: Priscilla Davis, Beverly Bass, and Bubba Gavrel. Priscilla had seen Stan Farr killed, and Bev had seen Bubba shot. The two women had given numerous accounts of what had happened at the mansion to different sources: ambulance drivers, passersby, police officers, security men, medical personnel. Some of these, perhaps all, could be used in court as *res gestae* statements, statements made during or immediately after a crime that are considered spontaneous and therefore not subject to the hearsay exclusion. Each telling appeared consistent with the others and the two versions jibed—the two women had run away from the mansion in opposite directions almost simultaneously.

"But neither one of them actually saw the girl killed?" Shannon clarified.

"That's correct," Curry confirmed.

Shannon made a face. It meant that the strongest case from a gut level, the murder of Andrea Wilborn, would have to be circumstantial. The prosecutors would have to show that the facts not only proved Cullen's guilt "beyond a reasonable doubt," but also that it could not be explained by any other credible theory. In a normal case, the additional burden was seldom a problem—the reasonable doubt requirement was already so strict. But—there was that "but" again—*this was no normal case.*

Curry went on to describe the physical evidence collected in the initial search. The crime scene unit was still at the mansion, but so far they had found four .38 caliber bullets: two where Farr was killed in the kitchen, one near the back door where Gavrel was wounded, and one under Andrea's body. They had also found bits of the black plastic bag in which Cullen reportedly held the gun.

The good news was that the location of the bullets and the pieces of plastic appeared to confirm the eyewitness accounts. Bullet holes in the door to the back stairs supported Priscilla's story of a struggle, and bits of plastic marked the spots where Priscilla said she and Farr were shot. Fragments of black plastic also marked the spot where Bubba Gavrel was hit, and some unspent cartridges mixed with the broken glass around the back door confirmed Bubba's story that Cullen had stopped to reload before shooting out the window. Farr's autopsy turned up two bullets, including one in his larynx that confirmed Priscilla's memory of hearing him gasp for breath. Bubba's X rays accounted for the other shot that the witnesses either saw or heard.

The preliminary autopsy of Andrea Wilborn indicated that the shot had entered slightly below her breasts and exited out the back—almost exactly the same path taken by the bullet that hit Priscilla, with only an inch or two difference.

"No wonder Cullen was surprised when Priscilla got up and ran," Shannon ventured. "He'd just shot the little girl in the exact same spot and killed her instantly."

Heads around the table bobbed in agreement.

"The problem," said Curry, "is that we're not sure where in the house she was shot. It might have happened someplace else and she was dragged to the basement."

"Was there a blood trail?" Shannon had just finished leafing grimly through the photographs of Andrea's blood-covered body. "She would have left a hell of a blood trail."

Curry shook his head. "Nope, nothing leading down from upstairs except the bloody handprint on the wall. So far we've got no ID on that."

"Figures," Shannon sighed. "What about the gun?"

"None found," said Curry. "Not yet, at least."

"Prints?"

"No matches yet."

"I doubt if we'll find any," Shannon concluded. "Anybody who's careful enough to keep a bag over his gun so powder traces don't get on his hands isn't gonna be stupid enough to leave his prints around."

That meant everything depended on the ballistics report. "If Andrea's bullet matches the ones the witnesses saw Davis shoot," Shannon summed up, "there's our circumstantial case. If not . . ." He didn't need to finish the sentence.

"I think they'll go for insanity," Curry said, as if he'd been waiting for hours for someone to ask his opinion. "Just like they did in the Parker case." In 1966, J. Lloyd Parker, overly eager to inherit his family's huge oil fortune, had killed his father. His lawyers had successfully kept Parker out of jail for almost a decade by rushing him off to Rusk State Hospital, where he was promptly declared insane and held for psychiatric treatment.

Shannon didn't buy it. If Davis got himself declared legally insane, he would have to give up his control of the business. His signature, whether on a check or a contract, would be worthless.

Tolly Wilson, the senior prosecutor at the table, suggested asking the judge for permission to have Davis examined by a psychiatrist immediately. "If we can get him declared sane before his lawyers can get ahold of some psychiatrist to say he's crazy," Wilson argued, "maybe we can head off that defense."

Curry liked the idea. "Get that started, Tolly," he said, motioning Wilson toward the door. Next he assigned Shannon to meet Priscilla in the hospital and "nail her story down." Over the next few months, Joe would become their "Priscilla expert."

On his way to the door, Shannon remembered to ask about bail. The judge would ask the D.A.'s office for a recommendation at the arraignment scheduled for later that morning. Curry suggested $40,000.

Shannon did a double-take. "That's peanuts to this guy, Tim!"

"Any bail we set is peanuts to Cullen Davis," Curry shot back.

Shannon tried to explain that normal rules didn't apply in this case. While no amount of money could ensure that Cullen stayed in the country, the public had to *believe* the bail was enough to keep him around. Anything less and they would accuse the D.A.'s office of favoritism.

Curry nodded—he wasn't convinced, but he wanted to avoid a disagreement. "All right, then," he said, "we'll double it to $80,000."

At one o'clock on the day after the murders, Cullen Davis was brought from the city jail to the county jail and arraigned before Justice of the Peace W. W. Matthews. In a departure from standard procedure, requested by Tim Curry, Judge Matthews came to the jailhouse for the arraignment. After a few questions in the booking department, Cullen spoke briefly to his attorneys, then left in an unmarked police car for the Beverly Hills Hospital in Dallas, where Tolly Wilson had arranged for a psychiatric evaluation. He was brought into the hospital chained at the wrists and ankles.

When Dr. John Holbrook came to escort him into the examination room, Cullen asked if he could make a phone call first.

Holbrook obliged, and a few minutes later Cullen returned. "The evaluation is over with," he announced.

"By advice of your attorney?"

Cullen looked him coldly in the eye. "I prefer not to answer any questions."

By the time the unmarked car arrived back in Fort Worth, Cullen's attorneys had $80,000 in cashier's checks waiting.

By evening, Cullen Davis was playing pool in the back room at the Petroleum Club.

24

Joe Shannon thought Priscilla Davis looked like hell: wrapped in tape and bandages, perforated by intravenous lines, feeding tubes, breathing tubes, drainage tubes, surrounded by IV stands, stainless steel machines that squeaked and whirred, and dark screens traversed by wavy green lines. Shannon could see her face, but it was the blonde hair that he recognized first. It looked like a fright wig: teased tufts in explosive disarray, platinum white turned to chicken-soup yellow in the cruel fluorescent glare. Without makeup, her face was pale as paper, nothing at all like the glamorous pictures he had seen in the press. She looked younger, plainer, sweeter, and impossibly pathetic.

If Priscilla looked like hell, it was because she had been through hell. The night of the murders they had brought her in, still conscious, but fading in and out of coherence. "Cullen is killing my children. . . . He had a wig on. . . . It was my husband. . . . They will never find them if he put them in the basement. . . . He shot me and my boyfriend. . . . I ran across a field. . . . Where's Andrea?" As they wheeled her to the trauma room, she grabbed the gown of a passing nurse and begged her, "Call my friend Judy McCrory, please."

In the trauma room, Dr. Minton Heard checked her vital signs. Her blood pressure was dangerously low. Heard started an IV and inserted a catheter in her back while nurses cut away her clothes and laid her naked on the table.

The hospital's director of surgery, Dr. Charles A. Crenshaw, arrived within minutes. He had been rousted from bed as soon as Priscilla's identity was known. Crenshaw examined the entry and exit wounds and discovered that the bullet had made a strange turn somewhere inside, a turn that had saved Priscilla's life. If it had gone straight, she would have died instantly.

She could still die, Crenshaw concluded, if she didn't get into surgery immediately.

They were still preparing her when Judy arrived. "What happened?" she asked softly.

The question jolted Priscilla into focus. "The sonofabitch shot me," she said fiercely. "Have the police found Stan and Andrea?" She was fighting the pain and dizziness to stay alert.

Judy didn't answer. "Bubba's here and he's in surgery," she offered instead. "Can't you give her something for the pain?" she snapped at a doctor standing nearby.

"Not for a gunshot wound," he replied "I'm afraid it's standard procedure."

At the first opportunity, Judy slipped outside and found a nurse. "Priscilla has a daughter who was at the house, Andrea. Do you know if she's here?"

The nurse was all business. "She's dead."

"Oh, God, no." Judy felt suddenly weak all over. "You haven't told Priscilla, have you?"

"No," the nurse said with odd indignation, "and don't you. We're trying to stabilize her for surgery."

Judy returned to the room, unsure of what to say. Priscilla grabbed her arm and tried to lift herself up. "Tell me what happened," she pleaded, suddenly, horrifyingly alert. "Is everybody all right? Where is Andrea? I haven't seen her. Where is she? Is she okay?" And then, "Did they catch him?"

Judy wanted desperately to say something. Not to say anything was to say everything.

"Have they looked for Stan and Andrea?" Priscilla pressed.

Again, no answer.

Priscilla didn't seem to notice. "Tell them to find Andrea. Tell them to let me know. It's driving me crazy. They won't tell me anything. I'm trying to find out about Andrea and they won't tell me anything!" She was almost hysterical by now. "I wanna *know*. What happened to Andrea? Where's Andrea?"

As more people arrived—Dee, Jack Wilborn, Pat Burleson, David McCrory, Larry Thomas—Judy had to keep them away from the door for fear Priscilla might overhear the truth. At one point a policeman wandered into the room. "Where's Andrea?" Priscilla pleaded. He shrugged his shoulders. "Well, get somebody here who can tell me something!" she demanded. When they finally came to take her away, she grabbed Judy's hand. "Keep Dee with you," she said in an urgent whisper. "Don't let her out of your sight." For all she knew, Cullen was still out there.

As they wheeled her into surgery, she saw Bubba's mother sitting on a chair down the hall, weeping hysterically.

"Why's she crying?" Priscilla asked Judy.

"Someone just told her that Bubba is paralyzed."

They waited to tell Priscilla about Andrea and Stan until the day after she emerged from surgery, when the heavy sedatives began to wear off and she began to ask the same questions over and over. Judy called Father James DeWolf, the pastor at All Saints Episcopal Church, where Priscilla was a parishioner. Perhaps he could find the right words. "We'll need them," Judy warned. "Priscilla's going to be a basket case."

At the appointed hour, Judy and several other friends assembled in Priscilla's hospital room. Priscilla was fading in and out of consciousness, still groggy from the anesthesia. Whenever she surfaced, she would ask about Andrea and Stan, and the question would suck all the sound from the room, leaving it suddenly, grotesquely silent. Then she would fade out and everyone could breathe again. The plan was to tell her just before the doctor gave her another sedative and she lost consciousness for the night. It was a cowardly plan, Judy conceded, but necessary.

DeWolf was an hour and a half late. He entered the room like a naked man stepping into a cold pool. The thought of being involved in a society murder, even in this small way, made him rigid with discomfort, almost angry. "All right," he said to no one in particular, "you just tell me what is required here, and I'll do it."

"*You're* the clergyman," Judy bristled. "You're the one who's supposed to know what to do when there's a death." She turned her back to him in disgust and stared out the window.

It was Priscilla who finally forced the issue, her frail voice rising up like a child's in the midst of the bickering: "Where is Andrea? Where's Stan?"

In the end, Judy bore the news. "They're gone," she said, leaning over the bed and holding Priscilla's tiny hand. "They didn't make it."

Priscilla started to cry, softly, privately—Andrea's way—until the nurses came and gave her the sedative. "That's the most compassionate thing anybody's done for her all day," Judy thought.

Shannon had tried to visit Priscilla once before, the day after the murders, but was told a clergyman was in the room. He decided then that his questions could wait. Now he had come back for Priscilla's version of that night.

Priscilla related the events of the murder with astounding clarity for a woman who had suffered both a gunshot wound and major surgery. But when her story was done, she leaned close to him and said softly, "I have to get out of here."

"Aren't the police giving you enough protection?" he asked, glancing toward the door on the other side of which stood a uniformed officer wearing a bulletproof vest. He wondered if she knew yet that Cullen had been released on bail.

She knew.

"Why did you let him go?" she demanded. For the first time Shannon thought he sensed panic in her voice. "He killed my little girl."

"We had no choice." It was a lame, dishonest answer, but he had no other. "He could have met any bail we set."

"But you don't know Cullen!" she said, her voice rising in distress.

"After all this, he wouldn't be dumb enough to try something," Shannon tried to reassure her.

Priscilla fixed him with a steely gaze. "You really don't know Cullen, do you?" Her hoarse voice grew suddenly calmer—resigned, contemptuous, and fearful at the same time. "He thinks he can get away with anything."

25

"What happened to the damn truck?"

For the hundredth time in three days, Joe Shannon found himself sitting at his desk puzzling over the fate of a 1975 green and white Chevy pickup truck, license plate BW 743. That was the truck Cullen Davis had been seen driving out of the parking garage at 5:30 on the night of the murders. It was the last time anybody had seen him until the police arrested him at Karen Master's house eleven hours later. But the car in Karen's garage wasn't the truck, it was Cullen's blue and white Cadillac. Where was the truck? If this case had a "murder vehicle," Shannon bet, it was that damn Chevy.

Through interviews with the attendants at the APCOA garage, where Cullen rented space for both the truck and the Caddy, Shannon had learned that the Cadillac was still parked in its space when the night attendant went off duty between 11:00 and 11:30 the night of the murders. The next morning, it was gone. Sometime during the night, before the police arrived at Karen Master's house at 4:30 the next morning, it had been removed.

Neither the Cadillac nor the truck had been back since.

There were two possibilities, Shannon figured. Either someone brought Cullen back to the garage and he picked up the Caddy, or someone else picked it up for him, rendezvoused with him someplace, and exchanged the car for the truck. Either way, the implication was clear: Cullen wanted the truck out of sight. He had driven it to the mansion sometime between 11:00 and 11:30, killed Andrea, waited for Priscilla to come home, then exchanged the truck for the Cadillac and driven to Karen Master's house.

It was a good story, but that's all it was. To turn it into proof, they needed the goddamn truck.

On Tuesday, August 10, Shannon received a call from Jim Kuykendall and Don Evans, two investigators on the case. They had found the truck. It was parked in the Continental Bank garage across Sixth Street from the Mid-Continent Building, diagonally across the street from the APCOA garage.

Shannon raced to the scene. The attendant told him that the truck had been there since August 4, two days after the murders.

Did anybody see who parked it?

No.

Shannon walked up to the fourth level, where he saw the truck, license plate BW 743, still parked in a slot near the northeast corner. A ring of police investigators surrounded it. As he approached, Frank Shiller came forward to meet him. Shiller was head of the police crime lab and one of the premier forensics men in north Texas, a spare, precise man whom even the big-city boys in Dallas respected. Just seeing him next to the long-sought truck was enough to make Shannon smile for the first time in a week. If there was a molecule of evidence anywhere on that truck, Shiller would find it. For the first time in a week, Shannon smiled.

Shiller didn't return the smile. "You're not going to believe this, Joe. It's clean."

Shannon's smile vanished. "Yeah, but . . ."

"No," Shiller insisted, shaking his head, "I mean it. It's *clean*, completely clean. Look, you can see the water streaks still on the windows. Somebody has cleaned it inside and out—and I don't mean at a local drive-through carwash." There were no fingerprints, not even partials. None on the glass, none on the dash, none on the rearview mirror, none on the door handle, none on the steering wheel—*none*. "Whoever cleaned this truck," said Shiller, "did it for one reason and one reason only: to remove any possible evidence. There's no other explanation for a vehicle to be this clean."

26

It was the fifteenth meeting of the prosecutors in as many days, and Shannon was fed up. They were getting nowhere. All they did was pass around the reports from the crime lab one more time, ask the same questions, and stare at each other through the same long silences. Tim Curry thought these frequent meetings in his trophy-lined office built esprit de corps and collegiality. Others dismissed them as "bureaucratic masturbation."

Either way, they weren't getting any closer to answering the hard questions.

What was the blood type on the palm print by the basement door? Was it the killer's, or his victim's? Cullen's, or Andrea's? The crime lab reports kept coming back inconclusive. The case threatened to unravel when the lab informed them that it was "probably type A." Andrea was type O. Only Priscilla and Stan Farr were type A, but neither of them had been shot at the time Priscilla said she saw the handprint. "How could it be type A?" everyone wailed at the next roundtable. When someone suggested, "Let's just forget about the handprint and move on," Shannon hit the ceiling. The defense could drive a truck through the hole that unidentified print left in their case. Any "reasonable doubt" about whose blood was on the staircase, or when the blood got there, could throw their whole chronology—and Priscilla's credibility—into question.

Besides, whose handprint was it anyway?

And where was the murder weapon? And what about the bullets? To make a circumstantial case, they had to prove that all the bullets were fired from the same gun. They had recovered all of them except one—the bullet that hit Bubba Gavrel. It was still inside him, lodged so close to his spine that doctors didn't dare remove it. The prosecution would have to go to trial minus one victim.

That raised the question of which charges to bring and in what order. Technically, Cullen had committed two murders (Andrea and Farr) and two attempted murders (Priscilla and Gavrel)—four crimes, any one of which could be the basis of a trial. From the beginning, Shannon had felt that Andrea's murder was the strongest case. He knew for a certainty that no jury in Texas would convict Cullen of murdering Stan Farr, the man who was "sleeping with his wife, staying in his house, drinking his booze, and bathing in his tub."

In fact, if Cullen had stopped at shooting Farr, he probably would never have been brought to trial. It had only been a few years since the repeal of a Texas law that excused "*in flagrante*" murder of a spouse or spouse's lover as justifiable homicide. For the same reasons, the attempted murder charge for shooting Priscilla was iffy.

But not Andrea's murder. Shannon called it "a gut crime, the kind of crime that makes your guts churn with outrage," the kind of crime that technical defenses don't stand a chance against, the kind of crime that makes jurors overlook lapses in logic, contradictions in testimony, inconsistencies in chronology, and all the other little flaws that even the best cases are heir to. Andrea's murder was just such a crime, and for once the other prosecutors agreed: It should go first.

There was just one problem. Andrea's murder was the crime they knew the least about.

The final autopsy report had told them only how Andrea died—a single bullet in the chest that severed her aorta—not where or when. The wound did tell them that she died instantly, or, as the medical examiner so sensitively put it, "she was dead when she hit the floor." She had either been shot upstairs and carried down, or shot in the little basement utility room. "Either way," said Shannon's assistant, Jim Bennett, "it makes for a pretty gruesome picture of the execution of a twelve-year-old girl."

But Shannon knew that jurors would want a hard story, not hypotheticals. Without eyewitness testimony to make the crime concrete, they would want to know—he wanted to tell them—exactly where and how Andrea Wilborn died.

"We've got to know where she was shot," he told Claude Davis, the chief investigator on the case.

Later the same day, Shannon, Davis, and Frank Shiller from the crime lab drove to the mansion on Mockingbird Lane. They searched the basement for some scar that a bullet might have left. It was hard to know what they were looking for. The bullet could have hit the wall at any angle, Shiller said, once it passed through Andrea's body. It could be anything from a deep gouge to a shallow nick.

Claude Davis was the first to spot it: a small, ragged indentation in the plywood wall, about three and a half feet off the floor, at the back of the room where Andrea's body was found. A tiny chip of wood lay on the floor directly beneath it. Frank Shiller thought it looked as if the bullet had impacted sideways and, given the depth of the indentation, was still traveling relatively fast.

Joe Shannon saw something very different as he stared at the little nick in the utility room wall. Suddenly, the crime that he had been investigating impassively for the last two weeks came vividly to life. He had seen pictures of Andrea in life and in death and now those pictures began to move in his imagination.

He could see her, upstairs, coming to answer the back door. There was Cullen, dressed in black and holding something in a plastic garbage bag. Did she suspect anything? Did she let him in? Did she run? Did she hide in the basement, or did he drag her there? Did she sense what was coming? If she did, how terrified was she? Was a spanking the worst she feared? What twelve-year-old girl would think an adult was about to shoot her? Did she see the gun? If not, did she die before she heard the gunshot?

Suddenly, the horrendousness of it all overwhelmed him, and he felt his stomach twisting into knots. "What do you think?" he asked Frank Shiller. "Did she run down here to hide from him, or did he bring her down here to shoot her?"

"I'm not sure we'll ever know," Shiller sighed.

With that, Shannon walked quickly up the stairs. He needed air.

One by one, the blanks in Shannon's case were filled in. A few days after the trip to the mansion, Shiller announced the results of yet another test on the bloody handprint. "It's either A or O," he said. "I can't tell which. I know it's not AB or B. The best I can say is that it's inconclusive."

Shannon didn't like it—an O would have been great,

but an inconclusive was a damn sight better than an A, which would have shot holes in Priscilla's story.

The same was true of the palm print, which Shiller finally identified as belonging to Arlelia Cooper, the maid. Apparently, the print had been on the wall long before the blood. Again, if Shannon couldn't have Cullen's print, he preferred to not have anybody's. "Nobody in the world is gonna believe that the poor little maid lady did it."

But there was still one unanswered question, and it was a big one. Shannon knew when Cullen had done it, and how. But he still didn't know why.

27

As Shannon had predicted, news of the $80,000 bail ignited a firestorm of criticism. Switchboards at city hall, the criminal courts building, and the local newspapers exploded with calls from irate citizens demanding to know why Cullen Davis's bail had been set so low. "This just shows conclusively there are two standards of justice," harrumphed one caller to the *Dallas Morning News*, "one for the rich and another for the poor. We have people who have been sitting in the county jail for weeks because they don't have the money to post bond on petty theft charges."

Tim Curry tried to explain. "A lot of people don't realize that a bond isn't to keep somebody in jail," he told reporters. "It's to ensure they show up at their hearing." But the explanations sounded lame and muddled. In one interview he argued that people misunderstood the purpose of bonds, in another that Davis's "murder bonds are about five times higher than usual," and in still another that "if the bonds had been set at $1 million, Davis could have posted them as easily as he posted the $80,000"— a "what-the-hell-difference-would-it-make" attitude that only reinforced the public perception that Davis's wealth put him beyond the reach of the law.

Many couldn't understand how a man accused of murdering a twelve-year-old girl could be set free at all, no matter how much money he put up. And no one believed that a paltry $80,000 was going to ensure that Davis showed up for *lunch*. "Here's a man worth millions," one Fort Worth attorney complained. "My gosh, all he's got to do is jump on a plane and he's gone."

Again, Curry struggled to explain: "There is no way under Texas law that we could keep him in jail. He was entitled under our state constitution to have bonds set." But the public wasn't in the mood for legalisms. People found it far easier to believe that the lenient treatment had something to do with Cullen's money or, more particularly, the $250 contribution Cullen had made to Tim Curry's last election campaign.

Even those who clung to Curry's initial explanations began to have doubts when Justice of the Peace W. W. Matthews, who set the bail, made the mistake of trying to defend it. "This man probably will never hurt anybody again," he told reporters. "The police told me he was quite drunk. And they said, when he gets drunk, he gets really mad." The police promptly denied that they had suggested Davis was drunk, or that there was any evidence to support Judge Matthews's "explanation," leaving Matthews lamely claiming that *someone* in his courtroom (the defendant perhaps?) had said that Davis was drunk, although he couldn't remember who exactly.

Around the county courthouse, the word began to percolate: Cullen Davis's next victim would be Tim Curry's career.

No one was angrier than Jack Wilborn. It was hard enough to believe that he had lost Andrea. When the phone call came around 2:00 A.M. on the night of the murders and he rushed to John Peter Smith Hospital, he kept telling himself, "It's just some wild dream. Who would want to shoot Andrea?" Dee met him at the hospital door screaming the answer: "Daddy, Daddy! Cullen killed Andrea!"

At first he couldn't comprehend it. "No, no. Not my baby!" he wailed. "It can't be true!" Then a policeman told him that Andrea would be taken to All Saints Hospital. Wilborn raced there and waited until almost dawn before the ambulance arrived bearing Andrea's body covered in a stained white sheet. Sobbing uncontrollably, he pleaded with the medical examiner's investigator, R. O. Parkey, to let him see his child.

Parkey considered Jack Wilborn a friend and wanted to help, but he urged him not to take a last look. "Believe me, Jack, you don't want to see her the way she looks now. It would leave a memory that you could never erase." Parkey had just come from the little room in the hospital's basement that served as the county's unofficial morgue, with its coolers full of blue bodies and the stink of putrefied blood. He had seen Andrea's body, covered with blood, clothes in disarray, hair matted and tangled. He knew *he* would have trouble forgetting it. "I beg you, Jack," he repeated, "for Andrea's sake, don't do it!"

Wilborn decided to take his friend's advice. He didn't say anything, just turned around and walked away, all his grief and despair suddenly replaced by one overwhelming desire: to kill Cullen Davis.

Since that moment, Wilborn had been consumed with hate. "I feel like my heart's gonna explode," he told his wife. He couldn't eat, he couldn't sleep. He lived on nothing but coffee, cigarettes, and hate.

Friends tried to coax him to church, but he refused. "I won't go," he insisted bitterly. "God did nothing for my little girl." All he could think about was Andrea and the man who had made her cry so many times, alone in that basement room. Every time the image formed in his head, he thought he would go mad with rage. But each time he vowed to kill Cullen Davis, he would think about what that might mean to the other people he loved, and the hate would dissolve back into thoughts about Andrea, and he would bury his handsome tan face in his big hands and weep like a child.

When Wilborn heard that Cullen had been released on $80,000 bail, a new emotion began to crowd out the hate and the grief: outrage. "It's clear the D.A.'s office isn't gonna prosecute Cullen Davis," he told a friend. "He's just too rich and too important."

Through an intermediary, Wilborn made an appointment to see Tim Curry. They met in Curry's office, behind closed doors. Aware of Wilborn's presence, Shannon and the rest of the staff went about their business on tiptoes.

Wilborn got right to the point. "Tim, I am *real* disappointed about the amount of bail that was set—and the fact that Cullen didn't stay in jail but just overnight." Before coming, Wilborn had subdued his demons. He didn't want a scene; he wanted action.

Curry's relief was almost palpable. "I understand. I don't blame you for being upset. That was a mistake. It should have been a lot more. We're going to do our best to get him back in jail without bond." It was a bold—and risky—promise.

"The pressure out there is enormous," Tim Curry began.

Joe Shannon had feared it would come to this. Everybody in the office had heard the phones ringing incessantly with complaints about the bail. Everybody was reading the papers. Everybody was feeling the heat. Curry was nervous and wanted to do something, *anything*, to relieve the pressure. They had to put Davis back in jail and keep him there—somehow.

But Shannon knew there were only two ways to do it. One was to raise the bail to a level even Davis couldn't afford—twenty-five, fifty, one hundred million, no one knew how high they would have to go. But they couldn't do that because the Texas Code of Criminal Procedure explicitly barred them from using a bail bond as "an instrument of oppression"—meaning bail couldn't be set so high that a defendant couldn't possibly afford it.

The other way was to charge Davis with capital murder. But that, too, looked impossible. For a murder to be considered "capital" under Texas law, either the victim had to be a policeman or the murder had to occur during the commission of another felony (robbery, burglary, arson, kidnapping). Another dead end.

Shannon's explanation met with frustrated silence all around the table.

"What if Cullen Davis *was* committing a felony that night?" suggested Marvin Collins, a relative newcomer in the DA's office. "What if he was committing a burglary?"

"For Chrissakes," someone laughed, "it was his own house!"

"But *was* he the owner of the house at the time of the murders?" Collins, a brilliant, bookish young lawyer who headed the D.A.'s appellate division, went on to list three definitions of "owner" under the law: 1) the person who has title to the property; 2) the person who has possession of the property, whether lawful or not; and 3) the person who has the greater right to possession of the property. "Number three is the key to this case," Collins insisted. Because of the divorce court injunction giving Priscilla exclusive access to the house, *she* had greater right of possession. Because Cullen entered without the owner's —i.e., Priscilla's—permission, he had committed burglary. Since he had killed Stan and Andrea while committing the burglary, he committed capital murder.

By the nods around the table, Shannon decided the discussion had gone far enough. "It's all academic," he said, striving for a tone of finality. "No jury will ever give a multimillionaire a death penalty, so there's no point in even discussing it."

But it was too late. Curry grabbed for Collins's theory like a drowning man reaching for the last life jacket. "Work up the case law on that, Marvin," he ordered.

"A jury's not gonna send someone to the chair for burglarizing his own house!" Shannon protested. But Curry had stopped listening.

The next day, Collins's theory leaked to the papers.

"CAPITAL CHARGE A POSSIBILITY" blared the *Star-Tele-gram* front-page headline. An unnamed courthouse source had told the paper, "If Davis is found . . . to have committed a burglary, then the murders with which he is charged could become capital murder cases." Shannon saw the headline and knew immediately he had been sandbagged.

On August 16, the prosecutors met in Tim Curry's office to discuss the capital murder charges one last time. By the time Collins finished his presentation of the case law, Shannon was convinced they were on firm legal ground. But that didn't change his opinion: "A jury will never buy it," he insisted, "not in a million years."

Once again, Curry reminded him of the "pressure out there" to put Davis in jail. Curry was sensitive to the fact that Shannon was one of the most seasoned trial lawyers in the room, so he couldn't just ignore him. For the sake of "team morale," Shannon had to be persuaded.

"Daggumit, Tim, we all know there's pressure," Shannon replied, "but our first responsibility is to get a conviction. If we put Cullen in jail now, they might love us for a while, but if it means we can't get a conviction down the road, they're gonna hate us forever."

Curry squirmed in his chair. "The public clearly wants a capital case."

"The public doesn't have to try the case," Shannon bristled in the low-key country way he had learned from his father.

"What if he leaves town, leaves the country?" Curry protested. "He's got his own jet and pilots on staff. He could be out of here in a minute."

"We'll keep him under surveillance," Shannon countered, "just like we've been doing for the last two weeks. And we'll keep a writ ready so we can serve him on a moment's notice. The first time he even looks in the direction of Meacham Field we'll pick him up."

Curry tried again. "If he's in jail, he's gonna want to get it over with. You know how long he could drag this out if he's sitting in a fancy hotel room somewhere and working out of the executive offices. We could all be retired by the time we're through with pretrial motions."

"Okay," Shannon said. "Assume I'm wrong. Assume we can find a jury that will agree that Davis burglarized his own house *and* is willing to put a multimillionaire to death." Curry nodded warily. "What about the advantages it gives the defense? First, they would demand an immediate bond hearing to smoke out our evidence. We'd have to show them our best to convince a judge to hold a man like Davis without bond. Then they freeze our witnesses up front, put their testimony down in the record early, and spend all their time looking for ways to punch holes in their stories. The longer we can hold back, the more work they're gonna have to do and the better our people are gonna look."

A capital charge would also open the door to individual voir dire, Shannon pointed out. In most cases, prospective jurors were asked questions as a group, usually about forty at a time. But in a capital case, the jurors would be questioned individually, one by one—not only an infinitely more tedious and time-consuming way to pick a jury, but also an enormous advantage to the defense. The odds in favor of the defense coming up with at least one sympathetic juror jumped off the scale.

The discussion went on for an hour. Toward the end, Curry backed off a little, "Well, we may do it. We'll get back together on it later." But it was only a bone to Shannon. Everyone leaving the room knew Curry had made up his mind: capital murder.

28

Shannon knew it was a bum decision—good politics, maybe, but lousy prosecuting. He feared they would regret it someday. Right now, Curry's decision created a new problem: the danger that Cullen would break and run. Before, Shannon had been confident that as long as Cullen was out on bail, living off room service in a cushy motel, surrounded by a phalanx of fulsome lawyers, his girlfriend, and other flatterers, he would stay put. The risks of fleeing (losing his share of the family empire) would outweigh the risks of staying (a distant, uncertain jail term). Even as the meeting in Curry's office broke up, Shannon guessed, Cullen's lawyers were telling him they could delay the trial for at least one year and, if they lost, stretch appeals out over another three or four.

But Curry's decision changed all that. Now, instead of ten-to-twenty-five, Cullen faced death by electrocution. Instead of the hot tub in the Ramada Inn Central, he faced the sink and seatless toilet of a six-by-ten-foot cell in the Tarrant County Jail while he waited for his trial to begin. The prospect of living in jail *immediately* was a powerful incentive to see the world. And the prospect of death . . . Shannon had never had a client like Cullen Davis, but he imagined it might even be enough to separate a millionaire from his millions.

So the race was on: Could they finish the new indictment and arrest Cullen before he learned of the capital charges and made his escape?

Tim Curry doubled the surveillance on Cullen, who had returned to Karen Master's house, and staked out both Dallas–Fort Worth International and Meacham Field, where the Davis company planes were hangared. Shannon prepared a grand jury subpoena with Cullen's name on it. If he did run, they could intercept him at the airport and haul him directly before the grand jury. It was only a stopgap solution—Cullen could refuse to testify, walk out of the courthouse, and head straight back to the airport —but until the new complaint and indictment were ready, it was the best they could do.

On the night of August 19, all five prosecutors worked late, frantically trying to finish the new complaint and indictment. Surveillance units checked in by radio, their voices now and then crackling loudly over the one-way monitor Curry had set up in his office and startling the coffee-wired prosecutors. Jim Kuykendall was watching Karen's house, where Cullen was apparently asleep. Karen herself had disappeared several days before, causing some alarm, but so far, at least, Cullen had made no move to join her.

Around two in the morning, Shannon took a break and looked out the window. If Cullen's people were watching the prosecutors as closely as the prosecutors were watching Cullen, they wouldn't have any trouble guessing what was going on that night behind the lighted windows of the D.A.'s offices on the second floor of the Criminal Justice Building. If Cullen was going to skip, Shannon decided, he would skip soon. If he wasn't gone already.

By morning, they were ready. Or at least they thought they were. "What happens if we get this indictment and then Priscilla won't testify?" Shannon asked. He didn't need to explain; everyone in the room knew that under Texas law a wife could not be forced to testify against her husband. "Suppose when Davis finds himself facing the death penalty he decides that Priscilla isn't so bad after all. So he turns around and says, 'I love you. Won't you please come back to me,' and she goes for it. Or suppose he offers her a fat divorce settlement if her memory of that night goes suddenly fuzzy."

An hour later, they had a solution. A young prosecutor, Jack Strickland, had dug up an old case from the Texas Court of Criminal Appeals that said if a wife voluntarily signed a complaint against her husband, she could not assert a marital privilege. She *could* be forced to testify against him.

Would Priscilla sign? All eyes turned to Shannon, who had visited her at the hospital the day before.

Shannon scratched his head in his best farmboy manner. "I told her Cullen could get the death penalty if she testified and she didn't flinch. The lady's got grit." He allowed a slight smile. "She'll sign."

There was one problem, however. If Cullen was brought in on the new indictments, his lawyers would demand a bond hearing immediately and Priscilla would have to testify. On that, Shannon was less encouraging. "She's a sick lady and I don't think she'll be ready to testify for at least another week, maybe longer."

That bad news was just sinking in when the radio monitor on Curry's desk exploded with the voice of Jim Kuykendall. "Subject vehicle turning westbound on Camp Bowie."

Curry looked at the men gathered around his desk. "Cullen's moving." It was 8:30 A.M.

"Turning right on 183," Kuykendall relayed. "You take him."

A different voice, Don Evans, came on. "I got him." Evans was in another car, a few blocks from Kuykendall.

Curry sent his chief investigator Morris Howeth to the radio room. "Tell them I want to know if he passes Roberts' Cut-Off." If Cullen turned off on Roberts' Cut-Off he was heading to his office at Stratoflex, a Kendavis Industries company. If not, Highway 183 would take him straight to Meacham Field.

Curry called Howeth in the radio room. He wanted to know who they had on the ground at Meacham Field. "Tell them to find out if that plane is in the hangar."

The next thing they heard on the monitor was Howeth's voice talking to Jesse Shaw, the investigator at Meacham Field. "What's that plane doing?"

"It's sittin' on the ramp with the engines turning."

Just then Don Evans's voice broke in. "Subject vehicle passing Roberts' Cut-Off."

Curry took a deep breath. "He's going for Meacham."

This was it. Davis was on the run.

Howeth hurried back into the room. "Did you hear that?" he said, unable to hide his excitement.

Shannon asked, "How many guys we got on the ground at the airport?"

"Three," said Howeth.

The radio monitor interrupted again. "Subject vehicle turning toward Meacham Field."

"Maybe he's just going out to Meacham to have breakfast with the boys," Shannon joked. It all seemed too dramatic to be real, too much like a movie.

Tolly Wilson laughed. "Yeah, maybe he's flying to Brazil for the sun."

"Not on my ulcer he's not!" said Curry, his eyes fixed on the radio monitor, his ear stuck to the phone with the radio room on the line. He refused to crack a smile.

A voice burst through the monitor. "He's at the hangar." Then again, "He's on the ground."

Curry barked into the phone, "We better get him."

A second later they heard Howeth's voice on the monitor. "Get him!" Then the radio went silent.

At Meacham Field, Davis's Cadillac pulled up alongside the whining blue-and-white Learjet. Davis stepped out, loaded something onto the plane, returned to his car, and drove it into the hangar. Don Evans pulled up behind him, followed by Jim Kuykendall. Cullen ignored them and began walking toward the plane. They caught up with him about forty feet from the Learjet's open door.

"Mr. Davis," said Don Evans as he slapped the subpoena into Davis's small, delicate hand, "I have an attachment from the grand jury. You'll have to come with me."

Later, airport officials would announce that Davis's plane was headed for Houston. But at least one of the pilots, Pat Asher, had been told a different destination: Caracas, Venezuela.

Joe Shannon jumped into his red Volkswagen and headed for Harris Hospital, where Priscilla Davis had been transferred. They had Cullen, now they had to keep him. To do that, they needed Priscilla's signature. Then they had to take the signed complaint, file it, get a warrant, and serve the warrant on Davis, all before his lawyers could pry him away from the grand jury.

"Cullen was arrested getting on the Learjet at Meacham Field," Shannon told her breathlessly.

Priscilla wasn't at all surprised.. "I bet he was going

to South America," she said, almost conversationally. "We've been there lots of times."

"We need to have you sign this complaint *now* so we can get him in jail." He handed it to her. "We want you to read it carefully before signing it, of course." He slowed down to avoid the appearance of pushing her. The signature had to be "voluntary." "It's a complaint for capital murder, Mrs. Davis. Do you know what that means?"

Priscilla was absorbed in the document and didn't answer.

"It means he could get the death penalty."

There was a long pause. When she finally looked up from the paper, he saw the same steely eyes as before. "He shot my little girl."

Cullen Davis waited outside the grand jury room of the Tarrant County Criminal Courts Building until his lawyers arrived. On their advice, he signed a statement refusing to go before the grand jury because to do so might violate his Fifth Amendment right against self-incrimination. Before he could escape, Morris Howeth arrived with the warrants based on Priscilla's signed complaint. The charges were capital murder of Stan Farr and Andrea Wilborn and attempted capital murder of Priscilla Davis and Bubba Gavrel. Howeth pulled a little blue card from his pocket and read Davis his rights:

> *. . . You have the right to talk to a lawyer and to have him represent with you while you are being questioned. If you cannot afford to hire a lawyer, one will be appointed to represent you . . ."*

Howeth handcuffed the prisoner, then took him to be arraigned before Justice of the Peace Bob Ashmore. From there, Cullen was led down to the county jail, past the big steel door posted with the ominous red-letter warning "STAY BACK."

About the same time, Joe Shannon got a call from his

office. "The grand jury indicted your man eleven to zero in all four cases," he was told.

Shannon suppressed a smile. "It won't be that easy in front of a jury."

29

Everyone else considered it a triumph. After two weeks of waffling, the D.A.'s office had come out swinging. Tim Curry called a press conference on Friday and his picture was all over the papers that weekend. Holding the revised indictments in his hand, looking grim and resolute, he stared into the blitz of flashbulbs and questions and talked tough. He described in dramatic terms how Davis had been apprehended just as he was about to step onto his jet: "The plane was fueled and on the apron with the throttle back."

When someone asked him if the capital indictments were filed in response to the public outcry after Davis's release on $80,000 bail, Curry looked even grimmer and shook his head. "Absolutely not."

Finally, he vowed through clenched teeth that *this* time he would contest any bond, no matter how high. Millionaire or not, Cullen Davis was going to jail.

The drumbeat of victory continued the following Monday, August 23, when the bond hearing opened in Judge Tom Cave's district courtroom. Amid armies of guards and a crush of reporters, the prosecution showed off its case.

First came Priscilla Davis. Looking pale and wan and long-suffering, she made her entrance in a wheelchair pushed by a uniformed nurse. Dressed simply in a cotton smock and a string of pearls, and clutching her brown handbag in obvious pain, she recounted her vivid story of the shootings: how she had watched Andrea turn on the security system before leaving that night; how, on her return, she had seen the bloody handprint and then, seconds later, Cullen stepped out of the shadows; how he shot her and then Stan, then dragged Stan's body into the kitchen; how she ran; how he caught her and dragged her back as she pleaded for her life—"I love you, Cullen, I always have"; how he suddenly left her again and she ran again; how she heard voices and a gunshot and screaming and she ran faster and faster.

Several times her eyes filled with tears and she couldn't go on. At one point, Judge Cave had to call a short recess. After that, her thin, faint voice grew even fainter, despite Joe Shannon's gentle urgings, until by the end it was almost a whisper. When it was all over, she covered her eyes with her hand, let her head sink to her chest, and cried quietly.

But there was more. To deprive Davis of bail, the prosecution had to convince Judge Cave that a jury would not only find clear and strong evidence that Cullen was guilty, but would also give him the death penalty. Under Texas's capital punishment law, a jury could only do that if they believed Davis was likely to commit acts of violence in the future; that he "posed a continuing threat to society." In short, that he was dangerous.

Under Shannon's direction, Priscilla led the rapt courtroom audience on a tour of the horror house of her marriage: the hotel brawls, the blood clots, the black-and-blue arms and legs, the fractured collarbone, the broken nose; how he snatched her crutch and beat her with it; how he threw her from pool table to pool table; how he beat her children; and then, finally, how he killed the kitten by hurling it repeatedly to the floor. As steeped as the public was in the details of the night of August 2, few in the audience had heard any of these lurid stories, and the courtroom fell into a stunned, mesmerized silence as Priscilla went from one harrowing episode to the next while Cullen sat at the defense table, glowering at the tiny, frail figure in the witness box, his brow knotting tighter with every word.

"Mrs. Davis," Shannon concluded on redirect, "has

Cullen Davis ever at any time apologized for breaking your nose or bones or any of your daughters' noses or bones?"

"No, sir," Priscilla answered firmly.

"Has he ever so much as said, 'I'm sorry'?"

"No, sir."

The prosecution rolled out more witnesses: Bubba Gavrel, also in a wheelchair, to tell how the man in black had shot him when Bev cried out, "It's Cullen"; Frank Shiller, to testify that the bullet that killed Andrea came from the same gun as the bullets that killed Stan Farr, thereby connecting Priscilla's eyewitness testimony to Andrea's murder. But after Priscilla's riveting testimony, it all seemed anticlimactic.

Until Ken Davis took the stand. The defense had called him to testify on his brother's behalf, but on cross-examination, Shannon asked him about the night of the murders.

"What did your brother say when you called him and told him about the shootings at the mansion?"

"He asked, 'Who was shot?' "

"And what did you say?"

"I told him a man by the name of Stan Farr and a little girl were killed and Priscilla was shot. I also told him the police were looking for him, and I asked him what he was going to do about it."

"And what was his response to that?"

"He said, '*Well, I guess I'll go back to bed.*' "

With those words, Shannon felt a wave of astonishment sweep silently across the courtroom from back to front and break over Judge Cave's bench.

On Friday, August 27, Judge Cave announced his decision: $500,000 bond on the murder of Stan Farr and no bond on the murder of Andrea Wilborn. The *Star-Telegram* trumpeted the good news: "DAVIS TO STAY IN JAIL." Tim Curry was elated. Surrounded by reporters, Curry preened: "We've taken the position all along that he should be held."

The only person not celebrating was Joe Shannon. Everything he had predicted about the bond hearing had come true, a fact that pleased no one less than Joe Shannon. Whatever Curry was telling the press, the reality was that more or less all of their case had been laid out in Judge Cave's courtroom: Priscilla Davis, Bubba Gavrel, the forensics. More worrisome, they had shown some of their key secondary evidence: Cullen's history of brutality and his chilling conversation with Ken the night of the murders.

If it was a victory, Shannon decided, it was a damned expensive one.

The morning after the bond decision, one of Davis's business attorneys, Hershel Payne, called Joe Shannon and asked for a private meeting. Payne, a well-connected corporate lawyer in one of Fort Worth's premier firms, arrived early. "You know, Joe," he began in a practiced, off-the-record voice, "as you can imagine, Cullen's not terribly thrilled with the results yesterday."

"I can imagine." Payne's seductive, unofficial tone had done its job. Shannon was intrigued.

Payne looked uncomfortable. "Can I ask you something?" he finally said. "If you were in Cullen's shoes, what would you do?"

"I'd hire the best lawyer I could find," Shannon joked.

Payne didn't laugh. "Who?" he pressed.

Shannon thought for a long minute. It was a perfect opportunity to stack the deck in his favor. He could think of a dozen lawyers who would make the case easier for him if they sat at the defense table with Cullen Davis. He played with that thought for just a second, then let it go. He might live to regret it, but he would give Hershel a straight answer. Anybody can shoot down a town drunk, he thought, but it takes a real lawman to go up against Billy the Kid. So he tried to think of a Billy the Kid for the defense.

Finally, with a broad smile: "I'd hire Richard Haynes."

30

Richard Haynes's career, like Priscilla Davis's, began in the bars of Houston.

Back in the early sixties, when, as old-timers used to say, Houston was still a part of Texas, the bars near the docks were no place for any self-respecting, churchgoing citizen. Yet among the grazing herds of urban cowboys in their boots and jeans and the hollow-eyed businessmen in their dreary coats and ties, there was the occasional "misfit," as Keith Harding, the late-shift bartender at one bar, called them. Houston, after all, was a rough and tumble town, and people inevitably got tossed together in unlikely combinations.

There was one misfit in particular who fascinated Harding.

He was short, barrel-chested, big-headed, and bowlegged—an unmistakable sight as he bullied his way through the crowd in his pinstripe suit and tight, neat tie. He was a regular—of sorts—coming often in the evenings, but seldom staying long. He had an odd ritual. On arrival, he would head straight for the phone on the back wall, place a brief call, then stride to the bar on his short legs and order a scotch. The rest of his stay was spent handing out business cards. When he had thoroughly saturated the crowd, he would return to the phone, place another brief call, then bully his way back out the door.

It wasn't until later that Harding discovered the bowlegged, pinstriped regular was a young attorney, and he was going through the same ritual at bars all around Houston, drumming up business for his new law practice. His specialty: DWI—Driving While Intoxicated. What better place to find a prospective client, he had figured, than a bar? The frequent phone calls he placed were to his office;

he was checking in to see if any of the cards given out so far that night had produced a desperate call from the city jail.

The name on the card was Richard "Racehorse" Haynes.

From a record string of DWI victories, Haynes soon moved on to richer clients and more lucrative cases. Fearlessly he took on what looked like sure losers and turned them around, charming juries, judges, and reporters in the process. By 1974, no one doubted his claim to be one of the best criminal lawyers in Texas. "If Nixon had hired me," he boasted, "he would still be President."

That same year, Dr. John Hill walked into Haynes's office. Hill was accused of killing his wife by slowly poisoning her and then withholding medical treatment. It was the Hill case, and Thomas Thompson's book about it, *Blood and Money*, that made Racehorse Haynes a familiar name in every state—and a legend in his own.

Richard Haynes took on his first "sure loser" the day he was born, April 3, 1927. The case against him was indeed daunting. The youngest son of a plasterer, young Richard was only two when the stock market in faraway New York City crashed, ending one of Houston's first building booms and throwing his father, along with almost everybody else in the rough immigrant neighborhood of Houston Heights, out of work. Reginald Haynes eventually found a job pumping gas but still couldn't make enough to keep food on the table for three boys. Or at least that's what young Richard was told when, at the age of six, he was packed off to San Antonio to live with his grandmother.

Elizabeth Haynes, a tiny, sinewy Englishwoman, took the rough Texas youth in hand and gave him the frontier equivalent of a British public school education. The skills that would later dazzle courtroom observers—the erudition, the elocution, the poise, the astonishing memory—were first learned at the foot of his grandmother's rocker in the big windowed dormer on the second floor of a little Victorian frame house near downtown San Antonio.

Elizabeth surrendered Richard to the Texas public schools only reluctantly. "Don't let them start you in the first grade," she instructed Richard on his first day. "You should be in the third grade, so make them give you a test, because you can do third grade work." It was a proud gesture—but a misguided one. Already small for his age, Richard was suddenly thrown in with children twice his size.

Underaged, undersized, and talking (to Texas ears) like British royalty, little Richard Haynes was easy prey. Every schoolyard bully in San Antonio left a mark on him. In later years, he would brag about fighting the older, bigger boys who picked on him in school. But that wasn't until high school. During what he called the "grim years" in San Antonio, there wasn't much to do but take the teasings and beatings, complain to his grandmother in his best rhetorical style, and lay deep plans for the day when he would show them all.

When, at the age of thirteen, Richard rejoined his family in Houston, it wasn't the joyous reunion it should have been. He had left home a rough-edged, hardscrabble laborer's boy and come back an insecure, self-impressed, fancy-talking "twit" (his own word)—nothing like his two older brothers, and not at all the son his father had in mind.

Locking his outsized jaw in determination, young Richard set out to prove himself. In a burst of optimism, figuring that his growth years were still ahead of him, he vowed he would someday run the decathlon in the Olympics. In pursuit of that distant goal, he bound himself to a puritanical regimen—no liquor, no cigarettes, no sweets—and drew up charts of the ideal weights and heights he would work toward on his road to athletic vindication.

But once again, fate played the bully. At the age of fourteen, Richard stopped growing. Soon, in addition to being small for his class, he was small for his age. Each year, he fell further and further behind the chart of ideal weights and the marks he had made on the wall.

In retaliation, he began lashing out at what he increasingly perceived as a hostile, even conspiratorial world, taking quick offense at the least slight and rushing into schoolyard fights with suicidal abandon. After school, he threw himself into any sport that would take him, even football—a dangerous game for a 125-pounder in a league of beef-fed Texas farmboys. The more brutal and punishing the sport, the more avidly he pursued it. Boxing was his favorite. By eighteen, he was competing in the Golden Gloves championships, welterweight division.

From football, boxing, and daredevil stunts like driving from Fort Worth to Houston steering with his feet or jumping back and forth between fast-moving cars, it was a short, inevitable plunge, at the age of sixteen, into the United States Marines. What better place for a short, angry teenager with so much to prove to prove it?

Over the years, Haynes learned to compensate in other ways as well. Disappointed with the odd physique God had given him, with its big head and short trunk, he claimed, "It wasn't always this way. Until I was thirteen, I was the perfect physical specimen."

By the time he returned from the war to college at the University of Houston, Haynes had perfected the art of self-invention. Eventually, he got himself elected student body president, largely on the basis of a mysterious rumor that he had announced his campaign by parachuting into the school's reflecting pool. When the story found its way back to Haynes, he modestly denied it, but by then no one believed him. It was a good lesson in the relative strengths of reality and illusion.

Like the name Racehorse.

Haynes told various stories to explain the origin of his famous and very flattering nickname. In one, he was playing in the backfield of his high school (or junior high) football team when the coach relayed instructions to run two plays through the middle. "I began the dive plays,"

Haynes would explain, "but I realized there was no hole, and I felt it was stupid to run into the line." So he began running back and forth parallel to the line of scrimmage, racking up a lot of yards but no gain. "What the hell do you think you are," he would quote the coach yelling from the sidelines, "a damn racehorse!"

To others, Haynes told the story of being caught in the boxing ring with a more powerful opponent. "I just kept running around trying to keep away from him," Haynes would explain, "and the coach yelled out from my corner, 'What the hell do you think you are, a damn racehorse?' "

Some who knew Haynes well took both stories, and the other ones as well ("My grandmother used to call me that"), with a grain of salt. The most likely explanation, they figured, was that like so much of the legend, Haynes had bestowed the nickname on himself—a last remnant, perhaps, of that early dream of running in the Olympics.

What was the key to Haynes's astonishing courtroom success?

Haynes himself might have said it was the lucky dogtags from World War II that he tucked inside his silk tie and custom-tailored suit every morning before going off to war, or the lucky penny taped to the inside of his wallet, or the lucky silver dollar in his pocket, or the lucky cufflinks on the French cuffs of his expensive starched shirts, or the battered lucky briefcase he carried with him into battle.

But others had their own theories.

Some thought it was his remarkable ability to delay. Like the time he dragged out jury selection for so long that the prosecutors were forced to settle. First he had the case transferred out of West Palm Beach to a small town in rural Florida. The prosecutors—far from their under-staffed home office and rapidly depleting their meager budget with motel and restaurant expenses—feared they would go broke before the trial ended. Their only hope was that the delay was proving equally burdensome for the defense.

Then one day a Western Union man stepped into the

courtroom with a "telegram for Mr. Haynes." Haynes took the telegram, read it, smiled, passed it around, then crumpled it up and threw it in the trash can. At the next break, after the defense team left the courtroom, the prosecutors fished through the trash for the crumpled-up message. "Dear Mr. Haynes," it read. "Fifty thousand dollars deposited this day to your account, Bank of Texas." It was signed by the defendant.

The next day, the prosecutors quickly agreed to settle the case on terms essentially dictated by Haynes. And all for the price of a telegram. There was no $50,000 deposit, of course. Haynes had sent the telegram to himself.

Some thought it was his ability to pick the right jury. Like the time he defended two white Houston policemen accused of kicking a black man to death, after arresting him for trying to "steal" what turned out to be his own car. Haynes had the case transferred to the small German-American community of New Braunfels, Texas, where the supply of potential jurors was more to his liking. "I knew we had that case won," he boasted later, "when we seated the last bigot on the jury."

Some thought it was his ability to generate sympathy for the defendant. Like the time he hired people to sit in the courtroom and pretend to be the defendant's family and friends. Critics dubbed the tactic "Rent-a-Grandmother," but Haynes defended it passionately. "I don't have any conscientious scruples about renting some nice, white-haired old lady to come down and hug my guy. The jurors say, 'He really must be all right if granny hugs him.' "

Or like the time he defended doctors and officials at a home for troubled children in Liberty County, not far from Houston, who were accused of withholding medical treatment and even food from some of the children in their care, some of whom died. The charge was murder by omission. Haynes convinced the court that the government regulations covering the treatment of the children were badly drafted and hopelessly confusing. How were the good doctors to know what they should and should not have done, victims as they were of poor draftsmanship?

Some thought it was his extraordinary skill at cross-examination. Like the time he defended a lawyer in Amarillo on charges of indecency and child molesting for fondling an eleven-year-old girl. The girl had bravely taken the stand and testified directly and convincingly how the lawyer had touched her and where. After four hours of Haynes's cross-examination, however, she was totally confused. Did he touch her left breast with the back of his right hand or her right breast with the front of his left hand? She didn't know! An associate of Haynes's later gushed, "It was some of the prettiest work I've ever seen. When Race was done, that child didn't know if it was day or night when the incident happened. It was great."

Some thought it was his ability to turn the tables and try the victim. Like the time he defended a motorcycle gang accused of nailing a woman to a tree. Haynes told the jury that the woman was "just a hooker who hung out with the gang." She had held back the gang's cut of her profit and they were only punishing her. It was strictly business—the kind of business you should expect if you're a hooker.

In the trial of the Houston policemen, Haynes suggested to the jury that the victim actually killed *himself* because of the internal injuries he suffered while struggling to get away from the policemen/defendants. He also accused the victim of being a dope addict and suggested yet another possible explanation for his death: a morphine overdose. His jury of New Braunfels "bigots" liked that version best.

Of course, Haynes had other skills: an extraordinary memory; a winning, self-deprecating sense of humor; an agile, gifted tongue; acute intuition; enormous physical stamina; and plenty of down-home Texas charm. But there were other lawyers—not many, but some—who had all those things. There were even other lawyers who saw the world through the paranoid eyes of an abandoned child and saw themselves as avengers on the bullies of that world. But even they did not have either Haynes's reputation or his remarkable streak of victories.

So what was the key to Richard "Racehorse" Haynes's courtroom success?

Joe Shannon and his fellow prosecutors would soon find out.

31

When Richard Haynes arrived in Fort Worth in November 1976, he was appalled by what he found. The case was only two months old and already a disaster. Cullen's lawyer, Phil Burleson, a big, silver-haired, boom-voiced lawyer from Dallas, whose considerable reputation was based on an inconsiderable role in the defense of Jack Ruby, had done his best. But his client's obsession with getting out of jail at all costs had virtually paralyzed the defense. At his very first meeting with Burleson, Cullen had demanded angrily, "Why am I still in jail?" Since then he had thought about nothing else. Despite relatively comfortable conditions—his own cell, private shower, and unlimited visitors—Cullen exploded with rage at the mere suggestion that he might have to stay in jail until the trial was over.

It was a problem for Burleson, too, because it deprived him of his favorite weapon: delay. With Cullen in jail, he didn't dare file the usual blizzard of motions that might put the trial off for another year. It only made the situation worse when he brazenly promised to have Cullen out in time for a midwinter ski trip to Colorado. In a desperate effort to make good on that promise, Burleson had thrown himself into preparation for the bond hearing, neglecting everything else.

When that fell through, all hell broke loose and Cullen started shopping for a new lawyer. To appease Burleson's considerable ego—and to keep control over him—Cullen fattened his fee and promised to continue running all secondary expenses (investigators, secretaries, etc.) through Burleson's firm. Haynes would receive just a flat fee of $250,000; the real money, in the millions, would continue to flow Burleson's way.

Meanwhile, public opinion had already reached a verdict. Joe Shannon's doubts aside, the bond hearing had been a public relations triumph for the prosecution. With its parade of wheelchair-bound witnesses and shocking revelations about Cullen Davis's history of brutality toward women, children, and small animals, the hearing had hardened the public's heart against "the millionaire who thought he could get away with murder." Long, lavish articles in *D* magazine, *Texas Monthly*, and local papers, based heavily on Priscilla's courtroom testimony, took Cullen's guilt virtually for granted and lingered sympathetically over Priscilla's grief. "All I ever wanted," she told the *Star-Telegram* after showing off her scar, "was a husband, babies, and a vine-covered cottage."

Fort Worth cocktail conversation tended to focus not on *whether* Cullen had done it, but on *why*. Then came three civil suits, filed in quick succession after the murders by Bubba Gavrel, Stan Farr's family, and Jack Wilborn. Even die-hard Davis supporters had second thoughts when Cullen was called to testify in one of those cases and refused to answer questions. It may not have been the law, but it was a fact in Texas—only guilty people took the Fifth.

Next came a string of losses on the bond appeal. At least once a week the papers announced, "DAVIS APPEAL TURNED DOWN AGAIN," or "NO FREEDOM FOR DAVIS." Each headline was like a lash. Each one represented another judge agreeing with Cave that, given the evidence presented, it wasn't just possible, but *probable* that Cullen would get the death penalty. When Burleson filed a motion to move the trial out of Fort Worth—essentially admitting that local public opinion had already convicted his client —the courthouse wisdom was that the defense had hit bottom.

Haynes's strategy for reversing the tides of fortune was brutally simple: attack, attack, attack.

"Your Honor, the prosecution has misused the grand jury." Haynes thrust his chin out and raised his voice in indignation on his very first day in court representing Cullen Davis. "We have reason to believe, and do believe, there are persons of influence who have access to this information who may use it to their best personal advantage. . . . The defense demands that the prosecution turn over transcripts of the grand jury proceedings to the defense."

It wasn't a bombshell, but it was a bomblet. It was both too vague to be easily disproved and too serious to be readily dismissed—the secrecy of grand jury proceedings being among the most sacred of legal sacred cows. On the other hand, it fell short of being preposterous. Prosecutors had been known to leak grand jury testimony, sacred or not, when it served their interests.

"Your Honor, the prosecution is harassing potential witnesses." To substantiate this claim, Haynes produced Cullen and Karen's babysitter. Under Haynes's sympathetic questioning, she told the court how investigators from the district attorney's office had "threatened" to haul her before the grand jury if she insisted on speaking to a lawyer before answering their questions. When Haynes began to supply words like "threaten" and "haul," Joe Shannon leapt to his feet to object: "He's leading the witness!"

Haynes turned to the judge, wearing a look of surprised indignation. "I believe he's trying to sully me, Your Honor."

"Your Honor, my client is a victim of selective prosecution." To charge Cullen Davis with burglary of his own home was a "freakish" application of the law, Haynes argued. To prove his point, he questioned Tim Curry and others about the case of Mrs. Judy Dow. Dow's estranged husband had broken into her house and assaulted her even though he, like Cullen Davis, was under a court order to stay away from his wife. Yet when Mrs. Dow brought her case to the D.A.'s office, she was told that no charges

would be filed. "How do you explain that?" Haynes roared.

"Your Honor, my client is the object of a vicious prosecutorial conspiracy." To make sure this accusation made the front pages, Haynes called the prosecutors themselves to the stand. Why was the grand jury still hearing witnesses after his client had been indicted? Wasn't there an agreement in the D.A.'s office to use subsequent grand juries as an investigating body on the capital murder charges? Wasn't the prosecutors' real objective to "harass" Cullen Davis?

Again, Shannon objected: "If it's possible for you to harass someone who's in prison for blowing away a twelve-year-old girl, then . . ."

Later, when the grand jury finally *was* dismissed, after returning indictments for assault and attempted murder, Haynes called its dismissal "a cheap trick."

Like shots fired at the floor to make a tinhorn dance, Haynes's accusations kept prosecutors on the defensive: evidence was illegally seized; a warrant was returned with a "deliberate omission in order to deceive the magistrate" (the policeman called it an oversight, Haynes branded it a "blatant lie"); the grand jury was illegally constituted (everyone on it was a property owner); Tim Curry kept a secret file rating potential jurors (Haynes wanted to see it); the police were hiding the fact that they had found unidentified prints at the crime scene (Haynes demanded to examine them).

By Christmas, the counterattacks had paid off—not in the courtroom, where Shannon successfully fought off most of Haynes's efforts to gain access to evidence and shut down the grand jury, but in the court of public opinion. There, Haynes had managed to turn a series of hearings on routine defense motions into a dazzlingly successful PR campaign. After a month of headlines like "MURDER CHARGE TO BE FOUGHT," "DAVIS' LAWYERS KEEP WORKING," "DAVIS' LAWYER WANTS CHARGES IN OPEN," "DAVIS CLAIMED NOT AT SCENE," and "DAVIS LAWYERS SAY WITNESS HARASSED," Fort Worth seemed ready for the first time to consider the possibility that Cullen Davis was innocent.

A private poll conducted by the defense in December showed such a shift in public opinion that three days after Christmas, Haynes felt confident enough to drop the defense motion to move the trial elsewhere. "DAVIS REQUESTS LOCAL TRIAL," cooed the *Dallas Morning News*. "MILLIONAIRE EXPECTS FAIR JURORS IN PLACE OF BIRTH."

The next attack came when Tim Curry took the stand to deny Haynes's charge that the prosecutors were withholding evidence. Were there any telephone logs or videotapes or police radio conversations the night of the murders? Haynes asked. "No," Curry insisted, wriggling uncomfortably in an unfamiliar role, "nothing relevant is being concealed."

Suddenly Haynes spun on his heel and faced the witness. He snatched off his glasses and bore down with a naked gaze. "Are you aware of any narcotics found in the Mockingbird Lane residence?"

Joe Shannon was out of his chair before Haynes could put a question mark at the end of his sentence. "Your Honor, is he taking the position that if there was a bunch of dope found in that house, it would give the defendant the right to kill someone?"

When the courtroom calmed, Curry answered the question: No narcotics were found at the house. But by that time no one was listening. At the next break, reporters crowded around Haynes demanding more details. Haynes set his jaw—as if the story he was about to tell was deeply distasteful to him personally, but he felt duty-bound to tell it—then dropped his bomb. The missing link in this case, he said, was the *motive* for murder. And that motive was drugs.

Somebody asked what kind of drugs.

"Society narcotics," said Haynes, without a trace of speculative shyness, "coke, marijuana, and possibly heroin." Pressed for details, he alluded vaguely to "a double cross on a drug deal."

Asked if he knew the identity of the real killer, Haynes smiled slyly and said he had to save *something* for the trial. But, he promised, "it's going to be shocking when the truth comes out."

The next day, headlines shouted, "CULLEN DAVIS DEFENSE LAWYERS HINT AT 'SURPRISE,'" "SHOCKING DAVIS REVELATION PROMISED."

Even as he said the words, Haynes knew that he had no surprises, no revelations, no story, no motive, no killer. Not yet, at least. Between now and the trial he would have to find them—or invent them.

Finally, Haynes launched his last and most important counterattack. "I've seen a lot of divorce cases where the wife is ready to assign everything, from the Kennedy assassination on down, to the man that she's leaving," he explained to reporters. "It's always been amazing to me how a female's mind works, but it was said long before I was born that the female is the more deadly of the species. And I think that's true. Females have an absolute tunnel vision for a project such as the destruction of a husband or boyfriend. . . . It's really a matter of genius."

Just how far would Priscilla Davis go to destroy her husband? Just how much of an "evil female genius" was she? Haynes soon supplied the answers to his own questions.

The affidavit Haynes filed in Tom Cave's 213th District Court purported to be a statement by David McCrory, and under the gag order placed on the attorneys by Cave, it should never have seen the light of day. But somehow a copy of it was left on the defense counsel's table, which was readily visible from the press area, and from there it quickly jumped to the front pages of every newspaper in Texas. Haynes expressed horror at the oversight, but others suspected that Priscilla wasn't the only one with "an absolute tunnel vision for a project."

"I personally have witnessed Priscilla Davis purchasing

drugs," the nine-page affidavit began. In addition, "I personally observed Priscilla Davis snorting cocaine and heroin." And alcohol to boot: "She would on occasion take pills and snort cocaine and heroin and drink, all in the same evening." According to the affidavit, Priscilla also had bad taste in friends, many of whom "were users of drugs and were also dealing drugs out of Cullen's house." Almost in an aside, the document mentioned that Priscilla also took too many Percodan, a prescription painkiller.

There was more: Priscilla was a sexpot as well as a drug addict, with numerous boyfriends both before and after the divorce proceedings began. There were dark hints of group sex and, even worse, corruption of a minor: in particular, Priscilla's daughter, Dee. "Priscilla said to me that she was taking Dee with her to some parties at the lake and in their home and thought it was funny that Dee was getting into the use of drugs and the participation in sex acts."

As for the murders: "I was aware of the drug trafficing [sic] that had gone on at the house," read McCrory's affidavit, "I knew Priscilla Davis's drug involvement, and I was thinking that these killings were probably related to some kind of drug deal." Specifically, the document (mis)named an "R. T. Rufner" as Priscilla's drug dealer and said he had once threatened to kill her and everyone else in the house.

The affidavit went to great lengths to rebut Priscilla's version of what happened at the mansion on the night of the murders. It quoted Priscilla, in the hospital only an hour afterward, telling McCrory: "You have to keep your mouth shut. For once in your life, if you keep your mouth shut, you will never have to worry about money for the rest of your life. I'll have at least ten million dollars when this thing is over with. Just remember, say it was Cullen who did it, because you know Cullen had to be behind this."

The document also quoted Priscilla admitting that she had met with Bev Bass on the lawn of the mansion after the murders but before running for help—presumably after both Priscilla and Bubba had been shot—to pin the blame on Cullen. This conveniently explained the damning fact that two people running in opposite directions from the mansion had both identified Cullen as the killer.

Even more conveniently, the affidavit quoted both Bev Bass and Bubba Gavrel giving statements to McCrory that directly contradicted the stories they had given police; statements which, not incidentally, exculpated Cullen Davis. The cherry on the sundae, however, was a statement, attributed to Priscilla before the divorce, that she "had to stay married to Cullen because I'd wind up with very little, since I signed a contract saying I wouldn't get any of his family money." Since Priscilla's divorce lawyers were denying that she had knowingly signed any such contract, the statement in the affidavit, if believed, could save Cullen Davis tens of millions of dollars.

It looked less like an affidavit than a defense wish list. There was only one problem: *It wasn't signed.* After the last line—"I sign this statement voluntarily . . . because it is the truth, so help me God"—there was a blank space.

Instantly the tinder-dry landscape of rumors and innuendo surrounding the case burst into flaming headlines: "AFFIDAVIT INDICATES PUSHER AT MANSION," "THREAT BY DRUG DEALER TO MRS. DAVIS CLAIMED," "MRS. DAVIS ALLEGEDLY OFFERED TO BUY SILENCE." The defense's "carelessness" with a copy of the affidavit had magically transformed all of Haynes's most insubstantial arguments and speculative evidence into hard copy.

Behind a mask of judicial calm, Judge Cave was livid. His careful efforts to contain an explosive case and keep the jury pool untainted through months of tedious jury selection had been undone overnight. The flurry of prejudicial headlines, combined with a scandal over the behavior of a juror already chosen, made a mistrial virtually certain. If that wasn't bad enough, the day after the sordid stories began appearing in the papers, David McCrory appeared in Cave's office and insisted that nothing in the affidavit that bore his name was true. As he later told a *Star-Telegram* reporter, the affidavit "was written, edited, rewritten, and reedited by Haynes and Cullen. It appears they're trying to use me as a scapegoat or an idiot, and I'd prefer not to be either.''

Cave immediately called Joe Shannon, who, like everyone else, had been frantically searching for the missing affiant. "Joe, there's a man down here that wants to talk to you. His name is David McCrory." Shannon came running.

Eight hours later, Shannon emerged from a meeting with McCrory in his office, waving some papers and shouting, "I got it!" "It" was yet another affidavit, this one *signed* by McCrory, that disavowed the most damaging statements in his earlier affidavit: the hospital conversations with Priscilla and Bubba, Priscilla's drug use, the conspiracy between Priscilla and Beverly Bass, and the sex orgies. In addition, McCrory provided an unsettling account of Haynes and Burleson's efforts to get his signature on the previous affidavit.

"I told them I would not sign it because it was not truthful," McCrory had told Shannon. "Mr. Burleson suggested that I have another drink. I visited with them most of the evening about the inaccuracies in the proposed affidavit. I told them to correct it, and that I would sign it if it were truthful. During this same conversation, Mr. Richard Haynes remarked about the ring which I had on my hand. It appears to be a diamond, but it was not. I told Mr. Haynes that evening that I wished the diamond were real. Mr. Haynes said that he had confidence in me and that someday it *would* be real."

In response, Haynes put on a scarlet mask of indignation and denounced McCrory as a damned liar even as he insisted everything in McCrory's first affidavit was gospel truth. But Judge Cave wasn't buying it. After giving himself overnight "to cool down," he called Haynes and Burleson into his chambers. The two lawyers didn't notice that Cave's voice was an octave lower than usual as he instructed the bailiff to hand them something. They were contempt citations: seventy-two hours in jail and a $500 fine. But the bailiff mixed them up, handing each man the other's citation. For an awkward moment, Haynes thought, "I'm sure sorry, Phil, this judge is citing you for contempt," and Burleson was feeling equally sorry for Haynes. Then suddenly, simultaneously, the truth dawned.

Burleson turned bright pink in shock and indignation. He was president of the Dallas County Bar Association, former chairman of the ethics committee. This was unthinkable! "Can't we find some other way?" he pleaded. "I can get you some authorities . . . this isn't the proper way to handle this . . . it's striking at our client over our shoulders . . ."

Haynes remained unflappable. "Well," he finally said, oddly expansive, "this is the first time I've ever been served with a contempt citation in Tarrant County."

In fact, it was the first time either man had been cited for contempt anywhere. (Not long afterward, at a judicial conference, Cave was approached by a fellow judge. "Congratulations," he said. "Thank God somebody finally had the guts to stick it to Haynes.")

Haynes had paid dearly for it, but the damage was done. And it was permanent. Now it was the prosecution that needed a change of venue. Within a week, on April 14, 1977, before a single word of testimony had been taken, even before a full jury had been seated, Cave declared a mistrial and sent the case west to Amarillo in hopes that a less angry judge and a fairer jury could be found to hear the case of *Texas* v. *Davis*.

But Shannon knew there was no watertight way to keep prejudice from seeping into a jury, wherever it came from. There would always be one prospective juror who said he didn't read the papers or didn't believe them or could ignore them but, in the end, did or couldn't. And the defense only needed one. Wherever the case went, the stories would follow. Every time the local newspaper summarized the case, right there next to Priscilla's name would be the rumors: the cocaine, the sex orgies, the lying, the conniving for Cullen's money. The papers would dutifully report them as "rumors" only, but most readers would devour the candy and discard the wrapper.

Even before the McCrory affidavit, Shannon had concluded that Priscilla was the key. If the jurors believed her, no high-priced lawyer or courtroom bluster could protect Cullen. If they didn't, no one could touch him. By the eve of the trial, it was clear that the defense had come to the same conclusion.

32

The long milk-white Continental pulled into the Mt. Olive Cemetery on the north side of Fort Worth, just across the street from the rusty tanks and towers of the Winston Oil Refinery. Not far past the entrance, in an area marked "Gardenia Garden" on the cemetery map, near a sculpture of an open book inscribed with the Lord's Prayer, the car came to a slow stop. A slim, leggy woman with long blonde hair stepped out from the driver's side. She opened the back door, then bent down and stuck her head inside. After a long time, she reemerged, gently helping another woman from the car.

It was Priscilla Davis. Her arm was hooked around Judy McCrory's neck, her tiny fingers crooked with pain. She tried to lift herself out of the car, but there was no strength in her legs. They felt as frail as dried leaves. The two women walked slowly, arm in arm, to the gravesite, about ten feet from the curb.

Andrea Lee Wilborn
January 22, 1964
August 2, 1976
Our Precious Little Girl

Priscilla sat on the grass and laid a big bouquet of pink roses beside the small plaque. When she started to cry, Judy went back to the car for tissues. They stayed almost an hour, Priscilla weeping quietly on the grass, Judy standing at a distance, watching to make sure no insensitive passersby, recognizing Priscilla from the newspapers, trespassed on her grief.

It was one of Priscilla's first trips out since returning from the hospital. There were times during those first few days back at the mansion when Judy wondered whether Priscilla would make it. Not because of the holes in her chest and back—the doctors had assured her that, to their amazement, Priscilla was out of danger. "She has the constitution of a horse," one of them had marveled. It wasn't even the pain, although the pain was relentless and, especially in her back where the bullet had grazed her spine, at times overwhelming. No, it wasn't the wounds or the pain that posed the greatest threat to Priscilla, Judy thought. It was the memories.

For that very reason she had urged Priscilla not to move back into the mansion on Mockingbird Lane. At Priscilla's bedside, she and Bill Davis had talked about where she should go when the hospital discharged her.

Judy suggested maybe a hotel.

"There's no security there," Bill objected. Cullen was still out on bail and Bill Davis was obsessed with security. "Why not take her back to the house? It's a fortress there."

"The *worst* thing would be for her to have to go back to that house," Judy objected. "How could she feel safe there?"

"Is there anyplace she'll really feel safe?" Bill asked.

Of course, Judy knew there wasn't. So she brought Priscilla back to the mansion.

But first it had to be made ready. The glass panel beside the breakfast room door had to be replaced. (The police had already taken the backstairs door, the one with the bullet hole.) The maids cleaned blood off floors, walls, and furniture, pouring bucket after bucket of bright red water down the laundry room sink. The sheets on Andrea's bed had to be changed and her room picked up to prevent Priscilla from doing it herself. There were black shreds of plastic garbage bag everywhere that had to be vacuumed up. Judy went over it again and again, imagining what would happen if Priscilla found just one stray fragment or one overlooked stain. One day, as Judy drove in, a tattered black garbage bag floated across the road in front of her like an apparition, then disappeared.

She locked the Hulen Street gate to keep out idle sight-seers who, ever since the house had appeared in the news-papers, considered it public property. Now, whenever she pulled in, she had to stop and unlock the gate, and the traffic on Hulen would slow as curious drivers craned their necks to see who was pulling into the notorious Davis estate.

But no amount of cleaning could erase the memories. The day Priscilla arrived, she made Judy and the police escort search every inch of the huge house, every closet, every dark corner, especially the dreaded basement. "She's terrified of someone lurking inside," Judy explained to the officer. Outside, she feared the prying eyes of strangers and put miniblinds in the windows to protect herself from binoculars and telescopic gunsights. She refused to use the security system—it was Cullen's system, after all, and what good had it done Andrea? If she changed the code, the installer would just tell Cullen. So she replaced all the locks and had only one key made—her key. She didn't even trust the twenty-four-hour police guard provided by the D.A.'s office, and recruited Pat Burleson to check on them late at night. Finally, just in case, she kept a silver-plated .32 revolver in a specially made holster attached to her right boot.

But it still wasn't enough to protect her from the past. Just when she thought it was safe, she would rummage through the huge commercial freezer for the makings of a meal and find something that Andrea had cooked and stored there. Suddenly the memories would leap out of all the dark corners and rise up from the darkened basement and chase her up the back stairs to the bedroom, where she would bury her head in the mountain of pillows and stuffed animals atop the silver-fox spread and weep inconsolably.

The friends who came to visit, to play backgammon and watch TV, did little to raise her spirits. She always seemed pleased to see Pat Burleson, the handsome karate instructor, or Stan's friend, Rich Sauer, who entertained her with his comic impressions or cooked dinner for her and the police guards. But she had nothing to give back. The rough, irreverent humor, the flirtatious warmth, the bubbly enthusiasm, had all vanished. Even friends found visiting a lugubrious chore—and she knew it. More and more often, she would simply retreat from the world behind her locked bedroom door.

It helped when Judy McCrory moved in. The marriage to David, always troubled, had finally disintegrated. After the murders, David had allied himself with Cullen, while Judy stood by Priscilla. The confrontation came to a head with the appearance of David's infamous affidavit, which Judy saw as both a sleazy bid for Cullen's favor and a desperate effort to get at her through Priscilla. After months of bickering, she announced she was leaving him.

David, of course, couldn't let her go without the mandatory melodrama. The next night, he showed up at her door brandishing a gun and threatening to kill them both. He seemed "dead serious" to Judy, who sat stone-faced in a rocking chair as David poured out his heart for the umpteenth time while holding the gun to her head. "We're gonna work this out or there will be nothing to work out," he threatened, tears running down his fat cheeks. "We're *both* gonna go."

He calmed down eventually, but Judy had finally had enough. After wasting eleven years of her life on him, she wasn't going to waste another hour. That same night, she fled to the mansion and, a few days later, moved her belongings into the basement.

Priscilla insisted that Judy sleep, not in one of the mansion's guest rooms, but in the master bedroom "right there next to her." She took Cullen's bed, a queen-size electric one that shared the huge silver-fox spread and a perfect view of the see-through fireplace and the triple TVs. At night, Priscilla would dim the lights and talk on the phone until a full pack of Eves was gone, usually 3:00 or 4:00 in the morning. When Judy, who had to be at work by 7:30 the next morning, would tuck her pillow under her arm and offer to sleep in another room, Priscilla would grow suddenly frightened and apologetic. "No. Please don't go," she would plead. "I promise I'll be quiet."

It wasn't easy sometimes, but Judy understood. She understood why Priscilla put off going to sleep as long as she could, and why she dreaded being alone. Judy had been startled awake many nights by the blood-chilling screams. She had seen Priscilla's eyes, frozen in terror after she woke up from one of the endless nightmares that haunted her. Was it Andrea alone in the basement? Was it Stan dying on the breakfast room floor? Was it the face of the man in black? Judy never asked. All she could do was get up and go through the house, checking all the dark corners one more time.

Not long after the trip to Andrea's grave, ignoring her doctors' objections, Priscilla again climbed into the back of the big Lincoln. With Judy McCrory and Lynda Arnold, Stan Farr's sister, and a roomful of flowers beside her in the back seat, she headed to Seimansville, Texas, where Stan Farr was buried. Riveted in pain to her hospital bed, she had missed all the funerals, all the condolences, all the opportunities to grieve. Now, a full month after the murders, just when everyone else's wounds were beginning to heal, Priscilla was feeling hers for the first time.

"She was quiet the whole way down," Judy later told a friend about the trip. "I'm sure she was in pain every inch of the way."

At the gravesite, a plain headstone in a small, ill-tended country cemetery surrounded by live oaks, something inside Priscilla snapped. "She just went to pieces," Judy remembered. "She bawled her eyes out. It was pitiful." So pitiful that Judy and Lynda Arnold broke down at the sight. The three of them wept together in a kind of awful chorus. Later, Judy would ask herself if Priscilla had blocked out the reality of her relationship with Stan. Had she forgotten how they were close to splitting up the night he was killed, how she had visited Cullen in the hospital and laid plans to ask him back? Or was all that just gone now, part of a different life?

Eventually they collected Priscilla from the ground, "like a limp kitten," and lifted her gently into the car, spread out across the backseat where the flowers had been. There, she curled up under her blanket and continued to cry quietly all the way back to Fort Worth.

A few miles before they reached home, however, Judy was startled by Priscilla's face in the rearview mirror. She was sitting bolt upright, her eyes dry as ash. "I know what I'm going to do," she said, her voice shaking with anger. "I am going to make sure that sorry sonofabitch gets what's coming to him."

After that, Priscilla was transformed. Fired by a determination to "put Cullen away," she began telling her story to anyone who would listen. She sought out reporters from local newspapers, wire services, and magazines, and invited them into the inner sanctum of her bedroom.

By turns coquettish, passionate, and breathtakingly open, she pressed her case. Sympathetic articles appeared in *Texas Monthly* and *D* magazine. But the press was often more interested in her life-style than her cause, and her openness backfired as often as it scored. Pointing to a revolving fixture over her bed, two AP reporters asked Priscilla to confirm the rumor that it was a camera to film her lovemaking with Cullen. Later, they wrote of her response:

> *A woman of some mystery, a target of high and low rumor, Priscilla swept away all pretenses, smiling wryly as she acknowledged talk about a movie camera focused from the ceiling on her bed below.*
> *"It doesn't even work," she said.*

Again the smile: "I know what I'm doing. I don't need an instant replay. . . ."

In fact, the fixture was a light.

True or not, such tidbits were raw meat to Fort Worth high society. They only confirmed what the "better people" had always known: that Priscilla was a low-rent girl from the wrong side of the tracks, a woman with too much hair, too much silicone, and not enough breeding; a woman with clothes that cost too much and covered too little. They would never forget (or forgive) the sight of her in her glory days with Cullen, dragging one of her mink coats across the floor of the Shady Oaks Country Club.

But Priscilla remained defiant. When, after months of legal wrangling, Cullen won the right to visit the mansion, Priscilla instructed the maid that when Mr. Davis arrived, she should tell him that his precious gold and silver chess set was in the upstairs safe. Then she packed the chess set in the trunk of her car and drove away, leaving in the safe only two framed pictures—one of Andrea and one of Stan Farr.

33

Even as she struggled to overcome the past and rebuild her life, Priscilla found there was one thing she couldn't put behind her: pain. "There wasn't a single instant I can recall," said Judy McCrory, "when something took her out of herself long enough that she forgot the pain. Everything else was experienced through that."

She tried everything, starting with a pharmacopoeia of drugs: Percodan, Tegretol, Dilantin, Maolate. None gave her relief. Many nights she would be propelled out of bed to John Peter Smith Hospital for injections in her back to deaden the pain enough to let her sleep. But the injections gave her spasms and severe cramps, and she would jolt awake at two or three in the morning with a lance of pain so sharp that, in her delirium, she thought she had been stabbed.

Then the hospital started turning her away. She would call to say she was on her way over and they would tell her, "You can't do any more injections now, Mrs. Davis, you have to give this a chance to work its way through your system." Priscilla would plead with them, "Please, you've *got* to help me!" as she doubled over in agony. When they still refused, she would slam the phone down and say, "I'll go anyway! Maybe if they see me, they can do something for me." And sometimes she was right. She would show up at the emergency room, writhing in pain and screaming for help, and their hearts would soften a little.

Eventually her arms grew puffy and abscessed from the injections, and they had to stop. "I just *can't* give her another shot," the senior nurse at John Peter Smith told Judy. "She is in no condition to handle it. I don't know why the doctors keep giving it to her. Something has to be done." So they moved the shots to her thighs for a while, until those muscles, too, collapsed.

More and more, she was forced to turn elsewhere in her search for relief: physical therapy, acupuncture, subcutaneous nerve stimulation, epidural blocks. And, of course, Percodan, the painkiller she had been using since her skiing accident years before. She took it like aspirin: at first, two every four hours, then four every four hours, then four every two hours—thirty-two a day, and some days more. Some days she lost count. She had prescriptions from different doctors and filled them at different pharmacies.

The more she took, the less effect they seemed to have. After so many years, they did little more than take the burrs off the pain. Friends like Rich Sauer couldn't believe her tolerance. A muscular ex-athlete, Sauer once took one half of one of Priscilla's Percodans for a sore back. It made him so dizzy he had to go to bed.

Judy McCrory worried about the effects of so many drugs, even on someone with Priscilla's iron constitution. "It's just unbearable watching her suffer," she told a friend. "The toxicity in her system alone should knock her for a loop."

Seeing the danger, Judy and other friends tried to warn her: she was addicted. But Priscilla brushed them off. "It's just for the pain," she would insist. "It's the only way of stopping the pain." So they tried other kinds of therapy. On a long weekend, they took her to a camp on Lake Granbury. She was still frail and sickly, depressed, and dependent on the huge quantity of prescription drugs that she carried with her everywhere. "When we went out on the lake," Judy remembers, "she had to be helped onto the boat like an old lady." Only two years before, she had frolicked like a girl with W. T. Rufner at Possum Kingdom Lake. But on this day she sat quiet and melancholy and clearly in pain under the awning of the barge boat watching, as if from a great distance, her friends cavort around her.

When a sudden breeze caught Judy's hat and whirled it onto the water, there was a flurry of concern but no one moved to retrieve it—except Priscilla. Frail and racked with pain as she was, she jumped into the lake.

Was she trying to save the hat? Or was she trying to kill herself? There was a moment of stunned indecision on the boat as they watched Priscilla flail against the water. Finally, Rich Sauer jumped in after her. When they pulled her out, clutching the hat, and laid her on the deck, she looked "like a drowned rat," Judy thought, "so small and pitiful looking, soaking wet and curled up like a baby."

When she recovered, Priscilla's pain and frustration turned to anger. She fixed her white-hot gaze on one of the guests, Charles Crenshaw, the doctor who had first treated her the night of the murders and who, ever since, had looked after her with something more than professional diligence. "Do something about this motherfucking pain," she demanded, her voice an animal growl, octaves lower than Judy had ever heard it, the words exploding out of her mouth in a crazed fusillade of spit and fire. *"Do something about this motherfucking pain!"*

Eventually, Crenshaw yielded to Priscilla's rage and wrote another prescription: one hundred more Percodan. Then Rich Sauer took her home.

Later that night, Priscilla called Judy, still distraught and depressed. "Oh, by the way," she said, "tell Crenshaw I've taken every one of those goddamn pills and it hasn't worked at all!"

Judy demanded to speak to Sauer. "Is it true, Rich?" she gasped. "Did Priscilla really take all those pills?"

"Yep," he said, stunningly calm. "She took every one of 'em. I watched her do it."

After that, something had to be done. Someone had to confront Priscilla. Inevitably, the thankless duty fell to Judy McCrory.

At the mansion, Judy sat Priscilla down and got straight to the point. "You have to stop taking so many drugs," she said. "You've *got* to get some help."

"I can handle it," Priscilla said coolly. "Besides, I don't have time to go away, I have to be on call for the D.A.'s office."

But Judy had the bit in her teeth now. "You're not gonna be good for anyone, not for the D.A., not for your lawyers, not even for yourself, if you don't *do* something about this. If you want to take this battle on, you've got to be in condition for it, and you're not. You can't handle it in this condition. You need to go to a detox center *now*."

Priscilla balked again and again until Judy backed her up against a wall and screamed into her face, "You've got to stop doing this! You're fucking killing yourself!"

Finally, Priscilla blinked. "I'll do it," she said. "But only because you all want me to. I still don't think I need it." It was all Judy could expect.

Priscilla was taken in secret to a hospital in San Antonio. After waiting anxiously for the first three days—during which no phone calls were allowed—Judy called.

"Well, what are you doing?" she asked, straining to be cheerful.

There was a long, wintry silence on the other end of the line. Then, finally, Priscilla's voice, black with anger: "Finger-fucking myself! What do you think?"

A few days before the trial was scheduled to begin, Joe Shannon met with Priscilla for the last time. She sat, as usual, in her silver-fox bed: on one side, a menagerie of stuffed animals; on the other, a Plexiglas nightstand covered with packs of Eves, an overflowing ashtray, a clutch of phones, and a little sign that had been Andrea's: "Love is being able to let go."

Shannon had seen Priscilla often since that first visit to the hospital, when she looked so "godawful." He had worked with her closely through the grand jury testimony, the bond hearing, the preliminary hearing. He had seen her at her best and at her worst, when she was sharp and energetic and almost too bright for her own good, and when she was so depressed that he began to worry when she lingered in the bathroom too long.

He had seen her pain: watched her shift in a hard witness chair, wince in agony, then reach behind to readjust the catheter that dripped painkiller into her back. He had seen her body grow frailer and sicker. He had also seen the pills, or, when he didn't see them, sensed them, as she ducked out of sight between sessions and reappeared with different eyes, or excused herself to the bathroom one time too many. He had heard them, hundreds of them, rattling in her purse. And he had heard the rumors. He didn't know the details, but he had his suspicions.

He had seen the articles in the papers and magazines and the news stories on television, the ones that pretended to flatter her even as they fed the public's ravenous contempt for her. Was she too vain to see how people would react when they saw her sitting on that lavish bed in the middle of Cullen's multimillion-dollar mansion? Or was she too honest to pretend to be anything other than what she was?

And why did he care? Not surprisingly, more than one friend had asked him that question as they followed the drama in the papers. Why was he so concerned about this "gilded whore"? Even if she lost her divorce case, she stood to make a million or more. Was it just that she was the star witness in what would undoubtedly be the biggest case of his life? Was he just worried about her credibility on the stand? He had often said that *Texas* v. *Davis* would rise or fall on whether the jury believed Priscilla's story. Was it just the stupid *case*, just the "stroke in the win column" he was worried about?

He was sure the answer was no. This woman had suffered in ways that most people couldn't imagine. So what if she slept around, so what if she did marry Cullen for his money? If everything they said about her were ten times true, it wouldn't change a thing. Her child had been murdered!

He knew that some on the prosecution team disagreed—or at least feared that a jury might disagree. The McCrory affidavit had unleashed a plague of doubts among the prosecutors, many of whom had never cared much for Priscilla anyway. They discussed not calling her as a witness at all. She was sick, they said, overly reliant on pills, often heavily sedated, slow on the uptake. Haynes would demolish her.

Was it that, Shannon wondered, or did she just not meet their moral standards? Were they doing what they feared the jury would do: judging the victim rather than the crime?

Shannon had gone to the mansion to ask Priscilla if McCrory's allegations of sexual orgies and drug use were true. "All lies," she insisted. Shannon wasn't sure he believed her, but what could he do? They had no choice but to put her on the stand. Andrea was her child. What would the jury think if she didn't testify? Haynes might destroy her if she took the stand, but he would destroy the *case* if she didn't.

And besides, he reminded his colleagues, in all the stories the defense and the media had spread about Priscilla, nothing had undermined or contradicted her account of the events of the night of August 2, 1976.

Would that be enough? Could someone believe Priscilla's story even if they, like so many others, thought she was a gold-digging whore? Shannon would soon find out.

In the meantime, he took what encouragement he could in something his father used to say: "Never underestimate a jury."

34

"Bitch" wasn't a word that R. C. Hubbard used often, and never in polite company; but around other men, it was the best word he could think of to describe Priscilla Davis. "Hub," as his friends in Amarillo called him, was a dutiful husband, driving his wife every weekend to the beauty parlor, the grocery store, and her sister's house. Some of his friends' wives considered Jessie Hubbard overbearing and overly religious, but R. C. never complained. Marriage was a sacred obligation, he would say, and he was bound by his vows to accept what God had given him.

During the summer of 1977, as the juggernaut of the Cullen Davis case lumbered toward Amarillo, R. C. spent the weekends Jessie gave him off in the mountains of New Mexico building a cabin where he could indulge in his favorite pastime: guns. But he was home enough to know something big was coming—the biggest murder trial in Texas history, in fact. He knew there had been a mistrial in Fort Worth, although he didn't know why, and he knew about Priscilla Davis. *Everybody* in Amarillo knew about Priscilla Davis—her boyfriends, her drugs, her schemes. Like a lot of other people, R. C. already had the case figured out: "Priscilla is just after her husband's money."

R. C.'s opinion of Priscilla Davis wasn't based on newspaper or television reports, most of which he missed while in New Mexico, or just plain avoided. He had other sources. Jessie was well wired into the network of Christian women's groups that broadcast frequent over-the-back-fence updates on the latest outrages of that most un-Christian of women. At Pan-Tex, a nuclear weapons facility (known around Amarillo simply as "the bomb plant") where R. C. worked, the transfer of the Davis case from Fort Worth had taken its place beside the usual sports talk as the hot topic of lunch-break conversation. No one cared too much about the legal niceties. People just knew that a bunch of big-city prosecutors had botched things up real bad in Fort Worth and now were bringing their problems to Amarillo for a jolt of old-fashioned West Texas justice.

As for the facts of the case, almost everybody agreed: Priscilla was guilty as hell. One reporter arriving from Dallas got an earful from her cab driver. "I sure hope they let Cullen off," he said, " 'cause I don't want to see that damn bitch get a damn thing." The second person the reporter met in Amarillo was the desk clerk at her hotel. "Well, I know what I'd do if *I* was on the jury," he volunteered. "That gal there just wants him convicted of murder so she can get all that property."

There was hardly a man at the bomb plant who hadn't heard the nasty rumors floating around town about "That Damn Bitch." More than one had talked to Ray Hudson, a big jowly man in cowboy boots and hat who seemed to know everything about the case and spent every evening going from one bar to another talking about the evil, conniving Priscilla Davis and how she had cooked up this whole case to get at her husband's money. A longtime local fixture in Amarillo, Hudson had moved to Arizona shortly before the storm broke, but came back to spread the word about Priscilla and buy drinks for just about every man in town.

R. C. Hubbard had heard a little about Cullen Davis, too. A number of his buddies down at the plant had friends who worked at Cummins Sales and Service, the big Kendavis Industries operation in Amarillo. They had the "inside line" on the defendant. According to them, he was a hardworking, straight-up, plain-folks kind of guy who got himself caught in the tangled web of a scheming wife. The men down at the bomb plant snickered sympathetically when they heard that. You didn't need to be a multimillionaire to know how dangerous a woman could be—especially when she was after your money.

R. C. was gratified to see that Mr. Davis had the good sense to hire a crack team of lawyers to defend himself. He didn't recognize the names of Richard Haynes or Phil Burleson—as far as he was concerned, they were just another couple of big-city lawyers—but he certainly knew the name Dee Miller, director of the North State Bank, past president of the Amarillo Country Club, and a popular former district attorney. R. C. and some friends from Pan-Tex had once gone down to the courthouse to observe the trial of a man who had injured a friend of theirs. Dee Miller was the prosecutor, and he won a conviction. "That Dee is a pretty sharp fellow," R. C. often said afterward. The fact that Miller was hired to serve on the defense team as local co-counsel showed what a "quality person" Cullen Davis really was.

R. C., of course, didn't run around in the same circles with Dee Miller (whose brother, G. William, would later serve as chairman of the Federal Reserve Board), but his bosses at the plant did. They had been to the country club and met Davis's other lawyers, the big-city ones, and damn if they didn't turn out to be "just plain folks" like Cullen. They wore jeans and boots and cowboy hats and talked like real Texans—not like the prosecutors. Word passed quickly around the plant: The Cullen Davis defense team was "the home team"—which only made men like R. C. Hubbard madder at That Damn Bitch for making so much trouble.

R. C. had escaped to his cabin in the mountains the weekend in June when Priscilla Davis arrived in Amarillo for pretrial hearings. But he heard all about it when he returned: how she and her "entourage" set down in a rented baby-blue jet; how they were whisked off in a limousine to the Presidential Suite at the Amarillo Hilton; how a photographer had caught her in the hallway of the hotel as she changed rooms wearing a white dress (white!) with ruffles, and *carrying a white leatherbound Bible and wearing a gold cross around her neck*! The religious women of Amarillo like Jessie Hubbard were up in arms. Jezebel Priscilla Davis with a cross and a Bible! As a deacon in the Church of Christ, R. C. shared their outrage. "From that first day," he said, "I knew she was a phony and a hypocrite."

Less than a week later, R. C. Hubbard received his summons to appear for jury duty at the Potter County Courthouse.

The name R. C. Hubbard, along with the other 249 prospective jurors who appeared at the courthouse on June 27, 1977, had already been typed into the computers at Cummins Sales and Service.

The presence of so much Kendavis "family" in a city of less than 145,000 was only one of many reasons the defense team was overjoyed with the choice of Amarillo. For the prosecution's sake, they put on a great show of head-shaking and hand-wringing over the choice: "Amarillo *is* in the northern, Bible-thumping half of the state," they moaned, "and everyone knows how hostile the born-agains are to defendants." One of the defense lawyers, Mike Gibson, told how he had tried a case in Amarillo once, and the jury almost convicted *him*.

But even as the complaints were being made, Kendavis companies were mobilizing their employees; local lawyer Dee Miller was introducing Richard Haynes to the town's landed gentry; and Karen Master's father, Ray Hudson, was being paid $45,000 by Cullen to spread the story of "that bitch Priscilla" all over Amarillo.

The defense also found much to like in their new judge, George Dowlen, a toothpick-chewing good ol' boy from Ralph's Switch, Texas. A graduate of the University of Texas Law School, Dowlen wasn't dumb, but he was no match for Haynes. Sources described him as "honorable," "trusting," "fair," "gentlemanly"—the quintessential West Texas rural aristocrat who considered a handshake a contract and tended to take lawyers at their word. It was just the Achilles heel the defense had been hoping for. Haynes would have free rein in the courtroom.

Dowlen also had a political side—another plus for the defense. After eleven years as the district attorney for neighboring Randall County, he had backed the right man for governor, Dolph Briscoe, and had been appointed to the bench only a year and a half before the Davis case landed in his court. Any man with that kind of political savvy would surely have one eye on the 1978 judicial elections, only a year away, when he would have to run for reelection. Maybe they couldn't manipulate Dowlen directly, but they were confident they could manipulate local public opinion—in fact, they already had—and that was damn near as good.

If Dowlen had one eye on his constituents, he had the other on women. At forty-two, he still savored the adolescent highs of dating too much to abandon his bachelor ways. Most nights, after leaving the courthouse, he would lope over to Rhett Butler's, a teeming local nightspot, hang his long, lanky body on a barstool, and order a "scotch and stick"—a celery stick, that is. "Does the celery make the scotch taste better?" some first-timer would inevitably inquire. "Naw," Dowlen would reply with a big, pliant smile, "but the scotch improves the hell out of that celery stick." When that story made the rounds to the defense team, everybody breathed a little easier. It sounded just like something Racehorse would say.

The Cummins computer check of R. C. Hubbard's address on Northeast 20th Street had kicked out the names of several Kendavis employees in the neighborhood who could be called in for their assessment of Potential Juror #167. Copies of the entire list were printed up by the hundreds and passed out to key company employees and anybody else who could be trusted in a search for "personal contacts." A phalanx of researchers went to work on public records: Where else had this "R. C. Hubbard" lived? How much money did he make? To whom did he owe money? How often had he moved in the last twenty years?

A few days later, a private investigator was dispatched to R. C.'s gray clapboard two-bedroom house in the Martin Addition area of Amarillo. First, he drove by. Then he stopped and snapped some pictures. Then he parked out of sight and walked by to get a better look. He made notes: type of house, size of house, size of lot, level of maintenance, current value, kind of car (or cars), yard condition, length of grass. He looked for signs in the yard, bumper stickers on the cars ("SUPPORT YOUR LOCAL POLICE"), political decals ("IF CARRYING GUNS WAS OUTLAWED, ONLY OUTLAWS WOULD CARRY GUNS"), club membership stickers (Rotary, church groups, country club). At R. C.'s house, the PI was lucky enough to run into a paperboy and asked a few questions, being careful not to arouse suspicion. If caught, he was instructed to claim that he worked for the prosecution.

In July, when the jury pool was reduced to 150, the questioning began to heat up; investigators interviewed R. C.'s and other prospective jurors' neighbors, coworkers, friends, doctors, even barbers. They asked about extramarital involvements, temperaments, prejudices, domestic problems. One man on the list turned out to be a wife beater. The defense team wasn't sure whether that made him more or less attractive as a prospective juror, but finally decided to exclude him as "unpredictable."

By the time the final selection process began in July, Haynes had in front of him a dossier on each of the prospective jurors, as well as analyses from Margaret Covington, a psychologist hired by the defense to evaluate the juror files compiled by investigators and provide a profile of the ideal juror. Her advice: Find jurors who would not overreact emotionally to the murder of a child but who were also "good, solid, basically conservative citizens who would have no affinity for Priscilla and might even find her revolting." In other words, jurors who would be morally outraged by a woman fooling around but not by the murder of a twelve-year-old girl.

If they could be found, Haynes would find them.

When R. C. Hubbard's turn came to be questioned, Haynes asked him about his hobbies. "I'm kind of a gun nut," R. C. said proudly. "I'm into guns, reloadin', and I do a lot of shootin'." Haynes seemed pleased to hear that, R. C. thought, although he figured his chances of being picked, especially by the defense, were slim. Earlier he had told one of the prosecutors, Tolly Wilson, that he supported the death penalty.

Mr. Wilson also seemed to like it when R. C. said that he hadn't seen any of the news reports or read any of the articles about Priscilla and the Bible incident. "I was in the mountains in New Mexico," he told them, "and I don't git any radio or TV up there." But with his attitude toward guns, R. C. felt confident that the prosecutors wouldn't want him either, which meant he was safe from both sides. Even so, they spent six and a half hours questioning him.

At one point, they asked him if he had heard anything about the people connected with the case. "Well," he said, "I read this article in the paper the other day about 'Wild-horse Haynes.' " Everybody in the courtroom chuckled. "You've got your horses mixed up," somebody said. But then they changed the subject, and R. C. didn't volunteer anything else.

Even after the questioning began, the defense had one last "safeguard" to ensure that "the state started as far behind the eight ball as possible." Whenever a juror like Hubbard was passed by the prosecution, a gofer stationed in the back of the courtroom would run to the phone and give the juror's name to Hugh Russell, the former county judge who had coordinated the jury research effort. Russell, perhaps the best-connected man in Potter County, would quickly place phone calls to the juror's employer, personnel director, banker, doctor, or whatever to get a last-minute assessment—"Is Hub on our side?" In the brief break before Haynes was required to give a thumbs-up or thumbs-down, Russell would call with the final word.

R. C. Hubbard got a thumbs-up.

It was an expensive system, but it worked. One member of the defense team proudly pronounced it "virtually fail-safe."

Wiley Alexander, the sage old sheriff's deputy who had been assigned to chaperone the jury, knew right away there was something wrong with juror #43, Roy Q. Biggers, a sixty-year-old retired railroad engineer. At first Wiley thought maybe it was just his imagination. After all, Biggers had been through the usual grinder: hours of questioning by the judge, prosecutors, even Mr. Richard "Racehorse" Haynes. Why, they asked him, had he never married? "Women don't do nothing but cause trouble," he replied. When the defense finally gave its approval, making Biggers only the fourth juror seated in as many weeks, he leapt out of his chair, stood at attention, and saluted Richard Haynes.

It seemed odd to Wiley Alexander, but, he thought, if all these educated lawyers can't find anything wrong . . .

Then Biggers showed up at the Executive Inn, where the jury was being sequestered. He had been instructed to go home, say his goodbyes, and come back with enough clothes to last at least a month. But all he had with him was a brown paper bag barely big enough for a lunch, an old straw hat, and the suit on his back.

"You're going to need some more clothes," Wiley told him, "because, you know, we're going to be here for a while."

Biggers smiled and held out the little bag. "This is all I'll need right here," he said cheerfully.

Again, Wiley didn't say anything. All those lawyers . . .

That night, when he came to take the four jurors to dinner, he found Biggers lying on his bed, buck naked—no covers—and the windowshade all the way up. It was summer, thought Wiley, and those attorneys did question this man all day long. And they were good attorneys, too, top-notch attorneys . . . At dinner, Biggers dumped all the food off his plate into his napkin, pulled the four corners into a pouch, and carted it off to his room to eat in solitude.

The next morning, walking down the hall, Wiley looked into Biggers's room and saw him standing in front of the mirror, buck naked again, talking to himself. Not just talking, *lecturing*; shaking his finger at the reflection, obviously giving himself some pretty emphatic advice. That was the last straw for Wiley Alexander. He and the other bailiff, D'Ann Hill, called the judge and announced: "We've got an idiot over here."

Biggers was quietly dismissed (under the subterfuge of "medical reasons"), avoiding yet another mistrial, but Wiley Alexander was still shaking his head over the incident months later. "Here's two million dollars worth of legal talent on each side of the case and they question this idiot all day long, and then here he comes and he's an idiot."

R. C. Hubbard was the eighth juror picked by the same process.

On August 22, 1977, R. C. shuffled out of the jury waiting room and into the fluorescent glare of the 181st District Courtroom in the Potter County Courthouse. In front of and behind him in the slow-moving line of jurors were three women and eight men: two salesmen, two utility company employees, two government employees, two white-collar office workers, one blue-collar factory worker, a grandmother, and a cowboy.

In the courtroom, every one of the fifty-two seats was filled, and lines of eager standbys waited just outside the doors. Reporters popped in and out of their chairs, sketch artists scribbled in a row, and six . . . eight . . . ten lawyers conferred around the big counsel table. So much energy and anticipation crammed into a space no bigger than the waiting room of a small-town bus depot.

Among all the faces at the counsel table and in the crowd beyond—mostly Cullen Davis sympathizers crowding the rows behind the defense team like the groom's side

at a wedding—R. C. found only two familiar ones: Dee
Miller, of course, and, sitting near him, Cullen Davis.

It wasn't until 3:30 that afternoon that Hubbard got
his first glimpse of the other star of this extravaganza. She
entered in a long dress the color of milk and honey. It
covered her neck, her legs, her arms. There was even a
matching ribbon in her hair. She didn't look nearly as
young or as pretty as she was supposed to. The pictures
had lied. He thought of Jessie's description of the photograph in the newspaper again: the ruffled dress, the
empty eyes, the white Bible. Then he saw the cross.

She was wearing the cross again.

35

"Will you state your name for the record?"

It was Tim Curry who stood up from the prosecution
table and asked the first question. Not Joe Shannon. After
almost a year of preparation, dozens of interviews, and
restless hours spent beside the silver-fox spread—not all
of them exactly enjoyable—Shannon had been replaced
as the prosecution's "Priscilla expert." At the last minute,
Tim Curry had decided that he himself would conduct the
direct examination of the state's star witness.

Shannon didn't have to ask why. The crush of reporters
filled all but four of the spectator seats in the Potter County
Courthouse that day. No trial in Texas history had been
awaited more breathlessly, and no part of that trial would
be more closely watched or more widely reported than
Priscilla's testimony. It was more than law, more even than
politics, that summoned Tim Curry, the courtroom novice,
to lead the prosecution into battle that day. It was history.

"Priscilla Lee Davis," Priscilla answered in her softest
little-girl voice.

That was as far as the proceeding got before Richard

Haynes made his presence known. "Can she speak up a little bit, Your Honor?" he said, his full baritone canceling out both Curry's shaky monotone and Priscilla's tentative whimper. Haynes was serving notice: He had no intention of waiting until cross-examination to join the battle.

Within the first few minutes of questioning, he stopped her twice more as she tried to describe for the jury her medical problems. A doctor's diagnosis was "hearsay," Haynes claimed, and a reference to the "rodeo" at which she met Stan Farr "not responsive."

Judge Dowlen sustained all the objections without comment, except for repeated instructions to the witness: "Don't testify as to what someone told you. . . . Listen to Mr. Curry's questions. . . . Just listen to the questions and answer them." Priscilla had been on the stand only five minutes and already impatience was beginning to show through Dowlen's country-boy bonhomie.

Curry stumbled ahead. "As a result of your injuries, have you been required to see an eye doctor and get glasses?"

"*Leading,*" Haynes objected and Dowlen agreed.

"Do you reside at 4200 Mockingbird Lane right now?"

"*Leading!*" Haynes boomed and Dowlen agreed.

"Did the court enter certain orders on August 2, 1976, concerning the temporary support payments you had been receiving?"

"*Leading!*" Haynes was on his feet again. "*Counsel* is testifying in these questions, Your Honor, and we object to them." Priscilla had been on the stand only ten minutes, and Curry was already rattled.

"Your Honor, I'm merely asking her questions that require a simple 'Yes' or 'No.' I don't believe that's a leading question."

In fact, it was practically the *definition* of a leading question—a fact that did not escape Haynes. "Well," he said, dipping his head in a lame attempt to conceal a smile, "it may well be that if he didn't supply all the information in the question, she wouldn't be able to answer it with a simple 'yes' or 'no.' "

Stymied and embarrassed, Curry took his frustration out on the person he thought most responsible for his predicament: Priscilla Davis. At best, his tone was that of a benignly tolerant teacher keeping a delinquent student after class. After almost every answer, he would add a curt, "All right," as if relieved and surprised that she had managed to traverse another question without a serious misstep. On those rare occasions when Haynes didn't object to an unresponsive answer, Curry would add his own churlish warning. "Now, Mrs. Davis, if you will, just try to answer the questions that I ask you."

If she became confused or misunderstood a question, it was always her fault, never his, and he made sure the judge and jury knew it. When she pulled out a monogrammed magnifying glass to examine some documents, he asked, "By the way, Mrs. Davis, prior to August the 2nd of 1976, had you ever been required to use a magnifying glass?"

"No," Priscilla replied. "I did, I believe, at that July 30th hearing, borrow my attorney's glasses . . ."

"No, no," Curry snapped, "I wasn't talking about glasses."

Through it all, Priscilla struggled to tell her story. She had thought the trial would be like the bond hearing, where her testimony had been so effective. Under Joe Shannon's gentle guidance, she had narrated the events of that horrendous night with passion and clarity. It was, after all, a dramatic story, and she was a gifted storyteller, with an eye for the poignant detail or the suspenseful moment.

But Haynes wasn't about to let her tell her story.

Referring to the murder night, Curry asked, "Eventually, during the night, did you and Stan leave the Old Swiss House restaurant?"

"Yes, sir," Priscilla replied. "I asked a group if they would like to go have a nightcap . . ."

"Not responsive!" Haynes yelped. "A recitation and we object!"

"Did you and Stan have an occasion to engage in any

conversation with the two girls in the restaurant that you've testified about?" Curry asked.

"Yes, sir," said Priscilla. "They were quite excited about . . ."

"Not responsive!"

"Now, Mrs. Davis, when you saw what you thought to be bloody handprints there on the wall and the door facing the basement stairs, did you stay where you were or did you go somewhere else?"

"I started walking through the kitchen, the way I had come, with the intention of going to Dee's bedroom . . ."

"Not responsive! She was testifying as to what she was intending to do and that is subjective and we object to it."

"Mrs. Davis, when you went out of the kitchen and back toward the back door and Dee's room, did you notice anything unusual, or did anything happen at that point?"

"Well, just as I walked past the staircase, I hollered very loud . . ."

"Not responsive! The question was whether or not she noticed anything unusual, and now she's making a narration, and we object to it!"

The last was the only objection that Dowlen overruled, but it didn't matter. The ruling was irrelevant; the interruption was all.

In his effort to break up Priscilla's story into the smallest and least persuasive pieces, Haynes found an unlikely ally: Tim Curry. In a wildly misguided effort to make his star witness's story clearer, Curry began introducing photographs of the interior of the house just as Priscilla started to describe what happened when she saw the bloody handprint on the wall.

"I looked up to push the button," Priscilla began, her changeable voice quickly finding the right narrative gear, "and I noticed bloody fingerprints going down the wall . . ."

"All right," said Curry abruptly. "Now take your pointer and show the jury what wall that is that you are referring to."

"It would be the wall . . ." Priscilla fumbled with the pointer. "Well, right here . . ."

"Would that be at the head of the stairs to the basement?"

"Yes, sir."

"All right. Mrs. Davis, I will hand you what has been marked as State's Exhibit No. 40 and ask you if you recognize the area that that photograph depicts?"

"Yes, sir."

"And is that a true and accurate representation of the area that it depicts?"

"Yes, sir."

"All right. We will offer State's Exhibit No. 40 into evidence, Your Honor. Now, Mrs. Davis, I will also hand you State's Exhibit No. 41, and ask you if that picture accurately portrays what it depicts in the photograph as it was on August the 2nd, 1976?"

"Yes, sir."

"All right."

Priscilla tried to pick up the thread. "As I said, I noticed . . ."

But Curry cut her off again. "Well, don't tell me what you noticed. Just tell me, is this an accurate picture?"

"Yes."

"All right. Your Honor, the state would offer State's Exhibit No. 41 into evidence. Now, I believe you testified, Mrs. Davis, that when you started to turn the lights off, you saw something unusual, is that correct?"

One last time, Priscilla tried to pick up the story, now little more than a frayed thread in a vast web of legalities. "Yes, sir, it just kind of looked like a globby handprint or something . . ."

And so it went: a tiny fragment of the story, and then another round of pictures, another tiny fragment, and then a leaping *"Not responsive!"* from Haynes.

She describes Cullen Davis coming down the stairs from the laundry room hall dressed in black . . .

"Do those stairs go up or down?" asks Curry.

The question rips Priscilla out of the memory. "They go down," she mumbles.

Curry hands her another photograph, State's Exhibit No. 42. "Is that an accurate representation of what that photo depicts?"

And the story is lost again.

A few minutes later, Curry asks, "Did you notice anything unusual about the defendant's hands when you first saw him that night?"

"He had his hands together . . ." Priscilla begins, the memory quickly re-forming. In just a few words, she conveys a sense of foreboding, a sense that terrible things are about to happen. ". . . They were in front of him but I couldn't see them . . . they were wrapped in something shiny . . ."

Haynes starts to rise but doesn't have to. Curry breaks the spell for him. "Now, Mrs. Davis," he says disapprovingly, "you're going to have to listen to my question and you're going to have to try to answer as best you can the question I ask you."

Glacially, Curry's questions inch toward the killing of Stan Farr. Despite every effort to prevent it, the pain of the memory begins to show in Priscilla's face and voice.

"What happened after Cullen shot through the door? Did you hear any sound other than the shot at that time?"

"Yes, sir, I heard Stan go like 'Uh,' only much louder, and I knew he had been hit."

Haynes jumps to his feet. "*Not responsive!* It's subjective, it's certainly speculative, and we object."

But Priscilla presses on. She tells how Stan came out from behind the door and grabbed Cullen's wrist. "They started wrestling, kind of back and forth. And they turned to where I could . . . I was lying there and I could see Stan . . ."

"All right," Curry interjects. "Now, did all of this take place in your view?"

"Yes, sir."

"And approximately how far away from you was the defendant at this time?"

"Well, it wasn't very far," says Priscilla, her voice rushing ahead, "because all of a sudden, Cullen jerked away and shot him . . ."

Curry struggles to keep up. "All right. Now . . ."

". . . shot *Stan*." Priscilla is answering the questions faster than Curry can ask them.

". . . Was that also within your view?"

"Yes, and Stan . . ."

Curry throws up his hands, palms out. "Now, *Mrs. Davis*," he cries, bringing Priscilla to a dead stop. "You're going to have to slow down and let me ask the questions and you answer them."

There is a long silence and the story starts again.

"After you saw the defendant shoot Stan Farr," Curry asks, his voice struggling to recapture its bureaucratic monotone, "what did Stan Farr do at that time?"

"He turned around and he fell down."

"All right. Now, could you see him when he fell down?"

"Yes, sir."

"Did the defendant do anything further with regard to Stan Farr?"

"Stan was lying there on his chin looking at me and he was breathing like . . ." Priscilla opens her mouth wide and makes a horrible gasping sound. Suddenly, Stan Farr's dying sounds fill the courtroom.

Haynes leaps in the air. *"That's not responsive,"* he shouts. "We object to it as not responsive to the question. The question was what the defendant did, and now she's offering some other recitation which is not responsive!"

But this time Priscilla has come too close. She can let go of the story, but not the pain. She begins to cry.

"And what did he do, Mrs. Davis, after the defendant shot him?" Curry asks, resolutely impassive.

"He just looked at me, and then he closed his eyes and let his head down and died."

"And all of this took place in your presence and in your view, Mrs. Davis?"

"Yes, sir." Priscilla whimpers, lowering her head to hide her tears.

"Would you like to have a moment, Mrs. Davis?" Curry offers, showing a shadow of emotion for the first time.

"I'm sorry," she says, looking up. "I'll be okay."

But now it's Judge Dowlen's turn to interrupt her story—one last time. Only forty-five minutes after the last break, he calls a recess. The jury is led out of the box, the judge and lawyers abandon the courtroom, and the crowd quickly disperses for lunch, leaving Priscilla alone to relive the rest of that night in private.

Priscilla returned to the stand, dry-eyed, after lunch and tried to pick up the thread—the struggle with Cullen, the voices in the driveway, the flight down the hill, the pleas at a stranger's door, the ambulance ride—but with no more success than before. At one point, frustrated and angry, she continued her story over a defense objection, sending Haynes into a red-faced rage.

"This witness has deliberately, and for about the tenth time, offended the rules of the Court," he fumed.

Dowlen, whose country-boy curiosity about this big-city *femme fatale* had worn thin early in the proceedings, scowled at Priscilla and, without taking his angry eyes off her, told the bailiff to "please take the jury out for a moment." His voice was that of a father whose patience has finally run out and is about to take his errant child out behind the barn for an overdue spanking.

For the jury, it was the final proof—if any was needed—that Priscilla Davis was, as one juror later described her, a "bad girl."

That afternoon, as Curry finished his direct examination and the courtroom began to buzz with anticipation of Haynes's cross, Joe Shannon was sure of one thing: Priscilla Davis would never look better in the eyes of the jury than she did those first two days. In cross, Haynes would do everything he could to destroy her. Shannon was sure of it. The only question was: How far would he go?

Without turning his head, he glanced down at the other end of the table where Haynes was making some last-minute notes on a yellow legal pad before beginning. Shannon noticed that one of the defense lawyers, Steve Sumner, had switched chairs and was now sitting next to Haynes, whispering in his ear.

36

Of all the attorneys in the courtroom, Steve Sumner was Cullen Davis's personal favorite.

In part, he liked Sumner's jock credentials. Sumner had spent the first twenty years of his life on the playing fields. And not just as some dime-a-dozen high school football star (although he had done that too). Sumner had risen all the way to the very pinnacle of the sports world: *pro ball*. The Houston Astros had signed him to pitch professional baseball right out of high school. He didn't even bother going to college; he just went on doing what he did best: throwing baseballs.

Cullen considered himself something of a jock, too. He took exorbitant pride in his prowess as a skier, making a great show of "getting in shape" by doing endless knee-bends and ostentatiously running up and down stairs for a week before every trip to Aspen. Occasionally he would argue that pool, his other leisure activity, was also a sport, but even he didn't seem convinced. As every Texas teenage boy—whatever his age—knew, there were *really* only two sports: football and baseball. Their stars wore letter jackets and dated cheerleaders and got their pictures in the paper and never gave the time of day to a geek like Cullen Davis, who charged money to ride in his car. Now he had one of those stars working for him. It was just the kind of sweet payback that Cullen relished.

In part, he liked Sumner's looks. With his boyishly handsome face, thick dark hair, and bedroom brown eyes, Sumner decorated even the dullest meeting. He had the easy, jocular manner of a true jock: the effortless camaraderie and randy, puckish humor of an adolescent boy, mellowed to perfection by decades of locker-room chatter and ballpark bonhomie. He was like a visitor from an idyllic male world that all the men on the defense team (and there were only men) had fantasized, but none, least of all Cullen, had ever known.

In part, he liked Sumner's inexperience. His pro career lasted only five years—most of that spent bouncing from one farm club to another. In 1970, a serious shoulder injury abruptly ended his career in baseball and forced a return to school. But after five years of college and law school, with his sights set on politics, the only niche he could find was in the fiercely competitive minor leagues of civil practice: representing mostly poor clients with insurance claims. It was there, however, that a scout for the majors, Phil Burleson, found him and, impressed by his performance in a suit that Burleson was defending, hired him.

The defense of Cullen Davis was Sumner's first major case—ever. Friends like Roy Rimmer and even Burleson told Cullen, "You need somebody with more experience," but Cullen ignored them. He *wanted* someone without experience: someone who wouldn't know what the limits were; what was possible and impossible; what was fair to ask and what was unfair; or how far was too far.

In part, he liked Sumner's simplicity. Fellow attorneys, even those who liked him, conceded that "Steve is no rocket scientist." Smarter lawyers like Haynes, Mike Gibson, and even Burleson intimidated Cullen, put him on his guard. Sumner never surprised him, never challenged him, never questioned him too closely, and never left him behind.

But what Cullen liked most about Steve Sumner was his eagerness to please.

Just how eager, Phil Burleson discovered one night when he returned to his Dallas office to pick up mail and catch his breath from the frantic pretrial activity in Fort Worth. It was only two months after Cullen's arrest and the defense was in disarray. All of his energies were being consumed by the bond appeal; Cullen was steaming about being stuck in jail. No one had yet mentioned the name Racehorse Haynes.

Waiting for Burleson outside his office door was his young associate, Steve Sumner. Since hiring him less than a year before, Burleson hadn't heard much from his newest protégé except that he had taken a criminal case that no one else in the firm wanted—defending a man accused of stabbing a friend in the face and beating him to death with a hammer. Sumner got him off, though, arguing that his client had acted in self-defense.

That night, over drinks, Sumner pleaded with Burleson to make him a part of "the Cullen Davis team." He would do whatever Burleson needed. "Hell, if you need somebody to empty the trash," he vowed, "I'll become the greatest expert on trash emptying in town!" He was hyped.

In fact, what Burleson needed, he told Sumner, that night, was someone to run the investigation. Cullen wasn't happy with the man Burleson had hired, Joe Meyers, an ex-West Point, ex-FBI man. He didn't seem to be accomplishing anything; he wasn't talking to the right people; his background was too FBI, too by-the-book; he "wasn't getting into the substance of the case"; he "wasn't finding out enough of the kind of evidence that they were searching for."

Sumner got the message: they desperately needed dirt to discredit the prosecution's witnesses—Priscilla first and foremost—and Meyers wasn't producing it. It was time to try "other strategies."

"Why don't I come over and help out," Sumner suggested brightly, barely able to contain the rush of team spirit.

After mulling it over, Burleson agreed—but only on a temporary basis.

It was all the opening Sumner needed.

That night he stayed up until dawn, reading every file he could find and writing a twenty-five-page memo on "how the investigation needed to be redirected." A few days later, he met Cullen in his cell at the Tarrant County Jail.

Cullen received him stiffly but cordially in his "jail whites," the white overalls with "Tarrant County Jail" on the back that all prisoners wore. Except for a small television, his cell was standard-issue: a seatless toilet, a sink, and a metal bunk with a mattress "no thicker than a good steak." Despite persistent rumors of special treatment, the only apparent "luxuries" being furnished by Sheriff Lon Evans were space and solitude. Cullen wasn't just the only prisoner in his cell, he was the only prisoner on the floor.

"I like your report," Cullen said tersely, barely moving his lips. He especially liked the dark recommendation to "go much more deeply into the backgrounds of the prosecution witnesses."

At an earlier, similar, meeting, Cullen had given Joe Meyers an idea of what he expected from an investigator. "You know how some of these lawyers—not necessarily the prosecutors, of course—but you know how they talk back and forth on the telephone?" Cullen had suggested cryptically, his syntax beginning to collapse on itself. "And it sure would be nice to know what their conversation is . . ."

Meyers's response had been quick and angry: "If you want to tap somebody, you go do it yourself. 'Cause you're the one who's going to court and be tried for wiretapping! I'm sure as hell not. I sent more wiretappers to the penitentiary than any other agent in the Bureau!"

Unfazed, Cullen continued: There was a lot of money involved in this case. And money, as everyone knew, could be a powerful motivator—"perhaps the most powerful there is." An investigator who was willing to "imply that money would be available" might find it a whole lot easier to get witnesses to come forward with the right information.

But Meyers, as Sumner knew, had lost the job.

37

Cullen Davis had one job and one job only for Steve Sumner. "You know, the reason Joe Meyers is gone is that he wouldn't listen to me," Cullen said, smiling his reptilian smile. "I told him to forget about the prosecution witnesses, forget about the hospital personnel and the cops on the scene."

Sumner nodded his head enthusiastically, unsure of what was coming next but eager regardless.

"I'll give you the same advice I gave Meyers," Cullen continued, "only I hope you pay more attention to it." He stood up and looked down with the coldest, hardest eyes Sumner had ever seen on a man. "Forget everything else," he said. "Just get the dirt on Priscilla."

That directive had brought Sumner to the dingy offices of a down-and-out Dallas lawyer to meet a man named Sonny Fortner. Rumor had it that Fortner and his wife Debbie were married at the mansion and that his car was parked in the garage the night of the murders. From this, Sumner concluded that Sonny had the dirt on Priscilla. A Charles Manson lookalike with long, stringy black hair, wild eyes, splotchy, semitransparent skin, and a wired, wasted, much-abused little body, Sonny was trying, in a manic, unfocused monologue, to convince Sumner that he was in a perfect position to provide the defense with all kinds of information with regard to Priscilla's activities and drug use and "goings-on" at the mansion, information that could help Cullen in the divorce case as well as the criminal case. He even offered a free sample of his wares: "Priscilla told me that she was going to take Cullen for everything he's got."

And what did he want in exchange for his "help"? Sumner wanted to know.

Sonny demurred. He knew Cullen was a generous man to his friends. Did he need to say more?

Sumner was new at the job, but not that new. Offering to pay a witness for his testimony, beyond simple expenses, was illegal. "How can we be sure that the information you have is helpful?" he asked. "First we got to know what you *have*."

Sonny sputtered. "Well, I'm sure as hell not going to *give* you anything."

Nevertheless, at the end of the meeting, Sonny agreed to put Sumner together with his wife Debbie to "check out" Sonny's claim. But he wouldn't let the two of them meet alone. He insisted on being there to protect his interests.

Debbie Fortner didn't look anything like the drug moll Sumner expected after meeting Sonny. An attractive, articulate brunette in her early twenties, Debbie could have been a cheerleader. She and Sonny seemed to come from two different worlds—except for the high-tension wire that ran between their eyes, from her frightened, mesmerized glances to his wild, mesmerizing glare.

"I got very close to Priscilla," she said, "and I used to stay up lots of nights all night talking with her."

Sumner got right to the point: What about Priscilla's use of alcohol?

Debbie couldn't wait to answer the question: "We can both testify that Priscilla stayed drunk all the time! She was always drinking and taking pills from the moment she woke up to the time she went to bed."

When Sumner asked if Debbie would be willing to testify about Priscilla's drug habit, she eagerly agreed, volunteering cheerfully that she had seen *both* Stan and Priscilla smoke pot and snort coke *all the time*!

And take a lot of pills, Sonny prompted.

And take a lot of pills, Debbie added.

Sumner asked about Priscilla's sex life.

"Priscilla told me lots of times how she used to run around on Cullen," Sonny offered, then added, *"while* they were married."

"She would have sex with *anybody*!" Debbie interjected.

"Just throw a little money on Bubba Palmer," Sonny suggested, "and he'll spill his guts."

Sumner didn't say anything, just wrote down the name.

Debbie added: "Another time, at one of Priscilla's parties, there were about ten guys sitting around the pool, and Priscilla took all her clothes off and jumped in the pool naked."

Did you see that yourself? Sumner wanted to know.

Debbie looked flustered. "Well, actually, I was in the kitchen when this was going on."

"Well, *I* saw it," Sonny added quickly.

Sumner asked Debbie what she knew about "Priscilla being AC–DC?"

"Priscilla never made advances toward me, or did anything that I can remember that way." A shadow of disappointment crossed Sumner's face. "But Judy McCrory was really weird and it wouldn't surprise me if Judy and Priscilla were gay for each other."

When Sumner asked for the names of others who might have "useful" information, Sonny and Debbie agreed that the two best sources by far were Larry and Sandy Myers. "Larry actually had group sex with Priscilla and W. T. Rufner and another girl," Sonny assured him. There was just one problem. Larry Myers was currently a guest of the state at the Texas Department of Corrections in Huntsville. Before he would be willing to talk, he, too, would need some "help."

"Larry's really down and desperate," said Sonny sadly. With a little "help" (that word again), however, Larry "could testify that Stan approached him to do some cocaine deals."

Sumner made a mental note: Stan Farr, drug dealer.

At the end of the interview, Sumner gingerly posed the question: "Why are you willing to give us this information?"

Sonny smiled. "Larry and I talked about maybe getting Cullen to help pay for some other lawyers to help Larry on his appeal. Larry doesn't think his lawyer is doing a good job." Another smile, yellow and ugly: "Larry and I aren't sure we can help Cullen in the murder case but we can save him a hell of a lot of money in the divorce."

And what about Sandy Myers?

"She lived at the mansion for a long time and was really tight with Priscilla," said Debbie. "She may have been the closest to Priscilla during all that time. She would be the best person to talk to. She'll give you the straight story."

Sonny grunted in agreement but reminded Sumner to talk to Larry before hitting on Sandy.

38

Sumner didn't recognize the slender woman with the wild auburn hair who approached him at the Rangoon Racquet Club on the evening of March 2, 1977, and purred in his ear, "I hear you want to talk to me."

"Who are you?" As if names mattered.

"I'm Sandy Myers."

He sure as hell did want to talk to her.

She slipped her supple body into a chair next to him.

To his own surprise, he stuck to business: How long had she lived at the mansion?

"I moved in about the same time as W. T.," she explained. "I was also there after W. T. and Priscilla split up, when Priscilla was going with Stan Farr." This was obviously going to be a damn valuable source, Sumner thought, and immediately began assessing her potential as a witness. Her tone was matter-of-fact, guileless. She was poised and, beneath too much makeup, not unattractive. Sumner decided on the spot that she would make a great witness.

What kind of drugs did Priscilla do? he wanted to know.

Sandy thought for a minute. "I only saw her take pills because of the ski accident. That's the only thing I know about."

There was a pause as Sumner recovered. Not even marijuana? he prompted.

"No," she said firmly. "Priscilla never used marijuana." Suddenly her guileless tone grated.

Sumner fumbled, covering his disarray with sarcasm. "I am sure you never saw so much as a marijuana cigarette pass the threshold of that mansion, did you, Sandy?"

"There was some marijuana in the house, on occasion," Sandy agreed, "but Priscilla didn't smoke it. She hated the stuff—it made her sleepy."

Until a better tactic came to him, Sumner pressed the sarcasm. "Then I am sure you never saw Priscilla snort cocaine, did you, Sandy?"

Very reluctantly, Sandy yielded. "Yes. I have seen Priscilla snort coke, but it was very rarely."

Sumner quickly changed the subject, trying to get the conversation back under control. "What about the sex parties and orgies at the house?"

Sandy's almond-shaped eyes went wide with indignation. "That is the farthest thing from the truth. I never heard of anything like that!"

The interview was not going the way it was supposed to.

Sumner tried hitting closer to home: Well, then, didn't your husband Larry have sex with Priscilla?

Absolutely not! Sandy huffed. Beneath the pancake makeup, her face was turning red with anger—genuine anger. Who told him that? she demanded, more out of disgust than curiosity. But Sumner took it a different way. She was fishing for information, he wrote in his notes of the interview: "When anybody starts trying to get more information from me than they are giving, I can't trust them. I didn't trust her at all."

Sumner changed the subject again: What were the parties in the house like?

She claimed not to know anything about what went on at the parties. And neither did Priscilla. She was just trying to be a good hostess, Sandy explained. "If you knew her you'd know what a down-to-earth person she really is. Actually, I don't think she ever really felt comfortable at parties."

Sumner contrived a smirk. "Right. That's exactly the image I have of Priscilla—the shy, retiring type, who longs for a quiet life in the country." The interview with Priscilla in which she claimed that her only ambition in life was to have a vine-covered cottage had just been published. No one who knew Priscilla well took it seriously.

Neither did Sandy. "No," she said to Sumner's invocation of the image, "that even bothered me."

Again, it was the wrong answer: too tempered, too even-handed. Sumner felt frustrated and betrayed. Sandy would have been the perfect witness for the defense. Now she threatened to become the perfect witness for the prosecution.

Sumner finally blurted out, "I don't believe I can get a straight answer from you. I think you'd just go back and report it to Priscilla." Steve looked her right in the eye and said, "I think that's exactly what's going on."

Sandy looked him back, right in the eye, calm and serene, and told him these *were* the straight answers. He just didn't want to hear them.

It was more than Sumner could take. He got up and left.

He rushed back to his room at the Green Oaks Motel and phoned Sonny Fortner. What the hell was going on with Sandy Myers, he demanded to know. She sounded like Priscilla's press agent.

Sonny didn't seem surprised at all: Sumner hadn't talked to Larry first, as Sonny had instructed him to do. "I told you so," Sonny scolded. The message was clear:

If Sumner wanted this information, he was going to have to get it Sonny's way.

Sumner wondered out loud if maybe Sandy was working for Priscilla.

Sonny laughed: "Naw," he said. She just hadn't been brought into line yet.

On March 7, 1977, Sumner drove to Huntsville and met with Larry Myers in a visitors room so noisy he feared his tape recorder wouldn't pick up Myers's soft voice.

He tried warming Myers up with some soft pitches. How had Myers met Priscilla?

Myers ran impatiently through a summary of their relationship: how W. T. introduced them; how he moved into the house soon after W. T. and Sandy were already there; how he stayed on and off for another six months, until he got busted. "Now," he said, "let's get down to business."

He leaned closer to Sumner's tape recorder. "Ever since Priscilla and Cullen separated, she's wanted to hurt him. She and Bev were so prejudiced, they were sure Cullen did the shootings *even though they really couldn't see the killer*."

He rocked back in his chair, put his hands behind his head, and smiled, indicating he felt *this* was the kind of information that would help Sumner out.

After that, however, most of what Myers had to say —the litany of drugs and sex—sounded like what Sumner had heard already from Sonny and Debbie Fortner—exactly like.

Sumner was beginning to think the long drive to Huntsville had been a waste when Myers dropped his bomb. Did Sumner know about the pictures of Priscilla and W. T.? Myers's face broke into a leering smile.

Sumner in fact had heard rumors of some homemade pornography starring the state's key witness. What kind of pictures? he asked, fighting to hide an adrenaline rush.

Myers smirked. Like the one of W. T. with a sock over

his dick. Or of them "doing it" in the lake at the Willie Nelson Picnic back in 1974.

Doing what? Sumner pressed.

Myers stuck his finger in his mouth: Get it?

Sumner got it, and he wanted those pictures. "Sure. I'd like to see those." He tried to sound nonchalant. "How can I get a look at those?"

Myers's smirk bent into a smile. "Get Sonny Fortner to call me, and I'll get them to him, and he'll give them to you."

The same curious thing happened when Sumner asked how to contact other witnesses. Myers gave him a list of people to follow up on—Bart Newton, Becky Ferguson, Marilyn Baker, Valerie somebody—but when Sumner asked how to contact them, Myers turned evasive.

"They're all my friends," he explained. "They'd be willing to help you only if they think you're trying to help me."

What kind of help did Myers need?

"I'm doing thirty years here," he said. "My conviction was just affirmed in the Court of Criminal Appeals, and I'm too broke to hire a lawyer. I need help on my appeal." In short, like Fortner, he wanted money.

Sumner and Cullen had anticipated it would come to this, and they had an answer already worked out. I can't give you an answer on that, Sumner would reply: We have to see how helpful you are first before we can make any promises.

Myers insisted he could be very helpful—even more helpful than he had been so far.

Sumner saw his opening. If Myers really wanted to be helpful, he hinted, he would talk to Sandy.

The deal was on the table.

Not to worry, Myers assured Sumner with another bent grin. He'd bring Sandy into line.

When Cullen read Sumner's memorandum on the prison meeting, his eyes narrowed as he read Myers's description of W. T.'s biker friends partying and plundering the mansion. He also identified "Valerie somebody" as Valerie Marazzi, a friend of Dee's and Bev Bass's. "I'll bet she could provide a lot of information about Bev using drugs," Cullen suggested. (Sumner had no idea where Cullen got his leads, and never asked.)

Finally, Cullen reached the part of the memorandum that related Myers's request for money. Cullen didn't blink.

39

Sumner met with Sandy Myers again on Monday, March 14. He had wanted to meet with her alone, but Sonny Fortner wouldn't allow it. He wanted the meeting at his house and he wanted to be there.

Sumner began with the same questions as before.

Did she see Priscilla using drugs?

"Oh, yes," Sandy chirped, "I saw her myself. I saw Priscilla doing cocaine and heroin *all the time*. Almost every time I was with Priscilla, she was popping pills and taking drugs . . ."

What about booze?

"*All the time*. Priscilla would start drinking at eight in the morning and never stop."

Any marijuana?

Reefers gave Priscilla headaches, Sandy conceded apologetically, but she *really* was into cocaine and heroin. "She said cocaine and heroin made her horny. Which is pretty funny, 'cause Priscilla was kind of horny all the time, anyway." Sandy smiled strangely between the dark, parted curtain of her hair.

She told Sumner about a trip she and Priscilla had taken to Dallas—the night Cullen moved out of the house: They'd driven to Billy Bob Harris's house, where he was giving a party for the Righteous Brothers, who were in town. Priscilla left Sandy there at the party and went to a motel with some of the players from the Cowboys.

Priscilla had also pimped for her, Sandy volunteered, setting her up with rich dudes in Dallas.

Group sex?

"Oh, yeah, sure. Priscilla had group sex all the time," Sandy chirped. She didn't elaborate.

Eventually, she looked at Sonny and asked if she had left anything out.

Sumner looked at Sonny Fortner in bewilderment. The questions were the same ones Sumner had asked at their previous encounter, but her responses couldn't have been more different. In his summary of the meeting, Sumner wrote: "She was like a whole different person."

As the meeting ended, Sandy, the former drama major, seemed pleased with the way the audition had gone. She sensed she had won a starring role.

But no one seemed more pleased than Sonny Fortner. He had delivered on his promise. Now it was time for Sumner to deliver on his.

The way Sonny saw it, Cullen needed information, Sonny had it—or at least could put him together with those who did. Sonny needed money, *Cullen* had it—or at least could put him in touch with someone who did, someone at a distance from the defense team (even Sonny knew the lawyers couldn't pay him directly; they had to preserve their deniability). If Cullen could get away with murder, Sonny figured, surely he could get away with palming money to a friend. The only question was how much to ask for. The first figure that came to him was $100,000. Surely Cullen wouldn't miss a measly hundred grand. Then he and Sumner flew to Oklahoma City to talk to Bart Newton. They flew on one of Cullen's Learjets. After that, the price went up—way up.

"I want five million," Sonny told Sumner as he held out the pictures of W. T. and Priscilla that Sumner had been hungrily awaiting. He counted out five snapshots and then stopped. There was a whole lot more, he said, but that's all Sumner would get until Sonny saw the money.

Sumner swallowed hard. He had been prepared for a money demand, but nothing like this. "That's completely out of reason," he said quietly.

If Sumner wanted the pictures, Sonny pressed, affixing his bent smile, that was the price.

Fortunately, Sumner and Cullen had worked out a reply for just such a moment and it finally kicked in. "Well, we might be interested in these," said Sumner, "so let me take them back to Haynes and Burleson and let them decide if these are something we need. If anybody's interested . . ." —he decided the more left unsaid, the better—"we'll see . . ."

Fortner's demand touched off a panic at the next meeting of the defense team. Sumner had a lot of explaining to do—certainly to Haynes. At his first and only encounter with Fortner, Haynes had warned Sumner, "This guy's a flake!" But in his eagerness to please Cullen, Sumner had refused to see it. "Yeah," he countered, "but he's the first witness we have with personal knowledge of Priscilla's use of drugs." Now they were again facing the ugly prospect of a "breakaway" witness—another David McCrory.

No one could have been worried about Sonny going to the prosecution or even the press. He had about as much credibility as his lookalike, Charles Manson—even less than McCrory, if that was possible. Besides, the defense had done nothing wrong, at least nothing provable. There were no written commitments, no record of payments, no trail of canceled checks. If, in his zeal, Sumner had stepped over the line, well . . .

Of much greater concern was salvaging the other witnesses. The defense could withstand a collateral row in the press far more easily than the loss of all that testimony attacking the prosecution's star witness. Just how strong was Sonny's hold over the other witnesses Sumner had "developed"? Could they be persuaded, intimidated, or seduced into breaking from him?

Sumner assured him they could.

Late into the night, Burleson, Sumner, and Cullen laid out the plan for damage control.

At the first opportunity, Sumner met with Sonny and returned the photographs of Priscilla and W. T. "I don't know . . ." he said cryptically, implying that Haynes and Burleson had shown little interest in them. In fact, he had already sent the photos in secret to Dallas (they would have been recognized in a Fort Worth photo lab) and had them copied and blown up into huge prints. Then, in so many words, he told Fortner to take a hike.

A few days later, on April 21, 1977, Sumner drove to Huntsville to see Larry Myers again. After getting the brush-off, Sonny had put out the word to shut down the "information machine," especially Sandy Myers. Sumner knew that the only way to cut Sandy loose from Fortner was to cut Larry loose. He began by telling Myers his version of the break with Sonny. He reminded Myers that, "always, from the beginning of our discussions, we only talked about the *prospect* of helping you on appeal." But Sonny had "become paranoid," said Sumner, and demanded money. "Apparently he would prefer to have money rather than have us help you on your appeal."

Sumner could read the doubts in the deepening crease of Myers's brow as he recounted the story. Had Sonny betrayed him? Was Sonny trying to strike a separate deal with Cullen at Larry's expense?

How much had Sonny asked for? Myers wanted to know.

"Five million," said Sumner. Myers's eyes bugged out. Clearly, Sonny hadn't shared *that* detail with him. "Of course, I explained to him that we were not going to purchase the photographs, and"—if that was a condition of turning them over—"then you would have to obtain your own legal assistance."

In fact, Sumner knew that a motion for rehearing in Myers's case had been denied just the day before. Clearly, the desperation not to spend another ten or fifteen years in Huntsville was, at that moment, far more compelling than any pact with Sonny Fortner.

"You know, there are still a number of appeal options open to you," Sumner pressed. "But, of course, at this time there is absolutely no work being done by us on behalf of you and your appeal because of Sonny's present attitude." The message was clear: Sonny's greed was killing Myers's appeal.

Unless, of course, Myers was willing to cooperate—without Sonny.

That was the carrot. Now came the stick. Sumner showed Myers an article from the *Fort Worth Star-Telegram*: "Defense subpoenas principals for Davis hearings." One of the "principals" listed was "Sandy Guthrie Myers." At the sight of it, Myers leapt out of his chair. Sumner didn't need to explain what it meant. Sandy was on probation for selling cocaine. Now the police and the prosecutors would be after her, looking for some excuse, any excuse, to bust her. Myers also saw the implicit threat. All Sumner had to do was subpoena him and *his* name would end up in the paper too, and if that happened, his chances on appeal would be zero.

Of course, no one *had* to know that he had cooperated with the defense.

Sumner handed Myers an affidavit to sign.

There was one more thing. "Has the D.A.'s office already been down to talk to you?" Sumner asked. He knew they hadn't.

"Not yet," said Myers.

"I'm sure they'll be down to talk to you soon. Now I want you to know what your rights are." In fact, Sumner was only interested in one of Myers's rights: "You don't have to talk to them." Again, the message was unspoken but clear: It would be best for everyone if the D.A.'s office didn't hear about this or any other conversation between Myers and Cullen Davis's lawyers.

Did Myers understand? Steve asked.

Myers nodded.

So, *now* did Larry have a problem with Sandy talking to them? Sumner tested.

Myers shook his head.

But Sonny had already gotten to Sandy.

"Steve?" Sumner recognized Sandy Myers's voice on the other end of the line, dangerously close to hysteria. She was in trouble. "Steve, I just got a call from Debbie Fortner. She and Sonny are planning to go to Florida on August 12 and they want me to go with them." The trial was scheduled to begin in Amarillo on August 20. Sonny was planning to disappear and make sure Sandy disappeared along with him. No money, no testimony. If Sumner was going to subpoena Sonny or Debbie, he was going to have to do it soon.

Sandy saw it too. Sonny wanted her out of town, and if she didn't go, he might suspect a double-cross. And you know Sonny, she added ominously; he would do *anything* if he thought someone were trying to pull a double-cross on him.

Sandy reminded Sumner of what had happened to Rick Self, a small-change drug dealer on Fort Worth's west side. Crippled from birth with polio, Self had only limited use of his legs and made a point of staying away from water. Larry Myers recruited him for a big mescaline and acid deal at a local motel, but the deal went bust when Myers jumped the buyer and discovered he was a narc. Although the police had helicopters out looking for them, both Myers and Self escaped. But a few days later, Self turned up facedown in a swimming pool.

At first, Sumner dismissed such dark forebodings as melodrama, the fevered imaginings of a frustrated drama student and novitiate witch. Sandy needed to feel important, important enough to be murdered on the eve of the trial. Suddenly all the attention would be focused, not on wrongly accused multimillionaire Cullen Davis or his wrongly accusing wife, but on slain star witness Sandy Myers.

On August 19, the day before the trial was scheduled

to begin in Amarillo, Sandy called Sumner in a state of panic. She had received a phone call at home the previous evening. The caller, a man, said, "Amarillo, haha," then laughed diabolically and hung up. This wasn't the first call, she reported. There had been many mysterious hang-ups during the three weeks leading up to the trial. Someone didn't want her to testify.

That morning, she had gone to her mailbox and found inside a small plastic gravestone inscribed "R.I.P." Several days before, someone had left a miniature toy coffin, complete with skeleton, in the same mailbox. It was a new mailbox with no name on it. One night, someone threw rocks at her window; another night, someone beat at her door. She was in mortal danger!

Sandy's friends and neighbors had other explanations. The girl she was living with, a heroin junkie, kept even worse company than Sandy. Neither she nor her ex-con boyfriend were happy about Sandy's repeated threats to kick them out of the apartment or leave and stick them with the lease. As for the Halloween toys, neighbors and roommates as far back as the mansion had seen boxes filled with similar ghoulish trinkets all around Sandy's room.

Others may have been skeptical, but not Steve Sumner. On the eve of the trial, he spirited Sandy away to an unknown "safe house" (actually, the Dusty Trail Apartments in Dallas) and began billing all of her expenses plus a comfortable daily allowance to the defense. Sumner insisted that Sandy's life was in danger and that such an "unorthodox" move was essential for her safety—he called it "the Cullen Davis Witness Protection Program."

Meanwhile, every bizarre detail of every bizarre story, and every melodramatic threat, were dutifully recorded and reported in Sumner's memos. Gradually, Sumner began to add his own stories to the memos: reports of death threats against *him*, anonymous calls in the night, break-ins at his motel room, mysterious disappearances, and clandestine meetings. The secretaries at Burleson, Pate & Gibson who typed the reports began to wonder if their Mr. Sumner had been "undercover" too long; if he too had fallen victim to the same strange, self-dramatizing disease that afflicted Sandy Myers.

But one person didn't question the reports at all: the client. The more melodramatic, outrageous, paranoid, and damning of Priscilla, the more hungrily Cullen Davis devoured them.

Finally, only days before Priscilla was scheduled to take the stand, after repeated pleadings from Sumner, Haynes skimmed some of the key reports. With all the pretrial motions and maneuvering and then the eight-week ordeal of picking a jury, he had barely had a chance to think about the facts of the case, much less devise a trial strategy. On August 20, after the prosecution made its opening statement to the jury, Haynes rose to tell a startled courtroom that he wouldn't bother with an opening statement for the defense—at least not until after the state rested its case. The truth was, he didn't *have* a defense yet.

Priscilla may have been mauled in the papers and in local gossip, but her story of the murders—Haynes always referred to them as "the shootings" or, better yet, "the incident"—had remained more or less untarnished through almost a year of hearings, interviews, and a string of interlocutory appeals all the way up to the United States Supreme Court. If that story emerged from the crossexamination still unshaken, the defense was as good as lost. And Haynes would need more than innuendo and general character assassination to shake it. He would need *facts*— or the rough equivalent.

That's what he found in Sumner's reports. When he finished reading them, he looked up and smiled at Sumner: "This is damn good stuff"—just the kind of stuff to inflame what Sumner had already taken to calling, fondly, "our racist, redneck jury."

40

Richard Haynes looked out over the rim of his half-moon glasses and smiled at the petite figure in the witness chair. "Now, Mrs. Davis," he began slowly, "would you please give the jury the benefit of the approximate number of times you have gone back over the story that you have repeated today?"

It was a standard defense opening, nothing flashy, nothing tricky, delivered in Haynes's most benign baritone.

But Priscilla had already made up her mind: She wasn't going to give an inch. "Oh, I really couldn't give you an exact figure," she said in a girlish singsong voice that sounded oddly seductive. "There haven't been innumerable times."

"I'm talking about the *number* of times," Haynes pressed without appearing to press. "How many times are we talking about? A dozen?"

The battle was joined. It had taken less than a minute.

"I wouldn't think a dozen," Priscilla scoffed. "It was just . . ."

"Excuse me," Haynes cut in, his smile already wilting. "I'm just interested in the number of times that you have gone over it."

Priscilla wasn't sure why he wanted a specific number, but if he wanted it, she didn't want to give it to him. "I really have not kept track," she said.

Joe Shannon had feared all along that Priscilla would do just this—try to match wits with Haynes, joust and parry as if it was a bedroom confrontation, wiggle out of tough questions, quibble over words, "zing" Haynes every chance she got. If she had been Shannon's witness, he would have told her: Just answer the questions, don't try to play tricks, you'll only get caught. The rules are stacked in the lawyer's favor on cross. You'll only end up looking evasive.

Oh, God, did she look evasive!

Haynes wanted to know how many times Priscilla had met with prosecutors to "review" her testimony. "A few times? Numerous times? More than numerous times?"

"Numerous times," Priscilla obliged.

"Dozens?"

"Several times."

Haynes did a double-take for the jury. " 'Several' means what, one or two?"

"Well, over a year's time, you know . . ."

"Yes . . ."

". . . it would be quite a few times, I'm sure."

Another double-take. "How often? I'm only looking for a number, ma'am."

After a long pause: "Very few times."

Shannon died a little death and Haynes did yet another double-take. "Very *few* times, you say?"

"Yes, sir."

"Which means four, five, six in the past year?"

"I would say numerous times."

Haynes looked at the jury and screwed up his face in exaggerated bewilderment. "Perhaps once a month, is that an unfair . . ."

"I really wouldn't be able to put an exact figure on it."

Haynes dropped the subject. He had made his point.

In Shannon's worst nightmares—and there had been many of them—it had not gone this badly. And it was only just beginning.

Haynes continued to pick at Priscilla's letter-perfect retelling of the events of the murder night. Was it the result of a vivid memory or countless rehearsals?

Had she given her version of the events of August 2 and 3, 1976, to friends?

Please, Priscilla, thought Shannon, answer yes or no, yes or no. It's okay if you talked to friends about the murder night. It wouldn't be natural not to. The jury will understand.

But Priscilla wasn't tuned to Shannon's wavelength. "No. Well, maybe in some . . . it would . . . not in great detail."

Haynes rolled his eyes in the direction of the jury. "All right," he said, his tone suddenly sarcastic. "Just so I don't misunderstand you, Mrs. Davis, you say, 'no,' 'maybe,' 'not in great detail,' which means, does it not, that you have given some version of the events of that night in 1976 to friends, does it not?"

"I guess I would have to say yes . . . ," she said, ". . . more or less."

Shannon cringed.

When Haynes asked Priscilla if her personal attorney had been present in the courtroom during her testimony, a strange look crossed her face and an even stranger sound came out of her mouth: a long, low, empty sound like a dial tone slowed down to a moan: "Uhhhhhhh." Meanwhile, her eyes appealed to Joe Shannon for help—a look that shouted, "What do I do now?" As soon as their eyes met, Shannon looked away.

It was too late.

"I noticed when I asked you that question, Mrs. Davis, you looked to the Counsel table." Haynes had seen. "They're not looking back at you, are they? You're not seeking some signal or device, are you, or clue as to what . . ."

Shannon jumped to his feet. "Your Honor, we object to any implication that the State has given this witness any signals whatsoever. It's highly improper."

Dowlen scowled. "I've seen no evidence of any kind of activity on the part of the State."

Haynes smiled slyly. "I saw none except the witness, Your Honor." He turned to the witness chair and repeated the question: "Your personal attorney, Mr. Ronald Aultman, has been present in the courtroom since you began testifying, has he not, Mrs. Davis?"

"Uhhhhhhh." That sound again, even longer this time, as if the question called for deep thought or, worse, quick thinking. "Yes, sir," she finally answered.

Shannon wondered what the problem could be. What was Priscilla trying to avoid? There was no reason to hide Aultman's presence. Any good lawyer in his position would have come to hear his client's testimony. Was there something he didn't know about? And what was that awful sound?

Haynes pressed: "And you have had occasion to talk to him about the testimony you were going to give, have you not?"

"Uhhhhhhhhh . . ."

If she had tried, she could not have devised a sound that sabotaged her credibility more effectively, Shannon thought. She was as good as saying to the jury: "I need time to think. I can't give you a straight, honest, spontaneous answer, but if I stall a few seconds maybe I can concoct one." Was it the painkillers she was taking, Shannon wondered, or maybe the pain itself?

Toward the end of the first day of cross-examination, Haynes set out to show that the woman before them was not the grief-stricken mother she appeared to be. In fact, she wasn't much of a mother at all. He began by extracting a chronology of her marriage to Jasper Baker that made it clear that her first child, Dee, was conceived out of wedlock.

Then he turned to her second husband. "As a consequence of your divorce from Mr. Wilborn in 1968," Haynes pursued, "did you retain custody of the two children born to that union: Jack Wilborn, Jr., and Andrea Wilborn?"

Priscilla answered reluctantly. "No, sir."

"And as a consequence of that divorce, did you have the custody of Dee Davis?" Haynes had a gleam in his eye.

"Uhhhhhh . . . yes, sir," Priscilla hedged, "after Cullen and I were married."

Haynes condescended to a smile. "Yes, but at the termination of the marriage between yourself and Jack Wilborn, you fought for custody of your children and lost. Isn't that true, Mrs. Davis?" Poor woman, his tone said, she wasn't even allowed to keep her child from a *previous* marriage.

Priscilla tried to fight back. "It was only a temporary order."

But it was useless. "And then later you agreed to let Mr. Wilborn have custody?"

Priscilla shifted in her seat. It had been a long day; she was in pain. "Yes."

Haynes triumphantly: "So you lost them and *then* you agreed to give them up, correct?"

Priscilla wanted to scream—and it wasn't the pain. "But, I had no choice, the circumstances . . ." She wanted to explain that it was Cullen who persuaded her to give up Dee, Jackie, and Andrea. It was Cullen's idea, not hers. Cullen had bargained away her children to protect Stinky's precious empire. She hadn't wanted it that way, she had cried for days, but Cullen had promised he would work it out. That man sitting not far from Haynes at the defense end of the big counsel table, that greasy little man with the foul smile and the empty eyes, *he* was the one. Yes, she had been guilty of being stupid, of being young, of being in love. Maybe she wasn't everything a mother was supposed to be to her children, but, goddammit, she didn't *kill* them!

But neither Haynes nor Dowlen nor even Curry would let her say any of that.

"No, I didn't ask you why," Haynes cut her off sharply. "I just want to know if it's a fact that you lost custody of your children?"

"Yes," she surrendered.

Shannon looked at the jury looking at Priscilla: her big, bright blonde hair, her Neiman-Marcus dress—a different one every day—her street-kid combativeness, her honky-tonk seductiveness, her wannabe gentility, and he knew what the jurors were thinking: This was a girl from the wrong side of the tracks who would do anything— *anything*—not to be thrown back. In a single afternoon, Haynes had managed to undermine both her credibility and her respectability. He had cast all of her testimony and all of her denials into doubt.

And he was only beginning.

41

"Now, Mrs. Davis," Haynes began the second day, "you are on medication now, are you not?"

"Yes, sir."

"And one of the medications you are on is Percodan?"

"Uh . . . yes, sir, that's true."

"And that is a medication that you have been on for some period of time, have you not?"

"Yes, sir." Priscilla rearranged herself in the witness chair. She had known this was coming, but that didn't help. She thought about what her divorce lawyers had told her again and again: The Percodan thing can hurt you. Whatever you do, don't say anything that might jeopardize the divorce. Remember. *Fifty million* hangs in the balance.

Haynes interrupted her thoughts. "You commenced taking Percodan when, ma'am?"

"When I broke my ankle snow skiing. I believe it was five years ago this last March." Priscilla wondered how much the defense knew.

"Did you take it on a daily basis while you were in a cast?"

"I didn't necessarily take it, unless I was uncomfortable."

"And when you got out of the cast, did you continue taking the Percodan?"

"Uh . . . I believe I did for a short while when I was still on crutches, as I said, if I needed it."

"When you got off the crutches, did you continue to take the Percodan?"

"For a short while, I believe."

"Did you then stop taking Percodan?"

"Yes, sir."

She hoped that might be the end of it, but Haynes wasn't about to let go. Slowly, methodically, he continued to explore her long, intimate relationship with painkillers. From the back injury in 1971 to the broken ankle in 1973 to cosmetic surgery in 1976, the prescriptions ran in an unbroken chain through the murders up almost to the start of the trial.

"How many Percodan did your doctors usually prescribe?" Haynes inquired.

"Like, possibly, a dozen."

"And how often did you take them?"

"I don't recall. I didn't take them unless I was in severe pain."

"You didn't take them every day?"

"It would depend on whether I was in pain."

"When you would get your prescriptions refilled, how many Percodans would you receive?"

"Thirty." By now, Priscilla knew she was in trouble. Her plan had been only to *minimize* her problem with Percodan, fudge it a little and hope Haynes would let it pass. It was only a painkiller, after all, not cocaine. How important could it be that she had a weakness for prescription drugs? It certainly didn't have anything to do with Cullen's guilt.

But the plan had gone awry. Now, suddenly, she found herself in midair, untethered from the truth, in a kind of free-fall of lies.

"Did you have any idea at all, Mrs. Davis, that you could become addicted to the use of Percodan?"

"No, sir."

"No physician ever told you that?"

"Uhhhhh . . . it's possible. I have been told that it's like anything, alcohol or anything, if one overdoes it. It can have harmful effects."

But Haynes refused to be distracted. "I think my question was, do you recall that a physician told you that?"

The little lies hadn't worked, so, in desperation, Priscilla tried a big one. "I have never been told that I'm addicted to Percodan," she announced firmly, "nor am I addicted to it." There, she thought, I said it, it's over. Even if they don't believe me, that'll put an end to it.

She couldn't have been more wrong.

Haynes pulled out a stack of papers and peered down at them through his half-glasses.

"Mrs. Davis," Haynes began, "on the tenth of April, 1976, did you obtain fifty tablets of Percodan from the Summit Park Pharmacy by prescription?" The papers in front of him were Priscilla's prescription records.

With her genuinely faulty memory, Priscilla didn't yet see the storm that was coming. "I don't recall," she replied honestly.

"On the twenty-first of that same month, did you obtain fifty Percodans from the Summit Park Pharmacy?"

"I don't recall the exact date. It's possible . . ."

"And on the thirtieth of April, you obtained fifty Percodans from the Summit Pharmacy?"

"It's possible."

"And during the same period of time you were getting prescriptions for Percodan from the Summit Pharmacy, you were also getting Percodan from the Whitten Pharmacy, were you not?"

"I used both pharmacies," Priscilla fumbled. "One delivers and one doesn't, but I have accounts . . ."

"Well, isn't it true, Mrs. Davis, that on the twenty-sixth of April, 1976, you obtained fifty tablets of Percodan from the Whitten Pharmacy?"

"I don't recall, sir."

"Then on the fifth of May, you obtained another fifty Percodans from the Summit Park Pharmacy, did you not?"

"I don't . . . it's possible, I guess." Surely, Priscilla thought, there couldn't be too many more.

But Haynes had only just begun. The questions accelerated, each one answered only by a faint "I don't recall" or "It's possible." On the fourteenth of May, another fifty Percodan from the Summit Park Pharmacy . . . On the twenty-fourth of May, another fifty Percodan from the

Summit Park Pharmacy . . . On the thirty-first of May . . . the seventh of June . . . the fifteenth of June . . . the twenty-first of June . . .

"Sometimes the pharmacy was closed over the weekend . . ." Priscilla tried to interject.

But Haynes ignored her. "On the twenty-eighth of June, the sixth of July, the twelfth of July . . ."

"It's possible."

"It's not only possible, Mrs. Davis—didn't it happen, now?"

"I only recall . . ."

"The seventeenth of July . . . the twenty-third of July . . ."

"Sir, I really don't recall the exact . . ."

"And *on the same day*, the twenty-eighth of July, you obtained fifty Percodans from the Whitten Pharmacy?"

That brought even Priscilla up short. "The same day?"

"The twenty-eighth of July."

"I don't . . . I don't know . . . I just can't . . . the doctor wouldn't have written two prescriptions right in a row."

"Were you giving Percodan away?" Haynes asked in mock bewilderment.

"No, sir," Priscilla lied. In fact, she had often given perks to W. T., but that subject was even more taboo than her addiction.

"So you were taking about *how* many Percodans a day?"

"It really depended."

"Depended on what?"

"On whether I was in pain or not."

Haynes cast a long, skeptical sideways look at the jury. "Well, you were pretty steadily in pain, were you not, from 1973 right up through last month when you entered the hospital, were you not?"

"Uhhhhh . . ." Priscilla searched desperately for something to say. "One time I lost a prescription," she offered lamely.

"Mrs. Davis, did you tell a doctor, in February of this

year, 1977, that you were taking up to about one hundred tablets of Percodan *weekly*?"

It sounded like a horrendous number, but she didn't dare deny it. Haynes undoubtedly had the records. "I don't recall."

"*Were* you taking about one hundred tablets a week?"

Finally, she capitulated. "Yes, sir."

Haynes went for the kill. "And did you tell this jury just a moment ago that you were *not* addicted to Percodan?"

Priscilla tried one last time to explain—"What I said was I realized that I was becoming . . . needing, you know, with the pain, more and more, and I stopped . . ."—but it was useless. There was nothing left to salvage.

"In fact, you *are* addicted to Percodan, are you not, ma'am?"

"Yes, sir, this is possible."

"And have been for . . . wait just . . . excuse me a minute. You say this is *possible*?" Haynes wasn't going to let anything slip by.

"There is a possibility," Priscilla continued to hedge, pointlessly.

"Well, don't you know it to be a fact?"

Priscilla nodded. "It's highly possible."

Haynes knew he only had to catch Priscilla in one lie to turn the jury against her, one lie to cast everything else she said into doubt, transform every denial into an open question and every "I can't recall" into a confession. Now he had it.

And Priscilla was just about to give him another one.

"Did W. T. Rufner live at 4200 Mockingbird after the time you separated from Mr. Cullen Davis and before August the second and third of 1976?"

The very mention of W. T.'s name set Priscilla visibly on edge. "If that's what you would like to call it," she allowed. "He stayed there recouping from an operation."

"He stayed there recuperating from an operation?" Haynes stroked his chin thoughtfully.

"Yes, sir."

"About how long did it take for W. T. to recuperate from this . . . 'operation'?"

"Probably about three or four weeks. He had his own home and he preferred to stay there." Even Priscilla realized how unlikely it sounded and she scrambled to explain: "It was easier for me than driving back and forth to see about him . . ."

Haynes mocked her. "You were being of some assistance to him in his recuperative period?"

"Well, I felt like I was."

Haynes smiled and shook his head. He slowly pushed his chair back, walked around in front of the big counsel table, and, from out of nowhere it seemed, produced a large photograph. "Let me show you here, ma'am, what's marked for identification purposes as Defendant's Exhibit 9."

It was a picture of Priscilla and W. T.—Priscilla was dressed, but W. T. was wearing only a Christmas stocking, hung strategically over his genitals.

To Haynes's astonishment, Priscilla reacted calmly. "Honestly," she said quickly, "I have never seen that picture ever."

Joe Shannon had a very different reaction. Sitting at the counsel table, behind Haynes, he could only see the back of the photograph. *But he could still see the image!* There, clear as day, was Rufner, buck naked, with his cock in a sock and Priscilla with a drink in one hand and W. T. in the other. Haynes had had the picture printed on paper so thin that with the courtroom's fluorescent lights shining through from the other side, Shannon could see the image perfectly. *And so could the jury.*

The realization catapulted Shannon out of his chair— *"Your Honor"*—demanding that the jury be excused "because of the nature of this material . . ."

Haynes interrupted. "If the Court please, we would object until I get a response to this question . . ." He wanted to make sure every juror got a good long look.

Shannon rushed to the bench. "Your Honor, that photograph is on thin paper and the way it is held up to the jury . . . I object to his displaying it in the fashion which he is because the jury can see through it and I ask the jury to be retired."

"I could put it on a piece of cardboard," Haynes suggested helpfully, as the jury continued to peer at the reverse image.

Once she had denied seeing it, Priscilla knew there was no turning back.

Haynes knew it too. "You can identify both persons depicted in that photograph, can you not?"

"Yes, I can."

"Was this photograph taken during Mr. Rufner's . . ." Haynes paused for full dramatic effect ". . . recuperation?"

Priscilla did her best to fight back. "I do not recall the photograph being made, is what I'm saying, sir." But it was futile.

"But there is no question in your mind, Mrs. Davis, that one of the persons in the photograph is Priscilla Lee Davis, is it not?"

"It appears to be."

"All right. And the other person depicted is the same W. T. Rufner that you assisted in his recuperation, is it not?"

"Well, I recognize his face."

"You don't recognize the rest of him?"

"I don't recognize his sock."

"And this particular photograph was taken at a time when you were in the presence and in the company of W. T. Rufner, was it not?"

"I do not recall."

"Do you recall ever on any occasion in your life seeing Mr. W. T. Rufner in a social atmosphere where he was running around without his clothes?"

"Truthfully, no."

"Your truthful answer in this District Court under oath is that you've never seen W. T. Rufner in this condition of attire or lack of it . . ."

Priscilla mustered all the conviction she had left. "Not that I recall," she repeated firmly.

"Is it your memory that W. T. Rufner could run around naked as a jaybird with his you-know-what in a sock and you not remember, ma'am?"

Priscilla stood firm. "Apparently he did."

Eventually, long after the damage had been done, Dowlen ruled the photograph inadmissible, despite Haynes's noisy insistence that the only way Priscilla could have forgotten seeing Rufner in that attire was "if she was dethroned of memory as a consequence of ingestion of a large quantity of narcotic substance, or some organic brain syndrome."

Many jurors had a simpler explanation: Priscilla was lying.

Haynes knew that from now on, Priscilla's denials would fall on deaf ears. From now on, he could say anything, no matter how outrageous, no matter how damning, no matter how exaggerated, no matter how baseless, and the jury would believe it.

With Steve Sumner's help, that is exactly what he proceeded to do.

42

"Now, with reference to Mr. W. T. Rufner," Haynes began, doting on Priscilla's discomfort with the subject, "did I understand you to say that your relationship with Mr. Rufner was strictly platonic until after your separation from Cullen Davis?"

"Yes, sir."

"And he, Mr. Rufner, moved into 4200 Mockingbird after the surgery, after his hemorrhoidectomy in late 1974;

is that correct?" Haynes succeeded in making the word "hemorrhoidectomy" sound pornographic.

"That's . . ." Priscilla's attention was interrupted as she watched Steve Sumner lean close to Haynes and whisper in his ear. ". . . correct." Sumner pulled out a sheet of paper from a large stack and positioned it on the table in front of Haynes.

"Mrs. Davis, do you recall an incident in 1974 at Larry Myers's house when you, Larry Myers, Valerie Marazzi, and W. T. Rufner were in bed?"

The oval of mascara around Priscilla's eyes expanded to a full circle. "No, *sir*," she huffed.

"You do not recall that incident at all?" Haynes gave the jury the same long, skeptical look he had used when Priscilla denied seeing Rufner naked. It said, "Here she goes again."

"No, sir," Priscilla insisted. "And what do you mean by 'in the bed'?"

Haynes flashed a grim, patronizing, "stop-pretending" smile at the witness. "I thought I said it, just 'in the bed.' "

"No, sir."

"That didn't happen?"

"Well, there was a situation at one time when Larry was with Valerie and, of course, I was with T on a bed talking . . ."

"*On* a bed, not *in* it?" Haynes shared his skepticism generously with the jury.

"Yes, sir, we were just sitting there."

"Fully clothed, I suppose?" By now his voice oozed sarcasm, disbelief, and condescension all at once. ("We understand why you feel you have to lie, dear.") "And just *sitting* on the bed?"

"Yes, sir."

Haynes glanced again at the paper in front of him. "Then I don't suppose you recall a drink being thrown on you and Larry Myers by W. T. Rufner while you were 'sitting' on the bed?"

"No, sir." It was the truth (the drink had accidentally spilled on Myers), but compared to the soap-opera drama and vivid details supplied to Sumner by Larry Myers, it *sounded* like a lie. More and more, everything that Priscilla said was sounding like a lie.

Haynes looked at the paper again. "All right, Mrs. Davis. Do you recall an incident at 4200 Mockingbird when Mr. W. T. Rufner cut your brassiere and panties off?" Another story from Sandy Myers.

"No, I do not."

"You don't recall *that*?" Haynes gave the jury a look of deep puzzlement. Several of the male jurors smiled.

"No, sir," Priscilla insisted.

"Well, then, do you recall an incident when W. T. Rufner started choking you so hard you believed that you were going to be killed by him . . ."

"No, sir."

". . . and that the only reason he stopped choking you was because a cigarette was burning a hole in the bedspread and he stopped to get the cigarette?" Haynes made sure to get all the details in. The more detailed the story, the truer it sounded.

"No, sir," Priscilla huffed.

"Very well, do you recall an incident when Mr. W. T. Rufner pulled a knife and cut your dress from the bottom up to the waist?" Another Sandy Myers story.

"No, sir."

"It was a wraparound-type dress?" Details, details.

"No, sir!"

Haynes smiled his we-understand-why-she-has-to-say-that smile at the jury and moved on to the next attack. "Mrs. Davis, have you ever used cocaine?"

"No, sir. I have not."

Steve Sumner passed a note to Haynes. Haynes read it in a glance, then looked back at the witness. "Did you make W. T. Rufner a birthday gift of a gram of cocaine wrapped in aluminum foil and placed on top of his birthday cake?"

"No, sir," Priscilla responded immediately, but the image was so sharp—a gram of white powder wrapped in aluminum foil sitting on top of a birthday cake—that no one heard her.

Haynes went on as if he had heard a "yes." "All right. Let me ask you this, Mrs. Davis: Have you ever used or taken LSD?"

"No, sir."

Haynes looked at the note Sumner had given him. "Did you give a party on September 20, 1974, for Larry Myers?" This was a party at which Myers had given out free LSD as a "promotional gimmick"—a fact that did not appear in Sumner's note.

Shannon rose to object, but Haynes cut him off. "Your Honor, we believe that we can prove that she in fact gave the party and in that particular party she committed some of the acts that she has in this court denied under oath."

But Dowlen, for once, agreed with Shannon. "She's already answered the question about use, Mr. Haynes."

For the first time, Haynes appeared visibly frustrated. At the bench, he complained to Dowlen. "What I think, Your Honor, is that this witness believes that she has absolute immunity from any prosecution for perjury."

"Well, I can guarantee you that I have given her no such immunity," Dowlen reassured him.

Unappeased, Haynes lashed out more sharply. "Have you ever used marijuana, Mrs. Davis?" He was genuinely angry now, and it showed. The questions came faster and sharper. Had she used heroin, he demanded, or methamphetamines or speed? What about L.A. turnarounds, black mollies, red birds, white crosses?

"No, sir," Priscilla answered each time.

"So you know what a white cross is?"

Priscilla was trapped. "I've heard of them," she admitted. It seemed almost as damning as having used them.

"Have you ever inhaled amyl nitrate? Amies?"

"No, sir."

"So you know what Amies are, too?"

"I know they're supposed to be for heart patients," Priscilla backed away.

"So that's what they're *supposed* to be for," Haynes mocked.

Shannon objected, "He's arguing with the witness . . ."

Haynes bristled. "It would be a travesty, Your Honor, to permit this witness or any other witness to sit in a District Court and deny a fact when it is a fact."

Shannon shot back: "The witness has categorically stated 'no' in answer to the question in regard to cocaine, LSD, and marijuana."

"Well," Haynes huffed, "it happens that we have witnesses who can provide independent proof that the fidelity of the responses by this witness is subject to question."

"Bring them in," Shannon shouted.

"We intend to," Haynes shouted back.

In fact, Haynes had no intention of bringing in his witnesses. Sonny and Debbie Fortner had disappeared to Florida. Larry Myers was still locked up at Huntsville, angry over Steve Sumner's failure to come through either with the $5,000,000 or with the promised help on his appeal. Sandy Myers was by now safely secreted in a hideaway known only to Steve Sumner.

Of this rogue's gallery, Sandy would have made the least risky witness, assuming she didn't start talking witchcraft and the prosecutors didn't find out about *her* history of drug abuse and sleeping around. After Haynes had hit so hard on Priscilla's drug habit and how it affected her memory, what would Shannon make of *Sandy's* memories, on which the defense was relying so heavily? As for the others—Sonny, Debbie, and Larry—what would the jury think of a defense built almost exclusively on the testimony of con men, call girls, and drug addicts?

Besides, the "testimony" they had provided Steve Sumner sounded far more credible coming out of Haynes's mouth. It couldn't be cross-examined, and Haynes, unlike Priscilla, *was* immune from prosecution for perjury.

And the fact that Priscilla denied it only made it more persuasive.

43

First a slut, then a dope fiend. As the cross-examination entered its fifth day, Joe Shannon couldn't believe Haynes had any mud left to throw at the state's star witness.

He was wrong.

With a righteous glint in his eye, Haynes now set out to expose the absolute worst about Priscilla Davis: *She kept bad company!* He wanted the jury to hear every sordid detail about the "rogues and scoundrels" who had invaded "Mr. Davis's home" following the separation. When Shannon questioned the relevance of such testimony, Haynes responded testily: "Surely, the criminal records of Mrs. Davis's friends and house guests, many of whom were given keys to the mansion, demonstrated her carelessness in matters of security."

But the larger message wasn't lost on the jury. What kind of woman would gather around her such a retinue of lowlifes and criminals? Even invite them into her home? A woman who would surround herself (and her children!) with such trash must be trash herself—just the kind of tramp who would marry a man for his money—or frame him for murder. During the questioning, one juror repeatedly looked at Cullen with glistening, sympathetic eyes that said, "Oh, you poor man! How you must have suffered."

And who exactly were these "rogues and scoundrels" whose very company marked Priscilla as a liar and a cheat?

"Let me ask you about Sonny Fortner," Haynes began. "Mr. Fortner stayed at 4200 Mockingbird at your invitation and with your permission—is that not so?"

"Yes. They asked me and I okayed it."

"All right. Now, Sonny Fortner had been convicted,

had he not, of a felony for possession of a controlled substance . . . ?"

These were exactly the same people who had supplied the defense with most of its "evidence": the "dirt" on Priscilla that Haynes had been hurling for the last two days, the "alternate theories" of the murder night—a drug deal gone sour—that he hinted at in court and announced to the press; all of it came from the mouths of the same "criminals and lowlifes" that he was damning Priscilla just for knowing. In Haynes's mouth, their words were transformed into golden, unimpeachable truth; but for Priscilla merely to associate with them marked every word she uttered "a damned lie."

Another name: "Mr. Larry Myers, he is a person that you let stay at 4200 Mockingbird from time to time, did you not?"

"Occasionally, yes, sir."

"And he, Mr. Larry Myers, was a person who was convicted for robbery, was he not?"

By now, Priscilla saw where Haynes was headed and her voice dropped to barely audible. "Yes, sir."

"Didn't you make a long distance call on behalf of Mr. Myers to your attorney Mr. Aultman at the time that he was appealing his conviction?" Haynes's inflections conveyed eloquently all the dark implications of conspiracy. Steve Sumner, of course, had made dozens of such calls and, even as Haynes screwed his face up into the skeptical look with which he received all of Priscilla's answers, other members of Cullen Davis's defense team were monitoring Larry Myers's appeal as part of the "bargain" for his testimony.

"No, sir, I didn't," she answered truthfully. In fact, it was another of the lies Myers had fed Sumner.

But Haynes saw it otherwise. "You did not?" he challenged, his voice halfway between incredulity and indignation.

"No, sir," Priscilla repeated vainly.

"In fact, you knew Mr. Larry Myers quite . . . intimately, did you not?" Haynes's voice oozed adolescent lust.

"What do you mean, 'quite intimately'?" Priscilla bridled.

Haynes smirked at the jury. "You all were more than handshaking friends, weren't you?" The smirk was followed by a wink.

"No, sir, we were not."

"You were *not*? All right." He had made his point.

Another name: "Mr. Bart Newton is a person who stayed at the house from time to time, is he not?"

"Occasionally."

"And he, Mr. Newton, was a person who had been convicted of the felony offense of possession of a narcotic, was he not?"

"I have no idea."

"You didn't *know* whether he was or not?" Haynes's inflection, accompanied by an incredulous look at the jury, said, "Can you believe she invited this man into her house and didn't even bother to find out if he had a criminal record?"

"No, sir."

"He, Mr. Newton, was coming over there for the purpose of visiting with you as a . . . social friend?" The sleazy suggestiveness again.

"Yes, sir," Priscilla responded, suddenly, finally affronted by Haynes's tone.

"And was he, Mr. Newton, dating your daughter, Dee?"

"Yes, sir."

"And your daughter, Dee, was what at the time, eighteen or seventeen." Haynes knew exactly how old she was.

"She was sixteen," Priscilla corrected.

A look of shock and dismay. "Sixteen?"

"Yes, sir."

Another name: "Do you remember a man named Bubba Harris, a black man who associated with Mr. Larry Myers?" The word "black" was sewn seamlessly into the question.

"Yes, sir," Priscilla replied, once again unaware of the trap ahead.

"He, Mr. Bubba Harris, then, had occasion to be at 4200 Mockingbird, did he not?" A black man in her house. She not only associated with criminals, she invited black men into her house!

"I don't recall his being there." To the jury, it was as good as a confession. Maybe she didn't just invite him in, maybe she seduced him in.

"You don't recall him actually in the swimming pool at 4200 Mockingbird?" They were right. She *had* seduced him, let him swim in her pool, swam with him, and had sex with him afterward, no doubt!

"No, sir," said Priscilla. "Yes, sir," heard the jury.

"You do not recall that incident?" Haynes pressed.

"No," said Priscilla. "Yes," heard the jury.

At the table next to Haynes, Steve Sumner concealed a smile. He knew when Debbie Fortner told it to him that that little nugget about Bubba Harris was "twenty-four-karat." He couldn't wait for that redneck racist jury to get ahold of it.

One name was conspicuously missing from Haynes's litany of lowlifes: Sandy Myers. She had been spared because Haynes had one more Sandy Myers story he wanted the jury to hear—and believe.

"Mrs. Davis, do you recall seeing Sandy Myers in your doctor's office a few days before August the second of 1976?"

"No, sir," Priscilla insisted, but it didn't matter any more. The jury was with Haynes. He had the date, he had the details. Whatever he said happened, happened.

"And did you tell Sandy Myers at that encounter that"—Haynes's voice downshifted to low and ominous—" 'something heavy was coming down'?"

"No, sir," Priscilla responded calmly, still clinging to the mistaken belief that the jury was listening. Haynes raised his eyebrows and glanced at the jury—the usual look of exasperation and incredulity. In fact, it was just another of Sandy's many lies.

"Your express recollection is that you did not tell Sandy Myers"—slowly, a second time, to ensure that it was firmly imprinted in the jury's mind—" 'Something heavy is coming down'?"

"No, sir," Priscilla repeated. "I did not make that statement."

Haynes smiled one last time at the jury, then announced, "I have no further questions of the witness, if the Court please . . ." a smile at Priscilla . . . "at this time."

The prosecutors disagreed about what to do next. Tim Curry wanted to skip the redirect and send Priscilla back to Fort Worth. Over the week of her testimony, Curry's distaste for his star witness had turned to deep loathing. He hoped out loud he never saw her again—on the stand or anywhere else—and the thought of shepherding her through another tortuous round of questions sent him into a rare show of petulance. He argued that for all the mudslinging, Haynes had failed to make a real dent in Priscilla's account of the murder night, so why put her back on the stand and run the double risk of Priscilla's mouth and Haynes's recross? Why prolong the agony?

Shannon didn't care about the holes Haynes had opened in Priscilla's story, and he knew the jury didn't either. Haynes had done such a devastating job of undermining Priscilla's overall credibility that "holes" were the least of their problems. The entire edifice of her story was in danger of collapsing if it didn't get some emergency reinforcement. If the prosecution cut Priscilla loose now, without responding, the jury would have no choice but to believe every last one of Haynes's dark insinuations. Indeed, they would assume that the prosecutors *couldn't* refute them.

Finally, reluctantly, Curry agreed. He would try to "rehabilitate" Priscilla on redirect.

It was a disastrous decision.

* * *

Curry's heart wasn't in it. And it showed. Against a steady ack-ack of objections, his listless, disjointed questioning recovered little lost ground. Almost for the first time since the trial began, a negative word was spoken about the defendant—over Haynes's bitter protest—as Curry questioned Priscilla about Cullen's abusive relationship with Andrea. Curry also hoped that some gruesome pictures of Priscilla's bullet wounds might elicit a little sympathy from the jurors. But when he tried to establish a motive for the killing by showing how much money Cullen Davis stood to lose in a contested divorce, Haynes leapt from his chair in indignation.

"Your Honor, it's just as impermissible to demonstrate great wealth as it is to demonstrate great poverty before a jury, if it's done so to create either antipathy on the part of the jury or hostility in the minds of the jury against a citizen that is accused."

The irony wasn't lost on Joe Shannon. For the last six days, he had sat and listened as Haynes hurled accusations at Priscilla with no purpose *other* than creating antipathy and hostility in the minds of the jury. Shannon had figured the cross to be long and rough; but "long" was one day, two days at most; and "rough" was . . . He couldn't remember what he used to think was a rough cross-examination—the standard now seemed part of the distant past, a past when Joe Sr. was alive and lawyers were admired and men used to pat him on the head when his father won a case.

Judge Dowlen had long since lost patience with Priscilla and her contentious ways, but even he wasn't buying Haynes's indignation. The objection was overruled.

At Shannon's suggestion, Curry ended the redirect with a question about Andrea Wilborn, the rarely mentioned victim whose murder was, nominally at least, the subject of this trial.

"Mrs. Davis, is your daughter, Andrea Wilborn, living or dead at the present time?"

Priscilla looked down into her lap. "She's dead."

"Where were you when you first learned of her death?"

"I was in intensive care after surgery." She showed no tears, but choked on the words. Her voice broke. No doubt tears were there somewhere.

"Tell this jury, Mrs. Davis, who it was that shot you and Stan Farr on the night we're talking about?"

Firmly, piercing through the tears: "It was Cullen Davis."

After such a long cross and brief redirect, Shannon expected Haynes's recross to be relatively short and sweet.

It was neither.

Haynes began sweetly enough: "Ma'am, I do not intend, by any question that I ask you, to unnecessarily distress you—do you understand that, please, ma'am?" But it was only a ruse to put Priscilla off guard. The truth soon became clear: He was out for blood.

First, he challenged the sincerity of her tears for Andrea. It was a touching scene, all right, but hadn't she staged the exact same touching scene in earlier courtrooms? In particular, he reminded her of her testimony in a divorce hearing called to determine if her alimony payments should be increased. "Do you recall testifying that your mother and father were divorced when you were a baby and that your uncle supported you and had been like a father to you? And do you recall saying, 'He's quite elderly, has TB, and nothing to live on but Social Security, and I'm the only person he can count on?' Do you recall that, Mrs. Davis?"

"Yes, sir," Priscilla answered icily.

"And at the time, you became emotional, and a recess was called by the Court—isn't that correct? Do you remember that now, Mrs. Davis?"

"Yes, sir."

And what about the time Priscilla asked the divorce judge to postpone the trial due to her "emotional and physical health"? "When Mr. Cullen Davis's attorneys requested that you be examined by an independent physician to determine if the delay was justified," Haynes pressed, "you again became emotional, did you not, and required a recess?"

"The situation . . ." Priscilla started to explain.

But Haynes cut her off. "Do you recall that you got emotional?"

"Yes, sir." She tried for icy again, but her anger escaped. "I don't know what you are talking about . . ." she snapped.

Haynes fought for control. "Excuse me! Excuse me!"

". . . You are making it seem rather light, and it was a very serious problem for me."

"*Excuse me!* It is true, is it not, that as a consequence of that, no doctor was selected by anybody to examine you?"

"All I know is the judge decided not to appoint a doctor."

At that, Dowlen finally sustained Shannon's objections, but the point had been made.

Next, only hours after bitterly resisting any evidence of Cullen's wealth as prejudicial, Haynes gleefully launched an attack on Priscilla's profligate spending during their years of marriage. "You did endeavor during the time you were married to Cullen Davis to spend his money, did you not?"

"I did spend money," Priscilla conceded, "but only because he allowed me to."

"But the *reason* for those expenditures," Haynes tried again, "was that you *knew* that there was a prenuptial agreement, and you were trying to buy all of these jewels and furs so that at a dissolution of the marriage you would have that community property to make your claim against. Isn't that why you made those expenditures, ma'am?"

"No, sir."

Finally, Haynes accused her of outright thievery. Referring to a valuable jade piece that disappeared from the mansion (it had, in fact, been taken by Dee), Haynes demanded:

"You took that particular jade piece and removed it from the house and sold it, didn't you, ma'am?"

Priscilla mustered all the vehemence she could. "No, sir, I did not."

The attacks grew increasingly personal and decreasingly relevant. Assuring Judge Dowlen that he would produce witnesses (he never did) who would testify that they saw Priscilla walking unassisted the same day she appeared at a writ hearing in a wheelchair, Haynes tried desperately to get before the jury an accusation that Priscilla's medical condition was nothing more than an elaborate charade.

"This woman," he argued at a bench conference, sputtering with rage, "*this woman* comes up here and announces to the court and the jury that she's here with her nurse and so forth, tactics designed to invoke sympathy for her and her condition. And I think that we can show that since day one she would ride a wheelchair to the courtroom with a nurse when she needed to invoke sympathy, but then go out and party at night, scantily attired and holding a drink. *It's all a fraud!*"

As the questioning heated up, Priscilla tried to defend herself. At one point, Haynes pasted on a smile and asked, "Now, the business of divorce is not something new to you, is it, ma'am?"

Priscilla, sick of his smarmy insinuations, shot back, "I don't understand what you are trying to say."

But Haynes turned her anger into just more fodder for ridicule. "Well, let me see if I can say it in a way that is easier to understand. You had been through a contested divorce, had you not, before the time that you filed the divorce suit against Mr. Cullen Davis, correct?"

Priscilla leveled her steely gaze at him. "Cullen and I have *both* been through divorces." It was the first time the jury had heard anything about the defendant's previous marriage.

Haynes was livid. "Now, *excuse* me, ma'am. I asked you if you had been divorced, and you want to volunteer that both you and Mr. Davis have."

Priscilla, defiantly: "Yes, sir."

Haynes, desperate to strike the last blow: "You do that out of acrimony and bitterness to this man?"

The usual belated objections.

Next, Haynes demanded to know why Priscilla, in recounting the story of how Cullen berated and abused Andrea for her poor performance in math, had put so many obscenities in Cullen's mouth. "You didn't use those obscenities when you were asked about the incident on August 10, 1976, did you, Mrs. Davis?"

"I told basically the same story," Priscilla insisted. "I just left out some of it."

"Wait a minute!" Haynes exclaimed dramatically. "Did you or did you not include in the story you told then the obscenities that you used before this jury?"

"Well," she started to explain, "it seemed rather foul . . ."

Haynes pounced. "Didn't they tell you to tell the truth?"

"I told them the truth."

"Did you use those obscenities or not?"

"Not at that time, no, sir."

The point was made, but Haynes wanted more: He wanted to punish her. "When you came into this courtroom, you included those obscenities and profanities, but when you were interviewed a year ago, you didn't use the profanity in describing that incident, did you, ma'am?"

But he had pushed too far, and now Priscilla pushed back. "No, sir," she said, "I also didn't tell anybody that he called her stupid . . ."

Haynes scrambled to back out. "Excuse me, ma'am, I'm not asking . . ."

". . . and kicked at her, either."

"*Excuse* me, ma'am, I'm not asking you to volunteer that."

Haynes fumed over the exchange for days. Later, at a bench conference, he complained bitterly about Priscilla "blurting out" unsolicited information and "dumping garbage into the record before the jury that has no factual basis."

By the second day of recross, Haynes's attacks had taken on the fever and pitch of a personal vendetta. Gone were the fake civilities, the elaborate apologies, even the plastic smiles that had begun every session. It was clear from the ice in Haynes's voice and the fire in his eyes as they volleyed back and forth between the witness stand and the jury box in an elaborate choreography of skepticism that the chief defense attorney hated the little blonde woman sitting alone in the front of the courtroom. Hated her with a passion so dense, so implacable, so single-minded that every other emotion in the room was simply overwhelmed.

Joe Shannon wanted to take him aside and say, "Stop! You've won. The job is done." But he knew Haynes was past listening. He was pursuing some other end now, beyond the needs of the case or the client, some personal demon who, in his mind, had taken the earthly form of a semi-pretty, dyed-blonde bar girl from the wrong side of the tracks. And now he *had* to destroy her.

On the third day of recross, Haynes rolled out "the ultimate weapon"—an argument that he considered so devastating, so definitive, that it would, at one stroke, demolish both Priscilla and the case against his client.

"I feel I'm entitled to show," he argued at the bench, out of the jury's hearing, "that during the time she was married to Jack Wilborn, and after suit for divorce had been filed, Priscilla Lee Davis had two acts of sexual intercourse with Mr. Jack Wilborn and then filed a motion to hold him in contempt on the grounds that he had raped her." And the purpose of this diabolical plot, Haynes concluded, was "to cheat Mr. Wilborn out of the community property." In response to Shannon's fierce protests that such an allegation was irrelevant and immaterial, Haynes insisted that it showed the witness was "capable of that sort of trickery and chicanery," *and* "that she has practiced it on the defendant, Mr. Cullen Davis."

In other words, Haynes had found the answer to the question everyone was asking: Why would Priscilla falsely accuse Cullen and let the real murderer of her child go free? The answer: "This woman's personal greed and desire to acquire the properties of Mr. Davis."

Appalled, Shannon demanded to know what independent proof Haynes had of this supposed "plot" against Jack Wilborn.

"We certainly have the sworn pleadings of Priscilla Davis claiming that Jack Wilborn had sex with her by force," Haynes offered lamely.

"That doesn't prove anything!" Shannon shouted, as the full scope of the outrage hit him. Haynes wanted to accuse Priscilla of serious misconduct in front of the jury without a shred of evidence—not even the money-induced inventions of some coked-out con man. No evidence of intent to deceive, no evidence of inducement, no evidence of a plot, no evidence of anything. All that mattered to Haynes was the accusation. He knew the jury would believe it, with or without proof—what a convenient way to explain away the whole case, pin it on the brassy blonde bitch with lousy taste in friends. All Haynes had to do was say it in open court. Priscilla's inevitable denial would do the rest.

This time, even Dowlen wasn't fooled. Over Haynes's last-bid protest that the plot against Wilborn was relevant because it showed Priscilla's knowledge of divorce law, Dowlen refused to allow it.

But Haynes wouldn't let it go.

"Mrs. Davis, you were familiar with the concept of restraining orders by the time you had completed your first divorce, correct?" he asked the next day, Priscilla's eighth on the stand.

Before Shannon could object, Priscilla answered the question: "To a degree." The ambiguity was all the opening Haynes needed to justify additional "clarification."

"Well, to a degree that you knew that you could move the court to hold Mr. Wilborn in contempt if you claimed that he was in violation of a restraining order—you knew that, didn't you, ma'am?"

"Yes, sir."

"And, in fact, you did exactly that, didn't you, after you obtained that restraining order?"

Shannon objected again, but Dowlen, eager to punish

Priscilla for her evasive answers, allowed "this one question."

Priscilla answered it: "No, sir."

But Haynes wasn't finished. "Your testimony is that you did not invite Mr. Wilborn to come and visit you after you obtained a restraining order against him?" The question allowed Haynes to get the allegation that she had entrapped Wilborn before the jury for the first time.

"No, sir, I did not."

"Is it your testimony that he came and visited you without your invitation then?"

Shannon rose to object. The court had allowed only "this one question." That was three questions ago.

Dowlen politely urged, "Let's move on to a different area, please," but when Haynes again proposed to ask "one more question," Dowlen agreed.

"As a matter of fact, Mrs. Davis, you set Mr. Wilborn up to have him held in contempt by the Court, did you not?" It was exactly the question Dowlen had disallowed the previous afternoon.

As expected, Priscilla replied, "No, sir, I did not," and Haynes gave the jury his we-understand-why-you-have-to-lie look.

After that, Dowlen managed to chase him off the subject—but not for long. Later that morning, Haynes demanded to know why, after their separation, Priscilla had given Cullen a key to the mansion.

"You weren't trying to set him up so that he would offend some restraining order and get himself in contempt of court the same way you'd done to Mr. Jack Wilborn, were you?"

When Shannon objected that "the question was already asked and she said 'no,' " Haynes's face flushed crimson and his voice rose to a petulant whine: "I don't know why I have to be married to her answers, Your Honor!"

Only fifteen minutes later, he tried again.

"Was Cullen Davis's reason for declining to come in at your invitation that he was aware of the manner in which, after the time that you and Jack Wilborn had sep-

The six-million-dollar Davis mansion sat like a fortress, alone on a huge expanse of horizon. (Photo: Ron Heflin, *Fort Worth Star-Telegram*)

Priscilla Davis (second from left) described her first year of marriage to Cullen (far left) as "like finding a genie in a bottle and having all your wishes come true." Carmen and Larry Thomas are at center; David and Judy McCrory are on the right. (Photo: Judy Brown)

Twelve-year-old Andrea Wilborn was more interested in the pattern of sunlight on a leaf than in something so evanescent as homework. "She's a dreamer," Priscilla said of her daughter. Andrea's murderer marched her to the basement and executed her.
(Photo: Jack Wilborn)

With her tiny body and "substantial balcony," Priscilla Davis drove the men of Fort Worth society crazy—and the women even crazier.
(Photo: W. T. Rufner)

At six feet, nine inches, Stan Farr was so big that when he stood next to Priscilla, they looked like a trick photograph on the front page of a tabloid.
(Photo: Judy Brown)

Beverly Bass pleaded with police to let her return to the Davis mansion, where she had seen her boyfriend shot. "There are other people up there," she screamed. "Cullen will kill them all." (Photo: Gene Gordon, *Fort Worth Star-Telegram*)

The policemen who arrested Davis were shocked at the comments he made on his way to jail. But the jury never heard their story. (Photo: Gene Gordon, *Fort Worth Star-Telegram*)

The Cullen Davis defense team in Amarillo. From left: Richard "Racehorse" Haynes, Sam Guiberson, Phil Burleson, Steve Sumner (standing behind Davis) and Mike Gibson. Sumner, the ex-pro baseball player, was Cullen's favorite. So eager was Sumner to play in the big leagues with Haynes and Burleson, he offered to do "anything, even empty the trash." (Photo: Pete Leabo, Associated Press)

Chief prosecutor Tim Curry (center) didn't know whom he hated more, the defendant or his own key witness, Priscilla Davis. After her testimony, Curry left the rest of the trial to courtroom veterans Tolly Wilson (second from left) and Joe Shannon (second from right). Also shown: Marvin Collins (far left) and Rufus Adcock (far right). (Photo: Gene Gordon, *Fort Worth Star-Telegram*)

Amarillo Judge Gordon Dowlen, a toothpick-chewing good ole boy from Ralph's Switch, Texas, was no match for Racehorse Haynes. The defense would have free rein in his courtroom. (Photo: David Bowser)

W. T. Rufner. "Even though I have long hair and am an arrogant son of a bitch and an alcoholic and a drug addict," he told Priscilla, "you may find I know something." W. T. was nothing if not honest, and Priscilla needed honesty almost as much as she needed sex. (Photo: John Ebling, courtesy: W. T. Rufner)

At the party after the victory in Amarillo, Haynes sang "The Ballad of Cullen Davis" and denounced the state's star witness as "the most sordid human being in the world." (Photo: David Bowser)

FBI agents took Judge Eidson to a parking lot where they burned cigarette holes in his undershirt, spread ketchup around, positioned him in the trunk of a car, and then took pictures to "prove" the contract killing had been done. (Photo: FBI)

David McCrory (left) and Cullen Davis in the parking lot at Coco's. Prosecutors had videotape, audiotape, and still photographs of the crime being committed. An airtight case— or so they thought. (Photo: FBI)

Houston Judge Wallace "Pete" Moore was an ex-World War II fighter pilot and an old friend of Racehorse Haynes. After the trial was over, he complained bitterly, "The entire system has been abused." (Photo: Ron Heflin, *Fort Worth Star-Telegram*)

Haynes knew that Jack Strickland (right) was going to be a problem. The lanky young prosecutor already had five death penalty convictions under his belt. (Photo: Pete Leabo, Associated Press)

Cullen's third wife, Karen Master, quickly learned that being married to Cullen wasn't all mansions, furs, and Lear jets. Soon after the wedding she was seen with bruises and black eyes. "That house is hard on wives," cracked Jack Strickland. (Photo: Ron Ennis, *Fort Worth Star-Telegram*)

arated and filed suits against each other for divorce, you enticed Jack Wilborn into the bedroom . . ."

Shannon objected, but it was already too late. In the last three words, Haynes had been able to suggest for the first time the charge of sexual enticement: that Priscilla hadn't just invited Wilborn in, she had *seduced* him into bed to further her plot. Bit by bit, he was finessing the whole story into the record. He still hadn't explicitly mentioned the rape charge, but he wasn't through yet.

By the fourth day of recross, Priscilla's tenth day on the stand, Haynes had lost all contact with reality. Some in the courtroom—not just at the counsel table—thought he had lost all control as well.

But, in fact, even his wildest attacks had a fierce, paranoid logic to them. He bore down hard on Priscilla's relationship with Beverly Bass, the prosecution's other key eyewitness. Just how close were the two women?

"You and Ms. Bass were a lot closer, were you not, than a thirty-five-year-old woman and an eighteen-year-old girl?" he inquired, his voice ripe with insinuation. How often had Beverly Bass spent the night at 4200 Mockingbird, he wanted to know. Did she *always* come to see Dee? Were there times when Bev and Priscilla were alone in the big house? Was their relationship of an "unnatural sort"?

The insinuations grew darker and darker. Did Priscilla assist Beverly Bass with a "serious personal problem"?

It took Priscilla a minute to realize that Haynes was talking about the time she had taken Bev to an abortion clinic. "I'm aware that she was upset that there *might* be a problem," she conceded.

Haynes exploded with accusations. Wasn't it true that Priscilla paid for the procedure at the clinic? Wasn't it true that she encouraged Beverly Bass to seek an abortion in the first place? Wasn't it true that Priscilla failed to inform Bev's parents of her "serious personal problem" after Bev confided in her? Wasn't it true that she posed as Bev's mother at the clinic because the law required parental consent to any procedure? Wasn't it true that she suggested Bev use a false name to conceal her identity?

And why had she done all these heinous things?

"To be of comfort and assistance to Beverly Bass," Priscilla explained.

"To be of comfort and assistance to Beverly Bass!" Haynes mocked.

"Yes, sir." Defiant.

"Have you performed the same sort of 'assistance' for other friends of Dee's as you did for Beverly Bass?"

"I have not."

Perhaps not, but there was something odd about Priscilla's relationships, Haynes went on to suggest. Take Valerie Marazzi, for example. "She was a friend of yours, was she not?" And wasn't she dating Larry Myers? And how old was Valerie Marazzi? Late teens? And Larry Myers? Mid-thirties? And what about Becky Ferguson, another brief resident at 4200 Mockingbird? How old was she? Late teens, early twenties? And who was she dating? Bart Newton? And how old was he? Mid-thirties? And who else did Newton date? Priscilla's own daughter, Dee? Who was how old? Sixteen?

"Now, those were all people that you were seeing socially at 4200 Mockingbird, isn't that correct, Mrs. Davis?"

"Somewhat," Priscilla hedged.

"All right," Haynes's voice began to ooze again. "That is, young girls in their teens or early twenties with men who were in their early thirties were seeing you socially at 4200 Mockingbird and other places, correct?" Of course, all of those named by Haynes had something else in common—all were defense informants.

Shannon objected, but, as usual, the insinuation was already burning in the jury's ears—put there as much by Haynes's dark, sulfuric tone as by the words themselves. Priscilla was a corrupting influence on young girls like Bev Bass. She possessed a malevolent, corrosive power over them. Maybe she even pimped for them. Maybe even for her own daughter.

* * *

Finally, on day eleven, after picking over Priscilla's accounts of the murder night in an unsuccessful search for real inconsistencies (Why had she placed her return to the mansion "about midnight" in one interview and "between 12:00 and 12:30" in another? Why had she told the jury the killer dragged Stan Farr's body "by the ankles" when she told the police "by the feet"?), Haynes could hold it in no longer.

"All right, Mrs. Davis. Then after Mr. Wilborn had the custody of the children, you got him to come over to your place of residence and you engaged in sexual relations with the man, did you not?" His face was red and his voice as high and heated as an engine in overdrive.

"I did not lure anybody over at all," Priscilla repeated.

Haynes pointed a short, crooked finger at the witness. "Isn't it true, ma'am, that you had relations with him and it was not because he, Mr. Wilborn, used physical force on you at all? That you made that up?"

"No, sir, I told the truth." Priscilla, too, still had some fire left.

"Did these 'rapes' against you occur in the broad daylight hours or the evening hours?" His voice shifted into snide.

"It wasn't late at night, I'm sure."

"Had to get him over in the daytime so that you could go to the doctor that same day and get it checked, didn't you?"

Finally, his questions drowned out in a din of objections, Haynes folded his arms in disgust and fell glumly silent. The message: He wasn't really finished with Priscilla Davis, just fed up.

After eleven days of testimony, Priscilla, too, was fed up, and from the safety of her hotel room, she could finally say what Haynes wouldn't let her say on the stand: "I know I'm not Miss Goody Two-shoes," she told a group of reporters, "but it's obvious they don't have a case if the only thing they can do is destroy my credibility. It doesn't matter if I was the biggest hooker, doper, or what have you. It has absolutely nothing to do with what Cullen did. . . . They are trying this like a smutty divorce . . . while in reality it is a murder. A twelve-year-old child was killed. They seem to forget that. I never will."

But no one was listening. Not even the chief prosecutor, Tim Curry, who flew back to Fort Worth on the first plane, relieved to be rid of his unpleasant duty. "If I never see Priscilla Davis again," he told a friend, "it will be too soon." Most of the courtroom spectators felt the same way. One told a reporter: "I don't have to be in the courtroom to tell you what I think. I think she's lying and Cullen is innocent." It was only the first indication that Haynes had achieved his most important objective: convincing the jury that if Priscilla was lying, Cullen had to be innocent.

No one was more convinced of Priscilla's "guilt" than Judge Dowlen's secretary, Helen Murphy. "If I write a book about this case," she joked bitterly, "it will be called *Silicone and Sex*." Whether talking with lawyers or reporters or the judge himself, she refused even to use Priscilla's name, referring to her instead, between clenched teeth, as "that woman."

44

Cullen Davis, meanwhile, had become a star.

In the courtroom, self-described friends and admirers (many of whom had never met him) filled row after row of spectator seats. Their Madame DeFarge was Rhonda Sellers, a Daisy-Mae Dallas Cowboys cheerleader, former "Miss Metroplex" of Dallas–Fort Worth (Cullen had sponsored her unsuccessful run at Miss Texas), and friend of Karen's who sat directly behind the defendant, generating a force field of fuzzy, down-home wholesomeness that enveloped the entire defense team.

Behind her gathered a gaggle of women in their forties and fifties, dubbed by a bailiff the "Menopause Brigade," who sat faithfully through every moment of testimony, making their sympathies known with applause (for Haynes) or jeers (for Priscilla). Between sessions, they crowded to the rail behind Cullen, passing cookies and pies, love notes, Lifesavers, and scraps of paper for him to autograph. Some brought copies of *Blood and Money* —the story of another handsome, wealthy Texan accused of murder—for Cullen to sign.

One woman begged to do his laundry. Another wanted to know if his jail sheets were being changed often enough. Some brought their children or grandchildren to meet the great man. "Mr. Davis," said one woman in wide-eyed admiration, pushing two little blond boys toward Cullen, "I'd like my two boys to meet you. They'll tell their children about you someday." When asked by reporters what they saw in Cullen, "brigade" members gushed about his boyish good looks, his charm, his poise, and, of course, his terrible, terrible ordeal.

To handle all the fan mail and sympathetic phone calls, Cullen needed office space, and what space could be more convenient than Judge Dowlen's office? With Dowlen's permission, Cullen had a phone line installed in the judge's outer office and Mrs. Murphy, giddy at the chance to help out, sorted his mail and screened his calls. After overhearing Dowlen's secretary answer the phone, "Good afternoon, Phil Burleson's office," Tolly Wilson warned Joe Shannon, "I think we're gonna have a hard time here."

Like any celebrity, Cullen enjoyed special privileges. Judge Dowlen made available a third-floor jury room for the defense team's daily luncheon: a hearty, often catered affair where Cullen entertained reporters as well as attorneys, investigators, and business associates while waiters in gold jackets served up inch-thick T-bone steaks. After a hard day sitting quietly in the courtroom, Cullen would host Kendavis company brass for an hour or so of business, then enjoy another catered meal in his private double-bunk cell. At six every evening, a sheriff's deputy would bring him fresh clothes and take him to see his chiropractor for "medical treatment." In fact, unknown to the prosecution, the trips were to see Karen and their purpose was therapy of a different sort.

No one, including Judge Dowlen, was rude enough to treat Cullen like a real prisoner. At the jail, he roamed freely around the corridors, chatting with guards (never other inmates) and even occasionally manning the booking office solo. One woman was impressed by the courteous voice that answered her call.

"County jail."

"May I speak to the sheriff?" she asked.

"He's not in," the voice responded cheerfully.

"Well, may I speak to one of his deputies?"

"There's no one here."

"Well, who is this?"

"Cullen Davis."

"My God! I didn't realize you'd taken over the place!"

When court was in session, bailiffs and sheriff's deputies kept a respectful distance, allowing Cullen to wander unescorted virtually anywhere in the courthouse. During recesses, he would wade out among his fans, receiving gifts and words of encouragement with a thin smile. At the lunch break, a bailiff might gently remind him, "Okay, Cullen, time to go on back to the jail," but no one dared the insult of escorting him there.

During one break, Jack Wilborn, who had come down from Fort Worth against his own better judgment and his doctor's advice, left the courtroom in search of a cup of coffee. A reporter directed him to an elevator lobby on the third floor. When Wilborn arrived, he found a big coffeepot sitting on a table and, next to it, a man talking on the phone. It was Cullen Davis. He looked around for guards or lawyers or somebody, but they were alone. Wilborn's blood pressure "went ten miles high." Before coming to Amarillo, he had vowed to keep cool, not to make a scene. Now his mind was filled with bloody thoughts.

Before he could say anything, however, a door opened and fifteen people crowded into the room, filling the space between them. For weeks afterward, his mind exploded with the things he should have said.

Joe Shannon and the other prosecutors watched the daily spectacle of Cullen's canonization with alarm and disgust. "Here's a guy on trial for executing a twelve-year-old girl in a dark basement," Tim Curry fumed, "and they treat him like a fucking hero!" Marvin Collins, who thought women were drawn to Cullen because he looked like Victor Laszlo in *Casablanca*, wrote it off to human nature. "There's a natural desire to do something to please powerful individuals. People think, maybe if I do something for the great man, he'll remember me." Curry put it more bluntly: "They think some of that money will fall out of his pocket if they stick around long enough."

Again and again, they complained to Dowlen about the defendant's special privileges. What would the jury think? Should Cullen really be allowed to send steaks to the jurors three times a week? But Dowlen was like everybody else: awestruck. He not only tolerated Cullen's perks, in many cases he *approved* them. At meetings in the judge's chambers, he was all West Texas charm and deference around the defendant, as if he couldn't wait to shake the man's hand and share a beer with him when this ugly business was over with.

Everywhere the prosecutors turned, the attitude was the same: Cullen Davis could do no wrong.

During a recess, Marvin Collins was working at the counsel table when he noticed Cullen, on one of his usual courtroom walkabouts, stop and strike up a conversation with an attractive middle-aged woman at the back of the room. Collins didn't recognize the woman, but a few minutes later, Haynes walked into the courtroom and Cullen called to him. "Richard, come back here. I want you to meet Kay Haessley's mother."

Kay Haessley was a juror.

Collins rushed to tell the other prosecutors. Joe Shannon threw a fit. "If the dadgum jury had been sequestered, *really* sequestered, this wouldn't be a problem. But no!

Dowlen had to give them weekend visits.'' They checked: Kay Haessley's mother *was* on the list of approved visitors. "Oh, that's just great," Tolly Wilson fumed. "Cullen talks to mama, then mama goes to talk with her daughter the juror and tells her what a fine person Cullen is, and that she's been talking to him. What a goddamn circus!''

Shannon and Wilson marched straight to Dowlen's office and demanded he declare a mistrial for improper jury contact. Dowlen smiled his don't-that-beat-all, that-Cullen-is-something-ain't-he smile and promptly denied the motion for mistrial.

Dowlen wasn't the only one who turned a benign eye to the defendant's "peculiarities." When Cullen boasted to a roomful of women, including Judge Dowlen's girlfriend and mother, "This jury is gonna find me not guilty, and when they do, I want you all to line up in a row, 'cause I'm gonna start at the top and screw back down," no one took offense. He was just being a man. When he called the judge in Fort Worth "a motherfucking, cocksucking, chickenshit son of a bitch," everyone figured, well, hell, he had a right to be angry. And when an eighteen-year-old boy was brutally gang-raped in an overcrowded cell while Cullen enjoyed his privacy and visits to "the chiropractor," everyone agreed that wealth was entitled to its privileges.

Priscilla was a whore, Cullen was just "randy," or "locked up too long." Priscilla was a greedy golddigger, Cullen was just a sharp businessman. Stan Farr was Priscilla's "live-in lover." Cullen and Karen were merely "living together." Toward the end of Priscilla's testimony, Joe Shannon inadvertently left near the witness stand a set of photographs from the medical examiner's office showing the bloody body of Andrea Wilborn lying on the mansion's basement floor. Recalled to the stand, Priscilla saw the pictures and began instantly to weep. At the defense table, in plain view of reporters, jurors, and many spectators, Cullen Davis smiled.

That, too, was forgiven.

In fact, the only thing that people had trouble forgiving

Cullen for was marrying Priscilla. In some ways, Haynes's cross-examination had succeeded too well. The stigma of associating with Priscilla, the brush with which he would tar many of the prosecution's witnesses, was beginning to rub off on his own client. People wanted to know how a man as admirable as Cullen could have married a woman as reproachable as Priscilla.

In a statement virtually scripted by Haynes, Cullen provided an answer. "I knew [Priscilla] was taking a lot of drugs, but only in retrospect did I realize how seriously they had affected her. During the past year of investigation, I have discovered that Priscilla caused my home to make Sodom and Gomorrah look like Petticoat Junction."

Also at Haynes's direction, Cullen challenged the only other blemish on his reputation: Priscilla's charges that he abused Andrea, calling them "unscrupulous lies." "It makes me cringe and disgusted," he told the press, "that she says things like I kicked Andrea and called her stupid. She has no one to back that up, and Andrea is not here to confirm it."

After that, all was forgiven, and Haynes could resume the attack.

45

His next victim was Beverly Bass.

When she walked to the witness chair in her loose, maidenly dress, with her long, honey-blonde, flower-child hair swaying behind, she may have looked to the jury like just another callow coed, all innocence and light. But Haynes would convince them it was all a lie; that behind her sweet face and guileless eyes, Beverly Bass was every inch a whore and dope fiend, as was her mentor and role model, Priscilla Davis.

As Tim Curry, who had returned from Fort Worth, led

her through the events of the murder night, Bev told her story with poise and conviction, and the story she told sounded true. As Joe Shannon explained: "She and Bubba are coming down this walkway, they hit this light, and she says, 'That's Cullen,' and *wham*, he turns around and shoots. If it hadn't been Cullen, he'd have kept on walking. He shot when he realized he'd been discovered." She spoke fondly and movingly of Andrea in life—until Haynes succeeded in blocking such "irrelevancies." When she pointed an accusatory finger at Cullen and their eyes met, his jaw muscles twitched and betrayed him; when Curry set before her a picture of Andrea lying dead in the mansion basement, she sobbed uncontrollably. All of which only redoubled Haynes's determination to destroy her, just as he had destroyed Priscilla.

What exactly was Bev doing at Brent Cruz's apartment—Haynes called it "that little back room"—on the evening of August 2, 1976, only hours before the murders? Who exactly was with her in that little back room? Brent, Dee, Bubba, and . . . ? Brent's thirteen-year-old sister! Haynes's face erupted in shock and dismay. They had allowed an innocent thirteen-year-old *child* to be present in "that little back room" when Bev and the others were . . . ?

"I don't understand what you're trying to do," Bev replied, puzzled and shaken by Haynes's sinister insinuations.

"You didn't have any sort of mood modifier while you were back there in that little room, did you?" The way Haynes said it, it didn't sound like a question at all.

Bev denied it—just as Priscilla had.

To prove that the witness was also a whore, Haynes returned again and again to the clinic visit in August 1975. Because Dowlen had forbidden the use of the word "abortion," Haynes was free to focus his vast powers of insinuation on the phrase, "your personal problem": How old was she at the time this "personal problem" occurred? Were there other such "personal problems"? Did she tell her parents about this "personal problem"? Did she use her own name when she sought help for this "personal problem"? The questions came like tongues of flame, white-hot and evanescent. By the time she answered one, it had been replaced by a different one. If she tried to stop and explain—"I have an explanation if you'll just let me . . ."—Haynes would lay on a hot iron of sarcasm—"I'm sure you do!" Even lawyers who had seen Haynes at work before were surprised at the ferocity and relentlessness of his attack.

At one point, he pulled out a transcript of a pretrial hearing from the previous December. "Do you recall, when you were giving testimony in December 1976, you were asked if your health was good and you indicated it was good and had always been good?"

"Yes, sir," Bev responded.

Haynes read from the transcript: "Question: 'Have you had any operations in the last five years?' And your answer was, 'I've had my wisdom teeth out, that's about all.' " He lowered the transcript slowly and grinned condescendingly at Bev. "Now, Ms. Bass, that answer you gave in December was not truthful, was it?"

"No, sir," Bev admitted, her voice beginning to break. "It was something I wanted to forget about, and I *had* forgotten it . . ." As her voice trailed off into sobs, Dowlen called a brief recess. Haynes scoffed audibly and walked away. When court resumed a few minutes later, he made no allowances.

"You had consulted with a medical person back in August 1975, hadn't you, Ms. Bass?"

"Yes, sir."

"So when you said 'no' back in December, you had just forgotten about the consultation, isn't that right?" The question was barbed with ridicule.

Bev tried to respond, but could only choke back more sobs.

Haynes bore in. "The truth of it is, you hadn't forgotten about that incident. You just decided that it wouldn't be discovered."

The words exploded out of her. "No, sir, Mr. Haynes.

I told you, I tried to block that from my memory—and I had!" And then more sobs.

Some in the courtroom, like Joe Shannon, thought Haynes's attacks were backfiring; that the jury would never believe Bev was just another Priscilla. But Haynes had an even more devastating charge.

"The relationship between you and Priscilla Lee Davis was a . . . personal relationship, was it not?" Elsewhere he had used the phrase "special relationship," hissing the first word like a snake to convey his meaning. Dee Davis had told Sumner that Bev never came to the mansion just to see Priscilla, and he himself on a hundred other occasions had portrayed both Priscilla and Bev as man-hungry nymphomaniacs. But none of that mattered now. Lesbianism was the insinuation of the moment.

"I don't understand," Bev replied. In fact, she was afraid to understand.

"So she was more to you than just Dee's mother!"

This was Haynes's most devastating charge against Beverly Bass: *She was a friend of Priscilla Davis.* By now every juror knew what that meant: She was in on the plot. To prove it, Haynes pulled out another transcript, this one of a statement Bev had made to Detective Claude Davis on August 3, 1976, only hours after the murders. "While we were walking on the walkway," he began reading, "I heard loud noises coming from inside the house. I heard a woman scream. I think I heard one shot. A man was walking in front of me . . ." The statement appeared to indicate that there was a *second* killer, inside the house, at the time the man in black was accompanying Bev and Bubba to the back door. No one, not even Bev, had ever mentioned a second killer.

Haynes fixed his gaze on the witness. "Is it your testimony now that the man in black was *not* walking with you and Bubba at the time you heard the shot?"

"Yes, sir."

"So what you said in the statement of August 3 is not true?"

"It's out of sequence," Bev protested. "Won't you let me explain?"

He wouldn't. He preferred the insinuation left hanging before the jury, the insinuation that Beverly Bass, like Priscilla Davis, was hiding something; that her story had changed over time for a reason; that the jury had yet to hear what *really* happened at 4200 Mockingbird Lane that night; that Bev had fallen under the spell of her "special friend," Priscilla (whom Haynes had taken to calling "the Queen Bee") and agreed to alter her story to slake Priscilla's thirst for money and revenge; that Beverly Bass was, in short, part of the conspiracy against Cullen Davis.

But what exactly did that mean? How could Bev and Priscilla have "struck a deal"? When? It had to be after the killings. But where? They turned up on opposites sides of the estate, both claiming that Cullen was the killer. Did they meet on the lawn of the mansion after Bubba had been shot? After *Priscilla* had been shot? Haynes, cannily, didn't attempt to answer these or any other questions. That was the beauty of an insinuation: No proof was necessary. Just plant it in the jury's imagination—like a grain of sand in an oyster—and by verdict time, presto, a pearl of doubt.

Joe Shannon couldn't wait for redirect to demolish Haynes's "conspiracy fantasy," but he never got the chance. Bev Bass never was allowed to explain the inconsistencies in her statements, and Detective Davis never took the stand to recount what trouble he had piecing together *any* chronology from Bev's fractured story in those confused hours after the murders. Why? Tim Curry, fearing that Haynes still had some unspent ammunition to lob at Bev, decided there would be no redirect. The witness was excused.

It was left to Cullen Davis, of all people, to say what Joe Shannon didn't dare say: "Curry fucked up."

That night, at the rented apartment that doubled as defense headquarters and barracks, Haynes celebrated the destruction of the prosecution's two main eyewitnesses with a bottle of cognac and a boast: "I dream of the day when I am cross-examining a witness and my questions are so probing and brilliant that the poor bastard blurts out that *he*, not my defendant, committed the foul murder. Then he will pitch forward into my arms, dead of a massive heart attack."

The prosecution brought on a parade of other witnesses: John Smedley, the security guard who had taken Bev Bass back to the mansion that night, the county medical examiner, police officers and crime scene investigators, the neighbors at whose house Priscilla had sought refuge, the doctors who treated her wounds. They added and explained, filled in details, bolstered this piece or that piece of Priscilla's story, or Bev's. Bubba Gavrel testified that he recognized Cullen in the instant before a bullet splintered his spine, but everybody, even the prosecutors, concluded that he was probably operating, whether in good faith or bad, under the power of suggestion.

There was one brief moment of excitement when Joe Shannon hinted to reporters that the state's fingerprint expert, Jim Slaughter, would drop a "bombshell" in his testimony: the mysterious bloody palmprint had finally been identified. Haynes responded with a fusillade of bluster: "You can damn sure bet it's not Cullen Davis's, and you can make book on that." In fact, the entire defense team was convinced of just the opposite: that the print belonged to their client.

The next day, Haynes tried every trick he knew to get Slaughter disqualified as a print expert. When Dowlen finally overruled the last objection and Marvin Collins began the questioning, Joe Shannon could have sworn he heard a collective intake of breath at the far end of the counsel table.

"And do you have an opinion as to who the print belongs to?" Collins asked.

"Yes, sir," Slaughter answered. No sounds of breathing at all from the defense team.

"And what is that opinion?" Collins asked.

"Arlelia Cooper," said Slaughter, "the maid."

At the defense end of the table, breathing resumed.

Finally, the state called its last witness, Frank Shiller, the forensics expert. In a soft, sleep-inducing monotone, Shiller testified to the nature and location of every bullet and bullet hole, every scrap of plastic bag, every spot of blood on clothes, walls, or floors—all of which corroborated Priscilla's account—until the courtroom was paralyzed with boredom. Then, for seven excruciatingly tedious days that drove away all but the hardiest of spectators and sent the jury's liquor bill soaring, Haynes cross-examined Shiller, going back over every scrap and spot until the jury never wanted to hear or think about forensic evidence again—which, of course, was exactly the point.

Then, after forty-seven days of testimony, the state rested.

Now it was Haynes's turn.

46

With the blue-haired groupies back in force and every courtroom seat filled, Haynes tugged at the vest of his custom-tailored pin-striped suit and checked the shine on his monogrammed ostrich-skin boots one last time. He could feel every eye in the place on the back of his neck, every ear waiting for the sound of his rich baritone as he began his opening statement. God, how he loved the law!

He knew what they wanted to hear. He had spent the last eleven weeks making sure they wanted to hear it, and now, as he shuffled his notes one last time and cleared his throat, everyone in the courtroom was wondering exactly what Haynes had programmed them to wonder: *What about the conspiracy?*

Haynes had talked about, talked around, and insinuated the existence of a conspiracy so often that most now simply took it for granted: Priscilla had conspired to pin the blame for Andrea's death on Cullen. But the questions remained. If Cullen didn't shoot Stan Farr and Andrea Wilborn, who did, and why? And why would Priscilla lie about it—allowing the real killer of her child to go free? What *really* happened that night at 4200 Mockingbird Lane?

Everyone was looking to Haynes for the answers.

Until just a few weeks before the trial, he didn't have them. For months after Cullen's arrest the defense had been scrambling to come up with a theory of what happened on the night of August 2. Haynes, Burleson, and then Sumner and the rest of the defense team had brainstormed late many nights concocting "alternate scenarios": who could have done it; who had the motive, the relationship, the access, the type of knowledge? Mostly the discussions had gone nowhere.

Then one day a tall, gawky stranger stepped into Steve Sumner's office and said he had some information that might be of interest. He had heard on the street that Cullen Davis's lawyers were looking for dirt on Priscilla and *anything* that would make their client look innocent. Sumner made the standard disclaimer—"we aren't paying any money, all we want is the truth"—but the man smiled anyway. The word on the street was that Davis's lawyers had to say that for the record, but that Cullen Davis was a millionaire who was looking at a long stretch on the inside, maybe even death row, and it was too late and the stakes were too high to play by the rules. The street knew that he would find a way to take care of anyone who helped him.

"I can give you the name of the real killer," the man was saying, his voice as nervous as a drop of oil on a hot griddle. "I know what happened that night out there." Sumner was used to this. From the day news of Cullen Davis's desperation hit the street, every junkie without the money for the next fix had materialized on Sumner's doorstep, eager—often desperate—to be helpful. Sumner was convinced the man who stood before him was one of them.

"All you need to do is deposit six million in a Swiss bank . . ."

That was it. Steve got up and herded him toward the door. The man sensed the brush-off and threw his story into high gear. "It was a dope deal, man, that's what was going down out there. It was a dope deal that went bad. I know the guy, the dealer who was there. . . . He's in jail in Colombia now, man, but he'll testify it was a drug deal that went sour." Sumner listened for another ten minutes before finally throwing him out.

Then he started thinking: a drug deal gone sour?

The more he thought about it, the better he liked it. A drug deal gone sour meant that Priscilla wasn't the intended target, thus removing Cullen's motive for murder. It also answered two questions left unanswered by the prosecution's case. Why was Priscilla only shot once and then "allowed" (Sumner's word) to escape? Answer: She wasn't the target. Why did the police find part of the garbage bag upstairs where no one had been shot? Answer: The killers searched the house looking for money or drugs.

A drug deal gone sour? Haynes liked it, too. He had heard from Glen Cooper, another inmate in the Tarrant County Jail, that Stan Farr was involved with drugs. Well, actually, Cooper didn't know Stan Farr, but he knew a girl who used to date Farr, and *she* was involved with drugs. "Here in jail, the talk is that Bubba and Stan were in a dope deal the night of the murders," Cooper reported to Haynes, "and they either got into a fight or were being ripped off."

As far as Haynes was concerned, that was all the confirmation they needed.

"Thus far, you have seen only the tip of the iceberg," Haynes told the jury. "All you know about what happened that night at 4200 Mockingbird Lane is what you have heard from the prosecutors." He dismissed all that with a condescending smile. "Ladies and gentlemen, we will show you something other than the tip of the iceberg." This was it. The packed courtroom fell into a dead silence.

* * *

In March of 1977, Sumner sat down with Cullen Davis and "fleshed out" the scenario: Stan Farr was deeply into drugs (dealt out of the mansion?); a big deal was scheduled for the night of August 2, 1976, but something went wrong; Farr was the killers' only target; Priscilla just got in the way; Andrea, too; Bubba, too (or was he in on Farr's deal?); Priscilla knew the killers but feared they would kill her if she named them; she concocted the story against Cullen for her own greedy reasons, and conned Bev into going along.

It may have sounded like the outline for a B movie, but at least it was a start. Now all they needed was something to support it.

So the word went out to the street: Cullen Davis's defense was looking for someone to say that a drug deal was going down on the night of August 2 at the Davis mansion.

The "testimony" poured in: Farr had been making frequent trips to Dallas, the scene of a big federal drug case involving Willie Nelson; Farr needed money; Farr had been asking around "to do any kind of drug deal—heroin or cocaine or anything to make money"; Farr had been seen with a suitcase in Dallas ("A suitcase," the source explained, "was a perfect place to hide drugs.").

Debbie Patton, a twenty-six-year-old socialite from a prominent oil family who had taken a wrong turn off the road to social prominence and respectability, told Sumner that Farr had bragged about having $160,000 cash to renovate a nightclub. Sumner concluded that there was only one way an unsuccessful businessman like Farr could put his hands on $160,000.

Eventually everything about Debbie's story turned out to be wrong, but it didn't really matter. The defense only had to *construct* a story, not prove it.

"We will demonstrate," Haynes assured the jury, "that Mr. Stan Farr, despite the fact that there was no way to show where it came from—proclaimed to have a large sum of money in cash at or near the time of the shootings that he could not put in the bank, but was available to him for . . ."

he paused to make sure he had every ear "... business activities." The words came out bathed in sinister implications. Everyone knew exactly what he meant. Haynes loved euphemisms. They allowed him to titillate the jury without appearing to lead it. They both informed the jury and left it craving to know more. They allowed him to transform a little, lifeless nugget of fact into a froth of insinuations.

In concluding his opening statement, Haynes had one last word to say about Priscilla Davis—although his comments, he added archly, were not intended "to disparage the character of Priscilla Lee Davis. I think she stands on her own two feet in that regard." Everything that happened that night, Haynes said, "Priscilla Lee Davis subjected herself to by her selection of the people that she made her entourage at 4200 Mockingbird, the people that she gave access to the house, and the type of activities that she allowed them to engage in."

In other words, as surely and inevitably as the bullet from the killer's gun had stopped Andrea's heart, Priscilla's wanton life-style had led to her daughter's death.

As repugnant as it was, nothing that Haynes said surprised Joe Shannon. To him, the defense position had been inevitable from the moment Priscilla took the stand. It was the conclusion that Haynes had been relentlessly driving toward with each baseless insinuation dropped into the record, with each carefully staged expression of indignation, with each condescending smile or ridiculing riposte directed at the state's star witness. Everything came down to this: *It was all Priscilla's fault.*

47

The one element Haynes's conspiracy still lacked was a killer.

From the beginning, there was no doubt in Cullen Davis's mind whom *he* wanted to pin the murders on: the only man who had slept in his bed, bathed in his tub, drunk his liquor, and was still alive to brag about it—W. T. Rufner.

Sumner liked the choice. Rufner had a rap sheet, a bad attitude, and a long association with drugs ("a hardened, proven criminal," Sumner called him). He knew the contents of the house intimately (including the safe and the $600,000 chess set inside), and, as a union electrician, he had the know-how to disarm the mansion's alarm system. Even better, he was well known to Andrea, which would allow the defense to insinuate that Andrea opened the door for him on that fateful night. Of course, as a spurned former lover, he had the most time-honored motive of all.

To drive the point home, Haynes had made sure that the jury heard every melodramatic detail of Priscilla's brief, stormy relationship with the mysterious man called "T": how he fought Larry Myers for trying to make it with his woman; how he brawled with Bart Newton in the mansion kitchen; how he lobbed a potted plant at Priscilla as she sat in the bathtub; how he cut the head off one of her stuffed animals in a rage; how he tore the transmission out of her car and then, when she walked away, slashed her tires.

Before it was over, the jury had seen the infamous "sock" photo, had heard the lawyers argue over admitting even more "prejudicial" pictures of "the two lovebirds" into evidence, and had heard enough stories about "T" to convince them that he had to be the most mean-tempered, dirty-minded, drug-crazed, murder-prone vermin to terrorize the state of Texas since the lawless days of the Wild West.

So it was with a shudder of apprehension that the jury greeted Haynes's announcement of his next witness: William Tasker Rufner.

A tall, spare figure in a loud print shirt and blue leisure suit swaggered to the front of the courtroom and arranged himself in the witness chair, hands clinging to the end of the chair arms, bow legs spread far apart, shoulders hunched, butt down—as if perched at the back end of a banana seat on a Triumph Bonneville motorcycle, ready to burn rubber.

At the defense end of the big counsel table, Haynes shuffled his papers and consulted one last time with Steve Sumner, trying to ignore the sudden vacuum in the room. For the first time in weeks, center stage had been stolen from him. Finally, he looked up from his papers and, over the top of his half-moon glasses, trained his laserlike gaze on the figure in the witness chair. It was a look of pure hatred.

"Would you state your full name for the court and for the jury, please?"

"William Tasker Rufner."

"Are you also known by any other names, Mr. Rufner?"

"Some of my friends call me 'W,' and some call me 'T' or 'T-man,' and some call me 'W. T.' " Rufner's eyes caught Haynes's look—and returned it.

For Haynes, W. T. had been nothing but trouble from the moment the defense subpoenaed him. "I'm never gonna go to Amarillo," he told them. "I'm not on your fuckin' side!" Why was that, they asked. "Because of Cullen killin' that little girl," he reminded them. They said they would call him as a hostile witness. *"You goddamn fuckin' right I'm hostile!"* he roared. When they finally corralled him into a pretrial hearing, he refused to answer all but a few of Haynes's questions, claiming his Fifth Amendment privilege against self-incrimination. "Haynes got madder than a sonofabitch," W. T. bragged afterward.

After consulting his lawyer, W. T. met with Haynes again, but still refused to answer all but the most innocuous questions. If the defense wanted to call him, they would have to do it without knowing what he was going to say on the stand. "They're going to be tough on you," his attorney warned him on the eve of his trip to Amarillo. "You were involved in a lot of shit." W. T. brushed him aside. "It's no big deal," he said. "I'm just gonna fuck 'em up as much as I can."

W. T. had his reasons for hating Haynes, too. He had been following the trial in the papers and on television and what he saw made him sick. Every day he would scan the articles looking for some mention of Andrea Wilborn. Andrea, the little girl with the pennant of auburn hair who loved animals and poetry and art, the girl who gave him a statue of a squirrel, saying it reminded her of him because he was "such a nut." He still had that squirrel. "They've turned the trial into a fucking circus," he complained to friends. "They've completely forgotten everything about Andrea." And W. T. knew why, too. "Haynes blows so much smoke at that jury, they get so fuckin' confused, they can't separate real things from false things—they keep forgettin'."

The antagonism between the two men made headlines when W. T. flew to Amarillo to present Richard Haynes with a "gift." After getting sufficiently drunk, Rufner arrived at the courthouse carrying only a small brown paper bag. Joe Shannon was the first to see him, peeking around the corner of the courtroom door. Then Haynes turned his head, then Burleson, then Cullen. None had time to hide his surprise. W. T. wasn't due to testify for weeks. What was he doing in Amarillo?

A few minutes later, Dowlen called a recess and Haynes emerged warily from the courtroom. A crowd of reporters and photographers, alerted in advance by Rufner, stood between him and the elevators. As he made his way through them, a solemn, glassy-eyed figure approached.

"Mr. Haynes," he said, "You remember me. W. T. Rufner."

"Yeah," Haynes said, "where's your girlfriend?"

Rufner ignored the reference to Priscilla. If he was going to do what he came to do, he had to do it quickly. He reached into the paper sack and pulled out a T-shirt emblazoned with a full-color picture of W. T., buck naked, wearing a Christmas stocking over his "business"—just like the photograph Haynes had tried to show the jury, only without Priscilla. Underneath the picture were printed the words "W. T. SOCKS IT TO 'EM." With a quick swing of his arm, Rufner held the shirt against Haynes's chest. The room exploded in flashbulbs.

"I'm selling these for a few hundred dollars apiece," Rufner announced as Haynes grabbed the shirt and wadded it into a ball. "Since you dragged my name through the dirt and made it a household word, I wanted to give you the first one." Amid laughter not of his own making, Haynes stomped off.

But Rufner wasn't finished. In a press conference after the encounter, W. T. mentioned the one subject that Haynes was determined to keep out of the trial of Cullen Davis. "This is *not* a divorce case," W. T. told reporters with real anger in his voice. "We're here about a murder of a twelve-year-old girl, Andrea Wilborn."

Three weeks later, Rufner was back in Amarillo to testify. "Don't let him piss you off," Joe Shannon cautioned him that morning. "He wants you to get mad. He wants to prove how arrogant and hostile you are, and what a temper you have." Shannon admired W. T.'s courage. He was sure the defense had tried to buy him off or turn him around. It took integrity to stand up to Cullen's millions.

"Well, fuck it," replied W. T., who had taken a Valium and several sunrise shots of scotch to help him relax, "I've been in a lot of pool halls. I won't let him know if I get mad." Then he reconsidered. "I may let *him* know, but I'm not gonna let those twelve people know."

"Mr. Rufner," Haynes began, "do you know a Priscilla Lee Davis?" Even the way he said the name conveyed disdain.

"Yes, sir."

Haynes got right to the point. "Are you in love with her?"

W. T. smiled. "I'm in love with a lot of women." The

jury smiled. There were even some chuckles. Rufner had won the first round.

Haynes scowled. "Does that include Priscilla Lee Davis?"

"She's a special lady to me, yes." Another guileless smile.

Haynes set out to prove that Rufner's affair with Priscilla had been longer, steamier, and more serious than Priscilla had admitted. "How long after Mr. and Mrs. Davis separated was it before you commenced to spend the night at 4200 Mockingbird?"

"I'm not for sure. It would have been the last part of August 1974."

"And when was it that you and Priscilla Lee Davis began to date each other . . . exclusively?"

Rufner gave his shaggy head an aw-shucks shake. "Boy, that would be hard to say, because I've always had more than one lady in my life." The tittering from the jury box washed away all of Haynes's oily insinuations.

"All right," Haynes tried again. "When was it that you began to date exclusively?"

"August, September."

"And was that at or near the time that you began to . . . spend the night at 4200 Mockingbird?"

"Yes, sir. At that time I put some cutoffs and blue jeans and a couple of T-shirts there."

Haynes pounced. "Are you telling the jury *under oath* that the most you ever had there in the way of clothes was cutoffs, a pair of blue jeans, and a T-shirt?"

Rufner looked at the jury and knitted his eyebrows in a puzzled "what-did-I-say?" expression. "No, sir, I am not."

Haynes forged ahead. "Is it true that you were living at least half of your time at 4200 Mockingbird and half your time someplace else by Thanksgiving?"

W. T. shrugged his shoulders. "I wouldn't say fifty percent either way. Like I said, I'm not . . ."

"Would you say *under oath* that you were not spending

at least half of your time before Thanksgiving at 4200 Mockingbird?"

Another shrug. "No, sir, because I was." By now Rufner's look of baffled bemusement had spread to some jurors.

Unaware, Haynes continued to press. "And in those evenings that you spent there, did you have . . . private quarters?" The insinuation oozed from Haynes's lips.

"If you mean one particular room where I stayed all the time," W. T. replied evenly, ignoring the innuendo, "no, sir, I didn't."

Once again, Haynes thought he had him. "Exactly what room *did* you stay in when you stayed there before Thanksgiving?"

W. T. responded without missing a beat, "At one time or another, possibly in all of them," then smiled his disarming smile.

Haynes pounced again. "Are you, saying *under oath* that you spent the night in all of the rooms?"

Rufner shook his head. "No, sir, I am not saying that. I'm saying that there was a time or two when I slept on the couch or in the master bedroom." He had slipped away again.

Haynes tried another attack. "Did you, during the time before Thanksgiving, have a key to 4200 Mockingbird?"

"No, sir."

"Do you say *under oath* . . ."

Finally, Joe Shannon had had enough. "Your Honor, I'm going to object to counsel repeatedly reminding this witness that he's under oath. That's improper."

Judge Dowlen agreed.

A few minutes later, however, when Haynes began excavating the story of Rufner's March 1974 drug bust, it was W. T.'s turn.

"Did the police find nine plastic bottles containing assorted drugs?" Haynes asked.

"I'm sorry," said Rufner, "I can't say *under oath* that there was nine or eight." Several jurors smiled. The courtroom audience rustled its appreciation.

Haynes ignored them. "All right. Did you have a matchbox containing two glass vials of an unknown liquid?"

W. T. nodded. "Yes."

"What was *that*?"

"I'm not for sure," Rufner apologized. "I cannot say *under oath* that I know." More smiles and rustling.

Haynes cleared his throat and tried again, carefully pitching his voice to rebuke the titterers in the audience.

"Did you have seventy-six grams of a white powder substance in two plastic bags?"

W. T. answered with a world-weary casualness that robbed the subject of interest even before it was broached. "I'm sorry, I can't remember the grams part of it. There was a white powder in the arrest, yes, sir."

"What was that?"

"I believe they call it . . ."

"You *believe*!?" Haynes thundered. "What was it that you had?" Haynes, his voice reflecting his incredulity, continued, "You were arrested for it!"

Rufner hung his head like a scolded dog. "I'm sorry," he said softly. "I can't give you the pharmaceutical name, or whatever . . ."

Haynes, in a voice laced with sarcasm: "What did *you* call this white powder?"

Rufner searched the ceiling with his bassett eyes. "White powder," he finally said. The audience and the jury burst into laughter.

And so it went: Haynes setting traps and Rufner deftly stepping around them. How could W. T. remember some events (like the long-ago trip to Boston) so well and others (like a recent rendezvous with Priscilla) so poorly? "Certain things stick in the back of a person's mind," W. T. explained, "certain things don't." Why was Rufner's memory a blank on one portion of a conversation with Priscilla but not on another? "I did not have a machine there recording everything that was said, Mr. Haynes."

Where Priscilla's denials never helped, W. T.'s admissions never hurt. And there were some eye-opening

admissions: the sex with Priscilla began far sooner than
she had acknowledged; Rufner had stayed at the mansion far longer; he and Priscilla had "coordinated" their
testimony regarding the famous sock photo. But the truth,
delivered in W. T.'s self-deprecating back-porch drawl,
had strangely little impact—far less than Priscilla's heated
denials. Where her "I can't remember's" drew scowls of
skepticism from the jury, his "I'm not for sure's" left them
grinning. No matter how sordid or steamy the accusations
sounded in Haynes's questions, in W. T.'s answers they
always came out sounding merely naughty—the high-
spirited high jinks of a Texas cowboy. Priscilla was the evil
slut; W. T., at worst, a low-rent roué.

Wasn't it true that Rufner and Priscilla were "paired
up" during the trip to Boston?

"I don't know what you mean 'paired up,' " W. T.
drawled in an accent even thicker than Haynes's. "If you
mean were we tied up together, no sir, we weren't tied
up."

Wasn't that a picture of Priscilla and Rufner naked
cavorting in a lake?

"I would say that, if that's not us," said W. T. with a
lecherous grin, "it sure looks like us."

Did Rufner drink so much water during his testimony
because the "mood modifier" he admitted taking before
coming to court gave him "a perennial thirst for water?"

"I couldn't say that, particularly," W. T. replied with
great seriousness. "I'm not a physician. But I do know
that if you drink at night, the next day you're awful
thirsty."

Wasn't it true that Rufner, like Priscilla, had spoken
to the prosecutors before coming to court?

"I sure did," W. T. admitted breezily. "I said 'Hello.
How are you?' And I would have done it to you, too, Mr.
Haynes, if you had been in the men's room when I was."

Wasn't it true that he poured a scotch and water on
Mr. Larry Myers?

"Oh," and a modest laugh, "I have done that more
than once to Mr. Myers."

Where was the hot-tempered, drug-crazed, spurned lover? Haynes tried to draw him out.

Did you throw a potted plant at Priscilla Davis while she was in the bathtub, Mr. Rufner?

"Yes, sir."

Didn't that indicate that his relationship with Priscilla had degenerated into a series of violent confrontations?

Not really, W. T. mused. "There was mornings when it was total harmony. There was mornings when it was total hell." More smiles from the jury.

Did you use profanity when talking to Mrs. Davis?

"I don't remember, but I'm sure I did."

Isn't it true that you met with Priscilla after she appeared in this courtroom and talked about her testimony?

"Yes, sir."

And how long did that meeting last?

"About a six-pack."

On his second day in the witness chair, W. T. showed the effects of a late night at the hotel bar on Cullen's tab. But even with Rufner drunk and hung over, Haynes couldn't break him. At one point, W. T. started rolling a cigarette. A buzz of whispering began in the back of the courtroom and, as W. T. spread a brown leafy substance on a little square of paper, slowly worked its way forward. Finally, somebody said it loud enough to be heard: "He's rollin' a joint!" Haynes, whose back had been to the witness chair, wheeled around just in time to see Rufner slowly licking the end of the paper with his lithe, narrow tongue.

"You got a light?" W. T. asked Haynes.

Haynes's eyes narrowed into a look that said, "I'm gonna get you, you sonofabitch!" He walked forward, pulled out a cigarette lighter, and held the flame close to Rufner's face.

W. T. took a drag and almost gagged. He never smoked. "I did it just to fuck with him," he said later. "Somebody had to do something. Plus I was pissed. I didn't want to be there."

Pissed himself, and frustrated, Haynes argued furiously that Rufner should be forced to testify about his drug use so Dowlen could determine if, in fact, his Fifth Amendment claims were valid—an argument that Joe Shannon summarized contemptuously: "In other words, he's got to waive the Fifth Amendment in order to take it!" Over howls of protest from the defense, Dowlen agreed with Shannon: There would be no more inquiry into the witness's drug habit.

That left Haynes only one last move: to try and place Rufner at the scene of the crime.

Where were you the night of August 2, 1976?

"I was staying at the Brown Trail Apartments."

And what were you doing there?

"Visiting a lady," said W. T., his eyes sparking.

To the jury, the whole picture was instantly clear. By the night of the murders, W. T. had moved on to another lady. Priscilla was a distant, bittersweet memory—a pain in the heart, perhaps, but no longer, if ever, the object of a murderous obsession.

Haynes tried to shake that image by accusing Rufner of threatening his "lady" at the Brown Trail Apartments with bodily harm if she didn't sign a statement that he was with her the night of the murders. "Did you use any sort of persuasion on the lady to get a statement concerning where you were August the second, 1976?"

W. T. looked puzzled. "Would you define 'persuasion'?"

"Did you threaten to kill her?"

"No, sir, I never threatened the lady with anything."

Then why was it almost five months before the lady signed such a statement, Haynes demanded to know.

W. T. shrugged his shoulders again. "Some women are just hardheaded, I guess."

On cross, Joe Shannon didn't even try to "rehabilitate" the witness. The jury didn't need his help to see that W. T. Rufner was no killer. Even Haynes was forced to concede—at a bench conference—that anyone who kept time by six-packs "can't be all bad."

Shannon decided instead to attack the defense strategy head-on. Clearly, somebody had tried to set Rufner up to take the fall. Who and why, Shannon wanted to know, and how far were they willing to go?

"Let me ask you this, Mr. Rufner. Were you afraid for your life during late '76 and early '77?"

"Yes, sir."

"Were you afraid you were being made a patsy in this whole deal?"

"Yes, sir."

"Had you heard, then, Mr. Rufner, that there was money out for people willing to assist in making you the patsy in this double homicide?"

"Yes, sir."

"Had you heard, too, that the police had not located a murder weapon in this case?"

"I had," said W. T.

"And had you not also heard that if there was nobody to alibi for W. T. Rufner, it would be a whole lot easier for him to be made the fall guy in this deal?"

"Very often," W. T. answered.

Shannon continued, more slowly, "And had you heard that it was the plan of the defense to try to lay this whole thing off on a dead man . . . ?"

Haynes sprang to his feet. "That's the rankest kind of gross attack!" he roared as the courtroom disintegrated into chaos.

Shannon's accusation may have been "the rankest kind of gross attack," but it was also dead right. Even before Rufner stepped down from the witness chair, the defense had decided that he wasn't "working out." He was too clever, too likeable, too alibied—just too damned *innocent* to make a credible murderer. They would have to find somebody else—preferably somebody who couldn't talk back, didn't have an alibi, and wouldn't object to being accused of murder.

In short, somebody dead.

48

On a steamy morning in August 1977, Horace Copeland could never have guessed that he would soon play a major role in the Cullen Davis trial just getting underway in far-off Amarillo. He had more important things on his mind.

Johnny Smith thought his old friend Horace looked like hell: his blue eyes bloodshot and wild, his curly blond hair matted with sweat, the veins on his forehead purple and bulging, his jaw muscles pumping, his smoke-stained fingers trembling. Not that Johnny hadn't seen Horace Copeland this way before. Copeland was heavy into pills —Quaaludes and Preluden, especially—and sometimes people into pills got that way: "quayed out." Johnny had seen it a hundred times.

What made this time different was that Horace was pointing a loaded gun in Johnny's face. "Gimme the fucking pills, man," Horace was saying. His voice trembled worse than his hands. He was strung way out somewhere. "Gimme the stuff you stole from my apartment."

Johnny felt a rustling next to him in the bed and suddenly remembered his girlfriend Kathleen. Horace jerked the revolver in the direction of the movement under the covers. "Gimme the fucking pills," he repeated. "Gimme the stuff you stole from my apartment, or I'm gonna kill you. I'll fucking kill you both."

Kathleen poked her head out from underneath the sheet. Her eyes struggled to focus on Copeland, then the gun. "Oh, go ahead," she finally said. "I've got nothing to live for anyway."

"No, wait a minute," Johnny interrupted, before Horace could register. "Man, let's talk about it. Yeah, let's talk about it!" He slid out of bed with his hands in front of his cock ("Whatever you do, man, don't shoot me there!").

"I want my fucking stuff!" Horace yelled as he pushed off the bed and headed for the dresser. "Where's my stuff?" Keeping the gun pointed in Johnny's direction, more or less, Horace attacked the dresser, yanking out the drawers and throwing clothes in the air. Johnny slowly picked up his pants and put them on. Kathleen, convinced that Horace wasn't going to do her the favor of shooting her, at least not yet, slid back under the sheet.

While Horace rampaged around the room, Johnny had a chance to think: The previous Thursday, he had seen Kathleen and Horace partying together; Saturday, Kathleen had called from Horace's apartment and asked Johnny to pick her up (she claimed Horace was going to "beat the shit out of her"—Johnny wondered why); Sunday, Kathleen ODed on 'ludes and Johnny had to rush her to John Peter Smith Hospital to have her stomach pumped; Monday, Horace comes looking for his missing 'ludes.

No wonder Horace was crazy. His supplier, Charlie Swagerty, had a reputation for being a heavyhanded collector. If Swagerty was after him, Horace was in deep trouble. He needed to find those pills and sell them in a hurry or Swagerty would gouge his eyes out. Johnny would have given the pills to him—only he didn't have them. He figured most of them were probably in a stomach-pump bag at John Peter Smith Hospital.

All Horace found were a couple of bills on the nightstand and a handful of costume jewelry.

By now, Johnny's roommate's girlfriend, Debbie, had appeared in the doorway to the living room. She watched Horace flinging clothes around the room for a few minutes, then turned and headed toward the kitchen to make some coffee. The roommate, Henry Byrd, had left an hour before for his job distributing milk and ice cream, and Debbie was eager to get started tracking down her car, which she had misplaced the night before.

The sound of the phone ringing brought Horace thrashing into the living room. It was Henry, wanting to know if Debbie had found her car yet.

"No," Debbie said in a whimper. She had cried herself to sleep just a few hours before. She started to hang up the phone, then had another thought. "Henry. There's some guy over here with a gun."

"Who?"

"How the hell should I know."

"I'll be right over."

Debbie turned to Horace, who had taken a seat at the dining room table, but was still waving the gun from person to person. "Listen," she said, "I gotta go. I lost my car and I gotta go find it." Without waiting for a response, she headed toward the bedroom to get her purse.

"You're not going anywhere," Horace barked, "not until I find my fucking stuff. No one's going anywhere. I'll kill you all if I don't get my stuff."

"Let her go, man," Johnny cut in. "She's not involved in anything. She's expected somewhere, and if she doesn't show up, she'll get in trouble." Horace didn't seem to notice the difference between the two stories.

A few minutes later, Henry Byrd walked in and saw Horace at the dining room table with his gun weaving back and forth between Debbie, Johnny, and Kathleen, who had finally gotten out of bed and put on some of Debbie's clothes, although she still had the same "shoot me first" expression on her face.

Henry looked at Debbie. "I don't know who the fuck he is either," he said, then walked past Horace, past the gun, and into the bedroom. He thought he remembered putting a revolver under his mattress, but when he looked, it was gone. Johnny was saying, "Keep cool, everybody. Just keep cool." But Debbie was tired of waiting. "I've just *gotta* go," she said, grabbing her purse. "I gotta find my car."

Horace waved the gun in her direction. "First, let me see what you got in there." He pointed the gun at her purse.

"Oh, fuck off!" said Debbie.

Horace leapt out of the chair, grabbed her by the arm, dragged her back to the table, and pointed the gun up her nostrils. His face looked like it would explode any second.

"Oh, all right," Debbie huffed, and spilled the contents of her purse onto the table. Horace's trembling fingers sifted through the debris and started to close on a blue stone earring. Debbie swatted his hand away. "That's *mine*," she said, snatching it up and quickly sweeping the rest back into her purse.

"Get the fuck out of here," Horace ordered.

As she walked to the door, Henry threw her the keys to his truck. The movement caught Horace's eye and he turned his back to watch Debbie make the catch. Johnny saw his chance. He pushed Kathleen back into the bedroom and leapt at Horace, pinning his gun arm against the chair. Henry grabbed the other arm. For a second, they seemed to have him under control. But Horace had been working out with weights a lot, and he was high to boot. The combination proved more than Johnny and Henry could handle. With a loud grunt, Horace reared up out of the chair, pushing the other two men back toward the kitchen door.

Johnny knew he was in trouble now. There was no way Horace wasn't going to shoot him dead first chance he got, so Johnny clung to the gun arm for dear life as they stumbled into the kitchen. Suddenly he felt the smooth black metal of the revolver in his hand and, a second later, Horace's grip broke free. He pointed the gun in Horace's direction and pulled the trigger. Three cracks. Horace's head jerked back, his body went stiff, and he fell backward. He hit the linoleum floor board-straight and didn't bounce once.

Johnny called his attorney. Henry told Debbie to go wait for him at the Tempo Club. Kathleen went to find some pills. Eventually someone called the police.

Not surprisingly, Horace Copeland's body was barely cold before he shot to the top of Steve Sumner's suspect list. He met all the requirements any defense lawyer could have asked for: a druggie and a lowlife, an ex-con known to carry a gun; he hung around with the wrong kinds of people, couldn't account for his whereabouts, and didn't have a single friend who couldn't be persuaded to testify against him. And now, thanks to Johnny Smith, he met the most important criterion of all.

Sumner had heard Copeland's name now and then almost from the beginning of his investigation. From Debbie Fortner, whose friend Kathleen Nitzinger had lifted the fateful pills from Copeland's apartment, Sumner knew that Copeland dealt drugs, always had some illegal scheme cooking, and hung around the Rhinestone Cowboy, where he had been seen with both Priscilla and Stan Farr.

It wasn't much, but with Copeland unavailable to fill in the blanks, it was enough. All Sumner needed was some contact between Copeland and Farr. His informants could do the rest. They needed to show, one, that the relationship between Farr and Copeland was close; two, that it involved drugs; and three, that it involved large sums of money. Anything less wouldn't provide an adequate motive for murder.

Eventually, word of the Cullen Davis defense team's needs reached Becky Burns, a barmaid with a drug habit. What was Burns willing to testify? One, that the relationship between Farr and Copeland was so close they often took out-of-town trips together; two, that she had seen Farr and Copeland in the kitchen of the Rhinestone Cowboy snorting cocaine; and three, that she had seen Farr and Copeland together in the same room with large sums of money.

It was certainly more than enough to convince a jury, especially a redneck West Texas jury, that the murders of August 2 were related to a drug deal involving Stan Farr and Horace Copeland. But Sumner wanted more. He wanted a home run.

Fortunately for him, the plight of a rich man in trouble had also attracted the attention of Charles Baldwin, a Fort Worth attorney, and one of Baldwin's clients, Polly Ware. Ware was Horace Copeland's girlfriend at the time of the murders on Mockingbird Lane, but subsequently had the good sense to leave him.

Before even meeting with Sumner, Baldwin proclaimed to the press that Copeland had threatened to kill Farr and that his client could produce the murder weapon. When Polly Ware finally did turn over a gun to the police, however, the forensics lab spit it up like a hairball: there was no way it was the gun used to kill Andrea Wilborn and Stan Farr.

But Sumner wouldn't give up. He went over even the minutest flaws in the state's evidence, determined to make them fit into *his* Horace Copeland scenario. When he heard that Copeland's wife had turned in a suitcase that belonged to Dee Davis, Sumner flew immediately back to Fort Worth, telling other members of the defense team that he had found something that would "blow the prosecution out of the water": the suitcase that had held the drugs that were the *real* cause of the murders at the Davis mansion that night.

Then, suddenly, none of it mattered anymore. The alternative scenario, the drug deal gone sour, Horace Copeland—all of it could be thrown out the window. Discarded, forgotten. The defense had finally found the "dynamite" witness they had been promising all along. A witness who had been to the mansion on the night of August 2. A witness who had *seen* the murderer.

"Would you state your full name for the court and the jury, please?" Haynes smiled unusually broadly for the jury this morning, November 11, the trial's eighty-fourth day.

"Arthur Uewayne Polk," said the man in the witness chair. It was clear from the looks on their faces that the jurors were having trouble puzzling out this strange man with the dramatic black hair and artfully cropped beard, dressed in a Sunday-best three-piece suit; this strange man with the strange name: "U-wayne."

"And where do you work, Mr. Polk?"

"My mother and I have a nursery in Wedgwood," the

strange man responded, his voice so calm it sounded almost mechanical, "the Wedgwood Nursery."

"In May 1976, did your nursery do anything for Priscilla Lee Davis?" Haynes couldn't wipe the Cheshire-cat grin from his face.

"Yes," said Polk, barely moving his lips as he began to describe how he had arranged indoor plants around Priscilla's sunken bathtub, repotted old plants, landscaped an ivy planter downstairs, and filled the house with caladiums in preparation for a party.

"As a consequence of the work that you did in May of 1976, did you present any statement for your services?"

Indeed he had. The first time he came to the house with a bill for $677, it was early June, and Priscilla told him he would have to wait. He came again in the last week of June, but again Priscilla put him off. In July, he tried twice more; the second time he came to the house, but Priscilla wouldn't even see him. Speaking to him over the house phone, she insisted she had never gotten a bill. Angry but ever poised, Polk said he would bring another bill.

And that's exactly what he did—on August 2, 1976. He arrived at the mansion around midday, only nine or ten hours before the murders. Once again, Priscilla would only talk to him over the house phone.

"What did you say in that conversation with Priscilla Lee Davis?" Haynes asked.

"I wanted my money," said Polk.

Haynes introduced a copy of the bill into evidence and handed it to the witness for identification. Polk looked at it, confirmed what it was, then folded it up and stuck it in his pocket. Judge Dowlen leaned forward. "Pardon me," he whispered to Haynes. "I think the witness just put Defense Exhibit 269 back in his pocket."

Haynes turned on Polk. "That's not yours anymore," he scolded.

Polk flared. "You gave it to me." It was the first sign of any emotion. Haynes apologized. "I'm going to collect this yet." Polk said darkly. The jury got a glimpse of the anger behind Polk's mortician's facade.

After leaving the mansion, Polk continued, he returned home angry and unpaid. Then, about nine o'clock that night, he loaded a trail bike into the bed of his yellow pickup, grabbed a burlap bag, and drove to a highway bridge over the Trinity River only a few miles from the Davis house. From there, he rode the bike through Forest Park to the Hulen Street bridge, where he hid the bike in some bushes and waded across the Trinity's three-inch deep water.

"And how were you going in relation to the Davis house at 4200 Mockingbird?" Haynes asked.

"Going straight to it," said Polk.

"And why were you going up to the Davis house late at night with a tow sack, Mr. Polk?"

"I was going to get my plants."

Haynes smiled as if to say, "We understand. It was all Priscilla's fault."

Polk went on to tell how, when he reached the other side of the river, he found a spot at the top of the embankment to sit down, dry his feet, and put his shoes and socks back on. Conveniently, he also looked at his watch.

"And what time was it?" Haynes asked.

"It was eleven minutes after eleven. That stuck in my mind: four aces, I thought." For the first time, the jury and the spectators began to understand what they were hearing.

Polk had reached the most dramatic moment of his story. "In between the trees, there was what I thought to be a hobo . . ."

"You saw a figure?" Haynes prompted.

"A man. I thought he was just a hobo or a wino. There's a bunch of them down in through there on the railroad tracks. He had a sack over his shoulder."

Polk described how the man came straight toward the spot where he was sitting, drying his feet; how the man passed just below him on the embankment, not eight feet away. And then—another stroke of luck for the defense

—the man stopped and lit a cigarette, illuminating his face for Polk to see.

"Did you get a look at him at that time?" Haynes asked, his voice hushed with anticipation.

"Yes, I did."

"And could you describe him?"

"He was about five-eight or five-ten, one hundred eighty-five, one hundred ninety pounds, kind of chunky." His face? "He had very big eyes, very big . . . you could see the white all the way around the pupil." His hair? It was blond, "short and curly."

The prosecutors and those few spectators who had been following closely recognized the description. Little whirl-pools of whispering broke out all across the courtroom. "It's Horace Copeland," they were telling their neighbors. Polk had given a perfect police-profile description of Horace Copeland.

"Did you see where this man went?" Haynes asked.

"No," said Polk. "But I could hear him. I knew he was headed up the same direction I had planned on going." That is, toward the Davis mansion.

But was Uewayne Polk discouraged by the sight of a strange man sneaking through the woods ahead of him? Did he turn back out of fear, resolved to come again some other night when the dark paths were not so crowded with bag-toting strangers? Certainly not. After giving the curly-haired man only a few minutes head start, he proceeded on toward the house on the hill.

And sure enough, as soon as he arrived, he saw the strange man again, this time crouching by the outside of the swimming pool.

"And did you see him do anything," asked Haynes.

"I saw him put something on his head," said Polk. "I first thought it was a stocking." *He put something on his head!* And Polk, who had admitted reading about the case in the papers, didn't know what it was? If he truly didn't, he was the only person in the courtroom, the only person in Texas who didn't. It was the *wig*! He had seen the murderer put on the infamous, inexplicable black wig!

Suddenly the last few spectators realized what was being said, and the entire audience snapped into recognition. It is 11:30 on the night of August 2, 1976, only minutes before the murder of Andrea Wilborn, and this man is *there*; he is *at* the Davis house, *watching the murderer!* Finally, after months of conflicting testimony and forensic puzzles and ugly photographs, this strange man with the strange name had brought the jury through the woods to the very threshold of the murders and, for the first time, they were going to *see it happen!*

"Where did the man go from there?" Haynes asked.

"He got up and went right around the corner of the house," said Polk.

Still undeterred in his mission, brave Uewayne Polk scurried to the pool area, where he saw the man again.

"Where was he this time?"

"*Inside* the swimming pool," said Polk. Now he was inside the house. The murders could only be minutes away.

Polk described how, at one point, he thought the man had spotted him. "But there was this palm between me and him, and he just walked up to the window and looked *over* me. It scared me."

Scared him enough, apparently, to make him finally reconsider his mission. As soon as the man turned and went back into the house—only seconds away from the murders now—Polk ran. The story ended. "If only he could have followed the man into the basement," Shannon complained, "and watched from the foot of the steps."

Haynes gave the audience, and the jurors, a chance to catch their breath before he asked his last questions.

"Had you ever seen that man before, Mr. Polk?"

"No."

"Could you recognize that man if you ever saw him again?"

"Of course."

"Was the man you saw in the swimming pool on the night of August the second Cullen Davis?"

Polk turned his head dramatically toward the defendant. "*Definitely not.*"

* * *

They've finally done it, thought Joe Shannon as he straightened his notes and prepared to cross-examine Polk. After almost a year of dangling Cullen's millions as bait, the defense had finally landed the big one, the witness that every criminal defense lawyer fantasizes about: the witness who "saw it all" and—surprise!—is stone-cold positive that the defendant ain't the man he saw do it.

Before now, the defense had been content with little lies—a whole string of witnesses eager to curry Cullen's favor in the hopes that, someday, they could redeem that for hard cash. In many ways, Polk was just like the rest of them, the Sonny Fortners and the Sandy Myerses. He had been arrested for robbing a Safeway Store at gunpoint and then trying to escape by dressing up in women's clothes—heels, hat, gloves, the works. But they caught him anyway. In court, the judge had to jail his mother for contempt when she lied repeatedly to protect her son.

But there was one difference between Polk and the others. Polk was willing to tell the big lie.

The thought of it made Shannon so angry that he worried what he might say during the cross (would "You dirty lyin' sonofabitch" get him a contempt citation?). Everything about Polk's story was phony. By his own admission, he hadn't discussed his murder-night trip to the Davis mansion with anyone until the month before. And then whom did he call? The police? The D.A.? Hell, no. He called his attorney. And whom did his attorney call? The police? The D.A.? Hell, no; Cullen Davis's defense team.

"You told your lawyers that you didn't want to talk to anybody for the State of Texas, didn't you?" Shannon began.

"I suppose so," said Polk, suddenly uncomfortable. Like so many eager witnesses, he had only anticipated telling his story, not defending it.

"You either know it or you don't . . ." Shannon snapped.

"Yes," Polk conceded.

"And you didn't want to tell anybody from the State

any of this . . ." Shannon searched for a word that conveyed his contempt ". . . *business* you've told the jury, did you?"

"No."

"But you're just here as a fair, public-spirited citizen, aren't you, doing your part?" Sarcasm. Bitterness and sarcasm.

"Yes, sir." Polk struggled to maintain his composure.

"And that's what you're telling this jury?"

"Yes, sir."

"You didn't tell anybody from the Fort Worth Police Department when you first learned about what happened August second, did you?"

"No."

"You didn't tell anybody from the District Attorney's office, did you?" Shannon could feel the blood rising to his face.

"No."

"Because you were worried about your business?"

"Correct."

"You didn't want to get involved?" More sarcasm. Shannon wanted to ask, "If you *knew* Cullen was an innocent man, how could you watch as the courts turned down his bond appeals and sent him back to jail again and again?" But Haynes wouldn't allow any mention of Cullen's confinement—that might prejudice the jury against him.

"Correct," said Polk, his teeth set against the ridicule.

"Afraid you'd lose money?" Shannon taunted.

"Correct."

"But you've just decided it's time to come forward?" More ridicule. Disbelief, contempt, anger, and more ridicule.

"Yes, sir."

"Have you quit worrying about losing your business?" It was more a statement than a question. More an accusation than a statement. It was the heart of Shannon's attack. Was there any doubt in anyone's mind why Polk had waited so long to tell his preposterous tale?

"Yes."

"I want to ask you just one more question, Mr. Polk: How much money have you been paid to come up here and testify to this cock-and-bull story?"

There! He had said it. Haynes was on his feet, bellowing at the judge: ". . . the most scurrilous remark that the prosecutor made . . . We object . . . improper . . . instruct the jury . . ." but Shannon barely heard him. He had said it and it was right and it felt dadgum good. For the first time in a long time, he was proud of himself, proud of being a lawyer, and, for the first time in this whole long trial, wished his father was there to see him.

"Pass the witness, Your Honor."

That same day in Fort Worth, state investigators tracked down Paige Polk, Uewayne's estranged wife. She told them that her husband's watch wasn't working on the night of August 2, 1976. She remembered because he had fallen into the lake a few weeks before and she didn't take the watch to the repair shop until November of 1976, four months later. Also according to Paige, Uewayne had indeed taken a nocturnal trip to the Davis mansion to repossess some plants—*but it happened a week before the murders*. That explained why the details of his story were so vivid and accurate. The morning after the murders, she had said to her husband, "I'm sure glad you didn't go up there *last* night."

Paige Polk also related a conversation she had had with Uewayne just before he left to testify in Amarillo. "I'm going to get involved in the Cullen Davis case," he told her, "so keep your mouth shut."

Why was he "going to get involved"? Uewayne was behind on his separation payments, said Paige—$350 behind to be exact. (Plus a much larger sum owed to his divorce attorney that she didn't know about.) In a phone conversation the day before he left for Amarillo, Uewayne reassured his wife that he would have the money soon.

Three days later, Paige Polk took the stand in Amarillo and testified about that conversation.

"Mrs. Polk, I want to direct your attention to the ninth

day of November, 1977," said Shannon, "and ask you whether or not you had a conversation about this case with your husband, Arthur Uewayne Polk, on that date?"

"Yes, sir."

"Now, did he say anything to you on that occasion concerning the money he owed you?"

"Yes, sir, he said that as soon as he came back from here, he would pay me the money that he did owe me."

As Paige Polk stepped down from the witness chair, Shannon wondered how many of the other witnesses who had sat in the same seat over the previous months had said, "I'll have the money when I come back from Amarillo."

Uewayne Polk came back from Amarillo and paid his lawyer everything he owed him—in cash. Then he went out and bought a brand-new Lincoln Continental. The salesman marked the bill: "Paid in full. Cash."

After Paige Polk stepped down, Dowlen gave Shannon a weary look and said, "Call your next witness."

"Your Honor," said Shannon, "at this time the State rests." The prosecutors had decided to end on a high note, and Paige Polk was about as high as they were likely to get.

Dowlen did an open-mouthed double-take. "The State rests?"

For the first time in anyone's memory, Haynes seemed at a loss for words. "I . . . I . . . I was under the impression they had several more witnesses, if the Court please." In particular, he expected them to call Priscilla again. Indeed, he had been looking forward to it.

Dowlen recessed early for lunch to give the defense team a chance to decide their next move. If they rested, the case was over except for closing arguments. If they called more witnesses, the jury would blame them for prolonging the agony through Thanksgiving, keeping them away from home and family for the holidays.

Steve Sumner, of course, was still out panning through the mud of Horace Copeland's past. But his only promising

lead was that suitcase belonging to Dee Davis that showed
up in the possession of Copeland's wife. For Sumner, this
constituted "explosive" proof that Priscilla, her kids, and
Horace Copeland were all involved in a major drug-
trafficking operation. But not everyone on the defense
team was ready to make that leap.

When court reconvened on November 11, Haynes
made the announcement. "At this time, if the Court
please, the Defense rests."

49

The first time Joe Shannon looked at his watch, it was
already almost 2:00 A.M. The sky outside the window of
his room at the Amarillo Hilton was as dark as it was likely
to get that night. The next day he was scheduled to give
the prosecution's closing argument.

For Shannon, it had been a bleak five months, even if
you didn't count the breakup of his marriage after all the
weekends away from home. To remind himself how bleak,
he only had to flip yet again through the yellow, dog-eared
piles of trial notes on the table in front of him. He had
been sifting through them all night looking for just the
right attack in his argument the next day. What struck him
every time, however, wasn't what he saw in them, but
what he didn't see. They had just finished the longest criminal trial in Texas history; listened to the most witnesses
ever to testify in a criminal trial in Texas history; conducted
the most costly criminal prosecution in Texas history; compiled the fattest court record in Texas history—yet two
names had barely been mentioned: Cullen Davis and Andrea Wilborn.

Day after day, Shannon had watched in frustration as
Dowlen let Haynes fill the jury's ear with the slow acid of
Priscilla's past: previous marriages, divorce maneuverings,

Percodan, marital infidelities, maternal lapses, rich taste in jewelry, bad taste in friends. "Make them connect it up!" Shannon had shouted each time. Make them show some relevance to the night of August 2. But each time Haynes would promise, "We'll connect it up later, Your Honor." He never did, of course.

Shannon didn't blame Dowlen. George couldn't help it. He was just being himself—an amiable, trusting West Texan who made deals with a handshake and always took a lawyer at his word.

Where were Cullen Davis and Andrea Wilborn?

Lost in the middle of an ugly divorce trial. Only in a divorce trial, Priscilla would have been able to smear back. She could have raised the issue of *Cullen's* affairs, of the violent beatings at Cullen's hands, of Cullen's addiction to bizarre pornography, of Cullen's irresponsible spending sprees and sudden inexplicable trips on the company jet to unknown destinations, of Cullen's strange relationship with shady characters like Roy Rimmer, of Cullen's previous marriage and the ugly way it ended.

If only there had been as much about Cullen's relationship with Andrea as there had been about Priscilla's relationship with W. T.; as much about Cullen's tendency to abuse women as about Priscilla's tendency to party late; as much about Andrea's fondness for animals as about Priscilla's fondness for painkillers.

Where were Cullen Davis and Andrea Wilborn?

To keep the jury's attention riveted in lurid curiosity to Priscilla, Haynes had skimmed the slime off the gene pool. Priscilla's affairs, Stan Farr's shady businesses, Horace Copeland's drug deals gone sour, all were based on accounts from witnesses with one thing in common: a proven willingness to do or say anything for money.

Did the defense actually offer money? Did they need to? The prosecutors had once considered trying to prove that the defense was baiting its hook with cash. They debated issuing subpoenas and dragging people before a grand jury. But Shannon knew "scuzzbags and druggies" like Sandy Myers and Sonny Fortner were worthless in a

case like that. Put them up against a "reputable" attorney
and have them say, "This guy offered me $100,000," and
who would a grand jury believe? The prosecution couldn't
have gotten a conviction with a case like that, and the
defense knew it. And if they had tried, Haynes would have
screamed foul and beaten them up good in the press, and
the defense knew that, too.

Where were Andrea Wilborn and Cullen Davis?

Would the jury find them? Through the smoke and the
mud, past the sensational irrelevancies and lurid distrac-
tions, would the jury see Andrea Wilborn in a basement
room staring up into the hawk eyes of Cullen Davis as he
raised his gun and pointed it at her heart and pulled the
trigger?

Tomorrow, Shannon would do his best to make them
see.

The huge courtroom gradually fell silent as Joe Shannon stood and reviewed his notes for the last time. Antic-
ipating a crush of spectators, Judge Dowlen had moved
the closing arguments to the biggest courtroom in the Potter County Courthouse, but even it wasn't big enough.
The crowd spilled down the aisles and out the doorways.

They had rustled and murmured their approval all during Haynes's closing statement, especially when he ridiculed Priscilla as "the Queen Bee," or "Dr. Jekyll and
Mrs. Hyde," or "the lady in the la-dee-da pinafore." When
he pounded on the jury rail and loudly denounced her as
"the corruptor of young people" and "the Machiavellian
influence behind this whole thing," they almost broke into
cheers. It was exactly what Shannon had expected. More
talk of drugs and sex and the "scalawags, thugs, skuddies,
and rogues" with whom Priscilla surrounded herself. As
examples, Haynes singled out Sandy and Larry Myers, two
of the many rogues he himself had invited into the defense
camp for the same reason Priscilla invited them into her
house: He needed them.

For a big finish, Haynes had resurrected the "bad
mother" charge. "Don't you wonder," he asked the jury

with a vicious squint, "why would a grown woman permit her own daughter to associate with those people?" The state's entire case, he concluded grandly, "is predicated on the testimony of Priscilla Lee Davis, who *is not worthy*." There was scattered applause as he took his seat.

Shannon glanced one last time at his yellow pad of notes and looked up at the jury.

"A good defense lawyer is a master of illusion," he began, gesturing deferentially toward Haynes. "He creates illusions by innuendo, by suggestion, by questions." That's all the defense's case was, Shannon argued: illusions. Like the illusion of W. T. Rufner as a killer. "He's a free spirit," Shannon conceded with a smile, "but does that make him a killer? No, it just makes him a patsy." The "peculiar relationship" between Bev Bass and Priscilla Davis? That, too, was an illusion—"Not one *shred* of evidence to support it." Dark, malevolent dealings between Horace Copeland and Stan Farr? Another illusion. "They were friends, perhaps," Shannon conceded, "but there is *no* evidence that Farr owed Copeland any money."

Without doubt, the cheapest and tawdriest of the defense illusions was Uewayne Polk. Shannon summarized Polk's incredible story: "This guy just *happened* to squat down under the bush where he saw this fellow coming. . . . He just *happened* to get a good view . . . just *happened* to get to the corner of the swimming pool . . . just *happened* to catch this fellow inside . . . and lo and behold, guess what, it's not Thomas Cullen Davis!" Illusions, illusions, illusions.

Of all the defense's illusions, Shannon continued, none was more pernicious than the illusion that this was not a murder case. "Thirty percent of this lawsuit has been devoted to trying a divorce case. Another fifty percent has been Priscilla's association with those skuddies that Mr. Haynes told you about. The remaining twenty percent has tried to answer the question: 'Who killed Andrea Wilborn?' "

Shannon approached the jury box. His voice fell to a hushed plea. "It really doesn't matter . . . what you think

. . . of Priscilla Davis. What in the world did Andrea Wilborn . . . have to do . . . with any of this . . ." he searched for a word to encompass a wasteland of testimony ". . . business?" Whatever business Priscilla and Farr were into, "it did not give anybody the right to go in there and slay a twelve-year-old girl."

He walked slowly back to the counsel table and picked up a picture of Andrea Wilborn—one of the grotesquely colorful shots of her lying in a pool of blood on the utility room floor. He walked with it back toward the jury box. He didn't need to show it; they knew what it was.

"So what is it all about?" he mused. "The people who were killed that night in August 1976 are real people—or were—living, breathing human beings." He brought the picture up, looked at it for a moment (still without showing it), and said softly, "This is not the 'deceased.' " He turned it toward the jury. "This is Andrea Wilborn. *This* is what it's all about." His voice rose in indignation as he pointed a finger at the defense team. "*They* want you to try a divorce case. They want you to try a drug case. *I* want you to try the murder case of a twelve-year-old child—a twelve-year-old child who had every right to grow up and have a date, every right to go to the high school prom, every right to have some guy bring her a corsage . . ."

From the back of the courtroom, a strange sound began to drift forward. At first it sounded like whispering, then like whimpering. Finally it broke into long, heartbreaking wails. It was Jack Wilborn.

Shannon let the unearthly sound fill the silence around his voice: ". . . And don't you know, ladies and gentlemen, that this little girl had a right to grow up and be a woman and have kids, grandkids, do all the things that the rest of us get to do."

Now, finally, Shannon turned to the other silent player in the drama of the last fifteen months: Cullen Davis.

He took the jury back to August 1976, when Thomas Cullen Davis was eleven million dollars in debt and shackled by a divorce court order that made it almost impossible for him to conduct his affairs. "But that isn't the worst of it," said Shannon. "The worst of it is that this man, Stan Farr, is living out there in *his* house, in *his* mansion, where *he* ought to be living—living with *his* wife, drinking *his* whiskey . . ." Shannon lowered his voice to a fierce growl, "and by God, he's just had enough. . . . He would go out there and wipe it all out in one fell swoop." Shannon fixed his eyes on the jury. "And I submit to you that that's exactly what he did."

Was Cullen Davis, the stone-faced, well-dressed multimillionaire they had seen every day at the counsel table, capable of such a thing? Yes, Shannon insisted, and the jurors knew it from their own experience. "What you've seen in this court is an attempt to run over everyone that gets in this man's way." Shannon pointed at the expressionless defendant. "Just like on August 2 . . . people were in his way, and he *fixed their twats*—that's exactly what he did!"

For the first time, a crack appeared in Cullen's mask. Only a few spectators seated in the front noticed it, but it was there, if only for a moment: a kink in the lips, a tightening in the brow, a sudden intensity in the gaze. It wasn't fear, or anxiety, or even anger, they agreed later. It was hate. Pure hate.

If Cullen was so eager to fix their twats, Shannon asked, why did he let Priscilla get away? Why didn't he finish her off when he had the chance? "I'll tell you why." One last time he slipped the color photograph off the table and walked with it toward the jury. "Cullen Davis had one more way of hurting Priscilla," he explained. "He wanted to drag her down to that basement and show her Andrea's body." Suddenly the picture was in front of them again. "That would be it—the final hurt."

Shannon let their eyes linger for a moment before continuing. Then, still holding the picture up, he directed their attention to the blood on the top of Andrea's head. "How does a person shot in the chest get blood on her head?" he asked. "I'll tell you how. She fell on her stomach in a pool of her own blood. The killer turned her over to make sure she was dead. That's how he got blood on him and at the top of the stairs." Several jurors nodded in appreciation. The riddle of the bloody handprint had been solved.

"Power! Greed! He was going to have it his way," Shannon exclaimed. "And that's what he did that night. The judge. The jury. The executioner."

For the first time, he turned and faced the defendant. Cullen's eyes shifted to avoid contact. "This man has been accorded a whole lot more rights than he gave Andrea Wilborn. He has had twelve people sitting up here in judgment of him. Andrea Wilborn didn't have anybody sitting in judgment of her."

Suddenly Shannon himself was back in the basement of the mansion on Mockingbird Lane, the day they had searched and found the bullet hole, the day he had stood in the little utility room and seen the phantoms reenacting their horrific drama. "I wonder what Andrea thought," he heard himself say, his voice echoing in the vast courtroom, "when she looked down the muzzle of that .38 before he snuffed out her life. I wonder if she pleaded with him, begged him."

Suddenly he was back again, and the eyes of every juror were fixed on him. "I don't know," he said, shaking his head, "and I guess we'll never know. But I submit to you, ladies and gentlemen, the time has come for you to make a decision."

50

R. C. Hubbard wanted out. It had been 124 days—more than four months—since his sentence began. Four months of the same bland hotel food, four months of beds that were too soft and steaks that were too tough, of nosy bailiffs and shredded newspapers. Now, by God, he wanted *out*.

The first few weeks of sequestration, before jury selection was finished, hadn't been so bad. That first Sunday, R. C.'s whole family had come by the hotel for a visit. Some of the other jurors also had visitors, families mostly. Then the prosecutors got wind of it—some meddlesome federal judge happened to be staying at the same hotel—and all hell broke loose.

R. C. couldn't imagine what all the fuss was about. So what if some jurors were making unmonitored telephone calls, or letters were coming in and going out without being checked by a bailiff? So what if they left the radios in the jurors' hotel rooms? They had taken out the TVs. So what if the deputies assigned to monitor the jury wandered away for a few minutes or left their wives in charge of the jury, or said to a group of jurors during an excursion to the mall, "We'll meet back here in an hour"? What was the prosecution so worried about? "Don't they trust us?" R. C. complained to the other jurors.

Apparently not. It wasn't long before every juror was dragged in front of Judge Dowlen to answer questions about "unmonitored contacts." It was humiliating. They had to give the names of everybody they had talked to or written since being sequestered and answer questions about "undue influence." R. C. tried to explain: "We've been hearing all this crap about being influenced, but when we get an opportunity to talk to one of our loved ones, the last thing we want to talk about is this garbage." The judge asked the questions, but it was no secret among the jurors that the prosecution was behind the whole ugly episode.

And then, as if that wasn't bad enough, they dragged all the jurors' *relatives* into court: mothers, fathers, brothers, sisters, wives, husbands, children—anybody who had had "unmonitored contact" with a juror—and gave them what R. C. described indignantly as "the third degree." Everybody who was questioned had to go over anything they had written or talked about with a juror, some of it quite personal: "What do the X's and O's at the bottom of this letter mean?" Not surprisingly, the defense kept a safe distance from this prying-eyes inquisition. Every time the judge asked the defense attorney if he had any questions for a witness, he would look up with a startled expression and say, "Why, *I* have nothing to ask." It wasn't the defense, after all, that distrusted the jury, it was the prosecution.

The jurors themselves probably never would have heard about the harassment of their relatives—the prosecution hoped they wouldn't until after the trial was over—if it hadn't been for R. C. Hubbard.

It started one night when he was visiting the room of Alma Miller, the sixty-four-year-old "grandmother" of the group. The bailiff came and told him that any conversation between jurors had to be monitored. That was all R. C. needed to hear. "Hey, look, guy," he flared, still burning from the way they had canceled the family visits. "*We* aren't the criminals. If you start putting all these restrictions on us," he looked the bailiff slam in the eye, "if you want another mistrial like they had down in Fort Worth, why, that's what you're going to get." Sure enough, the bailiff backed out of the room and never said another word about it.

Emboldened, R. C. wrote a note to Judge Dowlen and passed it around for the other married jurors to sign. It asked for the family visits to be reinstated for wives only. They handed the note to Wiley Alexander, who brought it to Dowlen. "Oh, crap," said Dowlen when he saw it. He knew the prosecutors would have a fit. If he said yes and the trial ended in a guilty verdict, the defense would have an automatic appeal and a likely reversal and they'd all be right back where they started. On the other hand, George Dowlen was a West Texas man, and he understood the needs of other West Texas men. "If we don't do it," he said, "there may be a revolution at the Executive Inn."

When the defense heard the news, they were elated. Dowlen had handed them both rock-solid grounds for reversal and a stock of happy jurors. As for the prosecution, Dowlen chose not to tell them about it just yet. And when they heard the rumor and asked him if it was true, he just shrugged his shoulders and looked away—a gesture they mistook for a no.

In addition to weekly "conjugal visits"—with a bailiff standing mortified just outside the door—the jurors got something else out of the bargain: a steady stream of news about themselves and the trial. When W. T. Rufner referred in court to his recent foray into the T-shirt business (something that had appeared only in the media), more than a few jurors smiled knowingly. Many had also heard from family members about "that nice man" Ray Hudson, Karen Master's father, who made a point of getting to know the jurors' families and filling their ears with Priscilla's evils and Cullen's virtues.

R.C.'s weekly conjugal visits from Jessie—who made no secret of *her* opinion of Priscilla Davis—helped make the long ordeal tolerable, but only just barely. He still had to sit through hours, days, weeks of Priscilla's lies. The sex, the Percodan, the drugs, the parties, none of it surprised him—he had her pegged from the start. But all of it revolted him. It got so bad that he and three or four of the other jurors would come back to the hotel at night and sing religious songs. They started off just listening to Fred Thompson, the cowboy, who played country music on his guitar. But after a few days of Priscilla's lies, they needed something more uplifting. They needed something to wash all that garbage out of their systems.

After Priscilla, the prosecution's case went from bad to worse. Poor prosecutors, R. C. thought, they seemed like good lawyers, but they were stuck trying to prove Priscilla's lame story. They should never have believed her in the first place. He felt the same way about Beverly Bass. Priscilla had somehow conned Bev into lying for her, convinced her to "go up there and match wits with Racehorse Haynes." It was just like Priscilla to think that a "confused, mixed-up" little girl like Bev could "beat Haynes at his own game." The result was a farce.

That was pretty much the way R. C. felt about all the prosecution's witnesses. They should have known better

than to get up on the stand and say things that they knew
Racehorse would attack. After a while, it got boring watching Haynes tear them apart.

Most of the time, though, Haynes did his best to keep
things interesting. When Haynes started bringing on his
own witnesses, the trial really picked up, R. C. thought.
He was fascinated and appalled by the stories about what
really went on at the mansion. He found it inconceivable
that a mother would allow those kinds of people in her
house, near her children. "That woman got what was coming to her," he said more than once. That's what Haynes
was saying in his closing argument.

R. C. believed Uewayne Polk's story. It sounded "fea-
sible" to him. Besides, R. C. could see himself in Polk's
shoes. He had been twenty-five once, and impetuous. If
Priscilla had done to him what she did to Polk, he just
might have taken the law into his own hands too. A woman
like that could make a good man do awful things. Awful
things.

Finally, toward the end, not even Haynes's theatrics
could keep R. C. from going stir-crazy. In four months, he
had cast thirty-five pounds of lead bullets in his little
electric melting pot. He had built both a rifle and a pistol
from kits. He had read his Bible so often it was falling
apart, sung every hymn he knew a hundred times, and
now, by God, he was ready to get out. Sometimes it felt
like even just one more cup of bad coffee, one more swim
in the cold hotel pool, one more meal in the Surf Room,
one more Saturday night watching the kids dragging along
Polk Street, one more table with the same eleven faces
around it, and he would lose control, bolt for the door
and head straight home to Jessie.

Fortunately, at just about the same time, the case came
to an end. Now all he had to do was vote and it would
finally be over. R. C. could hardly wait.

Outside the jury room, the bailiffs took up their posts.
Wiley Alexander, the cagey former police chief who had
sat through every word of testimony, same as the jury,

knew how *he* would vote. There was no doubt in his mind
that "Cullen Davis went out there that night and killed
that little girl."

But he wasn't at all sure the jury would agree. He had
watched them looking at Mr. Cullen Davis, with his fine
tailored suit on, not saying anything, looking all calm and
polite, and Wiley thought he could hear them thinking:
"Why, look at that nice Mr. Davis. He couldn't possibly
have done such an awful thing. Not with all that money."
And then they would look at Priscilla and say, "We're not
gonna let that hooker come in here and take control of
that nice Mr. Davis's hard-earned millions."

Deputy Sheriff Al Cross, referred to by the press corps
as "Deputy Dawg," wasn't really thinking about the verdict. He was thinking about how boring his life would be
after Cullen Davis departed—whether it was to Fort
Worth or to Huntsville. The last four months had been
the most exciting of his life. Reporters asked him questions, ladies in the gallery plied him with cookies. Everybody wanted the "inside" story on Cullen Davis—*his*
prisoner Cullen Davis—and to get it, they had to pay
attention to *him*, Al Cross. It felt good to have people pay
attention, even if it was only for a while. He was gonna
miss it.

If he had had a vote, of course, it would have been not
guilty. He was just so impressed with Cullen.

Inside the jury room, the twelve elected Gilbert Kennedy, the retired postman, foreman.

"I feel like Priscilla was telling the truth about who did
the shooting," Kennedy opened the discussion. "I realize
a lot of it was lies, but I believe that part."

Mary Kay Haessley agreed. She thought Priscilla
showed courage in standing up to Haynes's attacks.

"Haynes has such a mastery of the English language,"
said Alma Miller.

R. C. couldn't believe his ears. They actually *believed*
something Priscilla said. "Haynes caught Priscilla in so
many lies," he argued, "how can you pick out what was
truth and what was fiction? I can't."

"Even if you don't believe Priscilla," someone said, "you've got Bev Bass's story. No one contradicted her version of what happened."

R. C. gave them an earful of his opinion of Bev Bass: ". . . a confused, mixed-up little girl . . ."

Mike Giesler, a sheet-metal worker at Bell Helicopter, and at twenty-six, the youngest member of the jury, couldn't figure out why, if Cullen wasn't the killer, the killer had turned and shot Bubba Gavrel when Bev Bass said, "It's Cullen." "If I had been the killer and Beverly had mistaken me for someone else, I probably would have let her get away."

R. C. had an answer for that, too. "I think, if a person was that berserk, that would have been a logical thing to do."

"I wonder what Cullen's voice sounds like," Alma Miller mused.

Bettie Blair, a fifty-year-old secretary and divorcée, said she believed Polk's version of the murder night.

That caused another small eruption. "What a hoax," Haessley protested. Someone else called it "a farce."

"A lot of people lied," said Bettie, unmoved, "and they will be punished by God for it, but I think Polk was telling the truth."

R. C. seconded Bettie. He told the others how he would have done the same thing Polk did—in his youth.

Mike Giesler didn't think Polk had been to the house, but that didn't change the way he felt about Priscilla Davis. He blamed her for not trying to warn Bev and Bubba when she heard their voices, instead of just hiding in the bushes long enough to make a run for it. He blamed her for being addicted to Percodan and sex. Every time he looked at her on the stand, all hard hair and hard heart, he thought of his own ex-wife and the old anger knotted in his throat. All women were the same.

His anger brought a round of approving nods.

R. C. wanted to know why Cullen had only shot Priscilla once. "If I was mad enough to kill my wife, or anyone," he explained, "and I had a six-shooter, with five or six rounds in it, and I intended to kill a person, I wouldn't shoot them one time. I certainly wouldn't shoot them and let them run out of the house, and then go dragging them back in there, and, you know, do all this horsing around. I'da probably emptied the gun."

Someone reminded him of Joe Shannon's explanation in his closing statement: "He was gonna take her down into the basement and show her Andrea's body. He didn't just want to kill her, he wanted to hurt her." R. C. didn't remember that—and he didn't find it very convincing now.

R. C. didn't have much sympathy for Stan Farr, either. "If he was sleeping with my teenage daughter, I would have pulled out my .38 and saved Cullen or someone else the trouble." Coming from a man who cast lead bullets in his spare time, it sounded like a genuine threat.

Someone else wanted to know how Cullen could have dragged a huge man like Farr "all the way across the kitchen floor, and all the time he's got a gun in his hand, and it's wrapped up in a plastic garbage bag. How's a guy that little going to move that much dead weight?"

Karl Prah, the burly ticket agent for Braniff, pointed out that no matter how many small questions they found unanswered in Priscilla's story, it still matched almost exactly Bev Bass's story. Shannon had asked the question at the very end: "How do you explain two women running in opposite directions at the same time both telling the same story?"

"It was a conspiracy," R. C. insisted. "They were all in on it together: Priscilla, Bev, Gavrel. It was all Priscilla's plot."

But there was no *time*! came the response. Priscilla was shot and Bubba was lying in a pool of blood. Could they really believe that under those circumstances the two women met on the lawn and, on the spur of the moment, agreed to pin the murders on somebody who could have been at a party surrounded by a hundred witnesses or in South America that night for all they knew?

There was a long, percolating pause. Kennedy decided

it was time to send out for drinks: eight Cokes and four Dr. Peppers.

When they resumed, Karl Prah had a new theory. There *was* a conspiracy, he suggested, but it wasn't a *conscious* conspiracy; it was "coincidental." Cullen had confronted Bev and Bubba while Priscilla was still within hearing distance. So when Bev cried out, "Cullen, don't shoot, it's me," again and again, Priscilla must have heard her and got it into her head that Cullen was the gunman —like subliminal suggestion. "That's where Priscilla could have gotten Cullen's name," Prah concluded, "even if she knew it was somebody else who did it."

But why would she cover up for someone who had just killed her daughter and her lover?

Prah thought for a minute. "It was convenient to blame Cullen so she would be safe from the real killer?"

But why was Bev yelling Cullen's name in the first place if it wasn't Cullen?

Another long silence. Kennedy decided it was time to take the first vote. They had been deliberating less than four hours. Each juror wrote a vote on a piece of paper, folded it, and passed it to Kennedy at the end of the table. When they were all in, he unfolded them one by one and divided them into two stacks. When he was finished, there were ten slips in one stack and two in the other.

R. C. was shocked by the number of votes for not guilty.

Only a few minutes later, after a brief discussion of the meaning of "reasonable doubt," they took another vote.

This time, there was only one stack.

51

Judge Dowlen allowed a shallow smile when the bailiff brought him the message that the jury had reached a verdict. It was November 17, 1977. The night before, a reporter had asked him how long he thought the jury would take. "They'll be back around 2:30 tomorrow afternoon," he predicted.

He looked at his watch; it was 2:32.

In the courtroom, people scurried to their seats when they heard the news. Dowlen raised his voice above the chaos: "There will be no demonstrations or outbursts when the verdict is read. Is that understood?"

Joe Shannon fought through the crowd and took his place at the counsel table. It had only been twenty-four hours since his closing argument and *he couldn't remember a damn thing about it*. He recalled looking at his notes once before starting, but everything after that was a total blank. Still, he knew that he had done a good job—the best job of his career, in fact. If the jurors were movable, he had moved them.

But in only *four hours*? Four hours of deliberation after four *months* of testimony? Shannon shook his head. It didn't look, well, proportionate. It also didn't look promising.

At the other end of the table, the phalanx of defense lawyers had gathered. Dee Miller, who had successfully navigated the entire trial without uttering a word, made no secret of his concern following the prosecution's closing statement. "Shannon scared the hell out of me," he told a reporter.

But not Cullen. Seated between Haynes and Sumner, Davis ignored the pandemonium around him, his marbly black eyes fixed straight ahead as the jurors filed in like a choir. He didn't smile, exactly. The expression was closer to tolerance than concern. Someone called it Cullen's "you-can't-touch-me" look. The night before, he had heard from his sources that the jury was leaning toward acquittal, ten to two. Clearly, no one was going to touch him this day.

Richard Haynes had heard the same reports, but he still didn't sleep. He remembered a case where the jury went into their deliberations eleven to one for acquittal and came out a few hours later eleven to one for conviction. Even all the resources of Kendavis Industries couldn't make people predictable. He scanned the incoming jurors, hoping for some sign: a smile, eye contact, anything.

The bailiff took the verdict form from foreman Gilbert Kennedy and delivered it to Dowlen.

"The defendant will please rise," Dowlen said without looking at it.

Cullen stood, bracing himself with both hands on the table. Spectators in the front row leaned over the rail to see if they could detect any sign of weakness. There was none. He looked like a CEO at a board meeting rising to make a point.

Haynes's eyes jumped from juror to juror. A sign? A sign?

With agonizing deliberateness, Dowlen unfolded the verdict form.

Haynes looked and looked . . . and then he saw it. Alma Miller was smiling at Cullen.

"We, the jury, find the defendant, Thomas Cullen Davis, not . . ."

The courtroom exploded. Cheers, applause, whoops of triumph. A stampede of reporters toward the doors. In a mass, the spectators surged forward and broke over the defense table. The defense lawyers clutched at each other like World Series victors. Cullen hugged Sumner and Haynes. Karen Master, first over the rail, scrambled toward Cullen with tears streaking her cheeks. "I love you, I love you," she gushed again and again as they embraced. Then she turned and hugged Haynes. Someone thought he saw a tear in Haynes's eye, but the surging crowd quickly obscured him in a frenzy of congratulations.

Joe Shannon stood up and tried to feel his legs. They were numb. His whole body was numb. People were all around him, but he didn't want to see them. He stuck his hands deep into his pockets and refused to look up. His fingers felt the warm change in his pocket. For something to do, he pulled it out and held it low and close. It gave his eyes something to look at. His mind focused mightily on the five coins: a nickel, a dime, three pennies. Eighteen cents. The thought of Cullen's millions bullied its way into his head. There was a moral here, but he didn't want to think about it.

Meanwhile, at the other end of the counsel table, bailiff Al Cross had pulled out his revolver to "guard" Cullen. He waved it in the air with a grim expression, shouted at the crowd to "make way, make way!" and began pushing toward the exit, the gun in one hand and a startled Cullen grasped in the other. This was it: his last chance to shine in Cullen's reflected glory; his last chance to show Cullen how useful Al Cross could be; his last chance to be somebody.

A few minutes later, the phone rang at the mansion on Mockingbird Lane. An Associated Press reporter was calling to tell Priscilla Davis the verdict. After a long pause, she could only cry.

"Priscilla Lee Davis is the dregs of the earth," Richard "Racehorse" Haynes shouted into the microphone as his fellow revelers whooped their agreement. A camera crew from a local TV station had crashed the victory party at Rhett Butler's to broadcast the festivities live on the six o'clock news. As high on scotch as Priscilla had ever been on Percodan, Haynes grabbed the microphone and let the city of Amarillo know what he thought of the state's star witness.

"She's probably shooting up right now," he sputtered. "She is the most shameless, brazen hussy in all of humanity. She is a charlatan, a harlot, and a liar. She is a snake, unworthy of belief under oath. She is a dope fiend, a habitué of dope." Phil Burleson tugged at Haynes's sleeve, hoping to stop him, but Haynes was a man possessed. It wasn't enough that the jury had acquitted his client; he wanted to convict Priscilla. "She is the most sordid human being in the United States, in fact, *the whole world!*" His eyes narrowed. "Someone ought to put a barbed-wire fence around her house and not let her out."

Undaunted, the TV reporter followed up, "Do you

have any comment on Priscilla's statement that 'Now Cullen will have to answer to God. That's one he can't buy'?"

Cullen laughed so loud the room fell silent. "How would *she* know?" he said. Furtive, puzzled looks ricocheted around the room: Did he mean to say that?

Everyone was there: Sumner, Haynes, Burleson, Miller, Gibson, the investigators, the secretaries, Kendavis Industries executives, courtroom supporters, even four of the jurors, all one big drunken throng. Cullen strutted among them, Karen at his side, receiving their congratulations with nods and strange little smiles. "You're so brave," they would say, or, "How did you put up with it for so long?" To which Cullen would respond, "I guess I showed them," or "We sure kicked some butt."

Women panted their admiration and hugged Karen for standing by her man. Men patted him on the back and made squinty-eyed jokes about "doing without" and "abstinence makes the heart grow fonder." The raunchier the reference, the deeper the leer, the broader Cullen's smile. Someone called out above the din: "Rich men don't kill their wives." Bettie Blair, the juror, answered: "No, they hire somebody to do it." More laughter.

A short blonde woman appeared in the doorway, burst into joyful tears, and ran toward Cullen. "I'm so grateful you were acquitted," she squealed through the tears as she threw her arms around him and planted a bright red kiss. It was D'Ann Hill, one of the bailiffs.

Cullen smiled awkwardly. "Isn't this illegal or something?" he drawled.

"Not anymore," Hill shrieked.

Next to join the party was George Dowlen. Unaware of the celebration, he had brought a date to his favorite bar for a drink. But the crowd wouldn't let him alone. *"Hero,"* they called out, and "Great job, George." A voice rose above the others: "Get over here, Judge. Have a drink on us!" and the crowd picked up the chant: "Dowlen, Dow-len, Dow-len!" Dowlen smiled and waved and the chant grew louder: *"Dow-len, Dow-len, Dow-len!"* When he finally gave up and joined them, the crowd went crazy. Later, when the party moved downstairs for dinner, Dowlen took the place of honor next to Cullen.

Out of nowhere, a guitar materialized and Haynes grabbed it. "This is the 'Ballad of Cullen Davis,' " he announced in a voice as taut with screaming and drinking as a guitar string. In the roar of celebration and the rattle of drinks, the words were lost, but everyone figured it must be good because Racehorse was sure enjoying it.

Over in another corner of the room, Ray Hudson, Karen's father, was bragging about his role in "the greatest courtroom victory of modern times": "Those cocksuckers," he sputtered contemptuously, referring to the prosecutors, "they never realized it was put together that way. There wasn't nothing left unturned. It was all covered. . . . I knew when a juror sneezed or farted. I had the finger on the pulse. We had that son of a bitch won before the jury ever sat down."

Later, in a quiet moment when Ray Hudson found himself next to Cullen, he asked a question that had been on his mind for months. "The time you spent in jail, and going through the whole deal, has it made you more tolerant . . . more patient . . . more bitter? . . . Has it changed you in any way?"

Cullen's eyes went blank and there was a long, awkward silence as the two men just looked at each other. Then, finally, Cullen spoke. "No," he said, deadly earnest, "I haven't changed. I'm the same man."

52

Cullen Davis came home to Fort Worth a hero. The *Star-Telegram* embraced him with front-page photos, flattering articles, and a fulsome silence on the questions left unanswered by the trial. When one reporter inquired, "Do you know the identity of the true killer?" Cullen replied, "Probably. But I'm not going to do the D.A.'s work for them. Let them find out who it is." No one was so ungracious as to wonder publicly what kind of man would rather service a grudge than see the murderer of a twelve-year-old girl brought to justice.

On the streets, strangers would reach out their hands in congratulation, ask him to pose for pictures, or plead for autographs. And not just in Fort Worth. The same reception awaited him when he flew to Aspen soon after the trial on a long-postponed ski trip. He had become a *national* hero.

The elite of Fort Worth opened their doors and dining rooms to the city's newest celebrity, one of their own, and his "attractive girlfriend," as *Texas Monthly* referred to Karen. From the ladies of the Colonial Country Club to Cullen's pool buddies at the Petroleum Club, at every event from the Steeplechase Ball to Charles Tandy's sixtieth-birthday bash, they were embraced as honored guests. After a year's absence, Cullen's name was reinstated in the Fort Worth Social Directory. "It was almost as if Amarillo never happened," marveled Kendavis attorney Hershel Payne as he sat with a tanned, serene Cullen at the Merrimac Bar after work one day. In December, only one month after the trial, *D* magazine named Cullen one of the "People to Watch in 1978."

In the midst of so much celebrity, Cullen began thinking more and more about Hollywood. As the trial receded into the past, he wanted some way to "immortalize" his hold on the public's imagination. While still in jail, he had often thought about a book. He had even contacted his old classmate, Tommy Thompson, whose *Blood and Money* had soared to the top of every bestseller list. But Thompson begged off. "I've already done my Texas Gothic," he explained. (To friends, he confided the real reason: "I think he's guilty as hell.")

So Cullen's fantasies turned to a movie. Plans for a big-screen replay of the events of August 2, 1976, began to obsess him. He knew he wanted Ann-Margret for Karen and suggested jokingly that Phyllis Diller should play Priscilla and Mickey Rooney, Richard Haynes. But the critical issue, of course, was who would play him.

At first he favored Al Pacino, the moody, dark-eyed star of *The Godfather*, to whom many of his admirers compared him. But all that changed one night at the Old Swiss House restaurant when Cullen spotted James Garner at another table. He sent a bottle of champagne to Garner's table along with a message: "Mr. Davis might have a part for him in a film." Garner's reply: "Thank Mr. Davis for the champagne and tell him I wouldn't touch his film."

Inevitably, a fearless reporter brought news of Cullen's movie plans to Priscilla for a reaction. It came etched in acid: "Ask the sonofabitch who he's going to get to play Andrea."

The blitz of favorable publicity did not convince everyone. Pat Massad, a high school classmate of Cullen's, attended a dinner party one night when the subject of Cullen Davis came up—as it did at every dinner party, it seemed. "Let's take a vote," one of the guests suggested. "Who thinks he's guilty?" All but one person raised their hands.

Even Davis family friends and business associates were having second thoughts about Cullen. Hershel Payne no longer sputtered with indignation every time somebody suggested that being acquitted was not the same as being innocent. Little by little, Payne's rousing defense of Davis family integrity was reduced to lawyerly hedging. He still insisted to friends that Cullen "does not seem the type of person to me that could do such a thing," but now he felt obliged to add, "unless he were persuaded to do it, or at least had the idea planted."

Karen felt the backlash of skepticism when she returned from skiing in Aspen to find that her ex-husband had secured a restraining order preventing her from taking her two sons "around or near Cullen Davis." Walter Master claimed that his ex-wife was exploiting their children as "status symbols," that she was unfit to be a mother, and that continued exposure to Cullen would jeopardize the boys' "physical health [and] moral development."

Karen dismissed the attack as the rantings of a jealous ex-husband. But other defections were harder to explain.

Ray Hudson thought a long time before making the call to Jack Wilborn. "Mr. Wilborn?" he ventured tentatively. "This is Ray Hudson."

Wilborn recognized the name. In Amarillo, a man dressed in Western clothes and boots had approached him in the courtroom the day he went to hear Joe Shannon's closing argument. He seemed like a colorful local type, with a firm handshake and a warm hardware-store manner. He also seemed to know just about everybody in the courtroom, especially the bailiffs. Wilborn had assumed he was part of the prosecution team. "I know it's real hard for you," the man had said in his heavy, amiable accent. "I have a daughter of my own." Wilborn considered it a thoughtful gesture and later asked one of the D.A.'s assistants who the man was. "Why, that's Ray Hudson," he was told, "Karen Master's father."

Jack Wilborn had been sick at heart ever since that day. After the closing argument, he had waited in the parking lot outside the courthouse to congratulate Shannon. "You did a great job," he told him, the tears still welling up. "I really appreciate it." But he also knew it wasn't enough. He had heard the spectators cheering for the defense; he had seen the relatives of the jurors sitting cheek-by-jowl with Cullen's minions in the courtroom. On the flight back to Fort Worth, he had told his wife, Betty: "From what I've seen, they will never convict Cullen Davis."

Now the amiable hardware-store voice from that awful day was on the phone. "Mr. Wilborn, I wonder if you would meet me for lunch. I've got something I want to talk to you about."

Wilborn felt his blood rising. "I don't believe I want to," he said in a voice like stone, trying not to let his rage show.

There was a pause at the other end of the line. "Well, I guess I don't blame you," Hudson finally said. "I just wanted to tell you how ashamed I am and to apologize for taking any part in that trial . . ." another pause ". . . I'm so sorry." Then he hung up.

Ray Hudson wasn't the only one reevaluating his role in the Amarillo trial.

In the summer of 1977, during the trial, a woman named Martha Sloane walked into the office of the Tarrant County District Attorney and asked to speak to Bill Lane, one of the young prosecutors. She and Lane had dated for a while several years before.

But this wasn't a social call. The woman had come to talk about the Cullen Davis case.

In Lane's office, she clutched her purse tightly and tried to smile, but the muscles of her face, taut with anxiety, wouldn't allow it. "There is something I think you ought to know," she began. "I just think that somebody ought to know." She was obviously frightened.

She had been a secretary at Burleson, Pate & Gibson, Phil Burleson's law firm, for several years. She had been there all during the Amarillo trial. She had heard things. Things had gone on—were *still* going on—things that weren't right.

What things?

They all know he's guilty, Sloane said. The attorneys at the firm, they all believed that Cullen did it. The defense had evidence that Cullen was a "paranoid manic depressive," not only capable of murder but guilty of it. Among themselves, Sloane said, they referred to him routinely as "the killer." Mike Gibson had told her on several occasions to "stay away from Cullen," that even his own family considered him "crazy." Sloane added that when she asked Gibson point-blank if Cullen murdered Andrea Wilborn and Stan Farr, he replied, point-blank, "In cold blood." Jack Pate agreed. Gibson had also warned her away from Roy Rimmer. "Rimmer *has* and *will* do anything for Cullen," he said ominously.

"I just don't understand how they could be behaving the way they are," Sloane wailed. They had invited Cullen to the firm's Christmas party and then made jokes behind his back about "how glad they were that no twelve-year-old girls were present." It was also common knowledge in the firm that Cullen had a history of dressing up in women's clothes. According to Sloane, somebody in his own family—Ken, she thought—had confirmed it. Some time earlier, he had apparently been seen at the Albatross in drag—wearing a black wig.

There was more. The firm's all-out push on Cullen's behalf may have brought a million-plus dollars in billings, but it also brought a plague of embarrassing problems. Steve Sumner's so-called "investigation," in particular, had turned into a quagmire. Despite Sumner's assurances that none of his witnesses had been offered money, somehow the checks kept going out, especially to Sandy Myers. First to cover the legal expenses for her drug case, then to pay her telephone bills, apartment rent, furniture payments, and even miscellaneous living expenses as part of the "Cullen Davis Witness Protection Program." The bills continued long after the trial was over. The rental car she had been "lent" wasn't turned back to Hertz until August 21, 1978, nine months after the verdict in Amarillo. By then, the trust fund that Cullen had set up to pay these and other "collateral" trial expenses had run out, leaving Burleson to cover them with firm money.

How did Martha Sloane know all this? Her boss, Bill Gibson, was the firm's office manager. He was the one who cut Sandy's checks—and he wasn't happy about it. "Go talk to him," Sloane urged. "He's superstraight. He'll tell you."

Nor was Sandy Myers the only former witness on the company dole. The Burleson firm had paid Valerie Marazzi's bond too, after an arrest on drug-related charges.

Sloane knew what she was saying. She had worked for lawyers before. She knew what was allowed and what wasn't. "I feel insulted by what's been happening around me," she told Lane.

Everywhere Cullen went, it seemed, he left shadows; now the firm was falling under one, too—and there wasn't a thing they could do about it. Innocent or not, he was a client.

Bill Lane tried to reassure Sloane. She seemed so frightened that he was frightened for her. They met several more times, sometimes at the office, sometimes at his house. She brought documentation, including canceled checks, to support everything. For her safety, he never called; he waited for her to call. Immediately after that first meeting, Lane went straight to Tim Curry. Curry listened without expression and, when Lane was finished, thanked him, but decided not to do anything about it—at least for the time being.

By June 1978, only seven months after the trial, even Karen Master was having doubts about Cullen. Not about his innocence; she didn't dare think about that, no matter what second thoughts her father might have. Her doubts were about the future, not the past. For all the flattering pictures, favorable articles, and Hollywood fantasies, things had not been going well for Cullen. The trial in Amarillo had not solved his problems, only postponed them.

The divorce still loomed ahead, more ominous than ever. Priscilla's lawyers were threatening to use the proceedings to reopen the Amarillo case, rehashing every sordid detail. Only this time, Cullen wouldn't be able to hide behind his Fifth Amendment rights. "It will be a whole new ballgame," announced Ronald Aultman's partner Jerry Loftin. "There will be highly significant testimony which prosecutors could not bring out during the Amarillo trial." In other words, Cullen Davis would have to take the stand.

Nor would the judge be as genial and naive as George Dowlen. Despite a risky move by Cullen's lawyers to disqualify him, Judge Joe Eidson clung tenaciously to the case. If anything, his attitude toward Cullen had only hardened since the round of unfavorable rulings that, according to prosecutors, precipitated the events of August 2, 1976. Since starting up the case again after the verdict in Amarillo, Eidson had postponed the final hearings several times, he had refused to reduce Priscilla's monthly allowance of $5,000, and he had continued to control the transfer of funds into and out of Kendavis Industries—just as he had before the murders.

In addition to the divorce, there were now other lawsuits threatening, most of them related to the shootings: Bubba Gavrel's suit for $13,000,000; Priscilla's civil suit; Jack Wilborn's suit for Andrea's wrongful death; and two similar suits by Stan Farr's family. Cullen's legal bills were soaring and he still owed $400,000 to Burleson, Pate & Gibson for the Amarillo rescue.

At the same time, Kendavis Industries was in deeper trouble than ever. Despite a boom elsewhere in the oil industry, Stratoflex's profits had fallen 72 percent in 1977, and rumors abounded that Mid-Continent was desperately short of cash and might have to go public to survive. Yet, strangely, Cullen continued to pursue the high-risk, get-rich-quick schemes that were largely responsible for his companies' plight. After having lost $7 million on deals concocted by Roy Rimmer, he bought into yet another one—uranium leases in New Mexico—for $1 million. Rimmer's share: 25 percent.

Ken Davis, Jr., fumed about that for weeks. But the real explosion came when Judge Eidson ruled that a 250-page deposition given by Cullen could be made public. The deposition contained a bonanza of details about company assets and finances that had never been released. With the IRS and the SEC already on the scent thanks to Bill Davis's suit, such damaging revelations could put Stinky's entire empire in jeopardy. And all because of Priscilla. Again. Still.

To Karen, it all sounded ominously familiar.

It was a brilliant August day on Galveston Bay and Richard Haynes was entertaining friends aboard his forty-foot sloop, *L'Esprit Libre*, when someone asked him,

"What is a criminal defense lawyer's greatest fear?" Was it revenge from some disgruntled client after a guilty verdict? No, said Haynes, although he really didn't have enough experience with those circumstances to answer for all criminal lawyers. Was it the righteous retribution of a victim's friends or relatives? Haynes laughed, "You know I only defend innocent clients."

What was it then?

His worst nightmare, Haynes finally conceded, was that a client would later go off and kill or hurt somebody else. "People say, 'How in the world can you defend these people, knowing you are going to get them off, and they are going to go out and kill again?'" he explained between draws on his pipe. "Fortunately, I have always been able to say nobody I have ever represented has gone out and killed again." That, too, was one of the luxuries of being the best criminal lawyer in Texas.

"In the *country!*" shouted a guest.

Haynes flashed a smile and raised his glass in a toast. "I'll drink to that."

A few minutes later, the marine operator crackled on to the ship's radio. He had a call for Richard Haynes from his secretary in Houston. It was an emergency. Haynes excused himself from his guests and told the operator to patch the call through. A few minutes later he reemerged on deck, looking pale and puzzled.

"What was that all about?" one of the guests asked.

"Cullen Davis has been arrested." Even as he said it, he couldn't believe it.

"What for?" everyone clamored to know.

"Solicitation of capital murder."

"What does it mean, Race?" someone pressed.

Haynes looked around, taking in the *L'Esprit Libre* from stem to stern, and a smile curled across his lips. "A bigger boat."

PART
FOUR

PART

FOUR

53

"I'm in trouble."

Pat Burleson recognized David McCrory's high, plaintive voice. Then he looked at the clock. It was six in the morning, August 16, 1978. "David," he wailed, "can't it wait till later?"

"No it can't. I'm in big trouble. I need your help."

Burleson had known about McCrory's tendency to exaggerate long before the infamous affidavit that had brought Richard Haynes a contempt citation. The world may have been shocked and appalled, but McCrory's friends weren't surprised in the least; David was just being David. "He's a salesman," Burleson tried to explain to people, "and salesmen are intrusive by nature. They are pushy, and will say anything, do anything, to make a sale. He doesn't mean any harm by it."

Was David just being David again?

"Okay," said Burleson, resigning himself to consciousness, "what's this trouble?"

"You remember that job I told you I got?" Until eight months before, McCrory had been running Burleson's karate studio at TCU and doing pretty well at it. Then some company offered him big money and a company car. David was always a get-rich-quick type, not a plodder, so he jumped at it. Burleson hadn't heard from him since.

"Yeah, I remember," said Burleson.

"Well, what I didn't tell you was that I'm working for Cullen."

Burleson had a sudden urge to throw the phone across the room. "Aw, for chrissake, David! Haven't you learned your lesson with that guy?"

McCrory didn't answer. He had something more important on his mind. "Listen, Pat," he said lowering his voice. "I don't know what to do. Cullen's got a list of people he wants killed and he wants me to arrange it."

Burleson sat bolt upright in bed, suddenly wide awake.

McCrory went on, "I've come to a place with Cullen where I can't do anything more with it. I've either got to arrange to have a bunch of people killed right now, or I'm in big trouble, 'cause I'm in too deep."

Burleson sucked in a lungful of air and expelled it all in a long, low "Jesus." "Let's not talk about this on the phone," he finally said. "Get in the car, and meet me at the 7-Eleven on Jacksboro Highway."

On the way to the store, Burleson's mind ricocheted from thought to thought, but kept coming back to one: poor David. Just eight months ago, he seemed to be putting his life back together. He had come so far from that day in 1976 when Burleson visited him at home and heard him complain about what a mess his family life was. Burleson had told him straight out, "Get your ass in church, David. Get your family in *church*! Get straightened *out*!"

And, by God, David did it. He joined Burleson for a revival meeting at the First Baptist Church of Lakeside, where the Reverend Jesse Leonard showed David the fire and brimstone that were waiting for him at the end of a life of "wrong living." And there, amid the music and wailing, the shouted warnings of Hell and damnation, and the inspirational message of a 250-pound professional-wrestler-turned-evangelist, David McCrory dedicated his life to Christ. Afterward, in the pastor's carpeted office, he got down on his knees, cried, forswore "drinking, carousing, and having an unhappy life," and was reborn.

A few months later, he got the new job with the big money and the company car. He stopped coming to church and dropped the karate franchise. The few times Burleson had seen him, he seemed quiet and depressed. A rumor went around that he had been in the hospital for a heart attack. Now, for the first time since then, Burleson understood why everything had changed so suddenly. It was Cullen Davis. Again.

Suddenly Burleson realized he wasn't just driving to

the 7-Eleven, he was driving back across the border into Cullen Davis territory. The thought filled him with dread. His last time there, he had been luckier than most. But he had seen some friends, like McCrory, destroyed, and others, like Priscilla, almost killed. He had been with her during the worst of the terror, in the mansion after the killings, when she couldn't be awake without pain and couldn't sleep without pills, when everywhere she turned, something reminded her of Andrea. He had arranged protection for her—police by day, security men by night—but it always seemed futile. The real dangers couldn't be kept out by locked doors or armed guards; they were already inside, doing their murderous work, in nightmares by night and memories by day.

Was he entering that long tunnel again?

It couldn't have happened at a worse time. More than twenty years after his arrival in Fort Worth, fresh out of the Navy, Burleson's devotion to karate was finally beginning to pay off. He had bought the lots, built the buildings, and sold the franchises for fourteen karate schools. And he was still only thirty-eight. He would never be as successful as his friend and franchisee Chuck Norris, the movie star—although people told him he *looked* more like a movie star than Norris—but he was well on his way to being a millionaire, which was more money than he had ever dreamed of.

Burleson often wondered what his Japanese teacher in the fishing village of Iwakuni, near Hiroshima, would say if he saw all these white folk in their flowing *gi*. His teacher didn't think any Caucasian should learn the ancient Japanese art of self-defense, not even the eager young sailor who had wandered over from the Navy base. But with persistence and charm, Burleson had won him over.

Now he was doing the same thing with the people of Fort Worth. He did it by using karate not to "kick ass" but to build character; to give children as young as six or seven the self-confidence to stand up to bullies; to teach them self-control, courtesy, and respect. Parents brought their children to his schools not just because they learned to defend themselves, but also because they came home saying "yes, sir" and "yes, ma'am." Burleson had taught all three of Priscilla's children: Jackie, Dee, and, for a short while, Andrea. He had also taught Cullen's children—only they didn't stay very long. When someone suggested that Cullen himself take lessons, he said he already knew how to defend himself.

When Burleson pulled into the 7-Eleven, McCrory was already there, waiting by the door, pacing, shaking, alternating nervous little sips of coffee and deep, desperate drags on a cigarette. His eyes were red from sleeplessness. When his trembling hand reached out, Burleson noticed it was broken out in a rash. "You look whipped," Burleson couldn't help saying.

McCrory smiled pathetically. Even now, Burleson thought, he only wants to be liked. Then, just as suddenly, the desperate look returned. "Let's talk in my car," he said in a voice that seemed on the verge of tears, or madness.

As soon as the doors closed, his story came tumbling out.

Cullen had first approached him in February or March of that year, 1978, only a month or two after the verdict in Amarillo. "He wanted me to go to work for him," David said. Cullen had just bought a company called Jet Air, and the president, Art Smith, needed an assistant. The job paid $20,000 a year plus benefits, plus expenses, plus a company car, plus a $10,000 annual bonus. "Just go over and talk to Art," Cullen winked. "But don't worry. You're already hired."

It was a sweet deal—too sweet. There had to be a catch. "What do I have to do?" David asked reluctantly.

" 'I want you to do some investigating work for me,' " David quoted Cullen, " 'to help me through the divorce trial.' " Cullen especially wanted to know if Priscilla's attorneys, Aultman and Loftin, were paying off-hours calls on Judge Eidson at home. If Cullen could prove that, he could get Eidson off the case.

David said Cullen also wanted him to snoop on Bev Bass and Bubba Gavrel. Maybe he could confirm "reports" that they were dealing dope—in cahoots with Priscilla, of course. "See where they go, what they do, find out what kind of schedules they keep," Cullen coached like a pro, "get as much information on them as you can."

To prime the pump, Cullen gave him $5,000 and instructions on how to get in touch without "blowing his cover." "When you want to report back to me on the phone," Cullen directed, "call me and use the name Frank Johnson. Just leave a message that Frank Johnson called and don't leave any phone number. I'll call you back at home." Cullen's code name would be Dan Edwards.

Warily, David agreed. The money was just too damn good to turn down.

Then one day, at a meeting in the parking lot at Coco's Famous Hamburgers on Hulen Street, not far from the Mockingbird mansion, Cullen announced he had a new job for McCrory. "He said he had decided to go ahead and have Beverly Bass killed," David said, "because she was the only one anybody believed at the trial." Cullen didn't want McCrory to kill her, he just wanted him to find somebody who would, somebody who couldn't be traced back to Cullen. As for payment, "He said I would be well taken care of," David recalled, "and never have to worry about anything again."

"*David,*" Burleson yelped, "you *didn't* . . ."

No, David insisted, he told Cullen right from the start that he thought the whole idea was "ridiculous," and he didn't want any part of it. But Cullen wouldn't let it go. A few days later, they met again at Coco's. By now Cullen had become paranoid about eavesdropping bugs, telescopic lenses, and long-distance listening devices, so he turned the car radio up full blast. "You know, they can't tape you if you do this," he shouted to McCrory. "It washes out the recording."

He started talking about the plan again. 'I've decided

to go ahead and have Bev killed," he told McCrory, "and you are going to help me. You are going to hire somebody to have it done." When David tried to back out of the arrangement, Cullen fixed him with a glare. "And if you turn around on me this time, David, I will kill you and your whole goddamn family." The memory of it made David tremble so hard he almost spilled his cold coffee. "And you know," Cullen added, "I have the money and the power to have it done."

A few weeks later, they met again, and Cullen added Bubba Gavrel and his father Gus Sr. to the list of people he wanted "removed." "Jesus, Cullen," David exclaimed, "how many people are you going to have killed?"

Fifteen, Cullen told him.

He showed David the list: Priscilla Davis, Beverly Bass, Bubba Gavrel, Gus Gavrel, Judge Eidson, Judge Tom Cave, Bill Davis, Mitzi Davis, and then some names David didn't recognize or couldn't remember—Cullen snatched the list back before he could commit them to memory. Cullen made it clear, however, that no matter how long the list, the "priority hits" were Priscilla, Bev, and Judge Eidson.

"Why the hell didn't you just walk away?" Burleson shouted. This was crazy, talking about killing these people! Why didn't David just tell him so?

"I thought, maybe, if I went along with him, I could talk him out of it," David tried to explain, "get him to drop it. I felt like I could handle the situation without anybody getting hurt or anything happening." Besides, if he *had* walked away, who would Cullen have found to take his place? Maybe somebody who didn't think this was such an odd job and had the contacts to make it work.

So what *did* McCrory say?

"All right, we'll work on it."

After that, Cullen came to each meeting with a new idea for McCrory to pass on to the hit men he was lining up. For Bev Bass, he suggested the shooter hide in the bushes outside her house, wait for her to come home, then "shoot her, take her off, cut her body up, and leave it in different areas so she could never be found." For Judge Eidson, he recommended knocking him over the head, throwing him in the trunk, and killing him someplace else. "Offing" a judge could attract a lot of media attention, so maybe it was better to have him simply disappear. "People would think he ran away from his wife," Cullen speculated. Another idea was to drop a Mexican ID card of some kind next to the judge's body along with a brown beret cap, the trademark of a local Mexican gang that had already made threats on Eidson's life.

Burleson wanted to know if McCrory had ever actually *done* anything to further Cullen's plot.

No, said David, and that was just the problem. Months had passed since Cullen first proposed the murders, and nothing had happened. David had tried to put him off with excuses—"hit men are hard to find," "the man was supposed to contact me yesterday"—but now Cullen was demanding to see results. "He told me I better get something done," David wailed, "that he wasn't going to put up with it much longer. He had other people he could turn the job over to, and they *could* get it done."

Burleson had heard enough. "Stop," he said. "I don't want to know any more." He was already in deeper than he ever wanted to be. But his curiosity couldn't resist one more question: "What about me—am I on the list?"

David nodded. "Yeah, you're on it too."

Burleson couldn't control his anger any longer. "You stupid sorry sonofabitch! We just got through with all this, and now you got to get back in it." Even as he railed, however, Burleson knew it was too late for railing. If what David said was true, Priscilla and others were in serious danger. If he didn't do something, people might start dying—soon.

"David, listen," he said. "I can put you together with the right people to stop this thing."

David started trembling again. "I can't trust anybody in the D.A.'s office, or the police department," he said. "Cullen has got friends there. It has to be the feds. They're the only ones who can protect me." He was shaking hard now, spilling his coffee. "You don't know Cullen. If I don't do what he wants me to, he'll have me killed. Believe me. He will."

In late July, Theodore Shove pulled into the parking lot of the Holiday Inn on Regal Row and Interstate 35 in Dallas. Minutes later, a short, thin man with a cocky walk approached his car and slid into the front seat. He had a high forehead, birdy eyes, and thin, almost invisible lips. Shove thought he looked familiar.

"Let me get right to the point," the man said. "I want to hire you to kill someone for me. His name is David McCrory."

54

"Why me?" Shove demanded to know.

The man smiled—a slow, reptilian smile. "I've read about you in the papers."

The previous September, Shove had taken out two loans from the Citizens Bank in Richardson, Texas: one secured by some doubtful "receivables" in his business, the other by three cars. A few days later, the bank discovered some creative bookkeeping in Shove's application, called in the loan, and sent out its repo men to retrieve two of Shove's three cars.

Later the same night, bank officer C. J. Bell received a long-distance phone call from Las Vegas. "Do you know who this is, you rotten sonofabitch?" the caller screamed. It was Theodore Shove. Word of the repossession had reached Gambler's Alley. "You didn't keep our fucking agreement!" he roared. "I am personally gonna kill your ass if you don't have those cars back in my driveway by 5:00 A.M. tomorrow morning!"

Bell explained calmly that he couldn't return Shove's cars until Shove returned the bank's money.

Shove's tone grew even more darkly threatening. "I'm a mafioso. I'm a killer by trade. I've rubbed out ten people, and I'll have a contract out on your whole goddamn family if those cars aren't in my driveway by 5:00 A.M. I'll start with your grandchildren, then your children, then your wife, and *then* you." Shove was on a roll. "As God walks on this green earth, I make a vow to you that you are going to be a dead sonofabitch."

The next afternoon, a federal warrant was issued in Dallas for Shove's arrest. By making his threats long-distance, Shove had landed himself in the hands of the feds. Within hours, FBI agents arrested him at the Royal Inn in Las Vegas.

For weeks afterward, newspapers and TV stations all over Texas covered the story, every tragicomic detail of it. Even Shove might have considered it funny—if he hadn't been facing ten to twenty years in a federal prison on extortion charges.

The man in the front seat obviously knew the whole story, and the memory of it made him smile.

"This McCrory is doing some work for me," he continued without expression, "and when he's finished is when I want you to do it."

Shove clutched the steering wheel and stared grimly straight ahead. "I'm not in that business," he said, "and I don't want to talk about it any more."

"All right," the man said in a level voice, "if you don't do it, let me tell you what's going to happen. First, I will ruin you financially. Second, I'll make sure you spend a whole lot of time in jail. Understand?"

Shove nodded slowly. "I understand," he said, "but I'm not interested. I'm not in that business."

"All right," the man said, then opened the door, slid out, and disappeared.

A few days later, someone called the stereo shop where

Shove worked and told his boss about the pending federal indictment. He was fired that day.

Before long, the man called again. "Meet me at Coco's on Hulen Street at seven tomorrow night," was all he said. The next night, Shove pulled into the local hamburger joint not far from the notorious Davis mansion. The man was waiting for him in a light-colored Cadillac. He honked and Shove got in.

There was a long silence, then a little small talk. Finally the man said, "I heard you lost your job." Shove thought he detected a smile etched between those thin lips. "Have you decided to come around and do the job I want you to do?"

Shove didn't say anything. The silence conveyed his answer.

The man began to explain: "I have a list of people I want eliminated and McCrory is taking care of that. I want him taken care of after his work is done. I'm going to put off paying him until you take care of him." Shove noticed the man had an odd, disjointed way of talking—it was more than just the awkwardness of the subject. Was there a tape recorder going? No, he decided, a cop would be much more explicit.

"How much is this going to cost?" the man asked.

Shove thought a long time before crossing the line. Then, "Seventy-five thousand—plus a gun and a silencer."

"Shit."

"That's it."

"Shit."

"Thirty-five up front and the rest after the job is done."

"Shit."

"Take it or leave it."

The man sputtered for a moment, but in the end he said, "Okay."

"Why McCrory?" Shove asked just before getting out.

"He's the only link," the man said.

Shove couldn't stop himself from asking, "What about me? If I do McCrory, then I'll be the only link."

The man's lips stretched into a smile again. "Oh, you

don't have to worry about that," he said. "Nobody would believe you."

55

Why would Cullen choose David McCrory?

Pat Burleson had replayed his friend's bizarre story over and over in his mind, and the more he thought about it, the more it sounded possible. The more it sounded like Cullen. The high of beating the murder charge had lasted only a few months. After that, the anger had set in—that insatiable Davis anger—and with it, the overwhelming need to get even. Everything made sense—except . . .

Why would Cullen choose David McCrory?

After the embarrassment over the affidavit in the first case, after David's long history of shifting loyalties and erratic truthfulness, why would Cullen entrust him with such a sensitive mission? It was the one piece of the puzzle that Burleson couldn't make fit—until he spoke to FBI agent Ron Jannings, one of his karate students.

"There are several people who are locally prominent, and they're on a bizarre hit list," he told Jannings. "Some people are gonna die." Jannings was skeptical. "This is no bullshit," Burleson insisted. "It's real. I know a lot of the people very well. It has been tossed at me." Burleson again glimpsed the dark tunnel yawning ahead. "I don't want in it at all, but at the same time, I can't step back and let people die."

Jannings's first question was, "How reliable is your source?"

That was it! Burleson suddenly realized. *That* was why Cullen had chosen David. Because he *wasn't* reliable— and everyone *knew* he wasn't reliable. He was goddamn *famous* for not being reliable! Cullen must have been laughing to himself as he discussed the murders of all these people with David, thinking that if David ever turned on him, no one would ever believe him!

Burleson decided to let Jannings decide for himself if McCrory was worth believing. "I don't know," he answered. "Why don't I put you with the person and let him tell you."

Jannings agreed to the meeting.

Around four that afternoon, Burleson met McCrory outside the Botanical Gardens in Fort Worth. They drove around the gardens together in David's LTD. If anything, McCrory seemed even more nervous than before. The rash had spread to his arms and neck. "You know, I'm dead if Cullen finds out what I'm doing," he reminded Burleson. "Dead."

Such melodrama. Burleson beat back the question that kept sidling into his thoughts: Is David just being David? Then again, wasn't that the question Cullen wanted him to ask?

"I spoke to a friend of mine in law enforcement," Burleson said.

"Not local people!" David recoiled, his hands trembling and his voice near breaking. "I mean as far as leaks. Cullen has so much power." A car passed by slowly. McCrory was sure he had seen the same car behind him earlier in the day. "I knew it!" he cried out, as if in pain, "Cullen's fucking following me!" But the car moved on and Burleson dismissed it as a sightseer. There was no doubt about one thing: David was scared.

"Don't worry," Burleson reassured him, "my friend is straight down the line. Can't be bought. He's a little skeptical of your story, but if they can prove that it's real, they guarantee they'll protect you."

McCrory stopped the car and stared for a long time at the Japanese gardens. "Okay," he finally said. "Set up a meeting."

At 8:00 the same evening, the two men drove to the Lone Star Drive Inn in east Fort Worth to rendezvous with Jannings. In the car, Burleson told McCrory. "I want you to know one thing, David. I'm out of it. I'm putting you and this guy together. But I don't want to know the details. I already know more than I want to know." When they arrived, McCrory went inside but Burleson stayed behind in the parking lot, wishing he were somewhere else: in another city, in another country. Anywhere but back in Cullen Davis's life.

The same day, three hours earlier, Theodore Shove met his man at Coco's.

"I'm worried about McCrory," the man said. "He talks too much. I may need you sooner than I thought."

"As far as I'm concerned," Shove complained, "this whole thing has taken too fucking long already."

"Things are happening soon," the man reassured him. "I have the money, and I should have the gun and silencer soon. Maybe tomorrow. McCrory will be finished with his job by the middle of next week, then you can do your job." So businesslike, Shove thought. "It will all be over by the end of next week, and you'll have all of your money by then."

Shove asked how he wanted it to happen. Did he have a plan?

"I'll set up a meeting with McCrory in a parking lot to make the payoff. He'll come expecting me and the money, only you'll be there instead." Shove thought he detected a smile.

"Okay," said Shove, "but let's make it quick. I'm spending too much of my own damn money for gasoline, and spending too damn much time coming to Fort Worth to meet with you."

As Shove got out of the Cadillac, the man held out a $100 bill. "That's for the gas," he said.

Shove grabbed it. "You just get the gun."

56

At 5:00 P.M. the next day, August 18, McCrory met with Cullen in the parking lot at Coco's.

"I've got a little present for you," McCrory said as Cullen slipped into the front seat of his LTD. From a paper bag, he pulled a .22 caliber Ruger pistol and handed it to Cullen.

"That's nice," said Cullen, rubbing the smooth metal. "Just what the doctor ordered."

McCrory smiled like a little boy. "They haven't got the silencer made yet," he added, "but they're working on it."

Cullen frowned. "When will it be ready?"

"Just a few days . . ." McCrory explained, suddenly nervous. Cullen fumbled with the gun. "You have to pull this back," McCrory instructed, leaning over and cocking the Ruger. "Is that *sweet*?" Cullen gripped the gun's handle and pointed it at McCrory. "Don't point that son of a bitch at me," McCrory choked. "Hey now, we're friends. You're not gonna do something stupid with this fuckin' gun, are you?"

Cullen smiled. "Self-protection."

McCrory laughed, too loud. "Self-protection, my ass." Then he changed the subject. "We got somewhat of a problem. The man is here to put the judge away." The divorce judge—"fucking Eidson"—had been chosen as the first target. So what was the problem, Cullen wanted to know. "He found out he was a judge, and he wants a lot more fucking money." How much more? "The son of a bitch wants a hundred thousand dollars."

Cullen frowned again. "Bullshit."

McCrory's head bobbed nervously in agreement. "I told him bullshit, too, Cullen, but goddamn, he says that's a judge and it's gonna bring more heat. It's in the fuckin' paper every day. He's on TV. What else can I do?"

Cullen didn't have an answer.

"Priscilla is a different story," McCrory offered brightly. "He'd rather do Priscilla than the judge. He says he can do it easy."

"Like hell," Cullen spat, as if the comment had wounded his pride. "Priscilla's always got somebody around her. The judge doesn't."

McCrory pretended not to hear. "Give me a price on Priscilla," he said. "He says he'd rather do Priscilla than the judge, so if you give me a price on Priscilla, I'll just lay it in his lap. Unless *you* want to talk to the mother-fucker. He may trust you more than he trusts me."

"*You're* supposed to be handling that," Cullen snapped.

As for Priscilla, Cullen seemed strangely uninterested in talking about her. When McCrory pressed him on what to tell the "shooter," Cullen snapped, "Go back to the original plan."

"The original plan?" McCrory puzzled.

"Get the other one," Cullen explained, "the one we started this out with."

"Oh, Bev."

"Yeah."

McCrory shook his head. "Boy, Cullen, if you have that son of a bitch killed, I promise you, you're gonna have heat!" But Cullen didn't seem to be interested in warnings. "Well, okay," McCrory relented. "I'm sure you've thought it out. I'll do whatever you want done." But he still wasn't sure what that was. "You still want all three of them at once?" he tried to clarify. They had talked before about hitting Bev, Bubba, and Bubba's father all at one time, eliminating not only a key witness in the Amarillo trial, but also the sympathetic, wheelchair-bound plaintiff in a pending $13,000,000 lawsuit.

"Do it either way," Cullen replied cryptically.

McCrory played the scenario out. "Okay, what if he does all three of those, and just goes right on, and he wants his fucking money. He wants it immediately, and I don't have the money to pay him."

"You just get in touch with me anytime afterward," Cullen explained, growing impatient.

"Well, it's got to be immediately afterward. That's the problem, because I don't have the fucking money."

"You just call me and you got it."

McCrory wanted to recap. "So you definitely want her to go down before the judge?"

Cullen's eyes narrowed. "Yeah."

"What are you gonna do if the son of a bitch wants to do the judge first? If he grabs that judge up and puts him in his car, knocks him out, and takes him off, which is what he said he was going to do, there's gonna be a hell of a stink, but not near as much as if he left that son of a bitch bleeding in his driveway, or walked into the house and blew away the judge and his wife and anybody else that happened to be there . . ."

Cullen interrupted, "Well, he's not going to go wandering in there if there's anybody else there. He'll know what he's doing better than that." It sounded like the voice of experience. "Do the judge and his wife and that would be it."

"Yeah," McCrory agreed, "but he ain't gonna leave any witnesses. This man's good, Cullen. He's supposedly one of the best."

After some more discussion of the best way to deal with the judge—should the killer kidnap him and kill him or kill him on the spot?—McCrory turned to the subject he had been thinking about a lot lately: getting caught. He was concerned about his "exposure" when the shooting started. He needed an alibi. "If he moves tonight or tomorrow night," he explained to Cullen, "I've got to be out of the picture when it goes down."

Cullen dismissed his concern in an exasperated, that's-not-my-problem tone. "You know when it's happening. You can always get yourself covered real good."

McCrory wanted to know if Cullen was "covered."

"I'm covered all the time," Cullen assured him. "I'm

not taking any chances. If I'm not going to be covered, I'll let you know."

"All right." As for a signal, McCrory suggested that he would phone Cullen when the fireworks were about to start. "If I tell you I'm going out of town, that means he's going to work."

Cullen nodded. "All right."

Before leaving, McCrory returned one last time to the subject of money. "If he goes to work, like, tonight or tomorrow night, don't leave me hanging, 'cause that motherfucker will kill me, Cullen. Don't leave me hanging."

Cullen, impatiently: "I won't."

McCrory couldn't resist closing with a melodramatic flourish. "Now, he may take a bunch of them off at once. I mean, he's that kind of person. I mean, he may just waste the shit out of a bunch of them and get a bunch of it over with at once."

Cullen smiled. "That suits the shit out of me."

From the parking lot of Coco's, McCrory drove his LTD to a liquor store for a six-pack of beer, then to the south side Howard Johnson's motel. He walked to Room 315, where Agent Ron Jannings was waiting. While McCrory swigged beer and laughed nervously, Agent Jerry Hubbell removed the Nagra recorder and microphone taped to his body.

57

An hour earlier, Ron Jannings had suspected that David McCrory might be leading them all on a wild-goose chase. Did McCrory *really* expect him to believe that a multi-millionaire businessman was ordering up multiple hits on judges and prosecutors and twenty-year-old coeds?

Then he listened to the tape.

Jannings immediately called Tim Curry. "I need to see you as soon as possible," he said. "It's a matter of great importance." When Curry arrived at the FBI offices in the Federal Building, Jannings played the tape for him. Curry listened in mesmerized silence. When it was over, all he could say was, "I'll be goddamned."

Jannings wanted to move right away, but Curry balked. He had been burned once by Cullen and was still smarting from it. Following the acquittal in Amarillo, public sentiment had swung strongly in Cullen's favor. So much so that Curry had more or less decided not to pursue the other charges against Cullen: murder in the killing of Stan Farr and attempted murder for shooting Priscilla. It was an election year, after all, and there was no political capital to be made in pressing a losing case.

Nitpickers had already started counting up the costs of the Amarillo humiliation: $55,000 for transcripts, $65,000 for jury expenses (including $7,000 in liquor bills), $25,000 in "overtime premiums" for bailiffs and deputies. In all, Tarrant County had paid more than $300,000 for the privilege of being whopped by Cullen Davis, making it the most expensive prosecution in Texas history. It wasn't a story that Curry wanted to revive two months before the election by putting Cullen back in the dock.

On the other hand, there was this tape.

Later that night, Curry drove to the Howard Johnson's to hear McCrory's story firsthand. If he was going to stick his political neck out, he wanted to make sure McCrory wasn't suckering him the way he had suckered the defense in Amarillo, tape or no tape.

McCrory passed the test. Around 10:00 P.M., Curry called Judge Eidson and told him to come to the Federal Building the next morning.

"He might catch the judge coming in the house." Judge Eidson recognized Cullen Davis's voice.

"No, remember, the judge goes out and turns his fucking water off. That's when he's gonna get him." Ron Jannings

identified David McCrory's voice for Eidson. The judge's eyes were transfixed on the tape recorder.

"What good is that gonna do?" Davis's voice again.

"There ain't as much heat." McCrory's voice. *"They can't prove much unless they find a body."*

Davis's voice: *"Do the judge, and then his wife."*

Jannings figured the tape would scare Eidson. He was right. The judge had been concerned about his safety ever since the Amarillo trial, where he testified for the prosecution. Since then, with each adverse ruling in the divorce case, especially the refusal to step down, he had felt Cullen's cold, hateful gaze bearing down harder and harder. After years of dealing with him in court, Eidson knew Cullen wasn't the kind of man to hate idly.

Before Jannings even asked, Eidson volunteered: "What can I do to help?"

Jannings explained the plan. They would stage one of the "hits" Cullen had ordered; McCrory would arrange another rendezvous; and they would catch Cullen making the payoff. Eidson would be the bait. To convince Cullen that the hit had been made, McCrory would need photographs of the judge "dead," as well as some identification. Jannings assigned agents to take Eidson to the parking lot, where they burned three cigarette holes in his undershirt, spread catsup around, positioned him in the trunk of a car, and took four black-and-white Polaroids.

Next, McCrory set up the rendezvous. From a tapped phone at the Howard Johnson's, he called Karen Master's house. After several tries, he reached Cullen. "I may need to get ahold of you later on tonight, or early in the morning," he said, his voice cracking with urgency. "I been out checking. My man is still here. He's working." McCrory waited for some acknowledgment. There was none. He asked when Davis would return home that night.

"It'll be after 11:00 o'clock," said Cullen, or maybe later if he decided to go "partying."

"And you'll probably try to . . ." McCrory baited.

"Screw some," said Cullen, leaving out one of his favorite words, "pussy."

McCrory searched for a lighter tone. "Think about me while you're having all that goddamn fun."

"You'll be uppermost in my mind," said Cullen, not entirely facetiously.

McCrory returned to business. "I'll contact you either tonight or early in the morning, so hang loose and *stay covered*."

While Cullen and Karen partied, Ron Jannings marshaled his troops. By now, at least a dozen men had joined the operation, including investigators from the D.A.'s office who had worked on the Amarillo case. One of them, Rodney Hinson, asked the identity of the FBI's informant.

"David McCrory," someone said.

"Oh, shit," Hinson exclaimed. "I know McCrory."

At the Federal Building, they dusted the pictures of Eidson with fluorescent powder. If by some chance Cullen escaped the video and still cameras that would be trained on the exchange, they could still prove that he had touched the pictures by the telltale glow the powder would leave on his hands under an ultraviolet light. At the Pilgrim Inn Motel, not far from Coco's, another team of agents assembled and double-checked the cameras and recording equipment, then took the van on a practice run to Coco's parking lot, where they made a video survey of the scene. Meanwhile, another team of agents boarded a single-engine plane at Meacham Field and circled Karen Master's house, tracing the route Cullen would take to his meeting with McCrory.

By midnight, Jannings was ready.

At 1:00 A.M., McCrory started trying to reach Cullen again. He called four times and reached the babysitter each time. Finally, at 2:54, he found Cullen.

"I need to see you." Hours of frustrated efforts to reach Davis had pushed McCrory to the edge. The desperation in his voice was convincing; it was real. "He's finished with the job and he's wanting to get out of here, so, uh, we gotta do it now."

Cullen started to admit he didn't have the money ready.

"Shit, I haven't . . ." but then decided to stall. "How do I know the job is really finished?" he demanded.

"I got the proof," McCrory babbled. "That's no sweat."

Did McCrory really expect him to produce the money with no notice at three in the morning? "All that . . ." Cullen searched for a word that wouldn't arouse Karen's suspicion ". . . *information* is down at the office."

McCrory exploded, "Oh, shit, man. You're gonna have to go get it because he is . . . I can't . . . I'm not . . . I don't want to talk, but I can't fake it, you understand?"

Cullen wasn't about to be railroaded, not even by a man standing in the same room with a hired killer and understandably on the verge of a nervous breakdown. "What's the matter with in the morning?"

"He wants to get gone!" McCrory was losing control.

Cullen tried again to explain that it was just too late.

"Hold on just a second," McCrory said, reining in. He turned his head away from the phone and pretended to talk to the killer. "He's got to go to his office, and he can't get in there tonight. It's gonna have to be in the morning."

Back into the phone, to Cullen: "How early? Nine o'clock be all right?" This killer was proving to be a reasonable man.

"Yeah," said Cullen.

"And Cullen," McCrory added gravely, "for God's sake, don't leave me hung out on this."

Cullen's response, crafted for Karen's ears, wasn't much comfort. "No. That'll work out just fine."

When McCrory hung up, Jannings passed the word to his men: the rendezvous was postponed until nine the next morning; there would be no action tonight. Everybody should get some sleep.

Hardly anybody did.

Four hours later, Jannings met McCrory at a pancake house not far from the Pilgrim Inn. McCrory seemed calm. Jannings wasn't sure if it was courage, stupidity, or exhaustion. "It looks like I've gotten myself into a situation where I'm going to get killed either way," McCrory said philosophically. "There's no question in my mind that Cullen shot that little girl."

How could he be so sure? Jannings wondered.

"During one of our meetings, I told Cullen that I heard that one of the unusual things about that night at the mansion was that every door in the house was open. Cullen said, 'I didn't leave any doors open.' "

When McCrory returned to the Pilgrim Inn, Agent Joe Gray fitted him with another Nagra tape recorder, this time with two microphones. Gray thought McCrory seemed more nervous than before, and he understood why. When he was done, he spoke into the mikes. "I am Special Agent Joseph B. Gray, with the Federal Bureau of Investigation, Dallas, Texas. It is August 20, 1978. The time is 8:12 A.M. I have just installed a Nagra tape recorder on the person of David McCrory and I have personally inspected that recorder previous to its installation and found it to be in working order."

Just to be sure, Jannings did his own inspection. Clearly McCrory had had second thoughts since breakfast, because now he was jumpy as a fly. Patting him down, Jannings found a loaded .38. The two men exchanged glances. "Keep it," said Jannings briskly. Another agent handed McCrory the .22 Ruger from before, wrapped in a towel. It had a bronze silencer attached. McCrory would deliver the gun and silencer to Cullen, as arranged. Jannings suggested that McCrory put it in Cullen's trunk himself, immediately. The gun had been disabled, but if Cullen handled it, one of the agents watching from a distance might think he was making a move and shoot him.

Finally, Jannings gave him the envelope with Eidson's identification cards and the dusted Polaroids.

Cullen Davis was up early that morning, too. When the police plane flew over Karen Master's house around 8:10, the garage door was already open and Cullen's Cadillac gone. Not even Karen knew his whereabouts until he called from his office in the Mid-Continent Building around 8:15 and asked for the combination to the safe. She didn't have it, but she gave him the number of his secretary, Mary Anne Carter, who directed him to a piece of paper in her desk where it was written down. Cullen opened the safe and took out a brown envelope containing $25,000 in $100 bills.

A few minutes later, the police plane picked up his car at Sixth and Main. "He's moving," FBI spotter Larry Tongate reported over the radio to the dozen or more cars that were moving toward Coco's.

Agent Gray was the first to arrive. He parked the white surveillance van in a parking lot next to the restaurant and began setting up the video and still cameras. Gray watched from the driver's window, other agents from the side and rear windows. Another car picked up Cullen's Cadillac on the ground and followed at a safe distance, guided by directions from the plane. About 8:20, McCrory pulled into Coco's, followed by Jannings. D.A. Investigator Hinson and FBI Agent Bobby Oakley positioned themselves on Crowley Road, between Coco's and Karen's house. If Cullen broke and ran, they would intercept him. A shotgun lay between them on the front seat. They had heard that Cullen kept a gun under the driver's seat of his car.

"You know why we were selected for this detail, don't you," Hinson asked Oakley as they sat and waited.

Oakley shook his head.

"Because Cullen knows both of us, and he knows we're both law enforcement officers. If we get in a gunfight and one of us is killed, it's capital murder."

The observation plane reported that Cullen was "washing" any possible tails. He had taken a wrong turn onto the highway, made a U-turn, then circled back. Even with the evasive delays, though, he was ahead of schedule. In the surveillance van, Agent Gray feared he might arrive with too much time to spare, too much time to get curious about an empty van. Just to be safe, Gray pulled the cameras away from the windows, set boxes in the front seat, and put up blackout curtains. For the time being, they would have to fly blind.

Meanwhile, David McCrory sat oblivious in the front

seat of his LTD, smoking furiously. Jannings had ordered McCrory's car bugged, just in case—a T-2 device in the Kleenex box in the back seat—but McCrory knew nothing of what was happening around him. He had to take it on faith that they were there.

At 8:45, the radio cracked into the silence inside the surveillance van: Cullen's Cadillac was pulling into the parking lot. It was pulling up *alongside* the van. The men inside looked at each other with the same thought. They were trapped. If Cullen looked inside, there was no place to hide. If he started shooting, they were dead. Agent Gray whispered to his men, "If he makes us and starts shooting, get flat on the floor. Return fire through the wall of the truck. If we're lucky, we'll just lose our eardrums."

The next sound they heard was Cullen's car pulling up next to them, less than three feet away. With one hand, Gray slid the gun out of his holster; with the other, he turned down the volume on the radio. Cullen's car door opened, then shut. The sound of footsteps on the asphalt, moving slowly around the van, from left to right, around the front. When he passed a window, his silhouette rippled across the curtains. Even through the metal walls, his presence so close seemed to cast a shadow. The barrel of Gray's gun followed it around like a compass.

Suddenly there was a loud *bang*, and the inside of the van vibrated like a kettle drum. Cullen was pounding on the wall of the van, testing. He moved to the back and his silhouette hung in the window. He was trying to see inside.

Watching from Coco's parking lot, McCrory slipped the .38 out of his waistband and cocked it. The handle felt oily in his sweaty palm. Suddenly, for the first time, he realized he might have to use it. "Goddamit," the agent monitoring the T-2 device in the Kleenex box heard him sputter.

Then, suddenly, for no reason, Cullen turned away from the van, climbed back into his Cadillac, and drove to the other parking lot where McCrory was waiting. When Gray heard the car move away, he inched up to the back window where seconds before Cullen had peered in, and peered out. "Shit," someone said. "I thought sure he saw us."

Gray wasn't so sure. Just because Cullen didn't start shooting didn't mean he hadn't seen them. What if he knew he was walking into a trap? What would he do? Would he give up, shoot it out, or just dump as much of the evidence as he could? What was the most damaging evidence against him?

David McCrory.

Gray looked back out the window. Cullen had parked next to McCrory's LTD and was getting out of his car. It was too late to do anything. Any kind of rescue attempt now would be more likely to get McCrory killed than to save him. Gray lunged for the radio receiver and tuned into the T-2 unit in McCrory's car. Nothing. He turned up the volume and double-checked the frequency. Still nothing. The transmitter was dead. An hour earlier, it had checked out; now, nothing.

Gray went back to the window. Cullen was waving McCrory over to his car. Gray stuck a small video camera in the opening between the curtains. Whatever happened, he would get it on tape.

"Hey. I got something here," McCrory said as he slid into the front seat of the Cadillac. He handed Cullen the envelope with the pictures of Eidson. Cullen handed him the envelope with the $25,000.

"Goddamn," Cullen grumbled. "You just won't let a body sleep, will you?" He tried to hand the envelope with the pictures back to McCrory but McCrory wouldn't take it. "Damn. You keep it," he insisted.

But McCrory didn't seem to care about the photos. "Who do you want to go next?" he asked, voice shaking.

Cullen didn't answer. He was still trying to get rid of the photos. Finally, McCrory took them. "What are you going to do with those?" Cullen asked.

"I'm going to get rid of these motherfuckers," said McCrory with a weird smile.

"That's good," said Cullen, genuinely relieved. "Glad to hear it."

"Who do you want next?" McCrory asked again.

"The ones we talked about," said Cullen. "The three kids."

McCrory knew who he meant—Bev, Bubba, and Dee—but he needed names for the record. "Bev, Bubba . . ." he prompted.

Cullen cut him off impatiently, "Yeah, yeah," then started to get out of the car. The sudden movement made McCrory uneasy. "You going to get in the trunk?" he asked, trying not to show his apprehension. He had been afraid all along that Davis would try to kill him. Suddenly the fear gripped him body and soul. He was the only witness to Cullen's involvement in this whole scheme, which now included, at least as far as Cullen knew, a murder.

"I gotta go," McCrory announced.

Before he could move, though, Cullen's voice caught him. "Just a minute."

Seeing Cullen at the trunk reminded McCrory of the gun and silencer. "I got something for you to put in the trunk," he said. As he circled around to the back of the car, he watched Cullen open his trunk and peer inside. He expected to see a gun next.

Cullen reached deep into the trunk and pulled out something small and dark. "My sunglasses," he announced.

The tension proved too much for McCrory. "I'm a scared motherfucker," he blurted out.

Cullen didn't pay any attention, and McCrory slipped undetectably back into character. "I don't mind telling you. When you kill a man like Judge Eidson, hey, there is going to be more heat caused than you can imagine."

When Cullen started to close his trunk, McCrory jerked back into focus. "Hold on," he said. "Leave the trunk up." He motioned Cullen over to his trunk and showed him the gun. For a second, they both admired it in silence.

"Look at that motherfucker," said Cullen, in a voice filled with awe.

McCrory pointedly advised him to "leave it alone." Killing was only for professionals. He put the bundle in Cullen's trunk, closed his, and headed back to the car door. "Let's go," he said. "I got to get out of here."

Cullen was on the way back to his door when McCrory realized that he didn't have what he came for. Awkwardly, he tried to pick up the conversation again. "Now, you want Beverly Bass killed next—quick, right?"

"All right," Cullen replied.

McCrory wasn't sure "all right" was good enough. He pressed again. "Now, I don't want to make another mistake. You're sure?"

"Yeah." Bingo.

It was everything he needed, but McCrory decided to fish for more. "He's going to operate again tonight."

Cullen hesitated. "But I haven't got the money lined up."

"How long will it take?"

"I'll try to get it this week. I can get it in two days."

McCrory was feeling in control of the conversation again. He scratched his head. "I don't know whether I can keep him here two days or not." Now it was Cullen's turn to squirm.

"Couldn't he come back?"

McCrory shrugged his shoulders. "Fuck, I don't know. That's just what he told me."

"Why don't you talk to him?" Cullen suggested lamely. "Ask him, does he want to leave and come back, or do it and then wait three days for the money?"

"He won't wait for the money," McCrory predicted confidently. "If he kills all three of those people, he's going to walk."

Cullen nodded. "Yeah, well, I don't blame him."

"You know, you're talking about a lot of money," McCrory reminded him.

"How much?"

"Figure it up," McCrory snapped. Cullen shot him a look that made it clear he had gone too far. Instantly his tone changed. "I'm trying to do you a good job, Cullen."

Cullen looked at him askance. "Well, I was wondering whether you were going to . . ."

Run? Doublecross? Blackmail? Betray? "I know you were," said McCrory with a nervous, forgiving smile.

"Just don't give me too much pressure now," Cullen warned.

"I'm not going to give you any more pressure than I have to," said McCrory. "But, hey, look. This fuckin' murder business is a tough sonofabitch."

Cullen nodded impatiently. "Right."

"Now, you got me into this goddamn deal," said McCrory, as if taking offense and hoping maybe to win a few last-minute points. "I got Judge Eidson dead for you."

"Good," said Cullen, suddenly uncomfortable.

McCrory pressed: "I'll get the rest of them dead for you. You want a bunch of people dead—right?"

That was too much for Cullen. He tried to cut the conversation off: "All right."

But McCrory tried again. "Am I right?"

"All right."

A few more words and the conversation was over. Both men climbed into their cars and drove away as a light plane circled overhead. McCrory spoke into the microphone: "I have got the money. He has got the gun." Within seconds the order came over the radio in half a dozen cars parked nearby: "Take him."

When the first police car caught up to Cullen, he had pulled into a Kentucky Fried Chicken to use the outdoor public phone. In the first car was Morris Howeth, another of the D.A.'s investigators who had worked on the Amarillo trial. Cullen was just stepping out of the phone booth when he recognized Howeth. He tried to cover his face.

"You're under arrest," said Howeth. "Put your hands on the car." He searched Cullen—no gun—then handcuffed him and sat him in the backseat of the FBI car.

Minutes later, Rodney Hinson arrived. He walked up to the open door where Cullen was sitting and leaned in.

"Hello, Cullen," he said with a smile. "You remember me?"

Cullen nodded yes.

Hinson read him his rights.

Ron Jannings arrived and took Cullen to jail. When he was searched, he had $1,122 in bills, 15¢ in change, a photograph of a small boy with a huge phallus, and several telephone numbers written on scraps of paper. Two of them turned out to belong to well-known hired killers.

Eventually, Cullen was allowed to make a call.

Karen Master answered the phone.

"Guess where I am?" Cullen joked.

58

Karen Master didn't think it was funny at all. She cried for hours, wailing over and over, "I can't believe it's happening again!" At first, friends thought it was Cullen she was keening over, but it wasn't. For some reason, her attitude had changed since Amarillo. It wasn't Cullen she was worried about this time, it was herself and her sons. With friends, she openly discussed the possibility that Cullen was guilty, and debated whether she should leave him or not. When Steve Sumner called to express concern that Cullen might kill himself, she brushed the subject aside, complaining instead, "I can't believe this is happening to *me* again."

Curiously, public opinion in Fort Worth was more sympathetic. People saw Cullen as the hapless victim of either a frame-up or an official vendetta. Angry phone calls to the D.A.'s office accused prosecutors of "sour grapes" and "picking on an innocent man," and demanded they "just leave the poor guy alone." Joe Shannon wasn't the only one who noted the irony. "Last time they said Cullen wouldn't have murdered those people, he would have hired somebody to do it," he told a reporter. "Now he's caught hiring somebody to do it and they say he's being framed. You just can't win."

When reporters brought news of Cullen's arrest to Priscilla at the mansion, she fixed a steely I-told-you-so eye on them. "Cullen doesn't think like other people," she said. "If he gets away with something, he'll try it again. That's his way."

Did she blame anybody for what had happened?

"Yes," she snapped. "The Amarillo jury."

Steve Sumner was just putting a cooler of beer in the back of his car in preparation for a waterskiing trip to Lake Texoma when Phil Burleson called. "Cullen has been rearrested."

"What the hell for?"

"I don't know. Apparently somebody has been shot," Burleson misinformed him. "I think you ought to get over to Fort Worth as fast as you can."

A few minutes after Sumner left, a friend called the house and spoke to his wife, Nancy. "I just heard the news," he said, obviously elated. "I guess this means you'll be adding a swimming pool to your new house."

Sumner and Burleson rendezvoused at Tim Curry's office. When they went in, they found Tolly Wilson sitting at a desk with his feet propped up and his hands behind his head. When he saw them, he grinned. "It's gonna be different this time, boys."

A few weeks later, at a writ hearing, the defense attorneys heard the FBI tapes for the first time. Huddled around a single speaker in a courtroom, with David McCrory on the witness stand and a huge, teeming press contingent outside the door, they listened to a voice they all recognized.

"I got Judge Eidson dead for you."

"Good."   •

Afterward, they left the courthouse together and pushed, silent and stone-faced, through the throng of reporters shouting questions: "Was that Cullen's voice?" "Do you think the tapes were doctored?" They reached Sumner's car and escaped into it: Haynes and Sumner in front, Burleson and Gibson in back. Outside the windows, reporters were still hurling questions; inside, there was only moody silence. As Sumner drove off, Haynes began the elaborate ritual of lighting his pipe. The silence weighed heavier and heavier.

It was Sumner who finally broke the sound barrier. "Those sonsabitches really fell into our trap this time," he said with a snicker. "We've got them right where we want them!"

There was a pause as Haynes looked over his pipe at Sumner. Then a smile. In the back seat, Burleson chuckled tentatively.

"Yeah," Haynes added, grinning, "those sonsabitches, all they've got is a bunch of *evidence*." In another second the car was filled with uproarious laughter.

59

There were many stories Richard Haynes loved to tell about himself. This wasn't one of them.

It was about his undergraduate days at the University of Houston when, to help pay tuition, he worked up a novelty act and hired himself out to conventions and parties. Dressed in colorful outfits, he did slapstick, pantomime, and, best of all, pratfalls. Anyone else would have called him a clown. Haynes preferred the term "stunt act."

His favorite venue was the big pool at the Shamrock, the best hotel in Houston. From the Shamrock's ten-meter diving board, he could keep the conventioneers below in stitches with stunts like driving a tricycle off the end of the board. But by far his best gag was "the Trip." He would pretend to trip off the high board, plummet through the air head first, flailing madly, crashing toward the water at the most awkward, dangerous angle, until, at the very last second, he would flip his body around in a perfect half-gainer and enter the water feet-first. It was that last-second flip, that photo-finish escape from a speeding and seemingly inevitable calamity, that really wowed the audiences at the Shamrock.

"How do you do it?" they always wanted to know. "How do you know when to flip?"

But he never told them. Only many years later did he reveal the secret of the weathervane. It was on a building across the street from the Shamrock, and it was placed in just the right spot so that as soon as he saw it, he knew it was time to flip. That was his signal, and it worked every time.

Then one day he did yet another of his famous trips off the board and started falling. He fell and fell and fell. And he saw the water coming up on him fast, but he didn't see the weathervane. He kept waiting for the signal, but it didn't appear. He was still waiting for it when he hit the water. He slapped it so hard that it knocked the wind out of him and he almost passed out. Almost drowned. For an instant he thought every bone in his body was broken. When he finally dragged himself out of the pool, he looked across the street and saw that somebody had taken down the weathervane.

Only days after beginning work on his second Cullen Davis trial in less than a year, Richard Haynes was already looking for the weathervane. A few weeks before, he had lost a case defending one of his witnesses in the Amarillo trial, a private investigator named Sylvia Meeks. Meeks had testified that Priscilla tried to hire her before the mansion murders, a story that Haynes had successfully inflated into an insinuation that Priscilla knew "something heavy" was about to happen on the eve of the murders. A few weeks after testifying, Meeks shot another PI to death in a dispute over a polygraph machine. Despite Meeks's lack of funds, Haynes took the case (it was never clear who paid his fee, or why), and did his best. He was beaten by some hotshot young prosecutor, the kind of courtroom tenderfoot about whom Haynes often said, "I have suits older than him."

Haynes had lost cases before, of course, but never easily and never gracefully. He stewed for weeks, talking to friends about "losing his edge" and speculating openly that he wasn't able to focus because he no longer cared. Perhaps the all-out, year-long battle to save Cullen Davis's hide had drained him completely—even permanently.

Then, suddenly, before he had a chance to answer any of the questions left by the last Davis case, he was being sucked into the next Davis case. At first, he tried to resist. When Cullen initially approached him he said, flatly, "No."

"Name your price," Cullen tempted.

Haynes did feel that he had been cheated the last time around: he had made only $250,000 for a year's worth of hard work while Phil Burleson's firm raked in the really big money. He wasn't going to make the same mistake twice. This time, the fee would be ten times what he got for Amarillo—the largest fee ever paid for a criminal defense.

Cullen nearly choked, but he agreed. Desperate as he was, he recognized a good deal when he saw it. By offering Haynes a record sum, he was raising the stakes and daring Haynes to ante up. The ultimate fee demanded the ultimate defense—a virtual guarantee of acquittal. By accepting a miracle worker's wage, Haynes was promising a miracle. And besides, if there was one thing Haynes couldn't pass up, whether on the ten-meter board or in the courtroom, it was a dare.

Within a week of Cullen's arrest, Haynes was back where he had never wanted to be again, back where he had been only a year before, back at the defense table listening as Cullen stood and said in his tinny, bloodless voice: "Not guilty."

* * *

On August 23, 1978, Cullen Davis's bond hearing on murder-for-hire charges began in the big seventh-floor courtroom of the Harris County Courthouse in Houston, Texas. Once again, a blizzard of publicity and a groundswell of sympathy for the accused had driven prosecutors out of Fort Worth. The setting seemed strangely appropriate, however. Unlike the Amarillo courtroom, with its fast-food fluorescent glare and Holiday Inn decor, the big courtroom in Houston could have been a stage set for grand opera: high ceilings, mahogany-paneled walls, pewlike benches, and low, dramatic lighting.

But the setting wasn't the only difference between Houston and Amarillo. Houston was, after all, Racehorse Haynes's home court—an advantage that had the prosecutors worried. They would have preferred Dallas, a notorious hanging town where for years judges routinely handed down thousand-year sentences. But Haynes knew better. Houston was a city of two and a half million, far too big to be manipulated the way Amarillo had been. No amount of country-club schmoozing, rumor seeding, or contact buying would have a discernible impact on Houston public opinion. A Ray Hudson, even if they had one, would be useless. Even the wealth and power of the Davis empire, which had proved so potent in Amarillo, was diluted to insignificance in Houston's vast sea of prospective jurors.

It was a different judge this time, too. Gone was gentleman George Dowlen, whose country-store temperament and taste for singles bars had proved such an unexpected boon to the defense in Amarillo. In his place sat Wallace Moore, better known as "Pete," a fifty-five-year-old ex–World War II fighter pilot with a voice like gravel, a will like steel, and a gaze reputed to turn fools to stone. There was surely no mistaking him for George Dowlen. If Dowlen was the gentleman rancher, with his soft features, bedroom eyes, and pampered comb of curly dark hair, Moore was the ranch foreman, the wizened veteran whose heavy-lidded eyes, sharp and skeptical, watched from the wiry shade of his bushy eyebrows and saw everything. He looked the part: jowly cheeks, tanned and leathery like old saddlebags; a forehead so deeply creased it looked scarred; a few silver strands of hair combed over a bald, well-seasoned pate. Everyone agreed: Moore was a good man to have as a friend—as bailiff Grady Dukes found out when Moore rescued him from a crazed prisoner holding a knife to his throat—and hell to have as an enemy.

Like Dowlen, Moore didn't hold much store by courtroom ceremony. He rarely wore robes—"If you need a robe to instill dignity, you shouldn't be on the bench," he would say, "and besides, they get caught under the rollers of the chair"—and he could be unceremoniously blunt if he thought a lawyer was wasting his time or insulting his intelligence. It was rumored that he had once slipped out of the courtroom during a particularly tedious examination and overruled objections from his distant chambers. Although by no means a scholar, he was known and respected for his court smarts, efficiency, and fairness, but above all for his impatience. When, in a pretrial hearing, Phil Burleson suggested that the case would take three or four months to try, Moore scowled and leaned forward. "I can tell you right now," he said in a voice like an old truck on a rocky road, "it isn't gonna take that long."

That was the bad news for the defense. The good news was that Pete Moore and Racehorse Haynes were old friends. They had seen the bottoms of many glasses together at various lawyers' hangouts around Houston as well as on Haynes's beloved *L'Esprit Libre*. Just a pair of old vets—battlefield and courtroom—who understood each other. Surely Moore would indulge his old drinking buddy. Nothing conspicuous, of course, nothing that would betray his reputation for fairness, just a little slack in the reins for camaraderie's sake. As Haynes had demonstrated in Amarillo, he only needed a little to wander a long way off the path. In a case where he would need every advantage he could get, no matter how slight, Haynes felt sure he could count on this one.

* * *

On October 30, Judge Moore called the first panel of fifty prospective jurors. Haynes had requested individual voir dire, the excruciatingly tedious process of interviewing jurors one by one that had worked so well for him in Amarillo. Moore had said no. This wasn't a capital murder case, he reminded his old friend, just a garden-variety felony. He saw no reason to waste the court's time. It was Haynes's first hint of what was to come.

By the end of the second day, Moore had excused sixteen of the first group for bias or "extreme hardship." But when Haynes suggested that another group of fifty jurors be empaneled, Moore brushed him aside. "This will be enough," he said firmly. Deprived of background information and forced to address their questions to the remaining thirty-four as a group, the prosecutors finished their selection in two and a half hours.

For the next three days, Haynes struggled to keep the questions coming while Steve Sumner and his investigators raced frantically around Houston trying to find out something, *anything* about the remaining jurors. Without folders of background information, the jury specialist Margaret Covington was reduced to generalities. Engineers, she suggested vaguely, would be most likely to vote for acquittal because they were "obsessive compulsives, introverted, and good with details." In his desperation, Haynes considered turning for help to a Dallas "personologist," Bruce Vaughan, who claimed to be able to read people's characters in their faces and bodies. Others on the defense team laughed—until they heard that Vaughan had a perfect record in nine previous cases. Then Vaughan told the *Fort Worth Star-Telegram* that he had "read" Cullen's physiognomy and determined that "he is capable of everything he has been accused of—very capable." Vaughan was dropped from the program.

By the middle of the fifth day of voir dire, Haynes had run out of questions. Of the twelve jurors who remained, seven were men, five women. Eight were over the age of fifty and, much to Margaret Covington's delight, eight were engineers of one kind or another. The selection process had taken six and a half days. In Amarillo, it had taken two months.

For the defense, it was only one of many setbacks. When Haynes moved to waive Cullen's husband-wife privilege, hoping that the prosecution would call Priscilla to testify, Moore denied the motion. The only reason to ask for a waiver, Moore concluded testily, was "to stick it in the prosecution's ear at the end and demand to know why they hadn't called Priscilla if they had nothing to hide." When Haynes moved to sequester the jury—the defense had discovered in Amarillo that sequestered jurors could be monitored more closely, influenced more easily, and their families coopted less conspicuously—Moore denied the motion. "This is an ordinary felony case," he reiterated, "and we'll deal with it as such. I don't care if it's Cullen Davis, Joe Jones, Tom Brown, or whoever."

When Haynes requested that Cullen be allowed to move about freely in the courtroom during recesses, as he had in Amarillo. Moore again refused. Like all other prisoners, he would be permitted to speak only to his lawyers and other officers of the court. Could he be allowed more than the standard single change of clothes? No, said Moore, if he wanted to wear a different suit and tie every day, someone would have to bring it to him. Could he be allowed to speak to reporters? No, said Moore, and to make sure he ordered the press to stay behind the railing, well away from the defendant.

Finally, Haynes demanded that the jury should be allowed to hear character evidence relating to material witnesses. He was thinking in particular of David McCrory, who would be even easier to destroy on the stand than Priscilla. But Moore wasn't fooled. "I will have no character assassination in my courtroom," he warned in denying the motion. "I'm not going to let this trial become another circus."

That was the last thing Haynes wanted to hear. As Judge Moore entered the big mahogany-paneled courtroom to begin the first day of trial, a circus was still the only defense Richard Haynes had.

60

Tolly Wilson opened for the prosecution. The silver-haired, pixie-faced veteran prosecutor had played third fiddle to Curry, second to a much younger Joe Shannon, at the Amarillo trial. Now, with Shannon gone into private practice and Curry protecting his political flank back in Fort Worth (staying well clear of what was seen by many as a prosecutorial vendetta against Cullen Davis), Wilson was the man of the hour.

Richard Haynes wasn't altogether unhappy with the choice. Wilson's many years as a prosecutor had left him bitter as well as wise. A generally dyspeptic temperament and charmless, plodding manner made him no favorite of juries, and a quick temper kept fellow lawyers at a cool distance. Reporters found him stiff-necked and uncooperative. Even colleagues in the D.A.'s office, although fond of his acid tongue, often found him "weird" and "grumpy."

Haynes puffed his pipe serenely as Wilson made a brief, flat opening statement, then called his first witness. Ron Jannings, looking surprisingly shifty and ill at ease for an FBI agent, recounted his meetings with Pat Burleson and David McCrory. On cross, Haynes could do little except stir up the usual ink cloud of petty inconsistencies and memory lapses (Why did Jannings misplace McCrory's phone number?) and suggest with his tone of voice that these were, in fact, glimpses of something larger and more deeply sinister. He dropped mysterious names into his questions, another favorite trick, hoping to open an "unexplained" file in the back of every juror's mind: Why did Pat Burleson meet with Priscilla Davis immediately before Cullen's arrest? Who was David Binion? These were the facts they would ultimately *need* to know, Haynes's grave tone signaled, but the prosecution wasn't telling them.

When the next witness was called, Tolly Wilson sat down and the tall, lanky, curly-haired young man next to him stood up. His name was Jack Strickland, and Haynes already knew he was going to be a problem.

In fact, Strickland was not unlike Haynes himself. An air force brat who spent his youth in almost every corner of America and Japan, he was drawn to the military early on. Starting with Naval ROTC at UT Austin, through flight training, basic training, gunnery training, carrier training, and advanced fighter pilot training, he had chased the same adrenaline high. The jump from the sky to the courtroom ("Lawyers get killed less frequently than pilots," he concluded) hadn't slowed him down at all. Since being brought into the D.A.'s office by Joe Shannon in 1974, he had broken every speed record in felony court. His last five cases had been capital murders. All five defendants had been found guilty; all five had gotten the death penalty. He was on a streak.

Strickland was in the middle of the last of the five when someone slipped him a piece of paper announcing the verdict in Amarillo. He felt disappointment, of course, but also vindication. Soon after the first arrest, Joe Shannon had asked his opinion of charging Cullen with capital murder. Strickland told him straight: "I think you're out of your minds." Marvin Collins's brainstorm of calling Cullen a burglar in his own house was "too cute," Strickland told him. "It's the kind of thing some egghead might buy, but never a jury." When news came of the verdict in Amarillo, his only thought was, "maybe next time they'll listen to me."

Now it was his turn to show them how to do it.

Under Strickland's questioning, FBI Agent Jerry Hubbell, a handsome, burly ex–Marine, described how he had attached the Nagra tape recorder to David McCrory and then followed him to Coco's on the morning of the arrest. The big courtroom fell silent and the jury leaned forward in their seats as he described his close encounter with Cullen Davis.

"While that van was parked there, was that van approached by any person?" Strickland asked.

"Yes, sir, I could see a shadow cross the rear portion of the van where the windows were located. It was the shadow of an individual."

"Did you hear anything?"

"I heard somebody outside knocking on the side of the van."

"If you had nothing to hide," Strickland asked, "if your deeds were noble, would you be suspicious of an innocent-looking van?" Hubbell didn't have an opportunity to answer; he didn't need to. The question hung in the heavy courtroom air all during Haynes's disjointed, fruitless cross.

Frustration was beginning to show in the deeper teeth marks on Haynes's pipe. Soon after Tolly Wilson began questioning the next witness, it erupted. Judge Joe Eidson was recounting the long series of divorce rulings that had shackled Kendavis Industries financially and perhaps brought Cullen to the threshold of murder. Just ten days before Cullen's rearrest, Eidson had postponed a final hearing on the divorce yet again over bitter objections from Cullen's lawyers.

"Judge Eidson," Wilson asked, "did you ever excuse yourself from further participation in this case?"

"Yes, sir, I did."

"And can you tell the jury when that was?"

"Yes, August 29, 1978." Nine days after Cullen's arrest.

"Prior to that time, had any attempt been made by the respondent, Cullen Davis, to remove you from the case?"

Haynes exploded from his chair and filled the room with his angry, stentorian voice—*"Excuse me, Counsel!"* —so suddenly that the court reporter's hands jumped back from her keyboard, missing the end of Wilson's question. They had to consult the tape recordings to confirm that he had in fact asked what Haynes thought he asked.

Cullen Davis had *not* tried to remove Judge Eidson from the case, Haynes raged; his attorneys had merely requested that the case be transferred out of Eidson's court. When someone suggested with a smirk that this was a distinction without a difference, Haynes's face went so red with indignation it looked about to burst. *"He is accused of solicitation of capital murder,"* he thundered. Wilson's question, with its reckless use of the word "remove," might have suggested to the jury that Cullen had once before tried to *kill* Eidson. Furthermore, Haynes insisted, the question had "interjected matters of such prejudice before the jury that no instruction from the Court, however proper, can cure that prejudice." He therefore had no choice but to demand a mistrial.

Everywhere in the courtroom—at the prosecution table, in the audience, on the bench—eyes widened and jaws dropped. Was Haynes ready to call it a loser after only three witnesses? Before the FBI's tapes had even been played? Was he that desperate?

Moore denied the motion for a mistrial.

Eidson went on to score even more points, recounting the dramatic story of how the FBI had taken his undershirt, burned it, bloodied it, dressed him in it, then posed him as a corpse in the trunk of a car. "Frankly," he confessed, "I was pretty shaken up by it."

The prosecution's case only got better. George Ridgley, a cherub-cheeked photography clerk from the FBI, identified the still photos that had been taken of Davis and McCrory in Coco's parking lot on August 18 and 20. He also sounded the only negative note so far when he revealed that the FBI's plan to bolster its case by dusting the photographs of Eidson had run amok. An overzealous Fort Worth policeman had fingerprinted Cullen and then directed him to wash in naphtha *before* the FBI could run its test for traces of the fluorescent powder on Cullen's hands. In the oncoming rush of prosecution evidence, however, it seemed a minor lapse.

The stage was just about set. The FBI witnesses had

brought the jury to the threshold of the August 18 and 20 meetings at Coco's, into the curtained surveillance van, up to the moment when a wired David McCrory stepped out of his car and headed for Cullen Davis's Cadillac. There was nothing left to do but play the tapes.

To introduce them, Wilson called David McCrory to the stand. Through a blizzard of objections from Haynes, McCrory led the jury through a recap of his tortuous ten-year relationship with Cullen Davis. In a confident, almost cocky voice, he skipped quickly over the early years with Priscilla and Judy to Cullen's first mention of a "job" he needed done; the $5,000 for "investigative work"; the cushy job at Jet Air with the big salary plus bonus, company car, and expense account; the clandestine meetings and the code names.

More and more, the talk turned to murder, he said, and the list of victims began to grow. Bev Bass was the original target; then Bubba, wheelchair or no; then Bubba's father. Only if he got them all would the lawsuits go away. By McCrory's telling, Cullen took a hands-on interest in the project, suggesting helpfully that the killer spread cocaine around the murder scene to make it look drug-related; or, less helpfully, that the killer wait until Bubba was working at his father's cleaners, then "go in and kill everyone there."

Even a blizzard of objections—unmatched in ferocity since Priscilla's testimony in Amarillo—couldn't break up the story enough to make it sound anything but horrific.

Then they played the tapes.

Into two dozen bright yellow headphones spread among jurors and lawyers, judge and court reporter, and through two booming speakers that filled the cavernous courtroom with ugly sound, Agent Joe Gray sent the furtive voices of David McCrory and Cullen Davis:

"You still want all three of them at once?"

"Do it either way."

"Okay, what if he does all three of those and just goes right on and wants his fucking money?"

"You just call me and you got it."

"So you definitely want her to go down before the judge?"

"Yeah."

For the August 20 meeting, Gray had taken the audio- and videotapes to the FBI laboratories in Washington and combined them into a crude but potent sound-and-light show. Haynes objected furiously, but Moore overruled him. The lights in the courtroom darkened and once again, much clearer this time, the voices of Cullen Davis and David McCrory filled the dim air:

"Now you want Beverly Bass killed next—quick, right?"

"All right."

"Now, I don't want to make another mistake. You're sure?"

"Yeah."

"This fuckin' murder business is a tough sonofabitch."

"Right."

"I got Judge Eidson dead for you."

"Good."

When the lights finally came up, all eyes turned to the defense table.

There was loathing in Haynes's eyes as he approached the witness stand to begin his cross-examination. This was, after all, the same David McCrory who had accused him of suborning perjury in Amarillo ("I have confidence in you, and someday [your ring] will be real"); the same David McCrory who had brought down on him a contempt citation—a citation that still hung over him almost two years later even though it had never been pursued; the same David McCrory who now stood between him and the most astonishing, impossible, headline-grabbing, lucrative triumph of his or any other lawyer's career. Not since Priscilla Davis had he felt more hate or more determination to destroy a witness.

"What was the name of the company that you worked for?" asked Haynes, trying to establish that McCrory was a ne'er-do-well and hanger-on who had sought refuge in the

Witness Protection Program solely for the $950 per month stipend it provided.

"I don't remember the name of it," McCrory answered. "The supervisor's name was Bobby something."

"Bobby something?" Haynes repeated skeptically. "You are not saying that the last name is 'something'?"

McCrory smiled archly. "Mr. Haynes, do you really think I think 'something' is his last name?"

Haynes tried ridicule, sarcasm, and the full repertoire of looks to the jury—surprise, skepticism, disgust, irony —but McCrory held his own.

"Did you in this week before you went to Las Vegas have a prayer meeting with Mr. Pat Burleson present?" Haynes asked in the same mocking tone he had used to question Priscilla about religion.

McCrory cocked his head and looked at Haynes with his big cow eyes. "You say it like it is something wrong," he said. "Is there something wrong?"

Haynes fumbled. "I asked *you* the question."

Soon Haynes was reduced to blowing smoke in McCrory's face, sidling as close as he could and bellowing questions in his ear. One reporter compared him to "a demented dentist pulling teeth with a pair of rusted pliers."

"Did you see Priscilla Davis at a public restaurant in June 1978?" Haynes asked.

"I'm not sure what month it was," McCrory replied. "I did see her at a restaurant and I reported that to Mr. Davis."

"In June you reported that to Mr. Davis?" Haynes pressed.

McCrory smiled knowingly. "Would you have any other way of knowing, Mr. Haynes?"

Tempers flared. When McCrory slipped a mention of Cullen's murder plans for Bev Bass into a response, Haynes bristled. "I'm not asking you to go through that part. I think I know what it is you want to say." But when Tolly Wilson objected to his snide tone and Moore sustained the objection, Haynes detonated. "I don't ask the witness a question, and he starts rambling on. . . . I *ask* him a question, [and] I get silence and 'I don't know.' Could I have the Court instruct the witness not to make responses until I ask a question?"

Wilson countered, "Could we have the Court instruct the jury not to consider counsel's sidebar remarks?"

Moore gave Wilson's instruction, not Haynes's.

The frequent sparring destroyed what little continuity there was to Haynes's questioning. The jury drifted in and out of attention. Judge Moore grew increasingly irritated. "Let the record reflect that these two gentlemen do not like each other," he said as he broke up yet another squabble.

When Haynes repeatedly misquoted him, McCrory complained, "I have to keep correcting you so we will keep the facts straight."

Haynes's eyes bulged with indignation. "*You* have to keep correcting *me*?" he roared.

McCrory was uncowed. "Yes, you keep misstating the facts."

Strung between anger and astonishment, Haynes groped for a response. "What . . . How . . . How are you going to keep the facts straight when you can't remember anything?"

Jack Strickland rose from his chair. "Excuse me, just one moment. I think tempers are getting a little short."

Moore looked from Haynes to McCrory and shook his head. "I just don't know what else to say. I ran out of words to avoid this situation."

"We object on the basis Mr. Haynes is an officer of the Court," Strickland offered, "and I think that . . ."

Moore cut him off. "I would like to put it on the basis that Mr. Haynes is much more experienced in this than the witness."

While Haynes stood mortified and speechless, McCrory turned to the judge and apologized.

"When you strike out like that," Moore advised the witness, "he's going to bite you back."

McCrory turned his repentant eyes on Haynes. "I apologize, Mr. Haynes."

Haynes's eyes shot back silent bolts of anger.

None of the old tricks were working. Every time Haynes tried to undermine McCrory's credibility by dredging up something from his past, the prosecutors were on their feet demanding its relevance. "This is predicate," Haynes would respond to such challenges, as he had so often in Amarillo, indicating that his question would set up another, perhaps more relevant, one.

"Mr. Haynes's predicate questions could embrace the whole universe," Tolly Wilson responded.

"Yes," said Moore. "Sustained."

In Amarillo, too, there had been a motion preventing Haynes from impeaching witnesses on collateral matters —anything not directly related to their testimony or to the facts of the case—but Judge Dowlen's standards of relevancy had been limited only by his own broad, naive, and randy curiosity.

Pete Moore's standards were considerably more rigorous.

Did McCrory once try to pass himself off as an ordained minister? As a salesman? As a police officer? Did he claim on a job application that he had completed a year of college when in fact he dropped out of school after the tenth grade? Was he the karate expert he claimed to be? Did he have title to his own house, as he claimed, or did his mother? Did he pay her rent? Did he cheat on his taxes? None of it relevant, ruled Moore. Eventually he cut off any inquiry into *anything* that happened prior to 1978; no ancient drug prescriptions, no messy past divorces, no long-buried indiscretions. In short, no circus. And if Haynes persisted in trying, Moore would lean down over the bench and warn: "You're running up another rabbit trail, Mr. Haynes. Now let's move on to something else."

When Haynes tried to introduce the infamous affidavit that McCrory had refused to sign when the murder trial was still in Fort Worth, along with a statement issued at the time by Tolly Wilson's office that McCrory was "not to be believed," Moore refused to admit it. "The credibility of the witness is for the *jury* to decide," he chastised.

By the third day of cross-examination, Moore was losing patience with his old drinking companion. "You ask the question over and over," he complained to Haynes, "and you get the same answer, and it puts you in the same place, but it wastes a lot of my time." In the middle of an interminable series of questions on how often, when, where, and why McCrory had gone pistol shopping in the first eight months of 1978, Moore cried out in exasperation, "Mr. Haynes, the only thing we are really concerned with is, did he go anyplace looking for a pistol *for Mr. Davis*? Can we please stick to that?"

Tolly Wilson stood up. "I have a good idea," he offered helpfully. "Why doesn't he just *ask* him that?"

Moore nodded sadly. "Well, that's the easy way."

"I think that I would object to that if the Court please," said Haynes, knitting his high brow in distress, "as the comment affects the defendant over the shoulders of counsel." It was the response he always used when someone criticized him in court.

Moore ignored it. "I wonder why don't you just ask him the questions that are germane to this trial." There was both sarcasm and genuine bewilderment in his voice.

"I have asked him direct questions," Haynes struggled to explain, "and I get 'I don't know' and 'I don't remember.'"

Moore fixed him in the gunsights of his eyes and spat the words like bullets. "I can't help that, you know."

By the fourth day of cross-examination, Haynes was down to his last ammunition: inconsistencies between McCrory's previous statements under oath and his trial testimony. Did Cullen "tell" him he wanted fifteen people killed, as McCrory had testified at the bond hearing; or did he flash five fingers three times in answer to McCrory's question "How many do you want killed?"—the version he told on direct? Did he "hand" Cullen the envelope containing the pictures of a "dead" Judge Eidson (an earlier version), or did he "flip it" across the front seat at him? Every time McCrory tried to explain that these were only "semantic differences," Haynes pounded the table harder and demanded, "Which is the truth, Mr. McCrory?"

When McCrory complained that Haynes's questions were "confusing," Haynes reared back and his face turned red. "I *see*. Are you saying that I am trying to keep you in some confused state?"

"Yes, sir, that is your job," McCrory replied, his voice oozing sympathy. "I understand that."

The expression on Haynes's face turned vicious. "Did you inject that in there in some effort to demean myself or Mr. Davis?"

McCrory remained calm. "No, sir, not at all."

Strickland stood up. "Your Honor, I object to the constant argumentative . . ."

Moore didn't even let him finish. "Sustained."

As Haynes turned to Moore, an edge of petulance crept into his voice. "Your Honor, this witness has continuously endeavored to inject into his responses that which is not material to the response, only self-serving and bolstering and an effort to demean . . ."

"We object to that sort of jury argument," Strickland interrupted. "This is not appropriate. Mr. Haynes says that whenever he gets an answer he doesn't quite like."

In four tumultuous days of cross-examination, Haynes had managed only to open a few small holes in McCrory's account of the events leading up to Cullen's arrest, and to insinuate that in some mysterious way Priscilla Davis had played a role in those events. Left unchallenged—indeed, barely mentioned—were the money, the photographs, the gun, the silencer, and, most damning of all, the tapes.

After the Thanksgiving holiday, the prosecution came back with a closing barrage of testimony. Agent Gray returned to the courtroom with his yellow headphones to play his riveting sound-and-light show yet again. For days, Haynes tried desperately to shake his testimony with technical challenges that drove away most of the spectators and put several jurors to sleep. All to no avail.

Gray was followed by two secretaries from Cullen's

office. Brenda Adcock reluctantly testified that Cullen had given her a fat (with cash?) envelope in August and told her to lock it in the office safe. She also confirmed that David McCrory did indeed start coming around Cullen's office, just as he said he had, and once called using the code name Frank Johnson.

Mary Ann Carter admitted that Cullen had called her from the office on the Sunday morning of the arrest, asking for the combination to the office safe. When Brenda Adcock returned from a vacation a week later, the fat envelope was gone. No one else had the combination.

The prosecution's finale featured four law enforcement officials who had been in on Cullen's capture. Rodney Hinson told how he found the Ruger and silencer in the trunk of Cullen's car. Morris Howeth described how Cullen had tried to hide his face behind his hands when they approached to arrest him. John Hogg, a tall Texas Ranger, recounted how McCrory trembled and began to cry under the pressure of the moment. The jury was clearly moved —was this the cool, calculating conspirator portrayed by the defense? Haynes attacked Hogg "like a band of Apaches," spitting sarcasm and ridicule on his sloppy report, torturing minor inaccuracies (who first told Hogg about the $50,000?) into hints of a monstrous conspiracy. Some in the audience wondered if the handsome Ranger wasn't just the unlucky target of leftover bile meant for David McCrory.

Finally, the prosecution called its last witness: Larry Tongate, the FBI flight observer who had followed Cullen's car through the streets of Fort Worth from a plane on the morning of the arrest. He described how Cullen had clearly tried to "wash" any tail—zigzagging, backtracking—as if he knew or suspected someone might be following him. Jack Strickland best expressed the feeling that buzzed through the courtroom as Tongate gave his account. "Nothing suspicious in that," he cracked. "Doesn't everybody take those kinds of security measures when they go to meet a friend?"

As soon as the prosecution closed its case, reporters

surrounded Haynes. What was he going to do? Wasn't the prosecution's case devastating? Didn't things look bleak? Would Cullen Davis finally go to jail? Haynes smiled reassuringly, lit his pipe, and tried to quell the rush of speculation. "O ye of little faith," he intoned. "The opera ain't over 'til the fat lady sings."

But it was just a show—a quote for the next morning's edition. In fact, he didn't need the press to tell him how bleak things looked. He knew from experience. He had left the high board and the water was fast approaching—and there was still no sign of the weathervane.

Even as the press closed around Haynes, Karen Master sat on a bench outside the courtroom answering some of the letters that had poured into the Harris County Courthouse addressed to Cullen Davis; as many as fifty a week, most of them talking of God or Jesus and how "He" would deliver this fine man from his enemies. Many also asked for money. "There are so many wonderful people out there who want to help Cullen," said Karen with a beatific smile. "Total strangers willing to do *anything* they can."

61

"I'm going to walk in there and blow Cullen's head off." Priscilla Davis fixed her steely gaze on Jack Strickland as she prepared to enter the big seventh-floor courtroom.

"For God's sake, Priscilla, don't talk like that," Strickland recoiled, searching her heavily made-up face for some sign of a smile. "Don't say that." There was none. "Even jokingly."

She shook her huge mane of platinum hair. "Well, I ain't gonna spend one dime paying anyone else to do it." With that, she picked up her briefcase and headed into the courtroom. As she walked away, dressed in a high-collar, low-hemline, all-black dress, Strickland watched in admiration. Her resilience, her spontaneity, everything about her was genuine. So unlike Karen Master, whose studied sincerity had fooled so many jurors. It was just Priscilla's fate that her greatest asset off the witness stand was also her greatest liability on it.

This was Priscilla's second day of testimony. Richard Haynes had opened his defense by calling the witness he most loved to hate. There was just one problem this time, however. Because he called her, he was not allowed to impeach her.

Not that he didn't try. At times, it was almost as if they were back in Amarillo again, locked in their desperate duel. ("After Mr. Davis moved out of 4200 Mockingbird," Haynes asked at one point, "and during the period of time you were living there, did Mr. W. T. Rufner live there or stay there?") But Pete Moore proved again that he wasn't George Dowlen. When Haynes tried to delve into Priscilla's "personal" relationship with Pat Burleson, Moore cut him off. When Haynes began fishing in the dark waters of the divorce case, Moore cut him off. When Haynes tried to introduce Priscilla's phone records, Moore cut him off. He wanted their relevancy proved *first*. Haynes sputtered and fumed, but Moore wouldn't budge.

Haynes's attempt to establish a conspiracy between Priscilla, Pat Burleson, and David McCrory to "get" Cullen Davis also met with limp success.

Just before Cullen's arrest, didn't Priscilla offer to settle the divorce case for $20 million and wasn't that offer rejected?

Yes, Priscilla conceded, but she had also rejected Cullen's offer to settle for $1.2 million.

Wasn't the failure of these offers a likely motive for her to conspire? Haynes suggested.

No more so than for Cullen to commit murder, she replied.

As for her frequent meetings with Pat Burleson around the time of Cullen's arrest, Priscilla explained that she had hired Burleson to manage the security for her upcoming divorce trial. "He was the only one I could ask for help," she said. "I couldn't borrow more money. The divorce was running longer than I anticipated . . . and I knew I couldn't afford the police officers." She did not, however, know anything about David McCrory's troubles with Cullen Davis or his conversations with Pat Burleson around the same time. When Haynes pulled out a giant calendar and probed for holes in Priscilla's recollection of those critical days, one juror fell asleep and several others broke into yawns.

Every time Haynes tried to challenge one of Priscilla's answers directly, Wilson and Strickland would pepper him with objections ("impeaching his own witness") or Judge Moore would swat him down with an admonition ("You're walking on real thin ice now"). As a result, Haynes's bursting skepticism of his witness's responses was confined to mugging at the jury.

On cross the first day, Tolly Wilson ambushed the defense by playing the tapes yet again. Over Haynes's wild objections, Priscilla donned the yellow headphones and listened to her husband's acid voice:

"He'd rather do Priscilla than the judge. He says he can do it easy."

"Like hell. Priscilla's always got somebody around her."

"Give me a price on Priscilla."

It wasn't long before Priscilla began to tremble noticeably and the dim courtroom light caught the tears in her eyes.

When the tapes were finished, Wilson asked: "Did you conspire with Pat Burleson to get your husband to say any of the things he said on that tape recording?"

Priscilla spoke firmly, over the tears and trembling. "No, I did not."

"Did you conspire with David McCrory to get your husband to say any of the things he said on that tape recording?"

"No, I did not."

Later that evening, Priscilla's reaction turned from fear

to loathing. "I think Cullen has considerable firsthand information on how hard I am to kill," she said between gritted teeth.

She was in the same black mood the next morning when, unbeknownst to Jack Strickland, she slipped a silver-plated .32 revolver in her briefcase before leaving for court. Haynes had called her back to take some additional evidence.

When her name was read out, Priscilla walked to the front of the room, set her briefcase down and took her place on the witness stand. As Haynes began his questioning—"Did you at any time have a relationship with Pat Burleson that was more than platonic?"—Priscilla's heart began to beat faster and faster. For the first time since she began testifying, she looked at Cullen. "Everybody wonders how this is going to end," she thought, as she pictured herself opening the briefcase, pulling out the revolver, pointing it at the reptilian figure seated at the defense table . . . "Okay, everybody, here's your ending. *Bang!*"

Sitting at the prosecution table, listening to Judge Moore interrupt Haynes yet again—"This court is not a place for character assassination"—Strickland couldn't stop thinking about what Priscilla had said on her way into the courtroom about "blowing Cullen's head off." Then, suddenly, he remembered that she *did* have a gun—or at least she often carried one: a silver-plated .32 that she kept in an ankle holster. He tried to picture her walking away from him into the courtroom earlier. Did she have boots on? Could she have been wearing the holster? She wouldn't *really* . . .

His racing thoughts were shattered by a loud crack that echoed through the old wooden courtroom like a gunshot. He looked at Cullen; he was still staring straight at Priscilla. At least she hadn't shot *him*. He looked at Priscilla. She was staring down at her feet. "Goddamn," he thought, "she's dropped her gun right here in front of the jury."

But it wasn't even that. Her briefcase had fallen over.

62

The next day, Haynes tried again with Pat Burleson.

And failed even more miserably. Despite Haynes's repeated claims that he was showing them one of the key "co-conspirators" in the plot against Cullen Davis, the jurors noticed only two things about Burleson: that he was as handsome as a movie star, and that he was seething mad at Cullen Davis.

No one, except perhaps Priscilla Davis, had better reason to be. On the morning after Cullen's arrest, Burleson had awakened to a nightmare. His wife, Talana, a ravishing blonde from a deeply religious family, was reading the morning paper with an ashen face. "When asked what the defense investigation had turned up about the relationship between Pat Burleson and Mrs. Davis," she read, "Phil Burleson said: 'Nude swimming in the mansion pool together—and whatever that leads to.' "

It was only the beginning. There were more articles in the papers, more stories, all of them from Phil Burleson, the defense's designated hit man, about Pat's participation in drug parties and sex orgies at the Davis mansion. All of them lies. Pat tried to explain to Talana, and she nodded sympathetically, but he could tell it wasn't enough. She didn't look at him the same way anymore. The nastiness of it lingered between them.

Someone asked Phil Burleson if he and Pat were related. "I'm not sure, but I think we might be distantly," he said, as if he found even such a distant connection distasteful and embarrassing. When Pat heard that, he lashed back. "I don't want to claim that sonofabitch any more than he wants to claim me, but all I know is, his father and my father were brothers. Now, either we're first cousins or he's a bastard."

Then, suddenly, the attacks from the defense camp stopped. After Pat's testimony at the bond hearing in Fort Worth, someone apparently realized that he would make a better ally than enemy. Through a Fort Worth attorney who knew him personally, Burleson said, the offer was passed: "You know you're a critical player in this thing, Pat. All you would have to do is change your story a little and it would get Cullen off." It would be done inconspicuously, the attorney suggested helpfully, as simple as a mistake about times. "Where you said something about the timing, you could change it just a little bit, and destroy the case on that. You could just be a negligent witness," the attorney reassured him.

The next step, Burleson said, was phone calls. The callers identified themselves as "members of the defense team" but refused to give their names. They wanted to know if Burleson had decided to cooperate. "Name your price," they said, "unnumbered account. If you'll help us, you can have anything you want."

Burleson told them no: no, he wouldn't "cooperate"; no, he wouldn't name a price; no, he wouldn't change his story.

That was when the real nightmare began.

It started simply enough, Burleson said: two men, in two cars, in two shifts, around the clock, parked outside his home in the morning, outside his studio during the day, outside his home again at night. They took pictures of every place he went and every person he saw. One morning he came out and found that they had been through his garbage.

Then they began interviewing his neighbors. They would introduce themselves as "investigators," and people would assume they were working for the prosecutor's office. Someone subpoenaed the deacon of Burleson's church, ordering him to bring with him the church's tithing records so they could see if Pat had made any unusually large donations recently. Terrified, the deacon complied.

Eventually, to spare his neighbors further harassment, Burleson moved.

Next, Burleson said, they went after his business. They waited all day in the parking lots of his schools taking down students' license plate numbers. Then they called or visited students' parents. "We're investigators on the Cullen Davis case," they would say. "We just want to find the truth in this case, and we want to ask you some questions." A few parents asked to see identification or told them to get lost, but most didn't. Most thought they were officers of the court and that Pat Burleson was a criminal—after all, they had read the articles in the paper. They didn't want their kids going to a school run by a criminal. Within months, Burleson's enrollment dropped 90 percent. Rent and mortgages went unpaid. After twenty years of work, he was losing everything.

He had been right all along, from that early morning months before when David McCrory's phone call woke him up. He should never have gotten involved with Cullen Davis again.

Burleson gave Haynes nothing. For a full day and parts of two more, he was fire to Haynes's ice. Fearing that the witness's anger might erupt at any moment into a mistrial, Moore cornered Burleson and his wife in the elevator during a break. "Son," he said in his earthquake voice, "I don't want a mistrial. Race is pissing me off up there, too, but you just hold your temper. Don't let him get your goat."

Back in the courtroom, Haynes ominously directed Burleson's attention to an "inconsistency" in his story. At the bond hearing, Burleson had put one of his August meetings with McCrory at 10:00 A.M., Haynes pointed out with the usual arch in his voice, while, "to this jury," he had said the meeting took place at "midmorning."

"Well," Haynes demanded loftily, *"which was it?"*

Burleson looked at the jury knowingly and sighed. "I guess midmorning." To Haynes's mortification, several jurors smiled back.

On cross, Jack Strickland led Burleson through a description of his first meeting with McCrory. "He related to me that he was in a lot of trouble, that the company he worked for was owned by Cullen Davis, and his problem related to Cullen Davis. I told him I didn't want to hear about it, and I chastised him for being involved with Cullen Davis again." A sudden wave of conviction surged through his voice. "I was sick and tired of these problems with Cullen Davis."

"How did Mr. McCrory react to this?" Strickland asked.

"He hung his head."

"And what was his demeanor?"

"He was completely scared, totally, to death."

"What leads you to that conclusion?"

"The pallor on his face, the rash on his hands, and he was shaking."

Strickland nodded sympathetically, and his voice softened. "It is true, isn't it, that your relationship with Mr. McCrory is very much like that of an older brother to a younger brother?"

Burleson searched the courtroom walls for the right words. "It's been a very . . . hectic relationship." His exasperation was utterly convincing.

"Is the way you perceived it this time that 'Here's David in another jam again'?"

Burleson nodded slowly. "That's how I saw it exactly."

Clearly, this was not the clandestine meeting of co-conspirators bent on an evil plot to undo Cullen Davis that Haynes had tried so desperately to show. In a few brief strokes, Strickland had wiped out whatever doubts Haynes had managed to sow in the jury's mind about Burleson and seriously undermined weeks of innuendo about the conspiracy's "mastermind," David McCrory.

It was the second time in as many starts that one of Haynes's witnesses had been of more benefit to the prosecution than to the defense.

Clearly, Haynes needed help.

63

Cullen Davis provided it.

Some months before, foreseeing just such a strait, he had put out "the call" to the thousands of people who worked for or with Kendavis Industries International. Through the office grapevine, the word was passed: Anybody in a position to help Cullen Davis would be generously rewarded for doing so—no questions asked.

To a select few, the call was made directly. These were the people who had been identified by company computers (or by Cullen himself) as having special knowledge of the case. Bobby Smith was one of these select few.

A mechanic at Stratoflex, Bobby had taken karate lessons at Pat Burleson's studio. Over lunch, he told his supervisor, and the word was quickly passed up through the bureaucracy. It wasn't long before the call came back down: They needed Bobby to testify about Burleson's drug habit. "As far as I know, Burleson never did drugs," Bobby told the man who called him and identified himself only as "a member of the Davis defense team." "At least not while I was around. I never saw it."

Had Bobby ever seen Burleson drink? the man asked.

"Oh, sure," said Bobby, "we've shared some beers together."

"Are you sure that wasn't drugs and not beer you saw him with, Bobby?" the man pressed. "You know, it could have been cocaine. Are you sure it wasn't cocaine?"

"I'm sure," said Bobby.

"You know it would make a big difference to Mr. Davis if that was cocaine you saw him with and not beer. You do know what cocaine looks like, don't you, Bobby? You could describe it?"

Bobby said he could.

"So, knowing that it would make such a difference to Mr. Davis, and knowing how grateful he would be if you could come forward and say that you saw Pat Burleson with cocaine, are you still sure it wasn't cocaine and not beer?"

Bobby didn't know what else to say. "Oh, yes, sir. I'm sure."

The next Friday, Bobby was fired. When Bobby asked why, his supervisor shook his head and held up a memo "from the head office." "It says here, 'Drug use.' "

Bobby's story, and others like it, were picked up and carried to the furthest corners of Stinky Davis's farflung empire. The next time the call went out, no one ignored it.

Haynes first called to the stand a succession of baby-sitters, maids, and secretaries, all of whom testified that David McCrory was lying when he said he met and talked frequently with Cullen Davis during the first eight months of 1978. Next came Dorothy Neeld, a receptionist and secretary at Fan Clutch—not a Kendavis company, but a big client that shared an office building with Jet Air—who swore that she had seen David McCrory get into a burgundy car with a mustachioed man and a platinum-haired woman. To no one's surprise, she identified the man as Pat Burleson and the woman as Priscilla Davis.

A platinum-haired, bosomy divorcée herself, Neeld was known around the office for her ambition and her inability to keep a secret. The question of how she had managed to keep this one for so long—she contacted the defense only after receiving the call—went unanswered, as did the question of why, if McCrory, Burleson, and Priscilla were deep in a conspiracy against Cullen Davis, they would rendezvous in broad daylight in front of company offices.

Next came Mary Ramsey, the wife of an up-and-coming sales executive at Mid-Continent Supply. Prim and proper as a schoolmarm, she related her encounter with Priscilla Davis at, of all places, the Aladdin Casino and Hotel in

Las Vegas. Ramsey was on vacation with her husband. The day was June 13, 1978. It was about 8:30 in the evening when she looked up from the gaming table and saw Priscilla. They barely had time to exchange hellos, no more than thirty seconds, when Priscilla doubled up in pain and ran off to the bathroom. That was the last Mrs. Ramsey had seen of her.

Haynes smugly recalled that Priscilla had not only denied being in Las Vegas during the summer of 1978, but also knowing a Mrs. Mary Ramsey. It was a small victory (what did it have to do with Cullen's innocence?), but it was, at last, a victory, and Haynes celebrated it with a broad smile as he gallantly escorted Mrs. Ramsey from the stand.

The victory was short-lived. In rebuttal, Strickland called David Childers, Priscilla's brother, who testified that he and his wife had driven from Cincinnati to Fort Worth in June 1978 to visit Priscilla. They stayed from June 10 to June 17 and saw Priscilla every day, including June 13, the day Mary Ramsey had supposedly seen her in Las Vegas, and he had called her at the mansion on the morning of June 14. Furthermore, he had gas receipts and family snapshots to prove it.

Then there was Robert Brown, an employee of Cummins Sales and Service, another Kendavis company, who was married to W. T. Rufner's ex-wife. Brown testified that Rufner had called him in late June or early July with an ominous warning: "Something big is coming down."

Tolly Wilson couldn't help but laugh. It sounded suspiciously like what Sandy Myers had testified in the Amarillo trial that Priscilla told her on the eve of the murders: "Something heavy is coming down." Tolly wasn't surprised. After all, they had the same coach.

By the end of the first week of defense testimony, some observers were beginning to wonder if Haynes would ever get his case off the ground. But Haynes still had one source of witnesses yet to tap: Steve Sumner. If nothing else, the parade of Kendavis-sponsored testimonials had given Sumner and his team precious extra time to identify weak spots in the prosecution's case and scour the bars and honky-tonks of Fort Worth for witnesses to exploit them.

64

Before leaving for Houston, Steve Sumner had already begun the sophisticated process of collecting evidence. He had, for example, "developed" testimony that David McCrory was pimping for his wife as well as selling himself to "old biddies" at $50 a crack. He had even acquired photographs showing McCrory's wife "in various stages of undress." Much of his effort had been directed at proving his own theory that the conspiracy between Priscilla, Burleson, and McCrory actually "germinated" on the night of the murders at 4200 Mockingbird.

Lamentably, when Judge Moore ruled that nothing related to the 1976 shootings could be introduced at trial, all that work went down the drain.

This time around, however, Sumner wasn't the only one digging for dirt. Impressed by the importance of such "research" in the Amarillo trial, Cullen had hired an entire private investigation firm to continue the work Sumner had begun so admirably. The firm was headed by Jim Bearden, a plump, bland, and balding insurance-salesman type who looked even less the part of a PI than the jockish Sumner, but, like Sumner, knew what Cullen wanted and how to get it.

From Houston, as the prosecution made its case, Sumner fed Bearden a daily "to-do" list based on the day's testimony. He was especially interested in dates, times, and places—facts that the defense "needed" to challenge. Could Bearden find someone to testify that McCrory was someplace else at the time he said he was meeting with Cullen? Or that Cullen was someplace else?

Bearden's investigators usually didn't begin interviewing until after dark. But then, most of their interviewees didn't come out until after dark. Up and down Camp Bowie Boulevard, "Cullen Davis's men" were famous. Women propositioned them. Parades of people followed them from one honky-tonk to the next. Everyone wanted to be helpful: some because they thought Cullen was being ramrodded, some because they were just the helpful kind. "Even people who didn't like Cullen are awed by our celebrity status," Bearden boasted. When anyone approached them with an offer of information, he or she was given a phone number and told to "call the office."

The office was flooded with calls. For the benefit of those potential informants who did not frequent the bars and nightclubs that lined Camp Bowie but followed the trial in the papers, Bearden even set up a special phone line under Racehorse Haynes's name for "any witness who didn't agree with the state's version of things."

Of course, there were always callers who didn't understand the rules. "For $50,000 I think I can remember this, this, and this," they would say—often ten times a day—but Bearden had a standard response. "No, I'm sorry, we don't pay for information." After all, the prosecutors or police could be on the other end of the line. (One time, Bearden thought he heard a police radio in the background.) But every call was recorded, and every caller was scheduled for an interview.

Most interviews were conducted at the office, where it was easier to tape-record unobtrusively. "Well, gee, Mr. _____," the investigator would begin with a smile, "we're glad that you're here. Now, before you tell me anything, let me tell you exactly what we are focusing on at this particular point, and let me tell you how the facts have evolved up to this point. We rather expect, from what we have been able to learn, that your part in this is _____ . We rather expect that your testimony would be _____ . How does that square with what you are here to talk to us about?"

With uncanny frequency, it squared exactly. "That's

just what I was here to talk to you about," the witness would say. "I guess you already know about it."

When a potential witness expressed concern about Priscilla—would she be able to hurt them when it was over?—Bearden's investigators told them, "Look, at best, Priscilla's gonna walk away from the divorce with eight or ten million dollars, and she'll snort that up her nose. But Cullen's got all this other money. So, who would you rather work for?"

Fortunately, most knew better than to mention money. That was simply understood. "The witnesses felt money was possible," Bearden explained, "so we didn't need to talk about it."

For those who demanded more specific incentives, there was always Larry Boswell, Cullen's "private" PI. A one-man operation who claimed to be ex-DEA but wasn't, Boswell worked directly for Cullen, not his lawyers. Cullen loved his sleazy bail-bondsman look and pool-hall manner, and used him for all his most sensitive "personal matters."

The system didn't always work perfectly—as Haynes discovered when he called David Binion to the stand. A longtime denizen of the Fort Worth underworld, Binion fashioned himself a "used car salesman"—a notoriously rough business in Texas—but looked more like the hit man the defense claimed he had once pretended to be. As a paid police informant and a petty con man, he had slipped back and forth across the line between cops and robbers so often that no one trusted him—except, of course, the Cullen Davis defense.

As he slouched into Judge Moore's big courtroom, he looked every bit as rank as his reputation: a glassy-eyed, heavy-footed, overly muscled man with a half-crazed smile on his face. So rank, in fact, that Moore took one look at him and ordered Haynes to question him first out of the jury's presence. He wasn't going to let this seedy character open his mouth in court without first finding out what he had to say.

Binion did eventually tell his story, or at least part of

it, to the jury, but it didn't turn out to be the story Haynes expected to hear. He began by describing a visit to the mansion shortly after the Amarillo trial ended.

"Did Priscilla Davis say to you that 'Cullen will get his'?" Haynes inquired.

"No," said Binion, to Haynes's obvious surprise.

"What did she say exactly?"

"I can't remember exactly," Binion hedged. "It was in a religious sense, a religious manner."

"She didn't call you up there because you were a preacher, did she?" Haynes scoffed, losing patience with his own witness.

"No, sir."

"She didn't call you up there to buy a used car?"

"No."

Haynes bore down. "Did she say that Cullen Davis would get killed?"

But Binion refused to say what Haynes clearly wanted and expected him to say. "No," he insisted. "I already told you that."

"Well, what *did* she say?" Haynes demanded wearily.

"She said God would take care of these things, and he'll get what's coming to him."

"God would take care of things?" Haynes repeated scornfully.

"I think you and I are taking the conversation in a different light," Binion offered helpfully.

Haynes salvaged what little he could from the witness. "Did you leave the meeting with the opinion that she called you there to do harm to Cullen Davis?"

"Yes."

But it wasn't much.

On cross, Tolly Wilson scored an unexpected hit.

"During the entire time you say you were there, did Priscilla Davis ever ask you to kill or have her husband killed?"

"No," said Binion.

"And you reported the fact that Priscilla Lee Davis had

not asked you to get a hit man to kill her husband to Mr. Haynes *before* this trial, did you not?"

"Yes, sir."

Two days later, Haynes called to the stand Larry Gene Lucas, another product of Sumner and Bearden's busy witness factory. The look was unmistakable: fleshy face of indeterminate age, ruddy cheeks around a drinker's nose, disappearing hair, a screaming-print blue Hawaiian shirt, and a sharkskin suit the color of lima beans. His past was unmistakable, too. He called himself a "paint contractor," but from his lengthy police record it was clear he had spent precious little time with a paintbrush in his hand. He had been caught smuggling pot, burglarizing homes, and shoplifting—suits, of all things.

With all the dignity he could muster, Haynes led Lucas through a description of an encounter, in June or July of 1978, with David McCrory. Lucas was hanging out at the Sylvania Bar & Billiards when McCrory strutted in looking like he had just won the lottery. (Lucas described in loving detail McCrory's silk tie and $300 suit. How did he know? He had stolen some just like it.) Lucas greeted him as anyone in his position would—with a request for money. McCrory grandly handed him ten bucks, then took him aside. "You obviously need to earn some money," McCrory said, according to Lucas. "Let's go outside and talk about it."

Haynes stepped in to slow the story down. He wanted the jury to hear every detail. "What did you talk about outside?"

"He offered me ten thousand dollars to kill Cullen Davis." A startled murmur filled the courtroom.

Haynes gave it time to subside before continuing. "What did you say in response to that?"

"I told him, 'You're crazy, the man's got more security than the President.' "

"And what next did he say?"

"He offered me twenty thousand dollars." Another, louder murmur.

It was perfect. Here was proof that McCrory was trying to have Cullen killed only one month before he had him arrested. Clearly, when the plan for a hit fell through, McCrory and his co-conspirators dreamed up the FBI frame job. The defense could not have *invented* a more perfect story—even if they might have wished for a more perfect witness.

And that wasn't all. Lucas went on to testify that when he refused the $20,000 offer, McCrory said: *"Well, we're going to get him one way or the other."* It was the cherry on the sundae. The jury didn't have to make a leap of faith from the conspiracy to kill Cullen to the conspiracy to frame him: Lucas had made it for them.

But that *still* wasn't all. Just in case anybody might doubt Lucas's word, McCrory had been stupid enough to repeat the offer in front of a witness, a friend of Lucas's named Joe Espinoza. McCrory had followed Lucas to his car, where Espinoza was waiting, and said, one more time, "Gene, I'll give you twenty thousand dollars to kill him." "Forget it," Lucas recalled telling him. "I want no part of it."

At the next break, the courtroom exploded. The long-awaited reversal had begun—as anybody could see from the smile on Haynes's face. "Finally," veteran courthouse reporters declared, "ole Race has landed a big one."

On cross, Tolly Wilson struck some glancing blows by informing the jury, for the first time, of the witness's rich and varied criminal past and suggesting that money was responsible for not only refreshing but refurbishing Lucas's memory. But it was later, during rebuttal, that Lucas's ship, and Haynes's, took a torpedo amidship.

The woman who lived with Lucas, Mary Weir, took the stand and told how, shortly after Cullen's arrest, Lucas had said to her "that, since he knows David McCrory, and he felt like, if David could get into a good deal like that, there is no reason *he* couldn't be of some help to Cullen Davis."

Haynes objected fiercely that Weir was Lucas's

common-law wife and therefore, under Texas law, should not be permitted to testify against her husband. But Moore, clearly outraged that Haynes had put such a patent liar on the stand in the first place, dismissed his protests and allowed the witness to continue.

"What did Mr. Lucas say he was going to do?" Wilson asked Weir.

"That he was going to say that he met with McCrory, and McCrory offered him money to kill Cullen Davis." When asked whether she knew such a meeting had actually taken place, Weir said that Lucas told her it had not.

And what did Weir think of this scheme?

"I told him that he was very liable to get in a great deal of trouble," she testified. But that didn't stop him. Lucas had even asked her to come to Houston with him to testify that *she* had witnessed the meeting with McCrory. Why? "He thought I would be a more credible witness than Joe Espinoza," Weir explained.

On cross, Haynes attacked the witness with startling ferocity. He accused her of lying about her relationship with Lucas, of cheating the government out of Social Security payments, of operating a stolen-clothing ring (all of which she denied), and finally of prostitution (which she defiantly admitted). But it was no use. Waiting in the wings, ready to testify, was Weir's sister-in-law, Kimberly Vandever, who had brought with her a recent handwritten letter from Lucas in which the plot to "help Cullen" was immortalized ("there might be some good money in it," he wrote), as well as Joe Espinoza, who was also prepared to say that Lucas's "bombshell" testimony was all a scam.

Undeterred, Haynes called yet another witness to the "conspiracy" between Pat Burleson, David McCrory, and Priscilla to "get" Cullen Davis.

His name was James Edward Stephens and, like a surprising number of other defense witnesses, he listed his occupation as "used car salesman," although most of his income appeared to derive from unspecified nocturnal activities in and around Fort Worth's lawless south side.

Stephens's contact with the Cullen Davis defense began with a drunken phone call. He had been following with considerable interest the plight of Larry Gene Lucas in the paper, and, after a few six-packs of beer, decided to call the phone number for "Cullen's men" that had been circulating around the bars and beer halls of Fort Worth where Stephens spent most of his time. Within a day or two, Jim Bearden and several of his men paid Stephens a visit.

Although Bearden's men quickly dismissed Stephens as "a kook"—a hostile, drunken old con man who seemed to thrive on trouble, and for whom hardly a day passed without a death threat—Bearden himself wasn't so sure: just because he was a kook didn't mean he couldn't be a witness. Besides, with the trial going so badly, how picky could they afford to be?

Bearden ran a background check and was encouraged to find that Stephens hadn't killed anybody. There was the small problem of a rape conviction, however, made even more complicated by the fact that the victim in the case was Stephens's own mother. Around the Cullen Davis defense team, Stephens quickly became known as "our certified motherfucker."

In response to Haynes's effusively polite questioning, Stephens testified that he had been changing a flat tire in the parking lot of the Holiday Inn in Fort Worth when he saw three people, two men and a woman, emerge from the motel door. One he recognized as Pat Burleson, whom he had known "socially" for almost ten years. The woman he knew from television and newspapers as Priscilla Davis; and from a photograph Haynes showed him, he identified the other man as David McCrory.

And what was the date of this incident? Haynes inquired.

"Either Thursday the seventeenth or Friday the eighteenth of August 1978," said Stephens. It couldn't have been earlier in the week, he explained, because, "I had a hangover and didn't go to work."

For the first time, Haynes had found somebody who

was willing to put his trio of conspirators together at a critical time, right before Cullen's arrest. It didn't prove a conspiracy, but it did suggest one, especially since all three principals had denied such a rendezvous ever took place. Why would they have lied, Haynes hoped the jury would wonder.

The jury might have been more inclined to wonder if James Stephens had stepped down sooner. But since his initial contact with Jim Bearden, he had added a new twist to his story. He now claimed that two officials, a sheriff's deputy and an investigator from the D.A.'s office, had warned him not to testify. When Tolly Wilson demanded their names, Stephens defiantly refused to give them up. "I will not," he huffed, explaining that to do so would endanger his life.

Judge Moore leaned over toward the witness chair. "I will order you to."

Stephens folded his arms. "At this time, you will have to lock me up."

"All right," Moore smiled, "that's exactly what I'm going to do."

Suddenly facing six months in the county jail, Stephens threw his story into reverse. Divulging the names would jeopardize another case in which he was acting as a police informant, he argued. Moore didn't change expressions. "I don't remember the names," Stephens tried next, then, "I don't know the names," then, "Maybe it wasn't a D.A.'s investigator after all—or a sheriff's deputy, either." In fact, on further reflection, he couldn't remember *anybody* warning him about *anything*!

"I'm sorry I came down here," Stephens muttered as he left the stand. "I wish I hadn't."

It was a catastrophe for the defense, an utter rout, and no angry histrionics or accusations of prosecutorial misconduct or inflated indignation could cover it—although Haynes tried all of them.

When the prosecutors began cross-examining Stephens about his criminal record, Haynes exploded out of his chair. *"Your Honor!"* he roared. *"Counsel is not asking his questions in good faith!"* How did Haynes know? "Counsel is not operating from any printout reflecting reliance upon any computer facility," he explained, still shouting—as if he only had to shout loud enough and the memories of Lucas's and Stephens's dismal performances would be erased—"and for that reason it wasn't asked in good faith!"

Haynes demanded that Moore allow him to call the prosecutor to the stand to prove his accusation of bad faith. In response to a blistering barrage of sarcasm and outrage, Strickland calmly explained that the Harris County Sheriff's computer had been down, and that the information was obtained over the phone late the previous night from a staff investigator in Fort Worth.

Haynes, from whose mouth the words of whores, dopers, drug dealers, con men, and felons—even a certified motherfucker—had flowed unchecked for weeks, swelled up with indignation. How dare the prosecutors not verify their information *by computer* before smearing his witness in front of the jury?

Strickland explained that he had tried to check his information with Mr. Stephens the previous day—*but Haynes had told Stephens not to speak with the prosecutors, not even to spell his name for them*—although he did spell it later for the media.

The ambush threw Haynes into a blind rage. "Are you familiar with the case law which reflects the responsibility of counsel for the prosecution in asking questions of the witness about prior criminal history?" he demanded.

Strickland allowed a droll smile before answering, glimpsing for the first time the depth of Haynes's desperation. "The prosecutor is well aware of his responsibility," he said, lancing a look in Haynes's direction, "even if no one else in the courtroom is."

With his conspiracy theory in ruins, Haynes saw only one way out now.

65

Haynes had tried once before, in a backhanded way, to trap Pete Moore into a mistrial. He had called to the stand the person most likely to blurt out something that would burn the jury's ears and poison the record; the person most likely to be too drunk or too high to heed the instructions of lawyers or the warnings of judges; the person who, after Priscilla Davis, Haynes loved most to hate: W. T. Rufner.

From the moment Rufner stumbled into the courtroom during another witness's testimony, drunk and grinning from behind a pair of dark glasses, Haynes seemed to have finally hit on a winning strategy. From the tip of the feather on his burgundy hat to the metal points of his snakeskin boots, Rufner was a walking mistrial. His silver belt buckle boasted "I give joy to women," and his T-shirt showed a picture of two chimpanzees, one dressed as Richard Haynes, over the caption "Is this a courtroom or a circus?" By the time the startled bailiff began to move toward him, he was halfway down the aisle. "Hello, Mr. Davis," he called over to Cullen with a yoo-hoo grin, "how are you?"

After several tries, bailiff Grady Dukes finally wrestled W. T. to the door ("If you come back in this courtroom," Dukes snarled, "you're going to jail"), but even his angry mumblings were enough to fill Pete Moore with dread: "Motherfucking Haynes just wants to blow smoke up everybody's asses 'til they cut that bastard loose . . ." At the next break, Jack Strickland lamented to reporters, "The defense can't lose with Rufner. He creates a circus atmosphere. Jurors see it, wander around in it. All it takes is for Rufner to say something. If the defense gets a mistrial, they get to start all over."

Which was exactly what Haynes had in mind.

He called Rufner to the stand as quickly as possible,

before he sobered up, but Strickland headed him off, demanding that Haynes ask his questions first without the jury present.

"They are not entitled to a preview of the testimony from this witness," Haynes sputtered.

Moore wasn't fooled. "I want to find out for myself," he said.

"It's not going to be that long a witness," Haynes tried to assure him.

Moore smiled. "Well, I've heard *that* before."

"It depends on his responses," Haynes hedged. "If I get a lot of 'I don't knows' or 'I don't remembers' . . ."

"Talk's cheap," Rufner snapped from the witness chair.

Moore looked at Haynes—"See what I mean?"—then immediately turned to the jury. "Ladies and gentlemen, you are excused . . ."

"I wonder if we could have the Court admonish this witness regarding the rules of demeanor," Haynes suggested.

Moore looked Rufner up and down. "It may be already a little late."

The testimony went exactly as Strickland feared—and Haynes hoped.

"Do you know David McCrory?"

"I do."

"How long have you known him?"

"Too long."

When Haynes tried to determine how often W. T. and Priscilla had spoken to each other in recent months, W. T. shot back, "Oh, you can probably answer that better than I can, Mr. Haynes, with all your taps and all the things you have going."

Moore tried to be patient. "No," he chided the witness, "he wants it from you."

But chiding wasn't enough. After one particularly unresponsive answer in which Rufner again implied that Cullen Davis was "out to get him," Haynes protested to

Moore. "Could we ask the Court to instruct the witness to just answer the question?"

Moore obliged. "Listen," he said, leaning as close to W. T. as he could, "I'm running this show. We are going to do it my way or we're not going to do it."

But W. T. wasn't through. "If he has to back up what I say," he pointed at Haynes, "then I'm going to say a bunch of shit . . ." Apparently, someone had explained to W. T. that Haynes couldn't impeach his own witness.

"No, you're not, either," Moore snapped. "That's what I'm talking about. If you use some profanity like that before this jury, you will tie me down to a very short leash."

The anger on W. T.'s face as he stared at Haynes could be read all the way from the back of the big courtroom. "I'm sorry," he said between gritted teeth. "I apologize."

Moore wasn't fooled. "I've been here for almost seven weeks," he said, also between gritted teeth. "You think *you're* mad?"

W. T. turned to face him. "Has anybody tried to kill you about three times in the last three years?"

"Don't volunteer any information like that in front of the jury," Moore barked.

"Why not? Let's let them know what this man is charged with." W. T. shook his finger toward the defense table where Cullen Davis suppressed a smile, "and let this man," the finger moved to Haynes, "quit blowing smoke."

Moore's face turned red and his voice turned to lava. "Let me tell you something, one more time: This ain't Fort Worth. This is my show here. We are going to do it my way."

W. T. backed down. "I appreciate that."

"Do you 'appreciate' the fact that the jail is right back here?" Moore thrust his finger toward a door that led, indeed, directly to the Harris County Jail.

"Yes, sir, I do," said W. T.

"All right. You're going to do it my way, or you're going to go out the back door. It's as simple as that. I'm not going to let you blow seven weeks down the drain running off your mouth because you are teed off about something. You understand what I'm telling you? You say something in front of this jury to blow me out of the tub, and you're going to be safe for six months, anyway."

Against his own better judgment, Moore scheduled W. T. for the next morning—*with* the jury this time.

Jack Strickland didn't sleep all night.

The next morning, he cornered W. T. in the hall outside the courtroom. Even at 8:00 A.M., he was already buzzed on something: in control, but with a mischievous glint in his eye. "Look, I don't know you, but I've got some words of advice," Strickland began. "I know you feel strongly about this defendant, but I want to tell you something. If you go in there today and behave the way you did yesterday, I assure you you're helping Haynes more than you're hurting him.

"They *want* you to make a fool of yourself and blurt out something that's going to cause a mistrial. But if you go in there and be as cool as you can, you'll have them going crazy. If you really want to hurt that man, that's the way to do it."

W. T. looked unconvinced—so filled with anger at Cullen Davis, Strickland realized, that the slightest spark could set off an explosion.

Strickland tried again. "I'll tell you what, goddammit," he said, grabbing W. T. by the shoulders. "You go in there and do that, and you help convict this man, I will personally call you the day they put him on the bus and ship him to Huntsville. And when Cullen gets on that bus, you can wave good-bye to him. *That* will hurt Cullen Davis."

A light came on in W. T.'s eyes and a grin spread slowly from cheek to bearded cheek. "By God, I'll do that!"

From the time he took the stand to the time Haynes dismissed him in a frustrated huff, "T" was a perfect gentleman.

But Haynes had one last trick. "Your Honor, I may wish to recall this witness," he said to Moore as W. T. headed for the door. Strickland immediately saw what was coming and bolted from the courtroom. He caught up to a smiling W. T. in the hall.

"How'd I do?" Rufner wanted to know.

"Just great," Strickland assured him, "you did just great! But you know what they're doing now? They're going to call you back."

W. T.'s smile turned to a scowl.

"Don't you get it? They assume you're going to go out and get blitzed—take some pills or get drunk. And what they weren't able to do to you this morning, they're going to do this afternoon. I guarantee you, if you come back here sober, you won't be on the stand fifteen minutes."

W. T.'s eyes narrowed to a bitter squint. "I won't drink a drop."

He returned to the courthouse later that day rolling his eyes and weaving from side to side, hoping Haynes would see him. Haynes did, and immediately recalled him to the stand. He walked down the aisle steady as a rock, winking at Strickland as he passed, and took the stand sober as a judge. As Strickland had predicted, Haynes gave up in frustration in less than fifteen minutes.

If Haynes wanted a mistrial, he would have to do better.

66

"Your Honor, the prosecutors in this case have attempted to make deals with certain people to bring perjurious testimony."

It was a stunning charge—suborning perjury—and Haynes's booming baritone savored the high drama of it. "They did this as part of an ongoing conspiracy to get charges leveled against Cullen Davis to enhance the allegations that they have mounted against him in this trial."

And who were these "certain people" whom the prosecutors had pressured to lie?

Haynes called John and Salvatore Florio to the stand.

John Florio and his nephew "Sal" were no strangers to the Tarrant County D.A.'s office. According to his police file, John first arrived in Fort Worth in June 1975, a long way from his home in Manhattan and his regular job as a small-time enforcer for New Jersey mobster Joseph Zicarelli. He came on "business." A notorious Dallas–Fort Worth drug dealer, street name "Cosgrove," had crossed Florio's boss back in New Jersey, and now his boss wanted both Cosgrove and, for good measure, his girlfriend dead. John Florio was there to do the job.

Before he could, however, John found himself sitting inside the Tarrant County Jail on a check-forging charge. After being released, he returned to New Jersey for a few months, then set out again to finish the job. With his nephew Sal, a parole jumper and heroin addict, in tow, he stopped briefly in Grenada, Mississippi, to see his girlfriend and pick up a couple of guns, then drove to Fort Worth. The plan was simple: The mark, Cosgrove, not only sold drugs, he also fenced stolen property. To get to him, they would rob a house, take the booty to Cosgrove, sell it (this would provide them with some loose change for drugs), then kill him.

They picked a house at random and knocked on the door. John asked the lady who answered if he could use her phone to call a doctor. As soon as they were inside, Sal pulled a gun and held it to her head. He said he would kill her if she screamed. John did the same with her thirteen-year-old son. They ransacked the house, then forced the woman at gunpoint to drive to her bank and make a large withdrawal. If she didn't, Sal clarified, they would kill her son.

Afterward, they located Cosgrove in south Fort Worth and sold him the stuff, but decided to delay the hit until they had split the money so Sal could get a fix. Minutes after they sat down in a corner booth at the Torch Club to count it out, the police burst in. When investigators questioned him separately, John Florio swore the robbery was "all Sal's idea." The jury didn't agree: Sal got twenty years, John, sixty.

After that, the D.A.'s office didn't hear from the Florios again until May 1978. John, who had been following the Cullen Davis story closely on the prison's rec room TV, heard that District Attorney Tim Curry was trying to decide whether to file attempted murder charges against Cullen Davis for the shootings at the mansion. It was common knowledge around Huntsville that the prosecutors would give *anything* to nail Davis, especially after their humiliation in Amarillo. That gave John an idea. A few days later, an anonymous letter arrived at the D.A.'s office.

> *On several different occasions, I overheard conversations between Sal Florio and his Uncle John Florio regarding Cullen Davis. I explicitly heard Sal Florio tell John Florio that it's a good thing the police didn't find the tape recordings of Cullen Davis at the Ramada Inn, where the two inmates met him to discuss the prearranged killing of Priscilla Davis. From the drift of their conversations, I took it that they came here to Texas in 1975 for the sole purpose of carrying out a contract to kill Mrs. Davis.*

Curry bit. He scrambled his men to Huntsville to investigate. After a great show of surprise and consternation, the Florios admitted the whole sordid affair. Yes, they had met with Cullen at the Ramada Inn, and they described the encounter in great detail.

"My wife's name is Priscilla," Cullen had told them as he handed John a picture of her. "I want her dead." He gave them the name of a beauty shop that she used.

They met again the next day and Cullen gave them some more pictures, then repeated, "I want her taken care of."

Yes, they still had those photographs, the Florios told

investigators; yes, they had protected themselves by taping the conversation in the motel room; yes, those tapes still existed—in New Jersey—and, yes, they could be made available to the D.A. *if* "things could be worked out."

Tolly Wilson, one of the interviewers, recommended against any deal and suggested instead that Curry send investigators to New Jersey to see if they could locate the tapes and pictures themselves—if they existed. When the investigators came back empty-handed, skepticism began to set in. They gave John Florio a lie-detector test, which he failed miserably. Eventually he caved in and confessed to writing the anonymous letter. Furious and vowing revenge, both Florios were returned summarily to Huntsville.

Now they were back—on the defense side this time. Apparently, "things" had finally been "worked out."

The jurors in Pete Moore's big seventh-floor courtroom didn't need to know John Florio's criminal past. They could read it in his face: in the dark hollows around eyes so brown they looked black; in the long, greasy ringlets of black hair; in the permanent kink in a lip where a deep cut had healed badly; in the black corner of a tattoo showing just below the sleeve on his left forearm. (It was a naked girl surrounded by a wreath. On the other arm, unseen by the jury, were four aces.)

Judge Moore took one look at John Florio and sent the jury out.

Haynes protested, loftily accusing Moore of streamlining the trial "to the detriment of the citizen accused." Moore ignored him.

Haynes questioned Florio as if his every response might rock the courthouse to its foundation.

What did he tell the D.A.'s office when they first approached him about Cullen Davis?

"I said I didn't know him," Florio lied, "that I had never met him," that he knew "absolutely nothing" about the Davis case.

Was that the end of it?

No, said Florio. "They told me they could be of help to me."

"And who was it that represented to you that your cooperation with them would be helpful to you?"

"Mr. Wilson."

Haynes shot a look at Tolly Wilson, who was sitting at the prosecutor's table, listening without expression. "What did Mr. Wilson want you to do?" Haynes asked.

"Give testimony," said Florio, "perjurious testimony."

"Against whom?"

"Mr. Davis." Like Haynes, he uttered the name reverentially.

"And what did you tell them?"

"I told them I wouldn't do it."

Florio went on to deny all the contents of the anonymous letter that had brought the prosecutors to Huntsville. He did not come to Fort Worth on a contract to kill Priscilla—or anybody else, for that matter. No, he had not met with Cullen at the Ramada Inn. "Where they got this information, I just don't know," he complained.

But the prosecutors wouldn't take no for an answer, according to Florio. They kept pressing, "If I would cooperate with them they would be very helpful to me."

"When you say 'cooperate with them,' " Haynes asked, his brow knotted in distress, "cooperate in what fashion?"

"In the scheme they were trying to devise."

"What scheme were they trying to devise?"

"To frame Cullen Davis."

And what did the prosecutors offer Florio in exchange for his "cooperation"?

Florio explained that his case had recently been reversed on a technicality and remanded for a new trial. If he played along with the "scheme" and testified that Cullen had hired him to kill Priscilla, Florio claimed, Wilson had promised to dismiss his case—"just wipe the whole thing out."

Next came Sal Florio, John's thirty-four-year-old nephew, distinguishable from his uncle only by his abrasive

"New Joyzy" accent and a nasal whine that could penetrate steel. He also had a scar on his chin, tattoos everywhere, and, if possible, even shiftier eyes. He told a remarkably similar story: how the prosecutors had come to him un-invited; how he had "laughed at them, and said I didn't even know Cullen Davis"; how the D.A.'s men had dan-gled a deal in front of him if he would only testify that Cullen tried to hire him as a hit man. "They wanted us to come up with some ideas that would be strong enough to frame Davis," he added helpfully.

The spectators in the courtroom, including those at the counsel tables, were indeed rocked by the Florios' testimony—but not in the way Haynes had intended. It wasn't the story that stunned them—not a soul in the room, other than Haynes perhaps, believed it; it wasn't the Florios—"hardened criminals will be hardened crim-inals," said one reporter. What stunned them was that Richard Haynes would try to put this "evidence" before a jury. It betrayed a level of desperation that, until now, Haynes had successfully concealed behind the usual facade of humor, self-confidence, and histrionics. The secret was out: The defense was in deep trouble.

Convinced the jury would come to the same conclusion, Tolly Wilson breezed through cross-examination with breathtaking composure for a lawyer who had just been accused of suborning perjury. He merely reviewed each witness's lengthy criminal history, then dismissed him with a wave of the hand. On redirect, Haynes asked Sal what was perhaps the most startling question of all: "Despite your criminal record, isn't it true that the prosecutors were still willing to use you to testify if you would be willing to give perjurious testimony against Mr. Davis?"

Sal answered, equally incredulous, "Yes, sir."

At the end of the day, the courtroom was stunned one more time when Judge Moore ruled the Florios' testimony admissible. Haynes would be allowed to question them before the jury. "It's the defense theory," Moore said slyly. "If they put them on, they got to fly with them." Some in the courtroom heard it this way: "If Race wants to hang himself, then I'm sure as hell not gonna stop him."

That was the way Haynes's colleagues at the defense table heard it. They had been trying to talk Haynes out of putting the Florios before the jury since the idea was first circulated. Even Haynes, now that Moore had granted his request, began to reconsider the wisdom of it. Almost immediately, he started backpedaling in the press, calling the Florios "cuckoos" and openly doubting their accounts. He postponed their testimony before the jury several times, weighing whether to put them on at all.

It was Sal Florio, of all people, who finally made the decision for him. After spending several miserable days in the jail's cockroach-infested "holdover tank" waiting for Haynes to make up his mind, Sal asked bailiff Grady Dukes to "Tell Haynes, if he don't come back and talk to us, I'm going to blow his case out of the courthouse."

Haynes put Sal on—without his uncle this time—but steered the questioning safely clear of allegations about suborning perjury, with the result that his testimony had virtually no impact. Haynes's only message to the jury seemed to be: "Can you believe the prosecutors would stoop so low as to deal with a person like *this*?"

At the next break, as the attorneys filed out of the room, a spectator overheard one member of the defense team muttering to another, "You lie down with pigs, you get up smelling like shit."

But Haynes came back the very next day with yet another accusation. His voice spiraling ever higher in rage and indignation, he charged that the prosecutors had conducted an "after-midnight" gestapo raid on the home of defense witness Larry Gene Lucas. They had swept down on "Citizen Lucas's" little trailer home on Leisure Drive in Fort Worth, strong-armed his wife into signing a bogus consent form, then tore the place apart looking for something, *anything*, to impeach Lucas's testimony. Furthermore, the prosecutors had planned the raid in advance, specifically for the purpose of intimidating Lucas and any witnesses who might testify in his behalf.

Some wondered why the prosecutors would have gone to so much trouble to impeach a defense witness who was hardly credible to begin with, or why Haynes had waited more than a week after the so-called raid to stage this extravaganza of outrage. But even as his own witnesses stripped the story down to the tissue of fabrication and exaggeration it was (the trailer didn't belong to Lucas; he didn't even live there; the woman wasn't his wife; the search had been brief and cordial), Haynes shouted his protests louder and pounded the table harder.

"*It's a conspiracy,*" he thundered. "*It's all a conspiracy!*" There was almost a religious fervor in his voice as he boomed his accusations to the back of the courtroom, "a conspiracy to prosecute Mr. Davis, a conspiracy between witnesses and others, a conspiracy motivated by ill will and personal animosity." It was the voice of someone who believed not out of choice, but out of necessity. The defense was in shambles, Sumner's witnesses had self-destructed, and Haynes was headed toward losing the crowning case of his career in his own hometown. There *had* to be a conspiracy, the booming voice seemed to say, *there could be no other explanation.*

When an informant revealed that private investigators were shadowing the defense team, searching through their trash, tracking their cars, perhaps even tapping their phones, Haynes's indignation went ballistic. This was definitive proof, he roared, that both he *and* his client were the victims of a vast diabolical plot.

The revelation that Joe Shannon, now in private practice in Fort Worth, was directing the surveillance only seemed to confirm Haynes's most paranoid fantasies. He immediately summoned Shannon to the big courtroom in Houston and demanded to know who had hired him. Shannon explained that he had been contacted by a Colorado lawyer who "wanted to make sure the defense didn't go out and buy witnesses or do anything illegal, like they did in Amarillo"—an insinuation that sent Haynes into an apoplectic rage. How *dare* Shannon suggest that the defense would stoop to the tactics employed by the prosecution!

Besides, Haynes announced dramatically, he *knew* who had really hired Shannon, who was at the heart of this heinous plot—masterminding it, financing it, guiding it: Cullen Davis's brother, Bill.

To prove it, Haynes called witness after witness to show that Bill Davis was "hiding" from the defense's process servers and investigators. Only a man with something to hide would go to such lengths to avoid testifying, Haynes insinuated leadenly. When prosecutors tried to show that Bill Davis was terrified of Cullen and had taken extraordinary steps to protect himself ever since "the incident" at the Mockingbird Lane mansion, Haynes objected wildly to the prejudicial impact of such testimony. "I have an extensive security system at my home, too," he railed, "and I'm not afraid of *anybody*."

Why were the prosecutors fighting so hard to keep Bill Davis from testifying? "I can tell you why," Haynes announced. *They were in on the conspiracy*: if not actually helping direct it, at least condoning it, using the information the surveillance produced to prop up their shoddy case, and abetting it by putting pressure on witnesses like the Florios not to testify on Cullen's behalf. Their actions were "illegal, improper, immoral, and unethical," Haynes charged, spitting indignation and hinting darkly that somewhere lurking in the shadows of this demonic plot, the jury would inevitably find Pat Burleson, David McCrory, and, of course, the Queen of Evil, Priscilla Davis.

The more desperate Haynes's straits, it seemed, the wider he drew the conspiracy against him and his client. The more skepticism and contradiction he met, the louder and more strident his attacks. It wasn't just the prosecutors suborning perjury anymore, or the D.A.'s investigators harassing defense witnesses; now the conspiracy embraced Cullen's family, past enemies, and disgruntled former prosecutors as well as overzealous current ones, and it reached back years, to the previous trial and beyond. It was all the unchecked powers of the state *and* the wealth of a jealous brother *and* the implacable revenge of a vicious, conniving wife arrayed against "Citizen Cullen" and those who had so selflessly dedicated themselves to his defense.

As the witnesses mounted and the days passed, Judge Moore's bushy brow darkened, his ashtray filled earlier every day, and his voice sank to even coarser gravel. He sustained every prosecutorial objection to Haynes's conspiracy theories as irrelevant, and, when that didn't deter Haynes, raised some objections of his own.

"I think the whole system of justice is being abused," he cautioned Haynes, "and I don't like it."

Haynes responded with a fit of pique and indignation. "I want to know who paid these people! Who would go to the trouble to investigate us and why?"

But Moore had heard enough. *"Who cares?!"* he erupted.

Still, Haynes refused to let go. There *was* a conspiracy against his client—there *had* to be—and, furthermore, it was getting stronger every day. He could hear it in reporters' questions, wondering if the fat lady would ever sing, if there *was* a fat lady at all; asking about "Race's ego" and second-guessing his judgment on Lucas or Stephens or the Florios. He could see it every day in the courtroom: Even his old friend Pete Moore had gone over to the enemy. As far as Haynes was concerned, they were all co-conspirators now, unwitting perhaps, but no less a part of the plot against *him*—not even Cullen so much anymore—the plot to keep *him* from winning.

Haynes's outrage hit new heights when the *Houston Post* ran a front-page article on the arrest of Larry Gene Lucas for perjury. Haynes stalked into the courtroom that morning in a swirl of pipe smoke, chin high, chest thrust forward, his face red and warped with indignation. In a voice stretched almost to the breaking point, he accused the prosecutors of "deliberately orchestrating" the arrest and the news leak solely in order to prejudice the jury against Cullen Davis and his defense. He cited indignantly the sign-off line a local television newscast had used the previous night: "The Sheriff's office was instructed to keep Lucas from Davis or Davis from Lucas."

The conspiracy was at work again.

In apocalyptic tones, Haynes demanded a mistrial. Moore refused. Haynes demanded that Moore question each juror individually in his chambers. (Surely, if any juror thought the defense was responsible for perjured testimony . . . Haynes sputtered with outrage at the mere suggestion.) Moore again refused. He would simply instruct the jurors to disregard anything they might have seen or heard. Haynes demanded an immediate investigation of the leak to the press. A third time, Moore refused—but he did offer to let Haynes "take some testimony."

Haynes leapt at the chance. "We call the chief prosecutor."

Tolly Wilson didn't even bother to hide his bemusement when he took the stand, which only added fuel to Haynes's fire.

"Did you [have Lucas arrested and brought to Houston so] that it might be made a matter of attention in the news media?" Haynes demanded, his voice already several notches higher than usual, his anger already in full furl.

Jack Strickland shot out of his seat. "We object to that as being leading, Your Honor. Why doesn't he just ask him why he did it?"

"We get self-serving responses," Haynes lashed out.

"We get self-serving questions," Strickland responded.

"*We* are conducting the inquiry," Haynes bristled.

Moore finally wedged a word in. "Sustained."

Haynes turned his glare back to Wilson. "Do you know how it was that the fact of Lucas's indictment and the arrest got to the attention of the media?"

"I don't recall the first member of the media that called me," Wilson replied calmly, "but he said that his station had gotten an anonymous tip that Lucas had been arrested and wanted to know about it. They had told him they wanted to check it out."

Haynes screwed his face into a sarcastic half-smile. "The old anonymous tip trick, heh?"

"Yes, Mr. Haynes," said Wilson tartly. "I'm sure you are fully aware of that."

The half-smile instantly became a grimace. "You are not suggesting that *I* made the anonymous tip?"

"I don't believe *you* did," said Wilson, still unruffled. "You probably could have had it done."

Haynes exploded in red-faced rage. *"Are you suggesting that I probably had it done?"*

Wilson, dead calm: "Yes."

In fact, no one stood to gain more from revealing Lucas's arrest than Haynes. No one stood to gain more from a mistrial. He might not win, but at least he wouldn't lose. Was he capable of it? Wilson had no doubt. In the end, in the last two minutes of a losing game, Haynes was just like Cullen, Wilson believed: He would do *anything* to get his way. What was it Joe Shannon had said in his summation in Amarillo? "What you've seen in this court is an attempt to run over everyone that gets in this man's way . . ."

Haynes sputtered wordlessly for a second, as if unable to bring forth the huge fireball of indignation lodged in his throat. "Is that the result of some recent illness?" he finally spat.

Wilson fixed him with a hard glare from his pixie eyes. "Are you dethroned of your reason?" It was both accusation and ridicule: "dethroned of reason" was one of Haynes's favorite verbal pretensions.

Haynes was beyond rage now, approaching apoplexy. *"That is the most insane and asinine comment,"* he roared. *"You make a mockery of these proceedings."*

"A mockery?" cried Jack Strickland from the prosecutor's table, rising and pointing a finger at Haynes. "*You* are making a mockery."

Haynes clenched his fist and moved threateningly toward the young prosecutor. "Don't point your finger at me," he sputtered. "You're not big enough . . ."

"All right!" boomed Moore, his gravel voice filling the

big room like judgment day. "All right! Let's get on with it."

It was the week before Christmas 1978, and, after two months of trial and three weeks of defense witnesses, Haynes had yet to make a perceptible dent in the case against Cullen Davis. Karen Master had taken the stand and charmed the jury with her "Miss Flame" smile, but it would take more than Karen's iron effervescence to make the jury forget the evidence. Haynes had tried to break McCrory, and failed. He had tried to break the FBI, and failed. He had tried to break the tapes, and failed. He had tried to break Moore, and failed. He had tried to float a conspiracy theory, and failed. He had even tried for a mistrial, and failed.

He had, in fact, gone as far as he could go—some thought farther. If Cullen wanted more, he would have to do it himself. In their game of high-stakes poker, Haynes had anted up. Now it was Cullen's bid. After two years of avoiding it, after two years of listening by day and manipulating by night, after two years of sitting in the courtroom stone silent while Haynes put everybody else on trial but him, Cullen would have to take the stand.

67

Cullen Davis stood beside the witness chair in front of the crowded courtroom on December 27, 1978, and swore to tell "the truth, the whole truth, and nothing but the truth." Dressed in a suit the color of gun metal, a white shirt, and dark blue tie, his hair clipped and slicked back, he looked, according to one observer, "like a department-store mannequin."

As Haynes led him deferentially through a brief summary of his background, schooling, and business, Cullen fidgeted with his hands and, every now and then, stuttered over a word. Only a few in the courtroom knew that Cullen hadn't stuttered since the day his father died. Sitting in the witness chair for the first time, did he see the ghost of Stinky Davis—"the only man who could control Cullen" —stalking the courtroom?

If he did, the apparition had little effect. After only a few minutes, Cullen settled down into a board-meeting tone, equal parts self-confidence and condescension. He spoke with great—some thought too great—precision, especially about names and dates. Later, to reporters, Haynes would credit his client's "engineer's mind" for the care and conciseness of his responses. More likely, it was the dozens of hours he had spent over the Christmas holiday sitting in his cell, studying transcripts and making extensive notes. Jail officials had seen "jailhouse lawyers" before, but none who prepared for their testimony as thoroughly as Cullen Davis. "Telling the truth is like running a company," Cullen told a curious guard. "It takes a lot of hard work."

Eventually, Haynes came to the truth-telling that undoubtedly required the hardest work.

Why did Cullen hire David McCrory in the first place?

Cullen said he didn't really want to hire McCrory, and, indeed, after a brief encounter in January, successfully dodged McCrory's phone calls and pleas for help for several months. Finally, on May 1, 1978, he broke down and met with McCrory at Coco's. "David said that he was broke, and that he didn't have a job," Cullen explained, making sure to point out to the jury that McCrory's new wife was a prostitute, and that they discussed "the fact that David had been pimping for her." "He started crying, and he wanted to know if I could help him. He wanted to be friends with me again."

But that wasn't why Cullen hired him.

"I was motivated mainly by the fact that he was going to help me in my divorce," Cullen claimed, "particularly in matters pertaining to Priscilla." Exactly what kind of help wasn't spelled out, although Cullen suggested that it involved keeping an eye on Priscilla during the upcoming divorce and reporting back any "useful" information.

Why did Cullen ask McCrory for a gun and silencer? He didn't, Cullen corrected.

On June 9, McCrory had brought him the startling news that *Priscilla* was plotting to kill *him*! "McCrory told me that Priscilla was negotiating with other people to take my life," Cullen testified, his brow slightly furrowed as the memory of those dark days crossed his face. McCrory then showed him a pistol with a silencer attached and asked if he wanted one like it. "I told him I didn't know," said Cullen, "but if I did get one, I would have to register it."

According to Cullen, McCrory later offered to *give* him the gun and silencer. "He said he was going to make it a present to me."

Not a moment too soon, either, Cullen testified, because about the same time, he noticed that an "unknown white male" was following him around. Soon afterward, a friend overheard someone in a bar making threats against his life. After that, just to be safe, Cullen hired an investigator to follow Priscilla around.

Cullen continued: At their next meeting, on August 11, McCrory had bad news and good news. The bad news was that Priscilla had contacted hired killers "to bump [Cullen] off." The good news was that McCrory's magic tongue had convinced the killers to turn on Priscilla. If they testified at the upcoming divorce trial that she had tried to hire them to kill Cullen, the Kendavis empire would be safe at last. Best of all, it would "put Priscilla in her place," said Cullen, with what looked like an involuntary smile.

What did Cullen have to do to get the killers to turn on Priscilla?

"If I was willing to pay them more than she was going to pay them," Cullen said McCrory told him, "they would work for my side instead of her side."

There was just one problem, McCrory told him. "The killers are going to need proof that you are willing to cooperate with them and pay them."

What kind of proof?

Tapes, said McCrory, holding up a little Norelco tape recorder that he had brought along. They wanted Cullen to make tapes! Most killers wanted money, but not these. They wanted Cullen to make tapes in which he *pretended* to participate in illegal activities. That way, if he turned on them, they would have something incriminating on him. The tapes would be their insurance, McCrory explained.

Jack Strickland saw, for the first time, where Cullen was going.

What illegal activities did the killers want Cullen to pretend to engage in? Ever helpful, McCrory suggested: *Why not pretend to talk about having people killed?* "McCrory would do most of the talking," Cullen explained, "and I would say 'yes' and 'okay,' but he would talk about my wanting to kill Priscilla, and Judge Eidson, and Beverly Bass, [and] Bubba Gavrel, and his father."

Reluctantly, Cullen agreed.

Why would Cullen Davis, multimillionaire and semi-respected businessman, agree to such a preposterous scheme, a scheme that put his reputation and perhaps even his life in the hands of professional killers whose names he didn't even know? Surely he didn't expect the jury to believe that he would risk everything just to "put Priscilla in her place"?

No, Cullen explained, the real reason he agreed to McCrory's strange proposal was this: *The FBI told him to.*

Just the night before the August 11 meeting, in fact, he had received a phone call from a man who identified himself as "Agent Acree of the FBI."

"We think you're the victim of an extortion plot by David McCrory," said the caller.

"How do you know?" Cullen asked.

"Well," the voice replied, "we have informants."

"What do you want me to do?"

"We want you to play along," said the caller. "That's the only way we're going to catch him—for you to play along and follow his suggestions. . . . Just do whatever he says." The caller also directed Cullen to "keep our conversation confidential," promised to be "back in touch," and gave him a phone number where he could be reached.

So the next day, when Cullen agreed to David Mc-Crory's bizarre plan to make incriminating tapes about having various people killed, *he was just doing what "Agent Acree" had told him to do.*

Why was Cullen Davis willing to put his life and reputation in the hands of David McCrory solely on the basis of an out-of-the-blue call from someone who merely *claimed* to be an FBI agent—no confirmation, no badge number, no meeting at FBI headquarters, no discussion of safeguards or procedures—just a phone call?

Because, Cullen said, he *knew* Agent Acree.

In fact, so did the jury. Agent James Alex Acree, Jr., of the Dallas FBI had already appeared on the witness stand to describe his investigation of an extortion note that Cullen had received shortly after the Amarillo verdict. The two men had talked on the phone several times and even met once at Karen Master's house. That was why Cullen wasn't suspicious when "Agent Acree" called.

So then it *was* Agent Acree on the phone?

Well, no, said Cullen. Or at least he couldn't be sure. He *thought* it was Agent Acree—but he didn't recognize the voice. In other words, he knew Agent Acree well enough to rely unquestioningly on whatever instructions he gave, but not well enough to recognize his voice. Did the combination of a bizarre request and unfamiliar voice—no matter how familiar the name—make Cullen even a little skeptical? Skeptical enough, perhaps, to call the local FBI office for confirmation?

It didn't matter, Haynes insisted. All that mattered was that *Cullen thought he was acting on instructions from a federal agent.*

Jack Strickland scribbled a note on his legal pad and passed it around the prosecution table: "My eight-year-old writes better bullshit than this!"

At the same August 11 meeting, Cullen continued, he and McCrory also talked about money. Keeping Priscilla's hired killers in line would require money, McCrory warned him, maybe lots of it. But, Cullen insisted, he had refused to supply it.

If Cullen wouldn't supply it, where would the money come from?

From *McCrory*, Cullen claimed. McCrory had told him, "I'll put up my money if you will pay me back, and [pay my] expenses, plus a bonus, if it all goes through."

"If what goes through?" Haynes asked.

"If these people that he was in contact with would come forward with the information I could use in my divorce," Cullen explained.

Moreover, McCrory *did* come up with some money: $25,000, to be exact. He told Cullen he won it gambling in Las Vegas. "David said he didn't have a place to keep it," Cullen recalled, "and he figured that I had a safe at the office I could keep it in. He also didn't know whether he wanted the IRS to know about it."

Cullen then described how he took McCrory's money, in a bulky white envelope, to the office and told Brenda Adcock to put it in the office safe.

So the $25,000 that Cullen took from the office safe the morning of his arrest was really *McCrory's*. Cullen was just *returning* it.

"Did you promise to indemnify him?" Haynes asked.

"If everything went according to plan," said Cullen.

"What plan was that?"

"The plan was convincing these people to work with me, and turning them around so I could get information to use at my divorce trial against Priscilla."

"Did you really believe that McCrory was going to be able to do that?"

"I wasn't willing to put up my money to find out," said Cullen, offering the jury a rare, razor-thin smile. "I was willing to go along with the deal, and if it worked out, I would pay him for it."

So, according to Cullen, this was the "deal": At the appropriate time, McCrory would give *his* $25,000 to Priscilla's hired killers to try and turn them so they would help

Cullen's divorce case. If, and only if, they did, then Cullen would reimburse McCrory, pay his expenses, and throw in an undetermined "bonus." If the plan failed—if the hired killers skipped town, executed the contract on Cullen, or just sat tight—McCrory would lose everything, expose himself to criminal charges, and make himself the target of professional killers. Even for a veteran bargainer like Cullen, it seemed like an incredibly lopsided deal.

But why was Cullen still talking about the plan to "flip" Priscilla's hired killers anyway? By the time this discussion took place, Agent Acree had already called and "blown the whistle" on McCrory. Cullen knew there was no plan to turn Priscilla's killers. It was all just a come-on to get him to incriminate himself on tape and expose himself to extortion. Yet on the witness stand, he was still justifying his actions in terms of "the plan."

Judge Moore saw the contradiction immediately. For all his studying, Cullen was having trouble keeping his storylines straight. He should have dropped the whole "flipping Priscilla's killers" rationale, thought Moore, as soon as Acree stepped into the picture—and, presumably, McCrory could no longer be trusted. But he didn't—and now he was heading for trouble.

After the August 11 meeting, Cullen said, he called the phone number "Agent Acree" had given him. "Agent Acree" answered.

"I told him what had taken place with McCrory out at Coco's and what we had done," Cullen testified.

"What did he say, if anything?" asked Haynes.

"He said, 'Well, this is just fine, you keep playing along and we will be back in touch.' "

A week later, on the morning of August 18, Cullen said McCrory called him with yet another odd request. "He said the tapes that we had made a week earlier weren't good enough and he wanted to do them again . . . that day."

August 18 was the day of the first FBI tape. Strickland could see the pieces falling into place; he could also picture

Cullen, alone in his cell, carving out each piece to fit so neatly.

What was wrong with the earlier tape? *It wasn't incriminating enough*, said Cullen. "McCrory said I wasn't saying enough . . . and, if I was going to convince his people, he wanted me to quote a figure. I was to say something like twenty-five thousand dollars."

So, according to Cullen, they met that afternoon in the parking lot of Coco's solely for the purpose of making yet another tape on McCrory's little Norelco recorder. How was Cullen to know that the FBI was eavesdropping on the conversation—listening, minutes later, to the Nagra recorder taped to McCrory's body; misunderstanding his incriminating words; unaware of the bizarre circumstances surrounding them; unaware even that they were all just "part of the act"?

Now, finally, Haynes would give him a chance to put the tapes in perspective. The foundations had been laid; all the seemingly sinister subjects they discussed had been explained: the gun and silencer, the money, even the talk of murder. Now all Cullen had to do was explain the words.

68

Playing the infamous tapes yet again was a bold gamble. Haynes could have read the passages he wanted Cullen to explain, and the jury would have been spared another wallow in the background noises, the inflections, the pauses, the idiosyncrasies—the sheer overwhelming reality of what the state claimed was a crime in the making. But what would the jury think? That the defense was afraid of the tapes? No, if Cullen was going to convince them of his story, he had to confront the prosecution's chief witness head on.

One more time, the voices of David McCrory and Cullen Davis boomed through the old courtroom.

MCCRORY: *The man is here to put the judge away. . . . The son of a bitch wants $100,000.*

CULLEN: *Bullshit.*

"I'd never told McCrory I would pay any amount of money to do anything," Cullen insisted oddly, as though money was the only real proof of commitment. His "Bullshit" referred to the "whole plan," not the high fee. But which plan? He had already told Haynes he was impatient to "get on with [Acree's] plan" to trap the extortionists. As for the "plan" to make the tapes for the hired killers, he had promised Acree he would play along with that. Calling it "bullshit" to McCrory's face could have blown the very plan he was so eager to get on with.

CULLEN: *Go back to the original plan.*

MCCRORY: *The original plan?*

CULLEN: *Get the other one, the one we started this out with.*

MCCRORY: *Oh, Bev.*

CULLEN: *Yeah.*

"That related to the fact he wasn't producing what we were having the meetings for," Cullen explained, with a hint of exasperation. "I wanted to get the show on the road. And he kept wanting to make tapes."

And what was the "original plan"?

"To get Priscilla's people over to my side," Cullen insisted.

Once again, as Moore had foreseen, Cullen was getting his storylines tangled. If he was following Agent Acree's instructions, how could he still believe that McCrory was trying to win Priscilla's killers over to his side? How could he still believe there *were* hired killers?

MCCRORY: *You still want all three of them at once?*

CULLEN: *Do it either way.*

For the first time, Cullen looked slightly confused as he tried to explain. "McCrory had told me the conversation about killing people is how we would convince Priscilla's people I wouldn't turn on them."

He *was* confused. He had picked an answer from the wrong story. He should have said, "I was just playing along." Haynes tried desperately to straighten him out, to untangle the story-lines before his client tripped again. "Would you have made the initial tapes if you had not received a phone call or had a conversation with Jim Acree?" he asked, in a slow, listen-to-me-hard voice.

"I don't think McCrory could have talked me into doing it," Cullen replied in his bloodless monotone, "if I hadn't received a call from the person I thought was calling from the FBI."

But it wasn't enough. Cullen didn't take the hint.

CULLEN: *Do the judge and his wife and that would be it.*

At first Cullen seemed back on track: "I was just going along with him," he explained, "just like I thought the FBI wanted me to do. I was just following his cue. We weren't really talking about killing people." But then he was off again. "I was just trying to get his people to come around to my way of thinking. We were using those tapes he was supposed to be making as a tool."

Pete Moore yawned again.

Finally, Haynes came to the day of the arrest, August 20.

Cullen explained why he had inspected the white van so suspiciously: it looked like the van that belonged to the investigator he had hired to trail Priscilla. He banged on it a couple of times "for no reason"; then, as he drove to the adjacent parking lot where McCrory was waiting, he said, he had a reassuring thought: "Maybe that's the FBI."

According to Cullen, McCrory climbed into the front seat of his car and, before saying anything, opened his coat to reveal one of the two microphones Agent Gray had taped under his shirt. "He didn't say what it was," Cullen explained, "but I guessed. It looked like a bug." Cullen said he took that as a message that McCrory wanted to make yet another tape for Priscilla's killers as "insurance."

So the performance began.

Why did neither man mention it out loud?

According to Cullen, he *did*.

McCrory had testified that Cullen said "Damn. You keep it" when he handed him the envelope containing the Polaroids of Judge Eidson "dead." Not true, said Cullen. What he had actually said was "Damn. You're kidding," and he was reacting not to the pictures, but to the sight of the microphone under McCrory's shirt.

So what *did* he say when he saw the pictures of Eidson?

He didn't say anything, because *he never saw the pictures*!

Jack Strickland knew it was coming, but hearing it still put a knot in his stomach. He knew Cullen had to deny ever seeing the pictures. It was the one piece of evidence he couldn't explain away, the definitive proof that the talk of murder wasn't just a play-along game. Unfortunately, thanks to a dim-witted Fort Worth cop, it was also the one piece of evidence that he *could* deny. Without the telltale traces of powder on Cullen's hands, they had no incontrovertible proof that he had ever touched those photographs.

McCrory did hand him an envelope in return, Cullen explained (that much was clear from the surveillance photographs), but the envelope didn't contain pictures of Eidson. "I opened it up, and there were a couple of minicassettes in it," said Cullen, with just a hint of triumph in his voice. "I thought they'd come from his tape recorder, from our first attempts at making tapes"—the August 11 tapes that the killers had rejected. That was what McCrory showed him, not photos.

Haynes gave a signal, and the booming voices started up again.

CULLEN: *What are you going to do with those?*

McCRORY: *I'm going to get rid of these motherfuckers.*

CULLEN: *That's good. Glad to hear it.*

"So this was a conversation about tapes," Haynes clarified, "not photographs?"

"That's correct," said Cullen, greatly relieved.

"And how could you trust McCrory to get rid of the tapes?"

"Well, I couldn't," Cullen replied, with the slightest chuckle, "but they weren't damning to me in any way, so I didn't take them from him."

Not damning? thought Jack Strickland. Tapes that, according to Cullen's own testimony, included discussions of multiple murders?

MCCRORY: *I got Judge Eidson dead for you.*

CULLEN: *Good.*

This was, to many, the most damning of all the many damning lines on the tape, and now, finally, Cullen got his story straight. Sitting in the witness chair after two days of testimony, with his head at a jaunty angle, rocking back and forth in ostentatious ease, he explained, "Just going along with his conversation."

"Did you have any reason to believe Eidson was dead?" asked Haynes.

"None whatsoever," Cullen sighed.

"Would there be any reason for you to want Eidson dead?"

A blush of distress crossed Cullen's mask, as if the question offended him. "I had no reason to want him dead."

"Are you guilty of conspiring with David McCrory to have David McCrory employ someone to take the life of Judge Joe Eidson or anyone else?"

Cullen stopped rocking and held his head up straight. "As God is my witness, I most certainly did not."

"Pass the witness, Your Honor."

At a break in Cullen's testimony, sitting in the basement coffee shop, staring into a styrofoam cup of bad coffee, Judge Moore lamented to a fellow judge, "I wish I never took this case." In a voice even lower than usual from exhaustion and frustration, he also shared his opinion of Cullen's story. Recalling how Haynes had told the press "it ain't over till the fat lady sings," Moore growled, "I think the fat lady has fallen on her butt."

Later, over something stronger than coffee, he offered a more pungent assessment: "Horseshit."

69

Tolly Wilson agreed with Moore—and felt sure the jury did, too. Cullen's story was one big lie: a towering tale born of long, lonely hours in the Harris County Jail, a monumental ego, and an unshakable conviction that he could, in the end, get away with anything. The problem was how to attack it, how to disprove a defense based almost entirely on what was in Cullen's head when he said what he said. What did he *mean* by "Do the judge and his wife and that would be it"?

Cullen had also done his homework. His story wasn't just a big lie, it was an engineer's lie; it had been precision-tooled to fit every piece of prosecution evidence. Why wasn't he surprised when McCrory called on Saturday, August 19, to announce that the hit man was out "working"? Because, Cullen explained, McCrory had called him earlier that morning and *told* him not to act surprised because Priscilla's killers would be listening in. There was no evidence of such a call, but there was also no way to disprove it. And Cullen could always find some eager and pliant Kendavis employee to support his version of events.

But an engineer's lie also had an engineer's flaws. Cullen had accounted for the hard evidence, but ignored the soft. How, for example, did his story account for David McCrory's highly emotional state at the meeting on August 18, and near-breakdown on the twentieth? Why would Cullen, who made million-dollar decisions every day, show such poor judgment in relying on Agent Acree's telephoned instructions? Could he and McCrory really have turned in such a string of Oscar-winning performances without at least some stumbling that would have been caught on the FBI bugs? Why did Cullen wait until two months after the trial began to mention the phone calls from "Agent Acree"? Why didn't he blurt out his name as soon as the police tried to arrest him: "There must be some mistake. I'm acting on instructions from Agent Acree of the FBI!" Instead, what did he do? He tried to hide his face.

But these questions, and dozens like them, went to the *preposterousness* of Cullen's story, not its literal truth. It wasn't the best target; it wasn't the target Wilson and Strickland had hoped for; but it was the only one they had.

Wilson went at it with a vengeance.

Why did Cullen want to "flip" Priscilla's hired killers?

"To keep her from killing me," Cullen reiterated, "and to use them against her."

"Did you really expect they would come in and testify that they had made themselves available as her killers for hire?" Wilson asked.

"I don't know," Cullen mumbled. "I was skeptical about it."

Why did Priscilla's killers want the tapes?

"This was going to be their assurance that I wouldn't later turn against them."

"How would you have turned against them, Mr. Davis? If all they were going to do was testify?"

"I'm not quite sure," Cullen mumbled.

Why did Cullen wipe his fingerprints off the gun that McCrory showed him? "Was it because you trusted McCrory so much?" Wilson baited.

"It's because I *didn't* trust him that I wiped my fingerprints off the gun," Cullen huffed. "I was skeptical of his whole program. That's why I wouldn't put my money into it."

"However, you laid your *whole self* into his hands by making these tapes? Did the thought never occur to you, Mr. Davis, that he could take these tapes and use them to blackmail you forever?"

Softly, after a long pause. "Yes, the thought occurred to me."

"After you were arrested, you were taken to the office of the FBI, were you not, Mr. Davis?"

"I don't know whose office it was."

"Did you look high and low for Special Agent Acree down there?" Cullen had testified that he tried to call Acree from the phone booth where he was arrested but the line was busy and he got his money back.

"No, I didn't look for anybody."

"You didn't seek out Special Agent Acree of the FBI at the Federal Building that morning?"

"No."

"Did you tell the arresting officers about Agent Acree?"

"No."

Wilson had a tape recorder brought out, and replayed one last time the conversations that, by now, most of the jurors knew by heart.

McCRORY: *Just what you ordered.*

CULLEN: *Just what the doctor ordered.*

"Had you asked David McCrory to obtain a Ruger pistol for you?" Wilson demanded.

"No."

"So even though he said, 'Just what you ordered,' and you said, 'Just what the doctor ordered,' you had not ordered this pistol—are you telling the jury that is correct?"

Cullen, defiant: "Correct."

McCRORY: *He'd rather do Priscilla than the judge. He says he could do it easy.*

CULLEN: *Like hell . . .*

McCRORY: *Give me a price on Priscilla. He says he'd rather do Priscilla than the judge . . .*

"Mr. Davis, when McCrory said, 'He'd rather do Priscilla than the judge,' and asked you to give him a price on Priscilla, did you consider that to be talking about killing people?" Wilson's deep voice was frosted with contempt.

"No," Cullen responded in his flattest, businessman's tone.

CULLEN: *Go back to the original plan . . . Get the other one . . .*

McCRORY: *Oh, Bev.*

CULLEN: *Yeah.*

"When you were talking about 'getting Bev,' were you talking about picking her up and taking her to church?" Wilson shot a Haynes-like look at the jury.

"No, I didn't mean that."

"When McCrory said that the shooter wanted to 'hit Judge Eidson, snatch him up and take him off, they can't prove much unless they find the body,' did that conversation relate to killing?" Wilson's voice lingered on words like "hit" and "snatch" and "body."

"No, we were not talking about killing somebody," Cullen explained icily. "We were just making conversation."

Wilson pounced: Cullen knew someone would be listening to those tapes. According to his own testimony, he believed that the tapes were being made for Priscilla's hired killers. Why wasn't he worried that the killers, being killers, might "misuse" those tapes? Why wasn't he afraid they might fall into less scrupulous hands? Why did he leave it to McCrory to destroy the old tapes? "They weren't damning to me in any way," Cullen replied confidently.

"Not *damning* . . ." Wilson repeated to the jury as he started the tape back up.

McCRORY: *So you definitely want her to go down before the judge?*

CULLEN: *Yeah . . .*

"Didn't you consider *that* damning to yourself?" Wilson demanded.

"No," Cullen replied serenely.

McCRORY: *. . . he may take a bunch of them off at once, I mean, he's that kind of person. I mean, he may just waste the shit out of a bunch of them and get a bunch of it over with at once.*

"What did you answer him when he said that?" Wilson demanded.

Cullen glanced at the defense table. This was a part of the tapes that had not come up during Haynes's questioning, for reasons that would soon be obvious. For the first time since the first day, Cullen stuttered, "I . . . I . . . I said, 'That's all right with me' . . . or something like that."

Wilson smiled. "When he said that about wasting a bunch of them at once, did you think he was talking about killing anyone?"

"No, we weren't," said Cullen quickly.

Watching from the prosecution table, Jack Strickland thought he saw the first cracks beginning to appear in Cullen's composure. The syntax was always first to go.

"When you said, 'That is all right with me,' or something like that, do you think that was damaging to you in any way?"

"No," said Cullen, recovering, "we were just cutting a tape."

Wilson looked down at his transcript. "As a matter of fact, Mr. Davis, what you said was, '*That suits the shit out of me.*'"

Cullen didn't answer.

"Didn't you?" Wilson snapped.

After a few too many seconds, Cullen found his flat, casual tone. "Yes."

McCRORY: *This man's good, Cullen. He's supposedly one of the best.*

"When McCrory told you that," Wilson pressed his advantage, "did you consider McCrory to mean that he was one of the best witnesses?"

"I didn't know who he was talking about," Cullen replied warily.

"'The shooter,'" Wilson obliged, "was he one of the best witnesses that you could buy?"

"Whoever the somebody was going to be a witness I was hopeful for." The syntax again. More than syntax: The thoughts themselves were colliding. Cullen was fast losing sight of the trail of crumbs he had left through this forest.

Wilson pressed harder. "That's what you thought McCrory meant when he said, 'The man's good, Cullen, one of the best witnesses you could buy?'"

Cullen's neck stiffened and his jaw muscles began to pump. "That is *not* what he was talking about at that point." He seemed on the edge of losing control.

Wilson bore down. "He *was* talking about the shooter, wasn't he—about *killing* somebody?"

Cullen choked back his anger. "Yeah," he said, more in an effort to rid himself of the question than to answer it.

That was the closest Wilson would come to getting a rise—or a confession—out of Cullen Davis.

The one surprise among the rows and rows of cookie-cutter denials came in the middle of Wilson's review of the tapes. "When McCrory said, 'What if he does all three of them?'—did you think he was talking about killing people?"

Cullen answered on automatic: "We weren't actually talking about killing anybody."

Wilson followed up, "Did you think that statement was at all damning to you?"

Cullen answered "No," as usual, but then added, "Just talking about it, I found out, was not breaking the law."

Wilson looked startled. Apparently Cullen had discussed these tapes with someone else at the time, someone who could, presumably, confirm his story, preposterous or not. "Who had you found this out from?" Wilson asked.

Cullen unzipped a smile for the jury. "Hershel Payne."

70

The name Hershel Payne had punctuated Cullen's testimony like an exclamation mark. At each of the critical moments in Cullen's dealings with David McCrory, there it was. Did Cullen tell anyone about his first meeting with McCrory in January 1978? Yes, Hershel Payne. ("Mc-

Crory is trouble," Payne advised sagely.) Did Cullen tell anybody when he and McCrory started talking about killing people? Yes, Hershel Payne. ("Could a person go to jail for discussing such things?" Cullen inquired. "No," Payne reassured him, as long as they were "just talking.") Did Cullen tell anybody about the $25,000 McCrory gave him for safekeeping or about the "present" of a gun and silencer? Absolutely. Hershel Payne.

Up to that point, the prosecutors had found none of this either surprising or distressing. Payne's actions, as described by Cullen, were consistent with the defense version of the events leading up to the arrest, but they were also consistent with the prosecution's version. Of course Cullen would want to know what kind of legal risk he was running by discussing murder contracts with David McCrory, a man of legendary untrustworthiness, whether he was "just playing along" or dead serious. (What if Priscilla offered McCrory more money to "flip" yet again?) The same was true of the silencer. As a lawyer, family friend, and business partner, of course, Payne could be counted on to be discreet.

But Cullen didn't stop there. In answer to Haynes's questions about the call from "Agent Acree," he invoked Payne's name one more time. Did Cullen tell anyone (besides Karen) about the phone call from the man who identified himself as Agent Acree? Yes, Cullen announced, Hershel Payne! As soon as the prosecutors heard that, they knew Payne was headed for the witness stand. Excluding Karen Master, whose impossibly convenient, smile-filled testimony had been dismissed by virtually everyone, Hershel Payne would be the sole independent corroboration of Cullen's story.

Now, in cross, Cullen had once again sucked Payne into the eye of the storm.

"What had you talked to Mr. Hershel Payne about in relation to talking about killing people not being any crime?" Tolly Wilson probed carefully, trying not to alert Cullen.

Cullen, offguard, misheard the question. "After the meeting of August 11," he replied.

It was not only the wrong answer, it was a dangerous answer. Previously, Cullen had said that he asked Payne about the risks of talking about murder at a *June* meeting when McCrory first introduced the idea "in a general sort of way." Now he was suggesting that he had consulted Payne much later, at a time when the conversations with McCrory about killing people had progressed far beyond the innocent "just talking" stage.

Wilson saw the hole and went for it. "How long after that meeting did you talk to Mr. Payne?"

Cullen could tell he had slipped, but wasn't yet sure where. "I got him by Monday," he answered.

Wilson continued feeding him rope. "And where did you see Mr. Payne?"

"I believe I handled that conversation over the phone."

"You told him about your conversation with David McCrory, I take it?"

"Yes, in part."

"And just tell the jury what you told Hershel Payne."

"I told Hershel that David wanted to talk about killing people, and I wanted to know what he thought about it. And I said, 'Can he and I be prosecuted for it?' And he said, 'If you don't intend to do it, and then you don't consummate the deal, there is no law in this state that you have broken.' "

"Did he ask you who you were talking about?" More rope.

"Yes."

Finally the noose. "What names did you give him?"

"I gave him all the names that we have discussed on that tape right there."

"What names were those?"

"Priscilla and Beverly, Bubba, Mr. Gavrel, and Judge Eidson."

Wilson, fiercely casual: "Was Hershel at all disturbed that a judge would be mentioned as between you and McCrory?"

Cullen still didn't see it. "He didn't make any comment of being greatly disturbed."

Wilson had everything he needed now. It was time to show Cullen the trap. "And is Hershel Payne a licensed and practicing attorney in Fort Worth, Texas?"

Cullen began, "I had . . ." then he saw it; ". . . yes, but . . ." he backtracked instantly, ". . . but I had told him that we weren't *serious* about killing people. I told him what this was *for*." But it was too late; he had crawled out too far to crawl back in.

Wilson pursued him openly now. "He didn't give you any cautionary remark even after you told him about talking about killing the judge?"

Cullen struggled to regain control. "He said, 'You'd better be careful that you don't do something that David will try to blackmail you with.' "

"Did he express any concern at all about the identity of the other people that were being talked about? Beverly Bass was a potential witness against you, was she not?"

"Yes," Cullen conceded reluctantly, "*if* I was ever brought to trial again." Then he reconsidered. "She hadn't been any problem to me before." His disarray was giving way to arrogance.

"And Bubba Gavrel was a potential witness against you."

Cullen, chillingly: "He was no problem."

"So Hershel Payne expressed *no* concern that day other than telling you, as long as you just *talk* about it, you're not breaking any law?" Wilson's voice mixed anger and incredulity.

Cullen's voice was ice. "People talk about killing people without ever intending to do it or following through. There is no law against it."

Wilson ended in a blaze of sarcasm. "Did he charge you for that advice he gave you?"

"No," said the iceman.

The prosecutors didn't know what to expect from Payne. On the one hand, he was a respected corporate lawyer in the respectable Fort Worth firm of Hudson, Keltner, Smith, Cunningham & Payne. No history of shady dealings or marginal deals, a close friend of District Attorney Tim Curry, and a pleasant, friendly man, tending to be shy and bookish. On the other hand, they wondered, would Cullen have pinned so much of his story on Payne if the fix wasn't already in? Payne was, after all, not only a longtime friend and well-paid lawyer, but also, in one recent deal, a business partner.

In exchange for little more than shuffling papers, Cullen had cut Payne into a 6.5 percent partnership on a uranium property that had since tripled in value. Even as Cullen took the stand and constructed an alibi that embraced Payne, the two men were on the verge of making a killing (financial, that is), thanks to a seven-million-dollar offer for the company they jointly owned.

Which was the real Hershel Payne, prosecutors wondered: the strait-laced, pinstriped corporate lawyer, or the toady bagman for Cullen Davis? What surprises was Haynes still waiting to spring?

The surprise, it turned out, was for Haynes. When informed by reporters of Cullen's story, Payne appeared shocked. "Some of it is accurate," he said, "but a lot of it isn't." That comment, and speculation about what it meant for the defense, filled the papers and airwaves during the long New Year's break that interrupted Cullen's testimony.

71

By the time the trial resumed on Tuesday, January 2, Cullen's memory of his conversations with Hershel Payne had "clarified." His precise "engineer's mind," about which Haynes so often bragged, had apparently malfunctioned. On redirect, oozing apologetic charm, Haynes gave his client an opportunity to "correct" the record.

"Do you recall when it was that you had any conversation with Hershel Payne where the subject of killing people came up?"

"Yes," said Cullen, "it was right after David McCrory told me that Priscilla was trying to arrange to have me killed."

Jack Strickland saw instantly where Haynes was headed: There had been no discussion with Payne about Cullen's "killing" conversations with McCrory. They had talked only about *Priscilla's efforts to kill Cullen!*

"What was the nature of the conversation?" Haynes asked.

"Well, I asked Hershel if there was any way that I could file charges on Priscilla."

This was vintage Haynes, thought Strickland. In the same stroke, he wipes the shit off his client and smears it on somebody else.

"Did you have that conversation, or an additional conversation along that same line, with Mr. Hershel Payne?" In other words, did Cullen discuss with Payne *his* conversations with McCrory about having people killed?

Cullen touched his chin thoughtfully. "I don't think I did."

There it was.

But it wasn't clean enough for Haynes. "Subsequent to the June meeting with Mr. McCrory," he pressed, "was the name of Judge Eidson mentioned at any time in that conversation with Mr. Payne?"

Again. "No, it wasn't."

"Was there any conversation at all with Mr. Payne about Eidson's name being mentioned either on August 11 or August 18 or August 20?"

A third time: "No, we didn't talk about Judge Eidson like that."

But it still wasn't enough.

When Hershel Payne took the stand, he confirmed that

Cullen had told him about McCrory's sudden reappearance and had asked him about the legality of owning a silencer. Also, as expected, he supported Cullen's "corrected" memory that the names of specific targets, such as Judge Eidson, were never mentioned. But those were about the only scraps of Cullen's story that survived Payne's brief testimony. In rapid succession he denied that Cullen had told him of McCrory's "$25,000" in cash, denied that Cullen had mentioned the tapes, and denied that Cullen had told him about the call from Agent Acree.

He even denied Cullen's *revised* version of how the subject of killing people had come up. It wasn't in a conversation about Priscilla's efforts to have Cullen killed at all, Payne said; it was, as Cullen originally testified, in a conversation about *Cullen's* discussions with David McCrory. On redirect, Haynes invited him to correct that memory ("Are you certain about that, Mr. Payne . . .") but Payne politely declined ("That's the way I remember it").

Even as he disassembled much of Cullen's alibi, Payne tried, with scant success, to cast his old friend's bizarre behavior in a positive light. When he stressed the casualness with which Cullen had broached the subject of having people killed—"They can't have me arrested or put in jail for having talked to David about that sort of thing, can they?" he had "joked"—Cullen came off sounding more cold-blooded than casual. Besides, why was Cullen worried about going to jail if he thought he was working for the FBI?

Haynes's final question sounded more like a threat. "Do you still consider yourself to be a close personal friend of Thomas Cullen Davis?"

"Yes, sir," said Payne hopefully.

On cross, Jack Strickland passed quickly over the substance of Payne's testimony, much of which favored the prosecution, and went straight for the heart. He wanted to use Payne to show the jurors that Cullen Davis was *capable* of plotting cold-blooded murder. For months, all they had seen was a well-dressed, self-possessed, slightly

arrogant multimillionaire businessman. No matter how
many times the prosecution played the tapes or showed
the pictures, jurors still had trouble connecting the voice
and the picture with the man they saw every day in the
courtroom dressed in a clean pressed shirt, conservative
suit, and muted tie and surrounded by and waited on by
a bevy of fancy lawyers.

To make that connection, Strickland would show that
Hershel Payne—pressed-shirt, conservative-suit, muted-
tie Hershel Payne—was *terrified* of Cullen Davis.

The idea had come to Strickland the previous night
when he and Payne met for dinner. It was clear that Payne
wanted to be open. "I'll answer any questions you want
before we start," he told Strickland. "Ask me anything.
I'll tell you what I know. I'm not trying to hide anything.
I'm a corporate lawyer—I certainly don't want anyone to
think that I'm connected with anything like this."

But when Strickland began probing into his relationship with Cullen, Payne grew increasingly silent and subdued. Of course, he wanted to be as helpful to the
prosecution as he could, *but . . .*

But what?

He was afraid.

Afraid of what?

Cullen Davis. Afraid of crossing him, afraid of contra-
dicting him, afraid of alienating him, afraid of angering
him. Afraid that Cullen would end up hating Hershel
Payne just as he hated Priscilla, hated Stan Farr, hated
Judge Eidson, hated Bev Bass, hated Bubba Gavrel, hated
Tom Cave, hated Joe Shannon, hated Pat Burleson, and,
now, hated David McCrory. Afraid, not just for himself,
but for his family. Cullen was that kind of hater, he told
Strickland. "I don't want to be number sixteen on Cullen's
hit list," Payne said with a grim, hollow laugh.

Strickland was sympathetic, but he felt he had to let
Payne know: "I may have to ask you on the stand if you
have ever said to someone that you didn't want to be on
Cullen's hit list."

The next day, on cross, Strickland came quickly to the

point. "Mr. Payne, let me ask you, sir, whether it has occurred to you at this point, having been called as a witness in this case, that you were in some way being set up to provide an alibi for Mr. Thomas Cullen Davis?"

Payne took a deep breath. "I don't think my friend of ten or twelve years, Cullen Davis, would set me up for anything," he said. "*No, sir.*"

Strickland couldn't believe it. Payne had chosen to lie.

"Has it occurred to you, Mr. Payne," Strickland struck back, "and have you in fact *said*, you don't wish to be number sixteen on any sort of hit list?"

Haynes rocketed out of his chair—"Excuse me . . ."—and Moore sustained the objection before he had a chance to make it. After a furious whispered debate before the bench, Strickland tried again. "Mr. Payne, you indicated that you did not think your friend, Thomas Cullen Davis, would set you up in some way to provide an alibi for himself, is that correct?"

Payne eyed the young prosecutor warily. "Yes, sir."

"Whether you believe it, or want to believe it, has that thought crossed your mind in recounting the events of the last five or six months?"

Payne's eyes twitched in the direction of the defense table. Reporters in the audience saw that Cullen had fixed his laser glare on the witness box. Strickland didn't have to turn around to know where Hershel was looking. "Well," Payne finally said, "I guess it may have crossed my mind when I see the sequence of events, but I don't think . . ."

Strickland saw what was coming—another effort to defend his "friend of ten or twelve years"—and cut Payne off sharply. "We pass the witness, Your Honor."

There was no point in going on. Clearly, Payne had decided to put his money on Cullen. As he passed the defense table on the way back to his seat, Strickland wasn't sure who he feared more, the Hershel Paynes of the world or the Cullen Davises.

Not for the first time in this long ordeal, Strickland was

reminded of a story. A man asks a girl, "Would you sleep with me for a million dollars?"

"Yeah," she says, "I suppose I would."

"Well, how about five dollars?" he says.

She slaps him and says, "No way! What kind of a girl do you think I am?"

The man smiles. "We've already established what kind of girl you are," he says, "now we just have to know the price."

As he left the stand, Payne paused at the defense table to reassure his old friend. Pale with rage, Cullen refused even to look at him. Afterward, in the hall, Payne could be heard muttering in panic, "He's pissed. I've really done it. He's really pissed."

As soon as the prosecutors began calling rebuttal witnesses, it became clear that the refurbishment of Cullen's memory had not been nearly extensive enough. The real Agent Acree took the stand to say not only that he had not called Cullen in regard to David McCrory, but furthermore, that he had given both Cullen and Karen business cards with his *correct* phone numbers the previous December. These included a business number in Fort Worth, a home number, and a twenty-four-hour hotline in Dallas. He had also specifically instructed Cullen not to deal with any extortionist directly until proper "coverage" had been arranged and at least one FBI agent was present.

Next came more FBI men to testify that they had searched David McCrory and his car thoroughly both before and after the meetings on August 18 and August 20, and none had seen a Norelco tape recorder, or minicassettes, or any other recording device. Finally, one of the investigators from the team that arrested Cullen took the stand to reveal that Cullen had only 15¢ in change when he was apprehended at the Kentucky Fried Chicken phone booth. He could not have tried to call "Agent Acree" and gotten his money back, as he claimed; he needed 20¢ to place a call. Either he hadn't tried to phone Acree at all or he had completed a call to someone else.

* * *

Cullen had done his best, but by most estimates, it wasn't good enough. Now it was up to Haynes again. Cullen had shown how far he was willing to go to defend himself. The only question left was whether Haynes would go as far.

In the eyes of many, the answer came with his very next witness.

72

Harold Sexton didn't look like a "bombshell" witness—the Larry Gene Lucases and James Stephenses who seemed forever stepping out of the shadows to save Cullen Davis's hide and Racehorse Haynes's reputation. Tanned, silver-haired, well but casually dressed in V-neck sweater and khaki pants, Sexton looked more like a denizen of country club grills than honky-tonk bars; more like a white-belted, over-the-hill golf pro—which is exactly what he was.

Haynes couldn't be polite or deferential enough as he guided Sexton through a description of his background (growing up in Arlington, a suburb just east of Fort Worth); his source of income ("golf lessons and sales commissions"); and his current home (Southern California). In a voice as studiously informal as his apparel, Sexton described how he had first met David McCrory when the two worked together briefly for the Continental Life Insurance Company in the early seventies. Then, in 1972, he left Texas for California, returning only occasionally to visit his mother in Arlington.

On one such visit, in the summer of 1978, he had seen McCrory again.

"And would you tell the jury, please, where it was that you saw him?" Haynes prompted.

"On East Lancaster, at Sambo's Restaurant." The meeting was "by chance," Sexton explained. "David was sitting in a booth, and he drew my attention, and I joined him."

They had been talking for about half an hour, Sexton said, when David asked him, "Would you be interested in making some money?"

Jack Strickland's ears pricked up.

"And did you respond to that inquiry by Mr. McCrory?" Haynes asked, moving closer to the witness, his voice dropping—a sure sign that something big was coming.

"I inquired as to what he meant, 'make some money,' " said Sexton.

"And what did Mr. McCrory respond?" Lower, closer.

Strickland figured it out just as Sexton said it. "David said that he needed someone to place a phone call to Cullen and represent himself as being a peace officer."

Of course, thought Strickland. Others had speculated that Haynes would try to "find" an Agent Acree. But Strickland dismissed that as too risky; "Acree" would have to take the stand, take the rap, and go to jail (unless, of course, he turned up dead like Horace Copeland). This way was so much neater: Instead of *finding* Agent Acree, Haynes merely had to show that McCrory was *looking* for an Agent Acree. There was no crime in turning down such an offer.

Haynes was pacing the courtroom now, preening with satisfaction. "And what was your response to Mr. McCrory?" he asked.

"I told David I would not be interested in joining anything of that nature," Sexton answered, re-creating for the jury's benefit a little huff of indignation at the memory. "I declined."

Haynes picked up on the distaste in Sexton's voice, making it clear that he sympathized with the witness's low opinion of David McCrory. "Did Mr. McCrory ever, at any time, indicate to you some sort of money would be paid?"

"He didn't place a figure," said Sexton. "He just said considerable money, or good money—something of that nature."

Sexton went on to describe how he had been loosely following the story of the trial in the Los Angeles papers, unaware that David McCrory was involved at all, when he read in one article that Cullen Davis had received phone calls from a man claiming to be an FBI agent. That's when the light bulb went on.

"And what did you do after reading the item in the paper?" Haynes asked.

"I called you," said Sexton brightly.

Before concluding, Haynes made sure to underline how clear Sexton's memory of the meeting was. He remembered not only the exact time (10:30 A.M.), but even what McCrory was wearing (an open-collared shirt and sports coat).

"And was the meeting cordial?" Haynes asked finally.

"Yes," said Sexton with a smooth smile, "it was cordial."

On cross, Tolly Wilson tried everything.

He probed Sexton's vague and clearly precarious financial situation. Just how much money did he make as a "golf pro"? "Twenty dollars for a one-hour lesson," Sexton said. How many lessons did he give in a month? Sexton couldn't say.

"How much money did you make last month?" Wilson asked.

Sexton couldn't remember, although he reminded the prosecutor that the golf business was slow in December.

When Wilson asked how else Sexton supported himself, Haynes leapt to his feet and accused the prosecutor of trying to impeach his witness. Was this the same Haynes, thought Strickland, who forced Mary Weir to admit on the stand that she supplemented her income with prostitution?

Over Haynes's outraged objections, Sexton allowed that he had received unemployment benefits from the state of California. When Wilson pressed, he also admitted to "playing golf for money"—i.e., gambling. Again Haynes objected: "Lawyers, doctors, and judges likewise make small wagers on their playing."

Wilson moved on to another standard attack: the witness's cozy relationship with the defense. He pointed out that Sexton had refused to speak to a District Attorney's investigator who approached him in the hall earlier that morning.

"Did you have anything to hide from the District Attorney's office, Mr. Sexton?" Wilson suggested.

"No, I did not," said Sexton, with just the right hint of indignation.

"Did you call the District Attorney's office when you read the terrible thing in the paper out in California about what David McCrory said?" Frustrated in his questioning, Wilson was resorting more and more to ridicule.

"No, I did not call the District Attorney's office," Sexton lashed back in a small sortie of pique.

"Didn't you think it was something that the prosecution should know?"

"I thought it was something the *court* should know," Sexton snapped.

"Did you think Mr. Haynes was the court?" Wilson's voice was hot with sarcasm.

Sexton struggled to recover his poise. "He is representing the defendant."

"Did you attempt to call David McCrory to find out what the situation was, and why he was saying something like that?"

"No, I did not."

"Richard Haynes is the only one you called?"

"Richard Haynes is the man I called."

Finally, Wilson tested Sexton's strangely selective memory. Sexton may have remembered the exact time of day and exactly what McCrory was wearing, but when Wilson pressed him for the date, the day of the week, or even the week of the meeting, his mind was an obstinate blank.

Who was he staying with during the four weeks of his visit to the Fort Worth area?

His mother and "friends."

"Can you give us the name of any one friend that you stayed with?" Wilson asked. This was, after all, only five months ago.

"No," said Sexton firmly, "I'm sorry, I can't."

"Cannot?" Wilson puzzled. "Your memory does not permit you to recall *any* of those names?"

"No."

Wilson concluded with the question that had by now become standard for Cullen Davis defense witnesses. "Have you been promised anything in return for your testimony?"

And Sexton gave the standard answer: "I have not."

"Sexton killed you," a reporter told Jack Strickland that night at dinner. "If I was on the jury, I'd have to say your golfin' buddy created a reasonable doubt."

Tolly Wilson ate alone that night, for the hundredth time, in the restaurant of the Ramada Inn on Katy Street. It had been two and a half years since he first heard the name Cullen Davis. Two and a half years—with a short break out for a vacation in Europe—of anger and obsession; strategy sessions and witness preparations; weeks away from home and weekends gone by in a flash. Within a few days it would all be over, and now, thanks to Harold Sexton, it might all amount to nothing.

Unless.

During Sexton's testimony that day, something had bothered Wilson. He wasn't sure, but he had a vague memory that a Sambo's in Fort Worth had burned down the previous summer. How many were there? Was it the one on East Lancaster? Did it happen sometime before late July or early August, when Sexton said he met with McCrory? Was it a real recollection, or just desperately wishful thinking in the guise of memory?

After court, he called Coy Ray, an investigator in Fort Worth, and filled him in on Sexton's testimony. "Check with whoever ran those Sambos and find out if one of the danged things burned down," Wilson instructed, "and, if so, what date. Call me back if you get anything."

By midnight, when Ray still hadn't called, Wilson figured he wasn't going to. Joylessly, he went to bed. Sleep wasn't the release he was looking for.

Sometime after 2:00, the phone woke him up. It was Coy Ray. "I found the manager of Sambo's in Dallas. You were right, Tolly. There was a fire, and the place on East Lancaster was closed down."

"When?" Wilson asked, heart racing.

"All summer. May through August."

"On East Lancaster in Fort Worth, you're sure?"

"That's the one."

Wilson squeezed his fist into a tight little ball of joy. "Goddamn," he grinned. "We got him!"

73

Wilson called Sexton back to the stand the next morning, but chose not to close the trap quite yet. His witnesses, the Sambo's manager and fire department officials, wouldn't be ready until the next day—the last day of the trial. Their appearance would make for a hell of a finish.

In the meantime, he used the time he had to "stuff and truss" the defense's latest (and last) bombshell witness. To avoid arousing Haynes's suspicions, he began with some other discoveries his investigators had made about the mellow, suntanned Mr. Sexton.

"Do you know Mr. Tony Avarello, Jr.?" Wilson asked.

Haynes objected immediately and Wilson was forced to preview his discoveries to Judge Moore at the bench. "Mr. Avarello, Your Honor, is a well-known gambler in the Arlington area."

"That's what I thought," Haynes snipped.

"I imagine you would know that," Wilson replied with a smile.

Haynes stuck out his chin in a pout. "That's a sidebar, Your Honor."

Wilson turned back to Moore and explained. "When Mr. Sexton left Fort Worth, Your Honor, he left owing Mr. Avarello a great deal of money, and I want to know if anybody promised to pay Mr. Avarello off. Mr. Avarello could be dangerous to this witness's health."

Haynes objected ferociously, but he needn't have bothered. When Wilson confronted Sexton with the charges, Sexton blithely denied them. All he knew about Mr. Avarello, he said, was that he "used to be involved in selling insurance."

"He's also a gambler, isn't he?" Wilson asked.

"Perhaps," sighed Sexton.

Wilson continued with his list of names: Buddy Haas, J. B. King, Charlie Norvell—all major figures in the Dallas–Fort Worth gambling underground. Sexton acknowledged knowing all of them, but seemed surprised to learn they were gamblers, and flatly denied ever owing any of them money. But the point was made: For an out-of-town golf pro visiting his mother, Sexton kept unusual company.

At one point, Haynes objected loudly: "All they want to do is sully this man for the media!" and Strickland almost broke into laughter.

Finally, casually, Wilson turned to a series of brief questions on Sexton's testimony the previous day concerning the meeting at Sambo's.

"Did you pay your own check, or did Mr. McCrory pay it, or what?"

"I would assume we each paid our own check."

"Do you remember what you had?"

"No, I don't."

"Did you have a cup of coffee?"

"I'm sure I had coffee."

"Were there waitresses there in the restaurant?"

"Yes."

"Were there any other patrons there?"

"I recall it being rather few patrons."

"Were you sitting in a booth there at Sambo's?"

"I think so, yes."

"You are not sure of that?"

"I wouldn't stake my life that I was in a booth."

"But this Sambo's—you do remember it's on East Lancaster?"

"Yes."

Wilson nodded his head thoughtfully and turned to Moore. "We pass the witness, Your Honor." Then, just as Sexton began to rise from his chair, Wilson turned back. "Just a moment, Your Honor," and he took a step toward the witness. "Is that East Lancaster in Fort Worth, Texas."

"Yes."

Tolly Wilson spent the evening the way he spent every weekday evening, in Suite 70 of the Ramada Inn reviewing his notes for the next day. There was one difference this night: Tomorrow was the last day.

He had prepared his two witnesses, William Dunkin, a fire investigator for the Fort Worth Fire Department, and Ronald Soteros, a Sambo's executive responsible for remodeling. He even had photographs of the burned-out Sambo's on East Lancaster. (Jack Strickland suggested showing the pictures to Sexton and asking, "Now where exactly was it that you and Mr. McCrory were sitting, sir?")

Around 8:00 P.M., the phone rang. It was Ann McDaniel from the *Dallas Times Herald*. The sound of her querulous voice reminded Wilson of one of the many things he would *not* miss after this ordeal was over: the media. Unlike Jack Strickland, he loathed reporters, and had difficulty concealing that fact from them. By now, most of those covering the trial had learned to avoid him. McDaniel was probably calling for Jack.

"I've heard that the Sambo's on East Lancaster burned in May of 1978," he heard McDaniel say. "I was calling for confirmation or comment."

"I . . . I . . ." Wilson stumbled.

"We're planning to put this in our sunrise edition on page one. I'm also giving the story to the Associated Press. It will be getting to Houston early."

"I don't know what you're talking about," Wilson finally said, and hung up. It took a minute before he felt the full force of the blow. If Haynes found out about the Sambo's fire, he would throw Sexton on the stand first thing in the morning and retract his testimony—or as much of it as he needed to. Sexton wouldn't look good, but he would look a hell of a lot worse if they caught him in a red-letter lie.

By the time Strickland returned, Wilson had already been to McDaniel's room and been turned away. "The story's gonna go," he told Strickland, his voice crackling with anger. "Where the hell are her journalistic ethics? She's about to print something that's gonna affect the outcome of this case."

Frantic, Strickland called McDaniel back. "Jesus, Ann," he pleaded, "just hold off on this. We're not trying to get you to kill the story. You're just doing your job. But can't you just hold off telling them where we're going with this thing long enough so you don't give them time to come up with an answer? They will, too, believe me. I know it."

But McDaniel wouldn't budge.

Strickland did a quick calculation. The sunrise edition would hit the streets at 5:00 in the morning. By 6:00 the defense would have a copy. That was plenty of time. Given Cullen's resources, they would have an answer by 7:00, 7:30 at the latest. By 8:30, Sexton would be on the stand saying, "You know what I told you yesterday, well, what I *meant* was . . ."

Their only hope was that somewhere, somehow, the mammoth Cullen Davis defense machine would break down.

Ann McDaniel took care of that. She didn't wait for the defense team to read her article in the *Times Herald* the next morning to find out about the Sambo's fire. She called and told them that night.

Haynes listened to the news in stony silence, then turned to Mike Gibson. "Find me a Sambo's."

74

Gibson called Jim Bearden in Fort Worth. "Jim, we just found out from a reporter that our witness who testified today that something happened at Sambo's—well, the Sambo's burned down." Haynes wanted a confirmation that the story was true and airtight. "See if there's any room for error," Gibson suggested. If there wasn't, they would have to find another Sambo's—in a hurry. They had until 8:00 the next morning. It was already after midnight.

Bearden made some calls and scrambled his men. One group of investigators checked out the fire story, while another searched the area around East Lancaster for the "right" Sambo's. Even at 2:00 in the morning, the magic and mystique of Cullen Davis's name worked for them. Bearden called a contact who worked in the fire department offices downtown and "pulled in some chits." They needed the Sambo's file, he said, and they needed it by 8:00 that morning. The man wasn't happy about being woken up in the middle of the night, but Bearden reminded him that he "owed" Cullen Davis.

By 7:00, Bearden had a copy of the fire report in his hands.

Another investigator drove to the offices of the *Star-Telegram* to search through the paper's library. He had to wait until 6:00 for the library to open, but by 7:30, Bearden had copies of all the newspaper articles that had appeared on the fire and the follow-up arson investigation.

There was no doubt about it, Sexton had put himself and McCrory at a meeting in a burned-out building.

Meanwhile, the search for an alternative Sambo's turned up several possibilities in the Fort Worth area, but none close enough to make Sexton's mistake credible. Then Bearden thought to look farther east, in Arlington. The Sambo's he found was more than six miles away from the one Sexton had described, but *it was on the same road.*

The highway between Fort Worth and Arlington, Highway 80, was known as East Lancaster in Fort Worth and Division Street in Arlington. The Sambo's that burned down was at the Fort Worth end of the highway, on East Lancaster; the one Bearden found was at the Arlington end, on Division Street. "*If* you had your directions confused," Bearden explained in his telephone report the next morning, "and *if* you went almost exactly the opposite direction, you would get to the one rather than the other."

Bearden knew there were problems. Not only were there six miles between the two Sambo's, but some of those miles were nothing but country. That would make it hard for Sexton to argue that he just "lost track," or thought he was in Fort Worth when he was still in Arlington. Nobody who had lived in Arlington or Fort Worth for any length of time could get Division Street and East Lancaster Street confused. They were in different cities separated by miles of undeveloped land.

But Bearden was forgetting something Haynes wouldn't: The jury lived in Houston.

By 8:00 A.M., Bearden had filed his report and been assured that "a change would be made."

75

A few hours later, Richard Haynes called Harold Gene Sexton back to the witness stand.

He began by introducing the receipts from Sexton's trip to Fort Worth to prove he had indeed been in town during July and August of 1978. It was routine business, and Haynes's voice rolled through the questions as if this were just another witness on just another day. But Jack Strickland noticed something different. As Haynes showed Sexton a gas receipt, his hand trembled. And he was clearing his throat too often. For the first time in the trial, Racehorse was visibly nervous.

Haynes used a question about Sexton's mother, who lived in Arlington, to sidle into a new subject. "Now, Arlington, Texas, is where in relationship to Fort Worth?" he asked, his voice all charm and nonchalance.

Just east, said Sexton.

"And to get from your mother's address in Arlington, Texas, to Fort Worth, how do you go?"

The route described by Sexton mentioned both "Division" and "Highway 80"—interchangeably.

Here it comes, thought Strickland.

Haynes flashed a puzzled look at the jury. "Now you say 'Highway 80.' Is Highway 80 also known as Division Street?"

"They are one and the same."

"How about Highway 80 and Division and *Lancaster*? Are they one and the same?" Another puzzled look.

"Yes."

That was Haynes's opening. "You indicated in response to a question that you went into a Sambo's on Lancaster, did you not?"

Sexton nodded. "I think that was the testimony I gave."

"Do you know where Division Street changes from being Division Street to Lancaster in there?"

"No, I do not." Sexton's voice was dead level.

"Do you know whether or not in June or July there was one Sambo's on that street, or two, or do you know?"

"There's only one that I know of."

It was as simple as that. He hadn't been *wrong* about the Sambo's, merely confused about its location.

Tolly Wilson could barely control the rage in his voice as he began the cross-examination.

Was this the same Harold Sexton who grew up in Arlington, Texas? Who went to high school there? Who worked in Fort Worth selling insurance and making calls in his car to customers in Arlington? Who visited his mother in Arlington often, both when he worked in Fort Worth and later, after he left for California, on frequent return trips?

To each heated question, Sexton raised his bedroom eyes to half-staff and muttered an expressionless "Yes."

"Isn't there a big sign over Lancaster that says 'East Lancaster Street'?" Wilson continued.

"I don't know about a sign," Sexton shrugged.

"Haven't you been down that road many times?"

"I have been down that road," Sexton allowed.

Weren't there signs at every intersection in Fort Worth saying Lancaster Street and at every intersection in Arlington saying Division?

Sexton crossed his legs and shrugged again. "I don't inspect street signs."

Wasn't there a huge open area between Fort Worth and Arlington on that road?

"What constitutes an open area?"

Wilson erupted. "Are you telling this jury that you did not meet David McCrory in a Sambo's Restaurant in Fort Worth, Texas?"

Sexton, stonefaced: "I met David McCrory in a Sambo's on Highway 80."

Wilson turned to Moore. "Please instruct the witness to answer my question."

Sexton looked up to Moore. "I'm trying to . . ." he started to say before his eyes caught Moore's ferocious glare. Red-faced and white-knuckled, Moore, too, was struggling to keep his anger from the jury. Hell, he lived in *Houston*, and *he* knew the difference between Division and Lancaster. Every Texan with a car knew that Highway 80 was Davis Street in Dallas, Main Street in Grand Prairie, Division Street in Arlington, then a whole goddamn *prairie* before it became Lancaster in Fort Worth.

Gritting his teeth, but containing his anger, Moore told Sexton to answer the question.

But he wouldn't. "Should I say I don't know where it is?" he asked instead.

"Are you now telling this jury that you don't *know* where that Sambo's was?" Wilson exclaimed.

Sexton settled back in his chair like a pouting child and said firmly, "No, I don't."

Wilson exploded. *"Didn't you tell this jury that it was located on East Lancaster Street in Fort Worth, Texas?"*

"I don't know," Sexton muttered without looking up.

If Sexton didn't say where the Sambo's was located, Wilson demanded, why had Richard Haynes asked him about the Sambo's on East Lancaster, in Fort Worth? "Did Mr. Haynes just *guess*?"

For a moment Sexton pretended to be unsure where Haynes had gotten his information. "I told him that I met with David in *Sambo's*," he explained.

What about all those times during the last two days of testimony when he or Haynes or Wilson had said "the Sambo's on East Lancaster in Fort Worth"? Wilson pulled out copies of the transcripts and forced Sexton to read the exchanges. Why had he never raised a question or expressed a doubt?

Sexton pushed the transcript away: "Oh, Division, Highway 80, Lancaster, hell, they all run together, they're one and the same."

Wilson, astonished: "You're not honestly contending that Lancaster and Division are one and the same, are you?"

The pout again, and the defensive anger. "Are you contending they're not?"

"Mr. Sexton, don't you know that if you were trying to float this before a bunch of Fort Worth people or a bunch of Arlington people they would laugh you out of the courtroom?"

Defiance. "I've been laughed at before."

Wilson tried one last attack.

"Did you talk to any of the attorneys representing the

defendant this morning about this case or your testimony?"

Sexton looked at the defense table. A pause like an absolute vacuum. Then: "I don't know."

The answer left Wilson momentarily stunned. How could he not remember something that had happened within the last few hours? Was this an opening? Wilson didn't have to feign surprise. "You don't remember?"

But the opening, if there was one, had already shut. Instead, he hit the wall of petulance. "Have you ever been up here?" Sexton snipped.

When Wilson tried again with the same question—"Have you talked to anybody representing the defendant, Thomas Cullen Davis, about this case or your testimony this morning at any time?"—Haynes leapt to his feet to prevent Sexton from answering.

But Sexton had already recovered. He admitted talking to the lawyers, but not about the case.

The rest was pro forma.

"Have you read any news accounts of the condition of Sambo's Restaurant on East Lancaster?"

"No, I have not."

"Have you listened to any news reports on the radio?"

"No, I have not."

"Has *anybody* said *anything* to you since you testified here previously about the condition of the Sambo's Restaurant during the months of July and August that was located on East Lancaster in Fort Worth, Texas?"

"No. Nobody said anything."

Wilson stopped. After two and a half years of questions, there was nothing left to ask.

As Sexton brushed out of the courtroom, Haynes leaned back and lit his pipe. Around the stem, where his lips met the wood, hidden behind a rapid flurry of starting puffs, the telltale curl of a smile appeared.

He had showed them.

76

On the first ballot, on the first day of deliberations, the jury split eight to four: eight for guilty, four for not guilty. On the fourteenth ballot, six days and forty-four hours of deliberations later, the jury split eight to four: eight for guilty, four for not guilty. Pete Moore summoned the jurors into the vast, dark courtroom one last time and asked each one individually if there was *any* chance further deliberations might produce a verdict. Each one, in turn, gave the same bitter answer: "Never."

Moore had no choice but to declare a mistrial. With great dignity, he shook Cullen's hand and disappeared into his chambers. Later, he would concede that the four-month ordeal had "killed him," that the "entire system had been abused," and that he thought Cullen Davis "guilty as hell."

Haynes grinned and accepted the admiration swirling around him: "Your greatest victory . . . no other lawyer could pull off what you just did . . . resounding and incredible triumph . . . congratulations of the highest order . . ." "It's a great day for the system," he declared. He even managed to summon up a tear for the occasion and, lost in the spiral of celebration, an odd epigram: "They didn't get us, did they?"

As he slipped through the pressing throng of reporters and photographers toward a waiting limousine, Cullen was giddy as a schoolboy. "It isn't as sweet a victory as Amarillo," he complained, but no, he wasn't bitter. Within a few hours he was on his Learjet headed for Aspen.

Tolly Wilson disappeared as soon as the verdict was announced, leaving Jack Strickland to put on the noble face. "Coming in here we'd played one and lost one," he told a reporter. "Now we've played two, lost one, and tied one. Next time we'll even the score." But even he didn't sound convinced.

There would be another trial, all right. He and Wilson and Curry would have to play their hand out. But Strickland knew what the odds were on a retrial. Juries were notoriously reluctant to convict if they knew a previous jury had deadlocked. And where in Texas was there a jury that wouldn't know what had happened in Houston?

Not for the first time, Strickland wondered if maybe Cullen Davis was impossible to convict. Maybe the combination of Cullen's cold, conscienceless wealth and Haynes's cold, conscienceless expertise was utterly unbeatable. Maybe there weren't twelve people in Texas— hell, in the world—who could endure a trial like this one and come out with a unanimous "guilty." If that was the case, then maybe they hadn't done so badly this time. Eight to four. Maybe the system just couldn't do any better. Maybe Cullen Davis and Racehorse Haynes *were* above the law.

That, at least, seemed to be what some of the jurors thought. Four of them, including three women, had made it clear that they could not bring themselves to convict Cullen Davis *under any circumstances*. Their leader was Mary Carter, a prickly, self-righteous, out-of-work medical secretary who declared defiantly that she and her followers would have voted for acquittal *"even if the defense [had] presented nothing."* Merely *being* Cullen Davis was defense enough.

The prosecution, she maintained, simply "did not present a strong enough case." What about David McCrory's detailed account of murder for hire? (Not even Cullen disputed the substance of the conversations.) "There's nothing to substantiate it," she insisted. What about the tapes? She dismissed those because the prosecution had failed to explain why "a man like Cullen Davis" would want to murder a judge. Yet she bristled at suggestions that Cullen's station in life had influenced her decision in any way.

The bailiff, Grady Dukes, saw something else in Carter's vote. "I saw the gleam in her eye every time Haynes got up to speak," said Dukes, who, like the jurors, had listened to every word of testimony and deemed Cullen "guilty as homemade sin." It was Mary Carter, after all, who, during voir dire, had fluttered her eyelashes at Haynes and told him his name was "a household word" around her home. And Mary Carter who had dabbed the tears from her eyes as Haynes concluded his final argument with a plea for sympathy for Cullen Davis.

"You can see what the money does," Haynes had said in a voice close to breaking. "Were it not for the money," Cullen wouldn't have been victimized. "Were it not for the money," the evil conspirators—Priscilla, Burleson, and McCrory—would not have targeted him for their diabolical scheme. "Were it not for the money," he had concluded, with tears of sincerity glistening in his handsome blue eyes, "the press wouldn't be here, the crowd wouldn't be here."

"Were it not for the money," cynics in the audience had speculated, Racehorse Haynes wouldn't have been there, either.

But no such unkind thought crossed Mary Carter's mind. From her first sight of "Race" to her last, she was transfixed. And never for a moment did she consider any verdict other than not guilty.

Like the other jurors who voted to acquit, however, she was sorely disappointed when Cullen didn't throw a party for them like the one he threw for the jury in Amarillo. They had heard about that and were looking forward to it.

Priscilla Davis heard the news just as she returned from the Mount Olive Cemetery, where she had gone to put fresh flowers on Andrea's grave. By one last cruel coincidence, the day of the mistrial was January 22, 1979, Andrea's fifteenth birthday.

EPILOGUE

EPILOGUE

77

As Jack Strickland predicted, Cullen Davis was tried again—this time, for the first time, in Fort Worth. Disgusted by the mistrial in Houston, Pete Moore "washed [his] hands of the whole Davis mess" and sent it back to Tarrant County, where, he grumbled, "all this damn trouble started in the first place." The case was taken up by Judge Gordon Gray, a cantankerous good ol' boy with a weakness for lunchtime bourbon and branch that sometimes befogged his afternoon sessions.

Gray turned a deaf ear to the pleas of the prosecutors to move the case somewhere—anywhere—other than Fort Worth. Even when they produced a poll showing that 82 percent of the city's residents believed that Cullen was the innocent victim of an official vendetta, Gray insisted he could still find a fair and impartial jury. Prosecutors suspected the real reason for the judge's intransigence was politics. It was no secret that Gray had his eyes on Tim Curry's job. What better way to kick off a campaign for district attorney than to preside over the media extravaganza of Cullen Davis's first hometown trial?

On the first day of testimony, July 30, 1979, like swallows to Capistrano, the dozens of groupies who had dedicated their lives to the care, feeding, and moral support of Cullen Davis reappeared. After missing the season in Houston, chased away by a dour Judge Moore, they returned in even greater numbers than in Amarillo. Led by an earnest, rotund crusader named Joyce Smith, they flocked to the courtroom laden with the usual succor treats: pies, cakes, brownies, and apple turnovers, all for Cullen and his lawyers. They brought their children to see the great man—now, after his narrow escape in Houston, even greater. During breaks, they scrambled to touch him, crowded around to have their pictures taken with him, and held out their Bibles for him to sign.

Jack Strickland expressed surprise that they couldn't find something better to do—"like work in the animal shelter spaying cats."

Occasionally the women were joined by Cullen's former jailer, Fort Worth Sheriff Lon Evans, eager to show his support for an old friend. At a surprise birthday party for the defendant after the trial began, a beaming Sheriff Evans presented Cullen with a "key to the jail."

The gift was more than symbolic. In fact, for the first time in three trials, Cullen Davis was a free man. Released on a mere $30,000 bond, he could leave at the end of trial every day instead of returning to his jail cell. Even better, he could go home—home to the dream house from which Priscilla had expelled him five years earlier—home to his mansion on Mockingbird Lane.

The long, bitter divorce battle was finally over.

It hadn't been easy. The murder-for-hire trial did, at long last, remove the nettle of Judge Eidson, but soon Cullen was caught making a late-night visit to the hotel room of Eidson's more pliable replacement, Judge John Barron. Not only was Barron forced to withdraw, but in the resulting brouhaha, some embarrassing facts leaked from the divorce proceedings—facts that suggested why Cullen's thoughts might have turned murderous when Judge Eidson threatened to make the trial record public. One was a sales slip for a Smith and Wesson revolver, the kind used in the mansion killings, purchased for Cullen by Roy Rimmer sometime before the murders. Another was the record of thousands of dollars in personal checks that Cullen cashed just before his arrest in August 1978—at exactly the time David McCrory claimed Cullen was laying out money for hit men.

Still, all in all, Cullen could claim victory. The prenuptial agreement was ruled valid, and Priscilla walked away with a mere $3.5 million instead of the $50 million her lawyers had been noisily demanding up to the end.

Not only did Cullen get his beloved mansion back, but also, most important of all, he hung on to every single one of his half million shares of Kendavis stock. Stinky's empire remained unviolated.

Once the trial began, there were few surprises. The only difference in the prosecution's case was the prosecutor. Like Pete Moore, Tolly Wilson had walked away from the Davis case in disgust, leaving the unenvied mantle of chief prosecutor to Jack Strickland. The slender, curly-haired ex-pilot did not mourn Wilson's departure. They had argued bitterly during the Houston trial, both over courtroom strategy and Strickland's ardent courtship of the press. No one doubted the case would be better off without their feuding.

What wasn't clear was whether the handsome young prosecutor was up to the coming battle. He was smart, aggressive, and media-savvy, no doubt, but would that be enough against the now legendary Racehorse Haynes—who had recently taken to the lecture circuit describing himself as "just a simple trial lawyer from Texas representing the poor, downtrodden, and oppressed"—and the formidable Cullen Davis defense team, now numbering almost thirty?

If Strickland was intimidated, he didn't sound it. "I think that Racehorse is a tremendously talented attorney," he told a reporter on the eve of trial, "but I also think that, for whatever reason, he has lost too much of his professional objectivity. If you don't give testimony Richard likes, you're a damn liar or a slimy bastard. If you're a prosecutor who tries to go toe-to-toe with him, you're a clown or you're suborning perjury. I'm struck by the fact that Richard Haynes is motivated by two things—first, and foremost, the self-aggrandizement of Richard Haynes, and, two, the pursuit of money. I fail to see a thread of principle, a common denominator that runs through Richard other than those two."

Strickland may have presented his case more effectively and promoted it more aggressively, but it was, in essence, the same case Tolly Wilson had presented in Houston. Judge Eidson's chilling account of "playing dead" in the trunk of a car was followed by the identical parade of FBI agents: Ron Jannings, Jerry Hubbell, Joe Gray, and photographer George Ridgley. Jannings did take special care to describe his elaborate search of McCrory and his car prior to the meetings with Cullen (to head off the defense contention that McCrory secreted a tape recorder into those meetings), while Haynes modulated his voice and rolled his eyes more vigorously than ever trying to conjure up a conspiracy in the jurors' imaginations. But it all seemed like vamping as the courtroom waited restlessly for the headline act.

Much to Strickland's dismay, David McCrory did not disappoint. Finally in the spotlight he had been chasing his whole life, McCrory couldn't resist padding his part. Over the six months since Houston, almost every story he told had sprouted colorful, dramatic new details. At one point, he recalled how Cullen had talked about killing Priscilla by attacking her car with hand grenades and riddling it with automatic weapons fire in the driveway of the mansion. "Please, God," thought Strickland, "*anything but hand grenades!*"

In another conversation about killing, McCrory quoted Cullen as saying, "I've gotten by with it once . . ." But before he could finish the sentence, Haynes sprang from his chair. "Excuse me, excuse me, excuse me . . ." Later, to the press, he fumed, "The next thing you know, McCrory will be testifying that Cullen killed Kennedy and kidnapped the Lindbergh baby." Haynes, of course, demanded a mistrial—at this point, tantamount to an acquittal—but Gray refused.

Before long, McCrory was wishing Gray had agreed. For eight days, Haynes cross-examined the state's key witness, heaping him with scorn, lacerating him with contradictions, scalding him with sarcasm, yanking on every loose thread of his story hoping to unravel the whole. With a kind of sadistic anality, Haynes tore into McCrory's account of his conversations with Cullen, grubbing through every word of every phrase for inconsistencies, no matter how minor. And then, when he found one, braying and snorting and preening in a tantrum of satisfaction.

Early on, he locked onto McCrory's weak spot: his sense of self-importance, his tendency—his addiction—to self-dramatization. When McCrory claimed that "meditation and self-hypnosis" had permitted him to remember new details of his story, Haynes reminded him of another claim he had made once: that he could kill a rat by screaming at it. McCrory denied making such a boast, but no one in the courtroom would soon forget it—perhaps because they recognized, in this case, what a useful skill it would have been. "I was afraid McCrory was going to scream at Haynes and Strickland was going to fall over dead," quipped Cullen. To which Strickland replied: "I'll take my chances with those assholes. Line up all the attorneys and Cullen and let McCrory scream his fucking head off."

By the time the prosecution rested, the scales seemed to be exactly where they had been at the same point in Houston: McCrory's account was shaky but hadn't collapsed, thanks largely to the FBI's devastating tapes; the jurors were dozing off, thanks largely to the defense's interminable cross-examinations; and the judge was furious with Richard Haynes. "If we keep up with this," Gray wailed, "the judicial system is going to hell. Haynes could ruin the whole system."

In presenting the defense's case, Haynes, too, followed a familiar route, promising in his opening statement to take the jurors on a peep-show tour of Priscilla Davis's sordid world and show them the evil conspiracy that had been hatched there by Priscilla, David McCrory, and Pat Burleson.

As in Houston, however, the scheduled tour soon ran into roadblocks. When Priscilla, in a somber black dress and long, pioneer-day hair, appeared again as the leadoff witness, Cullen's groupies squawked their disapproval. But under a hail of objections from Strickland, Haynes had little success in portraying her as the evil queen his con-

spiracy theory demanded. Then, on cue, Judge Gray lost
patience with Haynes's plan to retry the divorce case in
an effort to show Priscilla's motive for plotting against her
husband. "You're going to have to produce some evidence
at this time of a defense," Gray warned. "If you don't,
I'm not going to let you prove up all this divorce trash.
I'm not fixing to make a circus out of a district court."

Deprived of the circus defense that had worked so well
in Amarillo, Haynes was forced to fall back on two old
standbys: first, Kendavis witnesses like Dorothy Neeld,
the ambitious secretary who claimed to have seen the three
conspirators rendezvous on the street outside her window,
and Art Smith, the president of Jet Air, whose testimony,
like McCrory's, had undergone significant improvement
with age; second, the latest-model "bombshell" witnesses
from Steve Sumner's witness factory.

To no one's surprise, Larry Gene Lucas failed to appear
and give his colorful account of a late-night meeting with
David McCrory at the Sylvania Bar and Grill. Lucas had,
after all, just pled guilty to perjury in connection with his
testimony on Cullen Davis's behalf. But Haynes didn't
disappoint. Standing in for Larry Gene Lucas this time was
Larry Kent Francis, who gave his colorful account of a
late-night meeting with David McCrory at the Tempo
Club. By the purest of coincidences, Francis had been
"found" by the same lawyer who had found Uewayne Polk
at an earlier opportune moment.

On cross, Strickland made short work of Francis. "Are
you the same Larry Kent Francis who was found guilty of
robbery, burglary, unlawful possession of a firearm, theft,
breaking and entering, receiving and concealing stolen
property . . . ?"

Of course, he was.

Once again, the defense came down to Cullen and his
bizarre story, which he proceeded to tell almost word for
word as he had in Houston. What was different this time
was the cross-examination. With his quick wit and sulfer-
ously sarcastic tongue, Jack Strickland was far better
equipped than Tolly Wilson to lacerate Cullen's thin skin.

And the one thing Haynes could not afford was an explosion of his client's widely storied but never-seen-in-public temper.

Strickland wasted no time, coming at Cullen first with barbed questions about Jerry Hittson, the hit man who claimed Cullen had hired him to kill his first wife, Sandra. When he asked next about Cullen's relationship with Larry Gene Lucas, Haynes leapt to object, accusing Strickland of playing to the press.

"Your Honor," Strickland smiled, "they haven't written any Sunday stories about *me* yet." The *Star-Telegram* had recently run a long, flattering portrait of Haynes.

"Well, any time he does something noteworthy," Haynes smiled back, "I'm sure they will."

"Such as what, Mr. Haynes," Strickland snapped, "such as sponsor a witness that is convicted of perjury? You think maybe that's something that's noteworthy?"

But riling Haynes was one thing; riling Cullen another. It wasn't until Strickland trapped him in the labyrinth of his own story that Cullen's stone composure began to crack. As Strickland led him line by line through the most incriminating sections of the tapes, responding to each explanation with a corrosively sarcastic "uh-huh," Cullen stuck fiercely to the same defense: "We weren't talking about actually doing it. We were just talking about something for his sham tape."

Finally, Strickland sprang his trap. "If your purpose in making these 'sham tapes' was to in some way aid David McCrory to get to these killers, to get these assassins, *why were you being so coy*?"

Cullen pretended not to understand. "About what?"

"Talking about money, talking about Priscilla, talking about anything about killing, about incriminating yourself. These tapes were supposed to be *convincing* these killers. How, if you give minimal responses and 'hums' and 'uh-huh,' how is *that* supposed to convince these killers?"

Cullen didn't have an answer.

Strickland never got the satisfaction of seeing Cullen's famous temper on the stand, but he knew he was having an effect. One day, through the courthouse walls, Davis's distinctive voice could be heard screaming at his attorneys: *"Get that sonofabitch off my ass!"*

After Hershel Payne, Karen Master took the stand. Only she wasn't Karen Master any longer, she was Karen Davis. Since Houston, Cullen had made her his third wife and the lady of 4200 Mockingbird Lane.

At 12:50 in the morning on May 24, 1979, less than an hour after the thirty-day waiting period following his divorce from Priscilla expired, Cullen Davis married Karen Master in a strange early-morning ceremony which Karen's father, Ray Hudson, refused to attend. "I don't want anything to do with either one of them," he said in unexplained disgust.

Why the rush? Why would a man whose disenchantment with the bonds of matrimony was legendary, a man who had found so little happiness within his two marriages and so much difficulty getting out of them, rush into a third without a single night of celebration? Cullen laughed off such questions with a weak joke: "I enjoyed my fifty minutes of bachelorhood." Far more convincing was the story whispered by friends that Karen had finally demanded compensation for her years of helpful testimony; that if Cullen didn't marry her *immediately*, her memory of the night of August 2, 1976, and of Cullen's conversations with Agent Acree could go dangerously fuzzy.

But like Sandra and Priscilla before her, Karen quickly learned that being married to Cullen wasn't all mansions, furs, and Learjets. Within the first few months of marital bliss, she "fell down the steps" twice. She was seen with both eyes blackened and once even had to be hospitalized. "That house sure is hard on wives," cracked Jack Strickland.

At the trial in Fort Worth, Karen appeared, sans black eyes, in an elegant gray suit, maroon blouse, and cherry-red lipstick, to smile at the jury and, almost incidentally, to confirm her husband's story. Once again, she demonstrated her uncanny ability to misjudge the importance of things. This time it was the meeting that Cullen claimed he had with McCrory on August 11—the initial tape-recording session which had to be "redone" on the eighteenth. Now Karen remembered that Cullen had said on his return from that meeting: "I've got to call this FBI agent's number and tell him I've met with David."

When asked why she hadn't told the Houston jury about this, Karen batted her eyelashes at the jurors and cooed, "I don't recall being asked the question."

And why hadn't she told the grand jury when Cullen was first arrested? "I don't believe I was asked," she repeated with a smile. For a woman who didn't think it was relevant to tell anyone that Cullen was beside her in bed when the police claimed he was out committing a brutal double homicide, it seemed a reasonable answer.

The trial ended with two surprises, one from each side.

Haynes had finally found a bombshell witness who was neither a drug addict nor an ex-con. He was, in fact, a handsome, horn-rimmed professor of linguistics from Georgetown University who had come to Fort Worth to testify that the FBI's devastating tapes weren't so devastating after all.

Haynes strutted proudly about the courtroom, beaming irrepressibly, as Professor Roger Shuy described how he had spent fifty hours (at $350 a day plus expenses) subjecting the tapes to "discourse analysis" and come to the conclusion that they didn't mean what they seemed to mean. On the August 18 tape, for example, a detailed "topic analysis" revealed that McCrory had initiated eighteen of the twenty-two topics discussed—including all of the topics related to murder—while Cullen had initiated only four. From this, and an equally detailed "response analysis," Shuy concluded that Cullen "had little control of the conversation." Haynes pointed out that this was just what Cullen had been claiming all along: that he was just "going along" with what McCrory said.

As for the most incriminating line, "Do the judge and

then his wife," Shuy dismissed this as a "hypothetical case." What Cullen was *really* saying, according to Shuy, was "He *could* do the judge and then his wife." And when McCrory asked Cullen if he wanted all three, Bev, Bubba, and Gus Gavrel, killed at once, Cullen's response, "Do it either way," really meant, "He *could* do it either way"— not an order, as the prosecution contended, just a passing fancy.

What about the August 20 tape in which Cullen responded to McCrory's news of Eidson's murder with a simple, cold "Good"? Shuy had an abstruse explanation for that, too. This was what linguists called a "simultaneous" or "dual" conversation, said Shuy. In other words, Cullen and McCrory *weren't really talking to each other*! It was purely *by accident* that Cullen's "Good" fell immediately after McCrory's "I got the judge dead for you."

On cross, Strickland ridiculed Shuy's contention that the discussion of murdering Priscilla was a minor "subtopic" and acidly reminded him that "Mr. Davis is not charged with being a good or bad conversationalist." Shuy had no answer to the question of what Cullen meant when he told McCrory to "go back to the original plan," or to the question that had stumped Cullen earlier: If the purpose of the tapes was to convince Priscilla's killers, why was Cullen being so coy—or, in Shuy's word, "passive"?

To Haynes's great relief, Strickland never asked Shuy about his own initial reaction to the tapes. "My god, they're talking about *killing* people!" he had exclaimed. "This is scary stuff!"

Strickland, too, ended with a bang. His bombshell witness was Gale Helms, a salesman and model-plane enthusiast who testified that he and David McCrory had traveled to a model-plane air show in Oklahoma City on June 9, 1978, and stayed until June 11. Haynes and Cullen understood its significance instantly, as anyone could tell from the ashen pallor that swept over the defense table like a shadow. In his testimony, Cullen had claimed that McCrory was with *him* on the evening of June 9, outlining for the first time Priscilla's plot to have him killed. If that meeting didn't take place, then Cullen's whole story that he was making tapes for Priscilla's killers collapsed.

And unlike Cullen, Helms had records and receipts from the Oklahoma City air show, as well as his wife's testimony, to back up his story.

Helms also testified that he and McCrory were together at Benbrook Lake, again flying model planes, on the evening of August 11, 1978, at precisely the time that Cullen claimed he and McCrory were meeting to make the first set of tape recordings for Priscilla's killers—the ones that later had to be redone on August 18 and that Cullen claimed were in the envelope that McCrory handed him on August 20.

For several days, Haynes hammered mercilessly at Helms while Sumner's investigators scorched the landscape in search of something that might cast doubt on his story. When nothing substantial turned up, Haynes had no choice but to rest his case.

On the day of closing arguments, Priscilla Davis (she kept his name) slipped into the courthouse and approached Jack Strickland in the hallway. She looked tinier than ever, Strickland thought, no more than ninety pounds, like a little girl. Unlike Joe Shannon, Strickland had seen little of Priscilla during his two trials, but still he admired her. She seemed to him one of those rare people who could be flighty and scatterbrained in their daily lives, but suddenly, inexplicably, rock-solid in adversity. "If the ship were to start sinking," he once said, "she would be a good person to have around—one of those people who, the worse it gets, the calmer she gets." He suspected that it was that calm at the center, that iron instinct for survival, that had kept Priscilla alive on the night of August 2, 1976.

"You know," she said, bowing her blonde head to avoid his sympathetic gaze, "I would really like to hear the arguments today. I'd really like to hear what you have to say."

"Come hear them, then," he said.

Priscilla, barely audible: "I can't."

"What do you mean, you can't?"

"I can't come up there 'cause I don't want to jeopardize this case."

"What do you mean?" He knew exactly what she meant. At this moment, though, he refused to acknowledge it.

"I know people hate me," she said. "I don't want them to see me having an interest in this and think that I want Cullen convicted. I don't want to hurt your case."

Hearing her say it, true as it was, filled him with outrage. "That's bullshit," he spat. "You're a victim, and your daughter was murdered." He bent down to catch her cloudy eyes. "I'd like to have you come."

Priscilla began to cry, something she rarely did any more. The thought crossed Strickland's mind that for three years now people had been treating her as if *she* were the guilty one. Now, for once, someone had treated her like the victim she was.

Priscilla did come to hear the arguments, but confronted by a gauntlet of jeers and insults from Cullen's groupies, she didn't dare sit with the audience and declined an invitation to join the press. Instead, she sat in a little hallway that ran beside the courtroom and watched the proceedings from a doorway that gave her a view of the lawyers and the judge, but hid her from the jury's sight.

The jury deliberated for two and a half days. During that time, the reporters who had been covering the case took a vote: eleven thought Cullen was guilty; none thought him innocent. When asked if they thought the jury would *find* him guilty, the result was almost the same: ten yes, one no.

On Friday, November 9, 1979, word came that the jury had reached a verdict. It was devastating news for the defense. The best they had hoped for was a hung jury. A jury that returned after only two and a half days wasn't hung. The verdict had to be guilty. "Our ship is sunk," said Phil Burleson when he heard the news. While waiting for the jury to return to the courtroom, Haynes approached Judge Gray. "What time are you going to start the punishment hearing?" he asked in a low, black voice. "Nine o'clock Monday morning," Gray replied evenly.

As the jurors filed in, Strickland looked to see if the women were carrying their purses. The rule in Texas was that if the women were carrying their purses, they were ready to go home—there would be no punishment hearing; the verdict was not guilty. Not only were the women purse-less, but a few were even crying, and some of the men looked visibly shaken—all signs that the verdict was guilty. Strickland turned to his assistant, John Bankston, and whispered ecstatically: "Jesus Christ, they've convicted him, John. They've done it to him."

The clerk handed the verdict form to Judge Gray, who looked at it a second too long. "Is this right?" he finally said, looking quizzically at the clerk.

The clerk shrugged her shoulders slightly. "That's right, Judge."

Gray didn't even look back at the form before blurting out: "The jury has acquitted Cullen Davis."

After an instant of stone shock, the room exploded into chaos. Cullen's fans surged toward the defense table, clapping and whooping in triumph, while rows of reporters sat stunned in their seats. Women fell on their knees and shouted their thanks to God. With a loud, piercing cry like a dying swan, Joyce Smith, the leader of the groupies, swooned and tumbled in a faint. Cullen and Karen wept. So did Haynes. Judge Gray muttered "Fuck!" under his breath and stalked to his chambers, surrendering his court-room to the bedlam.

As the crowd screamed and prayed around him, crush-ing toward Cullen and Haynes, Strickland looked at John Bankston and burst into laughter. The more he tried to control it, the harder he laughed. Yet his mind screamed, "If this is what the people of Tarrant County want, then fuck 'em, they can have it." Anger and laughter. In the din and confusion, everything made sense and nothing made sense. In one corner, Cullen Davis received the crowd's frantic adulation, while the jury filed back to their room and waited eagerly for a personal visit from the defendant. In another corner, Joyce Smith was being carried awkwardly away by four straining men. In another corner, Judge Gray watched from the doorway to his chambers, smoking, cursing, and sputtering to himself, "I just can't believe it. They actually acquitted the sonofabitch."

And everywhere, amid the loonlike laughter and cat-calls of victory, one could hear the same two words. On the lips of the jubilant groupies and in the mouths of tutored children, whispered in passionate gratitude by women clutching their Bibles and shouted by men as they clapped each other on the back—the two words that later, at the victory party that night, would break into ecstatic, full-throated chanting:

"Final justice! Final justice! Final justice!"

When asked why they had acquitted Cullen Davis, the jury members had no answer. Many still had doubts—why did Cullen have only fifteen cents on him if he made the calls he said he made, for example—but they had agreed to throw a party afterward and invite Cullen so he could answer their questions.

One juror claimed to have solved the case. After listening to the tapes over and over, he said he heard a "clicking sound" when McCrory handed Cullen the envelope that supposedly contained the photographs of Judge Eidson "dead." This juror had concluded that the clicking sound he heard was, in fact, the sound of the little Norelco tapes clicking together. That meant Cullen's story was true.

The other jurors had quickly agreed. After two and a half days of reviewing the testimony, they only had to take one vote: unanimous for acquittal.

Mostly, however, the jurors just seemed relieved—relieved especially that they did not have to convict Cullen Davis. "It's a pretty heavy thing having somebody's life in your hands," said one. "How does anybody ever get convicted?" More than a few skeptics wondered if it was a "heavy thing" having "anybody's" life in their hands, or just Cullen Davis's life?

"Why would a man with that much money have somebody killed?" one juror asked. "Why would he do something that low-down? He was above all that."

The Saturday after the verdict, Jack Strickland spent the day with his eight-year-old son, Geoff. It was their first weekend in fourteen months unhaunted by the spectre of Cullen Davis. Like his father, Geoff had paid a price for prosecuting Fort Worth's most popular defendant. His classmates at school, children of the city's affluent, had razzed him all during the trial and would undoubtedly ridicule him over the defeat when he returned to school on Monday.

When the doorbell rang, Geoff ran to answer it. It was Western Union with a telegram. Geoff, who had never seen a telegram before, pleaded with his father to let him open it. Strickland could tell by the way he tore into it that he was expecting a letter from the President of the United States saying "Nice going, Geoff's father, we're proud of you anyway."

But that wasn't it at all. Strickland read the telegram as his son listened: "You are a disgrace to the people of Texas . . ."

Meanwhile, Cullen Davis received a roaring welcome on "The Charlie Rose Show," a local TV talk show. Audience members rose reverently to ask their questions—"Do you see any relationship between the Iranian revolution, the war in Afghanistan, and the rise in gold prices?" And applauded lustily at Cullen's answers—"I think those are three separate issues."

The show's host, Charlie Rose, stared transfixed at his celebrity guest. "Do you think you should get restitution for the months and years that you spent in jail accused of a crime you didn't commit?" he asked.

Cullen smiled beatifically and the audience rustled with admiration at his composure. "That's a funny question," he said, "because there's no way I know of to get restitution for being improperly incarcerated."

"Has your life gotten back to normal," asked Rose in a husky, intimate whisper. "I mean, *can* you live a normal life ever again?"

Another smile. "Normal would be walking down the street without being recognized by anybody," Cullen replied. "That'll never happen."

Rose leaned closer to his guest, his voice even more intimate and earnest: "Tell me, Cullen. What is important to you? What does Cullen Davis *care* about?"

The audience leaned forward too, eager not to miss a word that passed from those thin, distinguished lips. "Well, that's a very broad question," he said with another smile.

Rose gingerly turned the questioning to the murders. "Are you afraid, living in the mansion?" he asked.

"Whoever did it was not after me," said Cullen nonchalantly, "and I see no reason to fear for my life."

Rose leaned in again. "Do you have an idea who did it?"

"Yes," said Cullen.

Rose, breathlessly: "Do you think you know?"

"Yes. I think I know."

Rose, after a pause, with a friendly, let-us-in-on-it smile: "Who was it?"

The audience broke into peels of laughter and applause. Rose grinned. Cullen laughed. "I can't announce that on public television," he joked.

78

The verdict was in, but Cullen Davis's trials were far from over. Even from the high ground of the victory party—"a Rhett Butler's repeat," Cullen drunkenly proclaimed it—

the view ahead was a daunting one. No less than six civil suits had already been filed against him, seeking a total of more than $30 million in damages. The list of plaintiffs included all the names that Cullen would have preferred to forget: Bubba Gavrel and his father, Gus, Jack Wilborn, Stan Farr's family, and, of course, Priscilla. Because Texas allowed survivorship actions, even Andrea Wilborn was suing him from the grave for the pain and suffering she endured while waiting to die on the basement floor.

Five years before, the prospect of a protracted legal battle, even on many fronts at once, would not have fazed Cullen Davis. In fact, he would have relished the prospect of crushing his accusers in court, paying his praetorian guard of lawyers to wear them all down with endless delays and costly skirmishes while he sunned in Mexico or skied in Aspen. Sooner or later, they would run out of money and, one by one, he could buy them off for a few hundred thousand.

But those days were past.

By the early eighties, it was clear, although not yet public knowledge, that Stinky Davis's empire was in trouble. The problem wasn't just the slump in the oil market, although that hurt, or even the nationwide recession. Kendavis Industries had emerged unscathed from earlier slumps and recessions. No, most analysts agreed, the problem was Cullen Davis. Unlike his father, who rarely borrowed and therefore never got caught overextended, Cullen had been borrowing and buying like . . . well, like Priscilla with a charge account at Neiman-Marcus. Convinced that the world's supply of oil would run out by 1990 and eager to diversify, he had ransomed the company's core businesses to pay for ventures into glamorous but unfamiliar new areas, especially real estate—after oil, the shakiest industry in Texas.

The first hint of the resulting disaster came when *Forbes* magazine dropped both Cullen and his brother Ken from their list of the four hundred wealthiest people in America. Less than a year later, Kendavis Industries International filed for Chapter 11 bankruptcy. In less than two decades,

Ken and Cullen Davis had taken their father's one-billion-dollar empire and reduced it to a rubble of debt.

Not surprisingly, the bankruptcy court soon removed the two brothers from their management positions at the company's major subsidiaries. A short time later, Cullen was forced to sell his beloved mansion and the 189 acres around it. Sale price: $33 million, although $16 million of that went to Ken, who owned half the land, and the remainder, according to Cullen, went to pay off debts. As always, however, the details of his personal accounting were kept strictly confidential.

Through it all, ironically, Bill Davis remained untouched. Ousted from the company years before by his brothers, he had invested his sizable cash settlement in safer places and now watched as his dire predictions about the fate of the company in Cullen's hands came true. But vindication had its price. Guarded by a massive fence and elaborate security system, he still lived in daily fear for his life and the safety of his family.

While some saw Cullen's financial fall as poetic justice, to many of the plaintiffs with lawsuits against him it looked more like Cullen's last laugh. In 1986, Bubba Gavrel agreed to drop his $13 million lawsuit in exchange for less than 1 percent of that amount, plus a piece of property that Cullen valued at $314,000 but which turned out to be virtually worthless. After the lawyers took their share, little was left for Bubba or his father, who had spent over $200,000 on doctors and therapy in the ten years since the shootings.

Not long after the end of the second murder-for-hire trial, Gus Gavrel had run into Cullen on the street—literally. He was driving his delivery truck when a man suddenly stepped off the curb and into his path. It was Cullen Davis. Gavrel slammed on the brakes and the truck skidded forward. In the next second, Gavrel thought of all the times he had wanted to kill Cullen Davis, the times he had vowed to make Cullen pay for what he did to Bubba, the time he had called Cullen at Karen's house and screamed,

"I'm gonna kill you! I'm gonna cut you up and feed you to the dogs!" In that split second, as the truck skidded forward and he saw the terror in Cullen's eyes as he looked through the window of the oncoming truck and recognized the driver, Gavrel thought, "I could get away with it."

But his foot stayed on the brake and the truck came to a stop just inches short.

Cullen hoped the settlement with Gavrel would break the ice and the other plaintiffs, especially Priscilla and Jack Wilborn, would quickly follow, convinced that if they waited too long nothing would be left of the fast-disappearing Davis fortune. "They might end up getting a judgment," Cullen told the *Star-Telegram*, "but they can wallpaper their house with it." His lawyers floated settlement offer after settlement offer, like feathers in a desultory breeze, all of them for the kind of painless money that had pacified Bubba, all of them angrily rejected. In typical fashion, Cullen had mistakenly assumed that Priscilla and Wilborn were only after money.

In May 1987, Cullen found himself in the path of an oncoming truck of a different kind: a lawsuit combining the claims of Priscilla, Jack Wilborn, and Andrea in a single $21 million action. The question for the jury was the same as it had been ten years before in Amarillo: Was Cullen Davis the "man in black"?

Everything else about this trial, however, was different. *There was no Racehorse Haynes*. Cullen could no longer afford the fee that, largely because of the Davis victories, Haynes now commanded. Instead, Steve Sumner defended him. For the same reason, there was no pretrial publicity campaign, no expensive jury screening process, no blizzard of motions. Jim Bearden, the private investigator, continued to work the case, but without the big staff or the unlimited budget of previous trials. Bearden made a point of keeping all his "sensitive" records under lock and key just in case Cullen balked when the bill came.

There was no Tim Curry. Instead of thirty minutes, Priscilla's attorney, Bob Gibbins, spent days "woodshed-

ding" his chief witness, reviewing every detail of her testimony, advising her on her clothes, hair, and makeup.
She made her entrance in a matronly dark-blue suit, her
platinum mane drawn back in a clip. She told her story
plainly, without the dreaded "Uhhhhhhhhh." She told the
whole story: how she had suffered through years of Cullen's
abuse, how he had beaten her, bruised her arms and legs,
blackened her eyes, and broken her bones.

There was no George Dowlen. Armed with the picture
of Priscilla and W. T. Rufner in the water at Benbrook
Lake, Sumner dived immediately into the muck of the
divorce and the "scumbags" who infested the mansion in
Cullen's absence, but Judge Clarence Williams quickly
hauled him out. "What we're talking about here is the
murder of a little girl," he scolded, "and I don't see what
that trash has to do with it." When Sumner tried to present
his own bizarre theory of the murders—even darker and
more conspiratorial than Haynes's—Williams cut him off.

(Outside the courtroom, reporters clamored for the
names of Sumner's killers, but he would say only that "two
or three" were involved, and that Horace Copeland was
one of them but he "did not pull the trigger." Would
Sumner reveal the names eventually? Only if the judge
allowed them to enter the names into evidence, he said.
After the trial, he refused to reveal the names until Cullen
paid him. The names, if they existed, were never released.)

There was no hearsay rule. The paramedics who rescued Priscilla that night could testify how she had cowered
in the ambulance when she thought a passing car was Cullen's. Lt. Gordon Box could quote Beverly Bass—"Cullen
did it." Was she sure? "Yes, it was Cullen"—and tell how
Cullen had laughed in the police car on his way to jail that
night. Jim Karras and Randy McCarger, two more policemen, could testify that Bev Bass also told them: "Cullen
shot my boyfriend." And Detective Claude Davis, the officer who had booked Cullen at the police station that
night, could recount his conversation with the defendant:

"Why did two people have to die?"

"There are some things you don't need a reason for."

One week into the plaintiff's case, Steve Sumner approached the lawyers for Priscilla and Wilborn with a new settlement offer. "Look, I don't know whether Cullen can get any money together or not," he said, "but if he could get $300,000, could we settle this thing?" It was twice what Cullen had offered just before the trial began, but the answer was the same: "Hell, no."

There was a victim. For the first time, a jury heard the details of how Cullen had abused Andrea, how he had screamed and cursed at her for being "stupid," how he had locked her out of the house for stumbling on her multiplication tables, how he hated her animals and killed a kitten.

Tracy Wilborn, Andrea's stepsister, roommate, and best friend, took the stand to talk about how Andrea loved animals, loved going to see them at the zoo, loved cooking, loved "making things." But she herself was the dead plaintiff's best evidence. Almost the same age as Andrea, Tracy had developed into a charming, disarming beauty, as guileless and goodhearted at twenty-four as she had been at twelve. It was as if Andrea had come back from the grave to testify in her own behalf: "This is what I would have become. This is what was lost. This is what Cullen Davis murdered."

Andrea's fourth-grade teacher testified that Andrea was, in fact, smart and gifted, not "stupid" as Cullen had accused. Jack Wilborn took the stand and tried for the hundredth time to express his loss in words: how he had never cried before Andrea's death but cried every day for years afterward; how for months he "could hardly put one foot in front of the other"; how he had suffered through three heart attacks and a bypass operation since Amarillo. When he tried to recall Andrea's favorite song, a sudden rush of memories overwhelmed him and the trial had to be stopped.

As a grim finale, a medical examiner recounted Andrea's last minutes of life: how a bullet had ripped through her liver and aorta, how she had bled to death "mostly into her own stomach," how she had not died instantly but instead lingered "for a while" after being shot, writhing on the basement floor in her own blood, her last sensation a blinding pain in her gut.

There was a killer. In Amarillo, Richard Haynes had successfully hidden his client from the jury's view. This time, there were no secrets. Even Cullen's psychiatric evaluation, the one ordered by his lawyers ten years before, was shown to the jurors. To help them understand it, the plaintiffs called Russ Vorpagle, a psychologist with twenty years of experience profiling killers for the FBI.

According to Vorpagle, Cullen Davis's psychological evaluation revealed a "cold, cruel, and callous" man—just the kind of man who would empty his gun into a person who was already wounded and lying helpless on the floor. Looking at the pictures of Stan Farr's bullet-riddled body and reading Bubba Gavrel's account of Cullen pointing an empty gun at his head, Vorpagle saw an egotistical, anti-social personality with a powerful drive to dominate others. "What I saw at this crime scene," he said, "was anger, was revenge, was cruelty, was overkill."

Clearly, the murders had been committed by somebody in the family, Vorpagle concluded—*not* a double-crossed drug dealer. The killer had laid careful plans—bringing plenty of ammunition for unforeseen contingencies (of which there were many, including Andrea, Bev, and Bubba)—and his target *was* Priscilla. It was the work of a sociopath, not a psychopath, said Vorpagle, someone who, in the words of Cullen's evaluation, "recognizes society's expectations without reacting to them emotionally," a man who "fears losing control of relationships, rendering him vulnerable and with an oppressively threatened feeling."

On cross-examination, Steve Sumner demanded to know why, if the killer came to the mansion solely to kill Priscilla, he had let her run out the door after shooting her only once. Why didn't he shoot her again? It was the same question that had stumped police and prosecutors from the beginning. But this time Vorpagle had an answer. "The killer has fired one shot into Andrea," he said, counting on his fingers, "one shot into Priscilla, and four shots into Stan Farr." He held up six fingers and smiled. "Now he has an empty gun." Sumner's face turned ashen.

Sumner's luck was no better with his own case, as one by one his witnesses self-destructed. One told the jury he was 100 feet from the Hulen Street driveway, then admitted he had told the Amarillo jury he was 1800 feet away. One said he had not contacted Cullen since Amarillo, then admitted the two had spoken on the phone and met often. (In fact, Cullen had "taken care of him financially" ever since the previous trial, his mother told prosecutors.) Another "testified" through an unsigned affidavit and conveniently couldn't be found for cross-examination. From his seat in the gallery uncomfortably close to Jack Wilborn, Cullen watched as his Amarillo defense, the pride of Racehorse Haynes, crumbled around him.

Deprived of Haynes's "drug and sex" attack on Priscilla, Sumner was left with only an alibi defense. Cullen took the stand early to reveal—for the first time in open court—his version of the night of August 2, 1976. After leaving the garage, he said, he ate at Kip's Big Boy, then drove to the Western Hills Theater to see *The Bad News Bears*, which ended about 11:30. Because the truck was having engine trouble, he exchanged it for the Cadillac in the garage, leaving the truck on the street so it could be more easily towed the next morning. He arrived home "about midnight."

Did anyone see him?

No one he knew, said Cullen with a shrug. He did bump into someone on the way out of the movie and exchanged words, but couldn't remember anything about him. Veteran trial watchers thought they heard the Sumner/Bearden witness factory cranking up even as Cullen said it.

Louis Claassen claimed he was working as an usher at the Western Hills Theater on the night of August 2, and that he *remembered* Cullen Davis being there. Strangely, when Jim Bearden had first interviewed Claassen, he couldn't remember anything about that night, but eventually Bearden "turned him around." After Claassen told his story to the jury, however, Sumner learned that the plaintiffs' lawyers had found proof that Claassen wasn't even employed by the theater on August 2, 1976, and were prepared to "blast him" the next day on cross. In a desperate bid to save his witness, Bearden tried to float a story that Claassen had worked at the theater for free before he was hired, but not even Sumner bought it. The next morning, Sumner stood up and withdrew the testimony of his latest bombshell witness.

That left only Karen Master Davis, who had made several more unexplained trips to the hospital since her last courtroom appearance on behalf of her husband. Smiling beguilingly at the jury, Karen testified that, at Cullen's request, *she* had moved the truck from the street into the wrong garage several days after the murders.

Why had she never before mentioned parking the truck, even though it had been a key issue at the previous trial? "I didn't think it was important," she cooed.

After both sides rested, Judge Williams reminded the jury that it did not have to find that Cullen Davis killed Andrea Wilborn "beyond a reasonable doubt." In civil cases, the standard was "by a preponderance of the evidence." If 51 percent of the evidence indicated Cullen was the murderer, then they should return a verdict for the plaintiffs. Nor was it necessary for their decision to be unanimous. Only ten of the twelve jurors needed to believe that "a preponderance of the evidence" indicated Cullen was the killer.

Soon after the jury retired, one member, a heavy-set woman named Warlene Davis, disappeared to the restroom. When she returned, she told the jurors that while in the restroom she had discovered that Priscilla and her lawyer had paid their witnesses $75,000 apiece to testify against Cullen Davis. Three other jurors, two women and a man, believed her.

Even after Judge Williams called the jury back and warned them, "You are absolutely not to listen to any conversation out of that jury room, anything that you didn't hear in court," the four refused to budge, reminding the others again and again that Cullen had been acquitted in Amarillo. After four days of bitter debate, more pointed instructions from the judge, and an unprecedented second round of closing arguments, the jury was still deadlocked eight to four.

On June 22, 1987, Judge Williams angrily declared a mistrial.

Afterward, Warlene Davis refused to explain her opinion of the evidence, insisting that it was the job of the other jurors to convince *her* of their opinion, which they had failed to do. She did offer one hint of her reasoning, however. Cullen Davis's testimony had to be examined in a different light than other testimony in the case, she explained. "He had to be given the benefit of the doubt."

Cullen threw the usual "victory" party at Duffy's after the mistrial and launched the ritual attack on Priscilla. His problems all began "when she got on drugs," Cullen said. "It was her cattin' around and getting into drugs, and then I wanted a divorce." After that, he added, confident that all Fort Worth agreed with him, "greed got the best of her."

But Fort Worth wasn't so sure anymore. In the ten years since the first trial, public opinion had been slowly turning on Cullen Davis. Some were offended by the hasty marriage to Karen, others by the long, slow slide into bankruptcy. The drawn-out civil suits had also shown the public a side of Cullen Davis that Haynes had managed to conceal during the first trials. Eventually, the repeated accusations of wife-beating, child abuse, and cruelty to animals, too many to deny, began to have an effect.

After repeated vows to fight his greedy accusers, Cullen's willingness to settle the Gavrel suit out of court read to many supporters like a confession. If he wasn't the man in black, why would he surrender even one dollar to Gavrel? And what about the repeated offers to settle with Priscilla and the others? When Priscilla's suit finally came to trial, many of the most sordid details of Cullen's private life finally burned their way through the fog of hometown favor, along with a new, more skeptical view of Haynes's defense in Amarillo. One defense witness too many had been caught lying on the stand or turned up years later with unexplained cash in his pocket.

The psychological evaluation done in 1976 immediately after the murders and leaked to the *Star-Telegram* also revealed for the first time the kind of I-can-get-away-with-anything arrogance that Cullen had successfully hidden from his adoring public for almost a decade.

> "I am afraid of *nothing*."
> "The men over me: *none*."

Now when he appeared on talk shows, there were no more fatuous questions or spontaneous rounds of appreciative applause. No one asked his opinion of world events or openly admired his grace under pressure. Indeed, the audiences seemed to share in his awkward secret: He was guilty after all.

The final blow came in early July 1987, only two weeks after the mistrial: Cullen Davis declared personal bankruptcy. According to the final tally, he had less than $2 million in assets and *$860 million* in liabilities. More than half of that total represented defaulted loans to Kendavis Industries for which Cullen had signed personally. Most of the loans were for real estate ventures in which his partners had already gone belly-up.

There was a silver lining in this dark thundercloud, however. The bankruptcy court froze all lawsuits pending against Cullen Davis, including those related to Stan Farr's death, which were scheduled to go to trial in September. But if Cullen hoped that the freeze would encourage his tormentors to settle or, better still, abandon their claims, he was disappointed again. Priscilla, Wilborn, and the Farr family vowed to continue their fight and even suspected that Cullen had staged the bankruptcy to rid himself not only of creditors but also of them.

There was something too neat about Steve Sumner's

statement to reporters that Cullen's bankruptcy "is going to have to reveal to the plaintiffs the futility of coming after him for his money." And the bankruptcy itself stank of another Davis trick.

No one was surprised when, only weeks after Sumner's announcement, the bankruptcy trustee accused Cullen of "transferring, removing, destroying and concealing property" in the months before declaring bankruptcy.

But Cullen didn't care anymore. Whether they doubted his sincerity, suspected him of cheating, or accused him of murder made no difference. Nothing anybody said bothered him anymore. He had found the final, the ultimate defense.

He had found God.

79

"My name is Cullen Davis, and Jesus Christ is my personal savior."

The huge audience in Dallas's Reunion Arena exploded into applause and shouts of "Praise the Lord!"

Cullen beamed back with a lipless smile.

When the roar died down, he turned to the tall, handsome man seated behind him, the Reverend James Robison, a galvanic young TV preacher with a crown of jet-black hair and a voice like the Old Testament God—with a Texas accent. Robison was already being called "the next Billy Graham."

"When James came to me," Cullen began, "he didn't have any trouble leading me to Jesus Christ."

The year was 1980, and Cullen and Karen were still living in the mansion. Robison had just been through a legal ordeal of his own when a local station pulled his show off the air because of an especially vicious attack on homosexuals. Robison, like Cullen, had been rescued from the hands of his tormentors by Racehorse Haynes, who defended his client's attack as "a call for moral excellence" and branded the effort to suppress his show "the outrage of the century."

Not long after Cullen's acquittal in Fort Worth, Robison was directed by God to the mansion on the hill to tell the Davises that "the reason for their trials was to draw them to Christ." For three hours, fire and brimstone echoed through the high white walls on Mockingbird Lane. Robison told Cullen about "God's plan for sinners," applauded his "strength and endurance" through "troubled times," and praised the "depth Karen had shown during the trials." When it was over, Robison asked, "Do you want to pray and turn your life over to the Lord?"

"Yes, I do," Cullen answered. "I'm ready."

Together, they got down on their knees on the plush carpeting and prayed for God to forgive Cullen's sins and "take over his life."

From that day forward, God came into Cullen's life and Cullen came into James Robison's life. Wherever the TV evangelist preached his fiery attacks on liberal theology, gay rights, abortion, the Equal Rights Amendment, pornography, and big government, Cullen was there, giving his Christian testimony and beaming serenely at the wild applause.

Robison proudly called Cullen "my understudy" and sent him as a representative to New Right religious-political rallies throughout the Bible Belt. When critics questioned Cullen's past, Robison would rise up to his full 6 feet 3 inches and thunder: "It doesn't matter if Cullen Davis did what they accused him of doing. Because *I* have been tried and convicted of murder. *I* am guilty of murdering Christ."

Cullen even offered to donate his collection of art treasures to Robison's ministry, but Robison refused the offer. Many of the objects were "graven images" and might still contain "evil spirits," he warned. "Well, if you can't have them," Cullen wailed, "then I can't have them." So, according to Robison, they took the objects—"more than $1 million in jade, ivory, and gold"—out to the driveway of the mansion and smashed them to pieces with hammers while Karen shouted "Thank the Lord! Thank the Lord!"

This night in Reunion Arena, the subject of Cullen's testimony was "one of the biggest problems in the country and the world"—evolution. "I'm a scientific person," he told his rapt audience, "and I was deluded by evolution." His voice rose in anger. "I was sold a bill of goods without *any* proof, and that was how I started out on the wrong path." He scoffed at those who pretended to have evidence that man was descended from the apes and dared them to come forward with it. "I'll tell you what I'll do," he smirked, "I'll give $50,000 to the first man who can prove the theory of evolution!"

When the shouting and applause died down, he turned to a third man on the podium with a look that said, "This is for you." Then he turned back to his audience. "The *Communists* preach evolution," he began. "The *Communists* preach atheism." He beamed at the crowd. "You can draw your own conclusions."

The hall erupted again and the third man on the podium smiled and applauded warmly. Later in the program, Robison would introduce him to the crowd as "the next President of the United States, Ronald Reagan."

Not everyone was convinced by Cullen's conversion. "If Cullen's got that close to the Lord," said Jack Wilborn's lawyer, Hal Monk, "it makes me wonder a little bit about the Lord." Jack Strickland dismissed it as just another of Cullen's tricks. "It's cheaper than hiring a press agent," he snapped. "Cullen has used his family, used his wife, used his friends, and, now that he has used them up, he is trying to use God."

The doubters claimed a victory when the fragments of Cullen's art collection were recovered from Lake Worth and pronounced by a curator at the Kimbell Museum to be "of no aesthetic or religious value whatsoever." Contrary to Robison's claims, there was no gold or silver and the jade wasn't even real jade. The truly valuable pieces, Cullen admitted, like the gold and silver chess set, had been deposited in the vault of Robison's bank.

Jack Wilborn, who after Andrea's death had found comfort only in his faith, wanted to believe Cullen's conversion was real. His generosity seemed vindicated when Cullen appeared one day at the Word of Faith Church in suburban Dallas where Wilborn regularly attended a prayer meeting. Wilborn turned around and found himself looking into Cullen's masklike face. "Hello," Cullen said, "how are you doing, Jack?"

"Fine," Wilborn recovered.

Cullen looked him in the eye. "Could you forgive me for what I did?"

"I forgave you a long time ago," said Wilborn. And he had. "If I hadn't," Jack would say, "I'd be dead today. I couldn't live with that kind of hate." Wilborn's wife, Betty, embraced Cullen with tears in her eyes.

But when word reached the press of Cullen's "confession," his story quickly changed. He wasn't talking about the murders at all, announced Steve Sumner, he was referring to the trouble he had caused Wilborn in his divorce from Priscilla.

Wilborn knew that was a lie. He had looked in Cullen's eyes when he said it and they both knew what he was asking forgiveness for. After that, his feelings about Cullen's conversion changed. "I hate to see Christianity used like that," he said.

W. T. Rufner, as usual, was more blunt. "Cullen will rot in hell," he spat. "Shooting Farr, shooting Priscilla, or Bubba, that's sad, you know. But he'll rot in hell for Andrea. No matter how close he thinks he gets to God, he'll never get that close."

On the tenth anniversary of the murders, Cullen Davis preached a seminar on "spiritual warfare"—how to combat demons—at the Western Hills Inn in Euless, a suburb of Fort Worth. "Before I came to the Lord," he told his audience, "I had a lot of money. I lived in a big house and I was constantly being attacked by the enemy—the enemy being demons." When asked about the anniversary and his long legal ordeal, he would say only, "As nearly all of you know, I spent several years in criminal trials. I never lost any of them, praise the Lord."

God no longer communicated with Cullen through James Robison. He spoke directly. And Cullen spoke with Him—often in tongues. God had also given Cullen the power to heal with his hands, the "spiritual gift of discerning demons." Just as David McCrory could kill a rat by screaming at it, Cullen Davis could drive demons from the bodies of sinners by laying his hands on them. Witnesses swore they had actually heard demons "cry out" when Cullen prayed for people and touched them.

But Cullen had not come to Euless that night to exorcise just any demons. He asked the audience to join him in driving out "the demons of bitterness and hate related to sins of the past."

"In the name of Jesus Christ, I put off all the old," he shouted, shaking his head as if caught suddenly in a huge invisible spider web. "In the name of Jesus Christ, I put off the sins of the father which are passed down from generation to generation."

Soon his whole body was shaking, his voice more a wail than a shout. "Satan, I declare myself loose from you and your demons. I break off all curses." But the shaking continued, and the voice, demanding and desperate: "Satan, I rebuke you now and all your demons. *Leave me now!*"

By 1990, the demand for his seminars and exorcisms had fallen off and Cullen Davis had largely disappeared from public view. That was why Jack Strickland took so long to recognize the man he saw outside the Cake Boutique on McClellan Street shuffling around in bedroom slippers. At first, he looked like a wino or a derelict homeless man: clothes rumpled and dirty; three or four days' growth of beard; a distant, unfocused look on his face.

But the eyes eventually gave him away. They were Cullen's eyes, all right—Strickland had stared into them often enough—only different. Where before there had been two hard coals, now there were two burned-out craters. "He looked like he had seen hell," Strickland said later, "and lived to tell about it."